ECONOMIC GROWTH
The Japanese Experience since the Meiji Era

PUBLICATIONS OF
THE ECONOMIC GROWTH CENTER

LLOYD G. REYNOLDS, *Director*

LAMFALUSSY *The United Kingdom and the Six: An Essay on Economic Growth in Western Europe*

FEI & RANIS *Development of the Labor Surplus Economy: Theory and Policy*

BALASSA *Trade Prospects for Developing Countries*

BAER & KERSTENETZKY *Inflation and Growth in Latin America*

REYNOLDS & GREGORY *Wages, Productivity, and Industrialization in Puerto Rico*

BAER *Industrialization and Economic Development in Brazil*

MAMALAKIS & REYNOLDS *Essays on the Chilean Economy*

MOORSTEEN & POWELL *The Soviet Capital Stock, 1928–1962*

SNODGRASS *Ceylon: An Export Economy in Transition*

HELLEINER *Peasant Agriculture, Government, and Economic Growth in Nigeria*

MEAD *Growth and Structural Change in the Egyptian Economy*

KLEIN & OHKAWA (Eds.) *Economic Growth: The Japanese Experience since the Meiji Era*

ECONOMIC GROWTH
The Japanese Experience since the Meiji Era

Proceedings of the
CONFERENCE OF THE JAPAN
ECONOMIC RESEARCH CENTER

EDITED BY LAWRENCE KLEIN

Professor of Economics
University of Pennsylvania

AND KAZUSHI OHKAWA

Professor of Economics
Hitotsubashi University

A Publication of
THE ECONOMIC GROWTH CENTER
Yale University

1968
RICHARD D. IRWIN, INC., Homewood, Illinois
IRWIN–DORSEY LIMITED, Nobleton, Ontario

Series Foreword

This volume is one in a series of studies supported by the Economic Growth Center, an activity of the Yale Department of Economics since 1961. The Center's Research program is focused on the search for regularities in the process of growth and structural change by means of intercountry and intertemporal analyses. The emphasis is on measurable aspects of economic growth and on the development and testing of hypotheses about the growth process. To provide more reliable statistical tests of theoretical hypotheses, the Center is concerned with improving the techniques of economic measurement and with the refinement of national data systems. The Center provides a home for the International Association for Research in Income and Wealth, which moved its headquarters from Cambridge University, England in 1962. The Center library endeavors to achieve a complete intake of significant economic and statistical publications from about 80 of the larger countries of the world.

Book-length studies supported by the Center are printed and distributed by Richard D. Irwin, Inc. Reprints of journal articles are circulated as Center papers.

GUSTAV RANIS, *Director*
R. ALBERT BERRY, *Assistant Director*

Editors' Preface

This volume is intended to provide English language readers with a record of the proceedings of the International Conference on Economic Growth—A Case Study of Japan's Experience, which was held September 5–10, 1966, at the Japan Economic Research Center in Tokyo. The objective of the Conference was to make a quantitative appraisal of Japan's economic development over the last 100 years from the viewpoint of growth analysis. The advances that have been made in such studies of Japan's experience gave rise to the feeling that the time was ripe for holding the first conference of this kind in Japan with an international group of participants. The Conference placed emphasis on the long-run view in analyzing Japan's economic development, with the historical scope being set as the century from the Meiji Restoration of 1868 to the present. In view of the unique postwar pattern of Japan's growth, however, intensive discussion was planned as well for the period since 1945. Papers depending largely on econometric methods were deliberately avoided, and emphasis was placed on the quantitative, historical approach.

To facilitate productive and intensive exchanges of views and opinions, participants were kept to the modest number of 38, which included 22 Japanaese and 16 foreign scholars. English was adopted as the language of the Conference, with provision for interpretation when necessary. The Conference was, in fact, able to proceed smoothly without interpretation or language barriers of any kind.

The Japan Economic Research Center, a private organization founded in 1964, was the Conference's sponsor. Dr. Saburo Okita, executive director, Professor Shigeto Tsuru, director, and Professor Kazushi Ohkawa, director, represented the Board of Directors of the Center for this particular purpose. At the Center, an organizing committee prepared for the Conference in collaboration with the above directors. The full committee included Professors Kazushi Ohkawa, chairman, Miyohei Shinohara, Shinichi Ichimura, Shozaburo Fujino, and Tsunehiko Watanabe. While the Conference was in progress, the organizing committee, headed by Professor Shinichi Ichimura, functioned as a management committee to ensure a successful gathering.

vii

In accordance with the usual practice at such meetings, the papers were not read at the Conference, but circulated beforehand. Discussants were chosen for each paper and asked to prepare written comments in advance of each session. The sessions began with the discussants' comments, after which the author was asked to offer his response. The meeting was then opened for general discussion and questions from the floor. The author was given a final opportunity to reply.

After the Conference an editorial committee was established, the members of which were Professors Simon Kuznets, Lawrence R. Klein, and R. C. O. Matthews in addition to the above-mentioned members of the organizing committee. The Editorial Committee agreed to publish both Japanese and English versions of the proceedings. Shinohara and Fujino were asked to be coeditors for the Japanese version, and Klein and Ohkawa were asked to be coeditors for the English version. (The Japanese version, entitled *Nihon no Keizai Seicho* [Japanese Economic Growth], was published on April 10, 1967.) It was also agreed that the editing of the 12 Conference papers selected to appear in the English version would be done by the following teams, each handling four papers: Klein-Ichimura, Matthews-Watanabe, and Kuznets-Ohkawa.

It was originally intended to include the written comments in this volume. This plan was, however, changed since most authors took the comments into account in revising their papers for publication. We, as editors, would therefore like to acknowledge the part played by the discussants in revising the papers included in this volume.

In conclusion, the Committee would like to extend its sincere thanks for the assistance rendered by the JERC staff and express its gratitude to the Ford Foundation and the Asia Foundation for their financial assistance in inviting the foreign participants. The Committee is also deeply indebted to Professor Kuznets who has generously consented to write summary statements based on his general discussion presented at the Conference.

Finally, we want to express our sincere thanks to the Economic Growth Center, Yale University, for its generous support of the publication of this volume. We are particularly indebted to Professor Hugh Patrick, Associate Director of the Growth Center, for undertaking arrangements for publication.

The selected papers are arranged in two parts: Part I consists of seven papers that deal with economic growth in historical perspective or prewar economic growth, while Part II consists of five papers that discuss particular aspects of postwar growth.

Part I begins with an overall presentation of long-term economic growth and structural changes in Japan (Chapter 1, Ohkawa-Rosovsky). This paper is mainly based on the authors' own estimates of output and investment. An accelerating mechanism, both in swing and trend dimension, is found. In terms of investment spurt, borrowed technology, and flexible supply of labor, they try to explain the mechanism. The long swings that are shown, among other things, in Chapter 1 are discussed in more detail both empirically and theoretically in Chapter 2 (Fujino). The monetary and financial characteristics of these swings are particularly taken up here, on the basis mostly of data estimated by the author. Construction is found to play an important role in causing Japan's long swings. There are two papers on industrialization (Chapter 3, Shionoya and Chapter 4, Watanabe). The growth pattern of manufacturing is clarified in terms of changing structure of both demand and supply in the former, while the speed and type of technological progress in imitative processes and dual structure of the Japanese industrialization are the core of analysis in the latter. Shionoya depends on the new production index of manufacturing which he himself recently compiled, and Watanabe uses new data that he estimated on profit and wage differentials. The discussion on technological progress is further developed with respect to agriculture (Chapter 5, Hayami-Yamada). The process of diffusion of improved varieties and related cultivating practices, centering on rice production, is analyzed in order to clarify the characteristics of agricultural development in Japan.

The role of foreign trade in Japan's economic growth is taken up from its initial development through prewar years (Chapter 6, Baba-Tatemoto). Japan's positive attitude to external changes, the process of strengthening her competitive power, and accelerated export contribution to GNP are analyzed. The discussion is based, in part, on new estimates of the foreign balance, made by Tatemoto. Finally in Part I, discussion of private consumption is presented (Chapter 7, Kuznets). This is intended to summarize the trends in private consumption suggested by the presently available long-term estimates of product and its distribution by use. An examination of the tentative "residual" estimates imply "peculiar" consumption patterns, which call for further investigation. In addition to pointing to the high rate of increase in personal consumption in Japan, Kuznets particularly suggests a need for integrated, consistent long-term data in order to analyze the Japanese economy in general.

Part II begins with an overall anatomical analysis of the factors making for rapid postwar growth. This is done through a system of national accounts (Chapter 8, Ichimura). Resource allocation and market mechanisms are particularly clarified on the basis of the data compiled for the Osaka Econometric Model of Postwar Japan. Next, there are the two papers on the rapid industrialization in postwar Japan: one pays special attention to the domestic patterns and structural changes in the manufacturing sector (Chapter 9, Shinohara), and the other concentrates analysis on the international aspect—exports (Chapter 10, Kanamori). The so-called "heavy" industrialization and the increasing degree of "fabrication" are, among other things, Shinohara's major topic, while Kanamori finds the most important reason for the spectacular growth of Japanese exports to be the economy's capability of changing commodity composition and fostering new export industries.

The last two papers deal with postwar growth in relation to the public sector (Chapter 11, Patrick and Chapter 12, Shishido). The former focuses on the specified problem of financing the public investment, and discusses certain policy issues emanating from it, while the latter takes up government activity, especially its fiscal policy. Patrick's finding is seen in the nearly exclusive reliance on internal financing as a result of a policy decision and, in the change since 1962 toward a greater reliance on external sources. Shishido's use of a simple simulation approach for the case of adopting a tax policy of the Western type in Japan brings out interesting suggestions for Japan's growth.

We hope that our readers will have the general impression that major objectives of the symposium were accomplished. We believe that this volume represents a first step towards the quantification of Japanese economic history. As a matter of fact, the participants found a great deal of agreement in most of the empirical findings. Through discussion, however, not a small number of important points were clarified and directed for further study. Concerning the approach as a whole, apart from the individual papers, we would like to mention the following points in particular.

The organizing committee intended to cover all the important topics of Japanese growth analysis, but some were missed. For instance, no paper presented a long-term analysis of savings. The main reason for this deficiency is incompleteness of data. As pointed out above, many papers contain great efforts in data preparation. And yet integrated time series based on national income accounts are still to be seen in order to reach a stage capable of really consistent analysis of the Japanese economy as a whole. A more integrated, consistent analysis was sought during the discussions on both methodological and substantive issues. For example, some papers stress the role of international trade, while others weigh the importance of technological progress or the function of the dual structure. No paper is comprehensive by itself. This is also pointed out to some extent in historical perspective: analysis of most aspects of the postwar high rate of growth is not integrated with the prewar experience. With regard to the hypotheses and the methods of approach, it is clear that some disagreement remains among the participants. The thesis of borrowed technology or of the advantage of the latecomers, and the thesis of dual structure or flexible supply of labor—these two, among others, were particularly criticized (see Chapter 13, Kuznets). Authors who dealt with these points did not develop their response enough in this volume. For this reason, Kuznets hesitated to include that chapter in Part III. But we persuaded him to do so because we believed further development of discussions on these hypotheses will certainly be fruitful.

Regarding the method of approach, particularly, let us say, the Kuznets versus the Klein method, an extra meeting was held to have an opportunity of exchanging freely questions and answers as well as views and opinions. This contributed, we believe, to some extent towards deepening "mutual" understanding. But disagreement remains. It was clarified, however, through the discussions on the significance and nature of the long-swings. As mentioned above, econometric methods were deliberately avoided by design in this symposium, so that another conference may be desirable for testing the fruitfulness of the econometric approach. On the other hand, future completion of the 13 volumes of the *Estimates of Long-Term Economic Statistics of Japan Since 1868,* edited by K. Ohkawa, M. Shinohara and M. Umemura (Toyo Keizai Shinpo Sha, Tokyo) will call for another conference more concentrated on a quantitative historical approach.

Four papers were not included in this volume. They are: Keiichiro Nakagawa, "Organized Entrepreneurship in Prewar Japan"; Tadao Uchida, "Structural Characteristics of Japanese Economy—An Appraisal of the High-Speed Growth Period of Postwar Japan through International Comparison"; Kotaro Tsujimura, "Rapid Industrialization of Dual Economy"; and Shigeru Ishikawa, "Net Resources Flow between Agriculture and Industry—A Comparison of Developing Asia with Industrializing Japan."

Nakagawa delineated the features of the entrepreneurial aspect of the Meiji economy by investigating the relevant historical facts such as the first step to foreign trade, development of the raw silk market, and the establishment of modern cotton mills. The principal point of his findings is the fact that enterprisers in various sectors made particular efforts to support each other firmly to make effective use of the limited resources. He labels this characteristic "organized entrepreneurship." Uchida builds a simple macrogrowth model of seven equations—a variation of Harrod-Domar type with the purpose of applying it for international comparisons. In so doing, he aims at finding the characteristics of Japan's postwar high rate of growth. The data, mostly since 1950 and extending through 1963, are used for the study of Western advanced countries, particularly West Germany, U.K. and Italy. Simulations could be applied in comparison with Japan. The main conclusion is that Japan's high growth rate depends on its high marginal propensity to save. Tsujimura draws particular attention to the recent rapid increases in commodity prices and wage rates in Japan. He intends to clarify the causes by referring to the dualistic structure of the economy. A model, designed specifically to be capable of treating that structure, is used. Econometric measurements are not carefully made, but quantitative treatments were made possible. Ishikawa takes up the problem of the sectoral flow of savings from agriculture to industry—one of the conspicuous experiences in the early phase of Japan's economic development. He presents a generalized conceptual framework to analyze it. India, Taiwan, and Mainland China are selected for empirical studies of comparison. He draws careful reservations as a result of the limited reliability of the available data in concluding that no net flow of resources from agriculture can effectively be used for industrialization in Asian countries unlike Japan.

June, 1968   LAWRENCE KLEIN
                                      KAZUSHI OHKAWA

List of Participants

1. ABRAMOVITZ, MOSES Professor, Stanford University, U.S.A.
2. BABA, MASAO Professor, Kyoto University, Japan
3. BRONFENBRENNER, MARTIN Center for Advanced Study in Behavioral Sciences, U.S.A. (Professor, on leave, Carnegie-Mellon University)
4. FUJINO, SHOZABURO Associate Professor, Hitotsubashi University, Japan
5. GLEASON, ALAN H. Professor, International Christian University, Japan
6. GOLDSMITH, RAYMOND W. Professor, Yale University, U.S.A.
7. HAYAMI, YUJIRO Associate Professor, Tokyo Metropolitan University, Japan
8. HORIE, YASUZO Professor, Kyoto University, Japan
9. ICHIMURA, SHIN'ICHI Professor, Osaka University, Japan (Visiting Professor, University of California, Berkeley, U.S.A.
10. ISHIKAWA, SHIGERU Professor, Hitotsubashi University, Japan
11. JORGENSON, D. W. Professor, University of California, Berkeley, U.S.A.
12. KANAMORI, HISAO Senior Staff Economist, Japan Economic Research Center, Japan
13. KEMP, M. C. Professor, University of New South Wales, Australia
14. KLEIN, LAWRENCE R. Professor, University of Pennsylvania, U.S.A.
15. KOMIYA, RYUTARO Associate Professor, Tokyo University, Japan
16. KÖNIG, HEINZ Professor, Wirtshaftschochshule Mannheim, W. Germany
17. KUZNETS, SIMON Professor, Harvard University, U.S.A.
18. MATTHEWS, R. C. O. Professor, Oxford University, U.K.
19. MIYAZAKI, ISAMU Chief of Domestic Research Section, Economic Planning Agency, Japan
20. NAKAGAWA, KEIICHIRO Professor, Tokyo University, Japan
21. OHKAWA, KAZUSHI Professor, Hitotsubashi University, Japan
22. OKITA, SABURO Executive Director, Japan Economic Research Center, Japan
23. OSHIMA, HARRY Professor, University of Hawaii, U.S.A.
24. PATRICK, HUGH Associate Professor, Yale University, U.S.A.
25. RAJ, K. N. Professor, University of Delhi, India

26. RANIS, GUSTAV   Assistant Administrator, Agency for International Development, Department of State, U.S.A.
27. ROSOVSKY, HENRY   Professor, Harvard University, U.S.A.
28. SHINOHARA, MIYOHEI   Professor, Hitotsubashi University, Japan
29. SHIONOYA, YUICHI   Associate Professor, Hitotsubashi University, Japan
30. SHISHIDO, SHUNTARO   Senior Research Officer, Economic Research Institute, Economic Planning Agency, Japan
31. TAIRA, KOJI   Associate Professor, Stanford University, U.S.A.
32. TATEMOTO, MASAHIRO   Professor, Kyoto University, Japan
33. TSUJIMURA, KOTARO   Professor, Keio University, Japan
34. TSURU, SHIGETO   Professor, Hitotsubashi University, Japan
35. UCHIDA, TADAO   Professor, Tokyo University, Japan
36. WATANABE, TSUNEHIKO   Professor, Kyoto University, Japan
37. YAMADA, SABURO   Assistant Professor, Tokyo University, Japan
38. YASUBA, YASUKICHI   Associate Professor, Osaka University, Japan

Table of Contents

PART I. 19TH CENTURY AND PREWAR
ECONOMIC GROWTH

1. Postwar Japanese Growth in Historical Perspective: A
Second Look, *Kazushi Ohkawa and Henry Rosovsky*   3
2. Construction Cycles and Their Monetary-Financial Characteristics, *Shozaburo Fujino*   35
3. Patterns of Industrial Development, *Yuichi Shionoya*   69
4. Industrialization, Technological Progress, and Dual Structure, *Tsunehiko Watanabe*   110
5. Technological Progress in Agriculture, *Yujiro Hayami and
Saburo Yamada*   135
6. Foreign Trade and Economic Growth in Japan:
1858–1937, *Masao Baba and Masahiro Tatemoto* ..   162
7. Trends in Level and Structure of Consumption, *Simon
Kuznets*   197

PART II. POSTWAR ECONOMIC GROWTH

8. Factors for Rapid Economic Growth: A Social Accounting
Approach, *Shinichi Ichimura*   245
9. Patterns and Some Structural Changes in Japan's Postwar
Industrial Growth, *Miyohei Shinohara*   278
10. Economic Growth and Exports, *Hisao Kanamori*   303
11. The Financing of the Public Sector in Postwar Japan,
Hugh T. Patrick   326
12. The Role of the Government in the Postwar Economic
Development of Japan, *Shuntaro Shishido*   356

PART III. SUMMARY REMARKS

13. Notes on Japan's Economic Growth, *Simon Kuznets*   385

Program of the Conference   423

xv

PART I

19th Century and Prewar
Economic Growth

1 | Postwar Japanese Growth in Historical Perspective: A Second Look*

KAZUSHI OHKAWA and HENRY ROSOVSKY

I. INTRODUCTION

The postwar Japanese economy is an outstanding example of the fact that rapid growth and a dualistic structure can coexist. Our paper has two principal purposes: to explain the specific growth pattern which made this coexistence possible, and to examine some of the long-run factors which prepared the Japanese economy for this particular style of growth.

Broadly speaking, Japanese economic development since 1945 has been dominated by three main influences. First came the effects of direct dislocation of economic activity, including large-scale capital destruction, associated with defeat inflicted by the Allies. This resulted in a period of conversion, recovery, and rehabilitation which is frequently assumed to have ended in 1952/54. (This assumption will be critically examined in the main text.) A second influence relates to longer lasting consequences of the war, particularly those associated with Japan's technological isolation between the late 1930's and early 1950's. It concerns primarily the opportunities for rapid technological progress, and this essay largely concentrates on this subject. A third category must rather vaguely be called "new elements introduced into the Japanese economy by war and defeat." Here we

* The authors wish to express their gratitude to Professors Moses Abramovitz and Simon Kuznets, and to all other participants at the Tokyo Conference for valuable comments and suggestions.

Our first look appeared as "Recent Japanese Growth in Historical Perspective," *American Economic Review*, May, 1963. In that article we attempted a brief but systematic comparison between the postwar growth spurt of 1953–60 and the prewar spurts of 1905–12, 1912–19, and 1931–38. Our second look is somewhat more ambitious in that it attempts to fit the postwar years into the general evolution of modern economic growth in Japan.

3

have in mind certain increases in the social capacity of the nation to utilize the international backlog of technological progress. If, in fact, increased social capacity exists and can be identified, it could raise the long-run growth potential of the economy. At present, however, we are not ready to deal with this subject. Its influence will have to remain implicit.

In studying the effects of Japan's technological isolation and what we believe to be a causally related investment boom, the framework of long-swing analysis will be utilized. The very high rate of aggregate growth which followed the end of rehabilitation as well as the somewhat slower rates of growth since 1961 seem to fit the long-swing hypothesis, and this framework also allows illuminating comparisons with similar expansions and contractions before World War II. Specific comparisons will be made with the 1910's and 1930's, when there was also considerable acceleration in the rates of growth of aggregate output. The long-swing framework has the additional advantage of providing a good method of observing changes in trends. Evidence will be provided to show that trend rates of growth—measured between long swings—have been rising, and while this observation is extremely difficult to "explain," its significance for postwar growth must be taken into account.

What has happened in Japanese economic history for the past decade and a half must also be examined in terms of economic structure. We will deal with these matters—currently and historically—by using the concept of "modern" and "traditional" sectors, which is a particular form of dualistic structure. This concept has been used by us on a number of previous occasions, and hopefully no elaborate explanations will be necessary. In the Japanese economy, modern sectors are those which use techniques and forms of organization imported from the West. Traditional sectors employ techniques and organization indigenous to Japan. We have found this dichotomy to be a useful heuristic device in studying structural change, despite the fact that neat classification or statistical measurement is not always possible. There are many blurred areas where traditional and modern facets intermingle—one might think of these as "hybrid" sectors—but on the whole the distinction is theoretically useful.[1] We hope to clarify the relationship between structure and aggregate growth of the economy, and also the influence exercised by rapid growth in changing the structure. These interrelations are complicated, but they are especially crucial at the present time.

---

[1] See our article "A Century of Japanese Economic Growth," in W. W. Lockwood (ed.), *The State and Economic Enterprise in Japan* (Princeton, N.J.: Princeton University Press, 1965).

II. LONG-RANGE GROWTH PATTERN: A STATISTICAL VIEW

A General Picture

Let us begin by looking at the long-range growth pattern of the Japanese economy in terms of GNP. It appears in Figure 1–1, in constant prices, for the period 1882–1963—almost the entire span for which a quantitative record is available. The graph contains two series: one simply depicts the annual values, while the other shows annual values of GNP smoothed by a moving average the duration of which is approximately equal to the average length of the business cycle.[2]

Three observations are suggested by Figure 1–1.

1. Most obvious, perhaps, is the enormous and unprecedented

FIGURE 1–1. An Overall Picture of Growth in Terms of GNP in 1934–36 Prices.

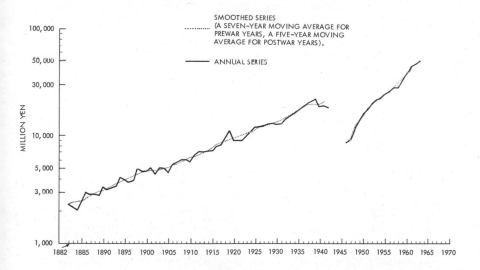

[2] Seven years before World War II, and five years in the postwar period. Prewar GNP is based on unpublished data of the Rockefeller Project, Institute of Economic Research, Hitotsubashi University; hereafter cited as RIH. Postwar GNP is from the official data of the Japanese Government Economic Planning Agency; hereafter cited as EPA. We have linked the prewar and postwar series. Some of the RIH series are now in the process of publication, and will eventually be available in 13 volumes under the general title of *Chōki keizai tōkei* (Estimates of Long-Term Economic Statistics of Japan since 1868), published by the Tōyō Keizai Shimpō-sha.

dislocation caused by World War II. In 1946, for example, the level of GNP abruptly dropped to the 1917–18 level, and although doubts must exist concerning the accuracy of statistical observations during the years 1946–50, there can be no question about the extent of economic disarrangement. A similar conclusion can be based on the observation that the prewar annual peak for GNP was reached in 1939, and was not attained again until 1954, although the quality of the statistics are doubtful especially for 1939–42 when military expenditures were very large.

2. A closer look, especially at the smoothed series, also indicates, in the long run, periods of faster and slower growth along the path of a rising secular trend. We consider these alterations to be long swings of the growth rate of total output (frequently referred to as Kuznets cycles), and we believe that the rapid postwar expansion, especially since 1954, is appropriately treated as a long-swing upswing.

3. That the trend is rising has already been mentioned, but a comparison of the prewar trend and postwar growth also reveals a clear acceleration in the last decade and a half.

These observations lead to a number of interpretative questions. Is the postwar acceleration of the GNP growth rate the "economic miracle" so frequently mentioned in connection with Japan? Does it represent a radical shift in Japan's trend rate of growth? If the prewar trend between 1919 and 1938 (long-swing peaks) is extrapolated, then postwar GNP only reaches the secular trend in 1961. Is this what some observers have in mind when they attempt to explain postwar acceleration as a process of catching-up with the historical growth trend?

These questions are too simple and it is our view that the postwar growth pattern is a mixture of elements only partially illustrated by these queries. Three things have to be considered: the influences of war dislocation and rehabilitation, of a long-swing expansion, and of the trend. In practice it is impossible to disentangle the weights of these influences in clear fashion. We shall, however, speculate about the relative importance of these separate elements in postwar growth, recognizing at all times that complicated interrelations must blur the analysis and qualify the answers.

War Dislocation and Rehabilitation

We can most conveniently begin by stating our views concerning the direct effects of war and rehabilitation. Increasingly in the 1930's, and most especially from 1939 onward, the needs of war affected the normal functioning of the Japanese economy. Total defeat came in 1945, leaving the national economy in great disorder—even income estimates are not available for that year. Between 1945 and 1952–54, Japan's economy was most heavily influenced by reconstruction and rehabilitation. During these years abnormal growth factors outweighed the normal. This situation changed after 1952–54, although some consequences of the defeat in World War II and its aftermath are still felt by the Japanese economy. Can these views be substantiated?

Both quantitative and qualitative evidence supports a 1952–54 demarcation. The 1939 prewar peak level of GNP was for the first time surpassed in 1954, and the same is true for GNP per capita. The aggregate capital-output ratio also rose to more usual values in 1953, indicating the end of a period in which previously existing excess capacity played a major role. Furthermore, the occupation ended in 1952 and Japan began once more to run its own affairs, both as a nation and as an economy. More confirmation of the demarcation can be found by looking again at Figure 1–1. Movements of the postwar growth rate are clear: a decline from the very high levels of the early postwar years reaching a turning point near 1954; after that the rate of growth accelerates. Our interpretation of this is that the high rates of the immediate afterwar years were heavily influenced by recovery factors which tended to fade away in the middle 1950's. The subsequent growth spurt must therefore be attributed to "new" factors having an existence relatively independent of direct war dislocation.

There are possible objections to the 1952–54 demarcation, and it may be said with some justice that our reasoning is too mechanical. Certain legacies of war dislocation and rehabilitation are still present in the Japanese economy. Some war-created shortages still plague Japan, and excellent examples are residential housing and social overhead capital. War-induced demographic factors are still significant. Also, advances in science and technology developed during the war combined with simultaneous manpower training are still relevant in understanding post-1952–54 rapid growth. It is also possible that the decline of the rates of growth near the turning point were caused by factors other than the exhaustion of war recovery: for example, the end of the Korean War may have been involved. We have no particular quarrel with these doubts—some of which we share—but we still believe that 1954 is the most appropriate year with which to begin the analysis of "normal" postwar growth. It represents a clustering of forces pointing to a reestablished normal economic situation.

Long Swings

The pattern of historical long-swing fluctuations is shown in Figure 1–2. In this graph, measurement is based on the smoothed GNP series, and two kinds of growth rates are shown: one simply takes the year-to-year changes, and the second indicates the intercyclical average rates of change. Both methods bring out the swings with clarity, but an unambiguous selection of peaks and troughs is not a simple matter. Our selection of long-swing peak and trough years depends on two principles: a trough year (or better "band of years," since each year stands for the center of a moving average) must precede a sharp and sustained increase in the average annual rates of growth; if a period of rapid growth is characterized by a plateau during which the rate of growth maintains a high level, the end of the plateau is selected as the peak.[3]

FIGURE 1–2.   Annual Rates of Growth in Terms of GNP.

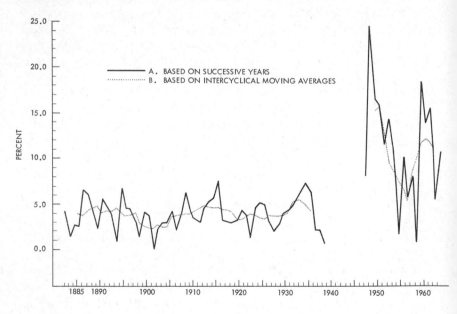

[3] Although prewar peaks and troughs were selected from the series smoothed by a seven-year moving average, an exception was made for the 1938 peak. The annual growth rate of GNP dropped sharply from 5.1 percent in 1938 to 2.1 percent in 1939, and a smoothing procedure lasting seven years would not adequately show this. Consequently a three-year moving average was used to center the peak in 1938.

In Table 1–1, the prewar long swings again appear clearly within the selected peaks and troughs. But how does the postwar period fit into this pattern? We will assume that 1954 represents a very special kind of long-swing trough, and that the years of rapid growth which follow form the first postwar long-swing expansion. This makes possible the historical comparison of four long-swing expansions: 1885–98, 1905–19, 1931–38, and 1954–61. At present 1961 seems a good choice for the first postwar long-swing peak—although it is much too early for a definitive opinion. In 1961, the real annual rate of growth of the smoothed GNP series (five-year moving average) peaked at 12.9 percent. After that, the rate of growth based on smoothed series has declined slightly, and we may hazard a guess that a downswing started in 1961.

There remains one more problem in the use of the long-swing framework. What should one do with the period 1938–54? Strictly speaking there was almost no secular growth between 1938 and 1954, but in fact those years consist of a decline occasioned by the war with a trough in 1946/47, followed by the abnormally high postwar recovery rates. Probably the wisest step would be to ignore this segment

TABLE 1-1

Average Annual Rates of Growth during Long Swings
Smoothed Series, Constant Prices (GNP)

		Rates of Growth (%)
1.	1885 (Trough) – 1898 (Peak).	4.33
2.	1898 (P) – 1905 (T).	2.27
3.	1905 (T) – 1919 (P).	4.21
4.	1919 (P) – 1931 (T).	3.56
5.	1931 (T) – 1938 (P)*	6.00
6.	1938 (P)*– 1954 (T)*	0.52
7.	1954 (T)*– 1961 (P).	10.86
8.	1961 (P) – 1964.	8.86

REMARKS: 1.   "Smoothed series" means a seven-year moving average in prewar years and a five-year moving average in the post-World War II period.   Some exceptional cases are marked with an asterisk and they are formed into three-year moving averages. The original series are in 1934–36 prices based on RIH and EPA data.

2.   Rates of growth are measured between moving averages centered on indicated years except line 8, which is measured between crude values of the EPA new data in 1960 prices.

of Japanese economic history entirely in long-run analysis, because of the overwhelming influence of noneconomic factors at this time.

The Trend

There are many ways to measure a trend rate of growth, and some can give misleading results. If the growth rate of real GNP in Japan is calculated between 1881–86 and 1931–38, the result is an average annual rate of 3.9 percent, and a comparison of this prewar trend with postwar values may lead to overemphasis on economic miracles and sharp breaks with the past. But this type of trend measure seems inappropriate when long swings are present. In that case complete swings are preferable as the unit of trend measurement, as has been done in Table 1–2 in terms of average level trend rates of growth, indicating the GNP growth rates between the average values of long-swing expansions and contractions.

If the specific experience of World War II is excluded the trend rates of growth show an accelerating tendency, already in evidence in rather weak form before the war.[4] The tendency of pre-World War II trend acceleration may appear even more clearly in the future when the moderate overestimation of late 19th-century growth rates is corrected. This would suggest that any explanation of recent growth

TABLE 1-2

Average Annual Trend Rates of Growth
Smoothed Series, Constant Prices (GNP)

		Rates of Growth (%)
1.	1885–98 to 1898–1905.	3.4
2.	1898–1905 to 1905–19.	3.4
3.	1905–19 to 1919–31.	3.9
4.	1919–31 to 1931–38.	4.1
5.	1931–38 to 1938–54*	0.7
6.	1938–54* to 1954–61	5.0

*Values for 1940–46 omitted.

REMARKS: The original series are the same as those in Table 1-1.

---

[4] Measures of the trend using long-swing peak-to-peak and trough-to-trough rates of growth show similar results.

must include as a contributing factor a rising trend rate of growth, and it would certainly be helpful to have a hypothesis for this phenomenon; unfortunately we are not yet ready to offer one.

Thus far results have been presented only for aggregate output, and in many ways this is a most appropriate indicator. A more balanced discussion, however, would require a broader analysis including input indicators and various output-input relations.[5] Some of these will be supplied in later sections, but to conclude with the main statistical presentation we would like to examine briefly the path of the output-labor ratio (Y/L) since it provides a good bridge between a discussion of the growth pattern in this section and the study of structural changes in the next section.

A number of observations follow from Table 1–3. First, the growth rates of Y/L and L conform to the output swings. Expansions mean more rapid growth of (partial) labor productivity[6] and employment, while contractions show a slowing down of both indicators. Secondly, one must note not only that the trend growth rate of the output-labor ratio has been rising during the prewar period, but also that the entries in lines 11 and 14 lie well below the prewar trend. The deviation from trend is obviously due to the negative entry in line 6. What happened between 1938 and 1954 can in large measure be ascribed to extraordinary factors, related to war and reconstruction. But line 6 includes the time span 1938–*54,* and the value for 1954 was still below the 1938 level. Consequently the very high-growth rate of Y/L for 1954–61 may still be influenced by recovery from war dislocation.

---

[5] A broader picture will be found in the following: Miyohei Shinohara, *Growth and Cycles in the Japanese Economy* (Tokyo: Kinokuniya Bookstore, 1962), ch. iv; Shozaburo Fujino, *Nihon no keiki junkun* (Business Cycles in Japan), (Tokyo: Keisō Shobō, 1965); K. Ohkawa and H. Rosovsky, "Economic Fluctuations in Prewar Japan: A Preliminary Analysis of Cycles and Long Swings," *Hitotsubashi Journal of Economics,* Vol. III, No. 1 (October, 1962).

[6] There may be some doubt about using simple labor force figures in a measure of labor productivity. It would have been more desirable to consider also changes in working hours. However, long-run series of working hours are not available. According to the Monthly Labor Survey of the Ministry of Labor, average man-hours in all industries increased 3.8 percent during the expansion 1954–61, and decreased 4 percent for the period 1961–65. For selected prewar years the Labor Statistics of the Bank of Japan provide similar data for factory manufacturing. According to this source, during the contraction of 1923–31, average man-hours decreased 8.4 percent, while they increased 8.2 percent during the 1931–38 expansion. These figures suggest that man-hours worked changed in association with long swings, and consideration of this fact would moderate the changes in (partial) labor productivity as shown in Table 1–3. For prewar years, see *Nihon rōdō undō shiryō* (Historical Materials on the Japanese Labor Movement), (1959), chap. x, p. 231; for postwar years, see the annual issues of *Rōdō tōkei nempō* (Yearbook of Labor Statistics).

TABLE 1-3

Output-Labor Ratio (Y/L) and Labor (L): Average
Annual Long Swing and Trend Rates of Growth

	Y/L (%)	L (%)
A. Long Swings		
1. 1887 (T) - 1898 (P).	3.38	0.91
2. 1898 (P) - 1905 (T).	1.41	0.86
3. 1905 (T) - 1919 (P).	3.20	1.01
4. 1919 (P) - 1931 (T).	2.90	0.66
5. 1931 (T) - 1938 (P).	4.82	1.15
6. 1938 (P) - 1954 (T).	-0.95	1.03
7. 1954 (T) - 1961 (P).	9.12	1.74
B. Trends		
(Peak to Peak)		
8. 1881-1898.	2.59	0.95
9. 1898-1919.	2.64	0.96
10. 1919-38.	3.56	0.84
11. 1938-61.	2.07	1.56
(Trough to Trough)		
12. 1887-1905.	2.61	0.89
13. 1905-31.	3.05	0.85
14. 1931-54.	2.54	1.36

REMARKS: 1. Linked RIH and EPA data.

2. The annual growth rate of Y/L for 1961-64 was 7.75 percent
(new EPA data in 1960 prices), and for L it was 1.13 percent (Labor
Force Survey data).

III. STRUCTURAL CHANGES

A General Picture

The form of dual structure defined in the "Introduction" implies differential productivity levels for the modern and traditional sectors in terms of product per worker. Modern growth in modern sectors is accompanied by increases in labor productivity due to technological progress and capital accumulation. The productivity levels of traditional sectors can also rise, as they certainly did in Japan, through traditional technological progress or in the form of induced progress on the part of the modern sector. In general, however, the possiblities of traditional productivity increases would appear to be much more limited, and in time they will fall behind the modern sectors. Changes in these sectoral productivity levels—particularly the rate of growth of the differentials—is one of the basic elements of structural change in Japan.

Another property of the dual structure is a differential rate of compensation for factors of production in the two major sectors of the economy. These are related to the productivity levels as well as to the techniques which the sectors employ, but the relations and inter-relations are far from simple. Ideally we would want information concerning all forms of factor compensation, but due to data limitations we will have to confine ourselves to wage differentials.

In a more general sense, it is very difficult to cast quantifiable structural change into "modern" and "traditional" categories. How-ever, since we believe in the validity and usefulness of the concepts, proxies have been employed. Manufacturing and agriculture are selected as the respective representatives of the modern and traditional sectors, and in our opinion this will realistically reflect the behavior of the two main sectors.

Let us start with the productivity differentials in Table 1–4. Using the long-swing demarcations of periods adopted in the preceding section, this table contains the average annual rates of increase in real product per worker for agriculture and manufacturing. For both sectors rates of increase (or decrease) on the whole conform well to the swing expansion-contraction pattern. One exception in the form of an inverse relation appears for each sector: a higher growth rate during a contraction in period (4) for manufacturing, and a lower growth rate during an expansion in period (1) for agriculture. And there is one other noteworthy item. Beginning with the 1905–19 expansion, the growth rate of real product per worker in manufactur-ing surges ahead of agriculture, and the differential is especially large during the 1919–31 contraction and the post-World War II expan-sion. This movement, in secular form, appears most clearly in Table 1–4 where the ratios of output per worker in agriculture and manu-facturing are compared at long-swing peaks and troughs. Until 1905, the trend of this ratio changes only little. But since 1905, and especially since 1919 (and with the insignificant exception of 1954), the ratio A/M declines steadily, indicating a widening labor produc-tivity gap which transcends long-swing expansions and contractions.

One should note also that this gap between the growth pattern of agriculture and manufacturing (or traditional and modern sectors) arises in spite of changing economic circumstances. Thus, in 1919–31

TABLE 1-4

Rate of Change in Real Product per Worker in
Agriculture (A) and Manufacturing (M)

		A (%)	M (%)	Difference (M-A)	Ratio of Output per Worker	
					Years	A/M
1.	1886-1898. . . .	1.25	1.96	0.71	1886	50.0
					1898	43.8
2.	1898-1905. . . .	1.86	-0.20	-2.06	1905	50.7
3.	1905-19.	1.99	2.88	0.89	1917	44.8
4.	1919-31.	0.51	5.68	5.17	1931	25.7
5.	1931-38.	0.80	2.93	2.13	1938	22.8
6.	1938-54.	-0.14	-1.52	-1.36	1954	28.1
7.	1954-61.	3.61	10.51	6.90	1961	19.9
8.	1961*-64*. . . .	3.44	8.14	4.70	1961*	27.8
					1964*	23.2

REMARKS: 1. *A*--(Forestry and Fisheries are excluded.) Output
data from Saburo Yamada and labor force data from Ryoshin Minami;
both contained in RIH. *M*--(Mining and Electricity included.) Output and labor force data from Ohkawa's compilations as contained in
RIH.

2. These series have been smoothed by a seven-year moving average, except for 1886 and the postwar years for which a five-year
moving average was used. For the years 1961-64 the RIH series were
not available. These years are marked with an asterisk, and rely
on the new EPA output series and the Labor Force Survey. For 1961-
64, agriculture includes forestry and fisheries, and manufacturing
excludes mining and electricity.

real product per worker in agriculture was stagnant while it was rising
sharply in manufacturing. At the same time, the labor force in manufacturing increased only very little. By contrast, in the post-World
War II period, labor productivity in agriculture and manufacturing
grew rapidly, and employment in manufacturing, during 1954–64,
increased at an average annual rate of 4.1 percent.

Differential Structure

The structural change which starts to affect the Japanese economy
slightly in 1905 and powerfully since 1919 is a specific form of the
general phenomenon of economic dualism which we call "differential
structure." To us, differential structure implies, besides the usual
different levels of productivity and capital intensity in modern and

traditional sectors, the rapid growth of modern sectors and the lagging growth of traditional sectors—in other words a *growing gap* in the structure of the economy. The years since World War II have not yet done away with the differential structure, and consequently the pattern of development since 1905 forms a particularly appropriate basis for historical comparison.[7]

We may begin a more detailed consideration of the differential structure by looking at what happened to the terms of trade between agriculture and manufacturing. This is relevant, because one might have expected the widening productivity gap to be counterbalanced by changing relative prices of outputs for the two sectors. That this did not happen in Japan is related to the persistence of this structure for over 50 years. Panel I of Table 1–5 shows the average annual rates of change for the output prices of the two representative sectors. Within the previously used periodization, fluctuations of relative prices are systematic: during expansions the prices of agricultural products rise more rapidly than those of manufactured goods (with the slight exception of 1905–19); during contractions agricultural prices decline more rapidly. In other words, the agricultural terms of trade improve during the upswing and deteriorate during the downswing, and this can be explained by the generally recognized phenomenon of a comparatively low-supply elasticity for agriculture—low, that is, compared to manufacturing. But Table 1–5 contains a more important observation. During almost the entire prewar period the trend of the terms of trade is rather level. Despite the declining relative productivity of agriculture beginning in 1905–19, its relative output price has risen only moderately up to 1961. This must be explained by the influence of imports competitive with domestic agriculture, and also by conditions of labor supply which forced agriculture to accept lower rates of compensation.

Table 1–5 also supplies some series which combine the influence of productivity movements and terms of trade. These are the columns which show output per worker in current prices, or simply "value

---

[7] By its very nature, the traditional sector is characterized by much self-employment and the use of unpaid family labor. This certainly creates great difficulties in measuring the "productivity" of labor. The simple exclusion of unpaid family labor does not seem to us justified, since this sector depends so heavily on this type of work. There are additional complications. The age, sex, and educational composition, and the proportion of part-time work, all differ between agriculture and manufacturing, and to some extent change over time. Continuous data which could be used to introduce necessary qualifications in sectoral behavior are not available for the long run, but we believe that the changing differentials in Table 1–4 are so drastic that no amount of adjustment would alter our argument.

TABLE 1-5

Changes in Prices and Value of Product per Worker
in Agriculture (*A*) and Manufacturing (*M*)

I. PRICES

		Average Annual Rates of Change (%)		*Terms of Trade (A/M) 1934-36=100*	
		A	*M*	*Years*	*(%)*
1.	1886-98. . . .	5.50	4.01	1886	81.4
2.	1898-1905. . .	1.37	2.60	1898	106.0
3.	1905-19. . . .	6.72	6.84	1905	87.3
				1913	113.2
4.	1919-31. . . .	-2.58	-2.06	1919	107.1
5.	1931-38. . . .	7.14	3.91	1931	89.1
				1938	93.0
6.	1954-61. . . .	4.53	-0.48	1954	125.7
7.	1961*-64*. . .	7.84	0.75	1961	139.9

II. VALUE OF PRODUCT PER WORKER

		Average Annual Rates of Change (%)		*Ratio A/M*	
		A	*M*	*Years*	*(%)*
1.	1886-98. . . .	6.75	5.97	1886	32.2
2.	1898-1905. . .	0.49	2.40	1898	36.3
3.	1905-19. . . .	8.71	9.72	1905	41.5
4.	1919-31. . . .	-2.07	3.62	1919	36.5
5.	1931-38. . . .	7.93	6.84	1931	22.9
				1938	22.4
6.	1954-61. . . .	8.21	10.03	1954	31.6
				1961	30.4
7.	1961*-64*. . .	11.28	8.89	1961*	34.7
				1964*	37.0

REMARKS: 1. Rates of price changes are approximations, calculated by taking the differences of rates of change between value
product and real product.

2. Sources and scope for value of product and number of workers
and smoothing of series, are identical to Table 1-4. An asterisk
continues to designate EPA data.

productivity"—a statistic highly relevant to the distribution of income. Once again the break associated with the differential structure
emerges clearly. Before World War I, the trend of the value productivity ratios (*A/M*) rose. Since World War I, however, this
situation has changed, and the trend of *A/M* has fallen more or less

continuously. (The reading for 1954 is still affected by remnants of war dislocation, but the decline from 1954 to 1961 is considered as the reestablishment of the prewar pattern.)

Wage Differentials

When a labor surplus situation prevails in a dual economy, the marginal worker who cannot enter higher wage modern industries normally finds employment (or partial employment) in the lower wage traditional sectors. Under these circumstances, total unemployment is rather uncommon. The requirements for labor, however, do not remain unchanging, and we will assume that wage differentials between modern and traditional sectors are a good indicator of changing demand-supply conditions in the labor market.

Before examining what happened to wages, a few words of caution are needed. Wages for "traditional" and "modern" sectors do not exist as statistical categories, and the wages of manufacturing and agriculture will again have to be used as proxies; and this creates problems. The average wage in manufacturing covers very different lines of activity associated with various levels of compensation, depending on the type and quality of the worker. As a result the changing composition of employment will affect comparisons over time. Furthermore, the very concept of agricultural wages in a society like Japan may appear questionable. Japanese agriculture has only very few independent hired workers, and their wages are subject to large seasonal fluctuations. Nonwage payments are also relatively important in Japan. All this means that our indicators must be presented with caution. Nevertheless we use wage differentials because they give the best available historical picture of the changing factor price position of the two sectors.

The relevant figures in the by now familiar periodic intervals are given in Table 1–6. Let us begin by looking at the wage ratio: Wa/Wm. We find that the ratio moves in perfect conformity with output swings. It rises during expansions (especially toward the end of expansions) and falls during contractions (especially toward the end of contractions). This seems to suggest certain demand-supply relations in the labor market: wage differentials narrow when the demand for labor in the modern sector is more active, and they widen in the obverse case. This has been also true during the post–World War II expansion.[8]

---

[8] Koji Taira observed a similar phenomenon using a different method. See *The Dynamics of Japanese Wage Differentials, 1881–1959*, Ph.D. thesis (Stanford University, 1961).

TABLE 1-6

Wage Differential and Its Relation
to Productivity Differential

	Ratio of Agricultural Wage (Wa) to Manufacturing Wage (Wm) Wa/Wm (%)	*Ratio of Wages to Productivity (P)*	
		Wa/Pa (%)	Wm/Pm (%)
1886.	69.9	67.3	34.9
1898.	76.5	46.2	22.2
1905.	69.6	53.4	32.0
1919.	73.7	51.8	25.0
1931.	53.8	65.9	27.8
1938.	56.7	42.5	22.2
1954.	37.3	40.0	33.1
1961.	42.0	46.8	27.9
1964.	48.6	36.0*	27.4*

REMARKS: The wage comparison is restricted to males and is taken from Mataji Umemura, *Chingin, koyō, nōgyō* (Wages, Employment, Agriculture) (Tokyo, 1961), pp. 193-94. The figures for 1959-64 are our own calculations, following Umemura's procedures. For wages in manufacturing and agriculture, no single continuous series is available. Umemura's series are preliminary, and also are composed of several linked segments. As usual, for prewar years we have smoothed the results with a seven-year moving average (a three-year moving average for 1886), while for postwar years we have used a five-year moving average.

Both *Pa* (value of product per worker in agriculture) and *Pm* (value of product per worker in manufacturing) are taken from Table 1-5. Years marked with an asterisk are EPA data.

Another feature of the *Wa/Wm* ratio deserves attention. The ratio sustains two distinct levels: a higher level through 1919 and a lower level from 1931 onward. This means that somewhere between 1919 and 1931 the relative wage of agriculture (or of the traditional sectors) fell sharply and remained in this position more or less until the present.

Next, let us look at the relation between wage rates and (partial) labor productivity. To begin with manufacturing, the ratio of wages to value productivity (*Wm/Pm*) in Table 1-6 behaves with considerable regularity: it falls during expansions and rises during contractions. Thus, in the modern sectors, during periods of more rapid growth wages lag behind productivity, but when the economy grows more slowly wages tend to make up for the previously lost ground.

Again these generalizations are valid also for the years after World War II.

The corresponding ratio for agriculture (Wa/Pa in Table 1-6) performs in the same fashion during long swings by falling during expansions and rising during contractions. One implication of this is that even in the traditional sectors the relative income of proprietors in comparison with wage income rises in upswings and falls in downswings. Special notice may be taken of the extraordinary entry for 1931 at the depth of the Great Depression, and also of the high value for 1886 immediately following the Matsukata Deflation. During the Great Depression, the fall in farm prices was unprecedented, and the relative income of farmers—many of whom were part-time agricultural "workers"—declined sharply, creating grave and lasting social difficulties. Matsukata's deflationary policies had somewhat similar effects. Once again, the overall pattern holds for the postwar years.

A Summary of Structural Changes

In this section we have analyzed primarily the path of (partial) labor productivity and wages in agriculture (traditional) and manufacturing (modern). The following results emerge:

1. Long swings appear in the movements of productivity and wage rates, and we will attempt to show in the next section that the relations between these two variables during the swing is especially important to the Japanese growth process.

2. From the standpoint of the historical trend, we have identified a major structural change called the differential structure—a specific form of the more general concept: dual economy. There are, as yet, some problems in dating this change with precision. As far as productivity differentials are concerned, the "gap" appears in rather weak form during the expansion 1905–19, and it is much more readily observable during the ensuing contraction of 1919–31. For wage differentials, the gap is in evidence beginning only with the years 1919–31. We will speculate about the reasons for this time pattern in the next section, but the main point is that the differential structure has as its characteristics both a pulling apart of productivity and wage levels.

3. Post–World War II growth until 1961 conforms to the structure outlined in this section. One can observe the typical productivity-wage lag associated with a long-swing expansion. The very recent—post 1961—narrowing of wage differentials will require separate analysis in later sections.

IV. THE MECHANISM OF GROWTH

An Investment Spurt

In the preceding two sections we have outlined some of the basic features of Japanese growth applicable to the period 1905–61, and now we must attempt the more difficult task of explanation. What gave rise to the Japanese growth pattern and economic structure during these years—these are the main questions. The questions are complicated, and we are not yet ready to suggest a comprehensive, definitive, or rigorous model. Our answers will focus on the interrelations of three factors: the investment spurt, the flexible supply of labor, and borrowed technology.[9] Primary emphasis will now be placed on the years following World War II.

First, let us examine the behavior of investment. The term "investment spurt" has been used to imply an explosive increase in the rate of fixed capital formation, accompanied by an accelerated rate of output growth. The adjective "explosive" calls attention to a sharp discontinuity with which the increase in investment begins. Two more empirical properties of Japanese investment spurts should also be noticed. Normally they last some six to seven years, a period longer than investment booms associated with ordinary business cycles, and the investment spurts are broadly based in many sectors of the economy. This does not deny higher-than-average investment activity in certain sectors, as was the case for chemical and engineering industries in the recent past, but it does underline an overall higher level of investment in all modern sectors. And this is important in understanding the association between accelerated investment and output.

Economic growth of the postwar period features a typical investment spurt, and the particulars can be examined in Figure 1–3 which shows rates of increase in total and sectoral domestic gross fixed investment in 1960 prices. The series of total investment contain several marked increases. A preliminary rise can be noticed in 1952–54, when the average annual rate of increase was 14.7 percent. A sharper increase took place in 1955–57 when the rate rose to 31.9 percent. Then, after a few years of less-rapid growth, the annual rate of growth of total investment again attained 30.3 percent for 1959–61. We will consider the years 1956–61 as forming the core of the

---

[9] A more comprehensive analysis would certainly have to take into account the role of international trade (and the balance of payments), and the domestic savings position. In the discussion which follows we can safely assume that both international trade and domestic savings supported the investment spurts.

FIGURE 1–3. Domestic Fixed Investment in 1960 Prices.

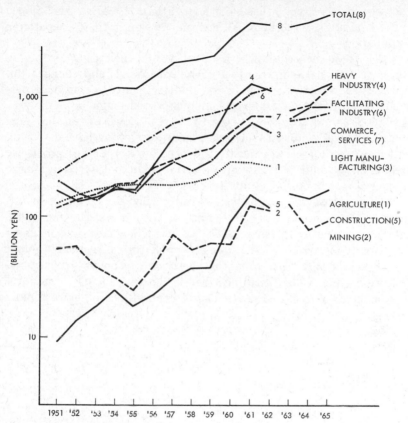

EPA data: 1951–62 A series
           1962–64 B series (excluding Public enterprises)

NOTES: 1. No continuous series of sectoral investment is available for the postwar period in constant prices. The "A Series" are based on unofficial data compiled for the medium-range economic plan (EPA, Planning Bureau, 1964, mimeographed). The "B Series" are derived from estimates of gross capital stock in Economic Planning Agency, Economic Research Institute, *Keizai bunseki* (Economic Analysis) No. 17, (March, 1966).
    2. (4) Engineering, steel, metal and chemical industries; (3) all manufacturing other than the industries included in (4); (6) transportation, communication, utilities; (7) banking, insurance and real estate are included; (1) forestry and fishery are included.

postwar investment spurt, even if this includes a couple of years during which investment remained stable, though at a very high level. At that time—specifically 1957–59—the underlying strong predisposition toward investment growth was merely dampened temporarily by a tight money policy occasioned by a foreign payments deficit. Investment incentives reappeared as soon as the policy was changed.

By contrast, after 1961, the rate of growth of investment slowed down, and this situation lasted at least through 1965; an easy money policy did not seem to help. All this supports the 1956–61 separation into periods.

A look at the sectoral series confirms the pervasiveness of the investment spurt. It is true that engineering, steel, and chemical industries shown as "heavy industry" (4) in Figure 1–3 produce particularly high speeds of investment increase through both the first (1956–57) and second (1960–61) waves. However, at the same time almost all sectors display spectacular rates of investment growth. There is no shortage of statistical evidence to bolster this point: we know, for example, that investment acceleration took place in all size ranges of manufacturing establishments.

In the postwar period, as well as historically, the timing of investment and output spurts is closely related. The evidence for the aggregates is contained in Table 1–7. No claim is made for an exact conformity in terms of duration of these spurts—actually output expansion usually lasts somewhat beyond investment expansion—but we do believe that, both now and in the past, the acceleration of investment is one of the major causal explanations of more rapidly rising output.

TABLE 1-7

Capital Formation: Average Annual Rate of Growth during Long Swings ($\Delta I/I$) and Its Ratio to GNP (I/Y)

(1)	$\Delta I/I$ (%)	(2)	I/Y (%)
1. 1898 (P) – 1905 (T).	3.53	1898 (P)	12.6
2. 1905 (T) – 1919 (P).	6.67	1905 (T)	12.6
3. 1919 (P) – 1931 (T).	4.99	1919 (P)	16.0
4. 1931 (T) – 1937 (P).	13.97	1931 (T)	16.5
5. 1938 (P) – 1954 (T).	0.55	1938 (P)	27.6
6. 1954 (T) – 1961 (P).	20.89	1954 (T)	20.9
7. 1961 (P) – 1964.	8.70	1961 (P)	35.2
		1964	32.9

REMARKS: Lines 1 through 4 are from RIH data primarily derived from H. Rosovsky, *Capital Formation in Japan* (1961). These show gross domestic fixed investment (including military investment), and the growth rates are calculated from smoothed series (seven-year moving average) in 1934-36 prices. Lines 5 through 7 are from Economic Planning Agency, *Kokumin shotoku tōkei nempō* (Annual Report on National Income Statistics) (1961); smoothed by five-year moving average. Lines 6 and 7 are in 1960 prices.

Another notable feature of the investment spurts viewed historically is that they exhibit increasing vigor. For the three investment upswings since 1905, one must conclude that both their rates of increase and the proportion of investment to GNP have risen. Post–World War II years indicate the highest entries in Japanese economic history, and this raises a point related to long-run perspective. Astonishment about the growth and level of recent Japanese investment has been expressed by numerous observers, a feeling that has perhaps been fortified by comparisons to a long-term prewar average. This is a rather meaningless comparison, because account must be taken of the spurts and the nature of the trend. In this light, what has happened after World War II appears to be much more reasonable; the trend of investment spurts has been accelerating and we would suggest that this is related to similar accelerations observed for productivity and output.

We think that the accelerating pattern of capital formation—both in its swing and trend dimension—was the dynamic force behind modern economic growth in Japan. But it is a very difficult matter to explain why capital formation should have proceeded in discrete movements or why its ratio to total output should continue to rise secularly. Three ranges of factors may be relevant: each investment spurt is affected by exogenous or *ad hoc* factors; there are causes common to all spurts; there are relations between specific industries and investment spurts.

The 1956–61 spurt provides an excellent example of *ad hoc* elements. War dislocation, discussed in Section I, obviously had indirect effects which lasted well beyond 1952–54. One of these is the enlarged technological gap, which the years of isolation and abnormal international relations created between Japan and the more advanced countries. This must have been an important factor in the postwar investment spurt, and it has often been labeled "short-term catching-up." Another factor, though of lesser importance, was the pressure for greater competitiveness injected into the economy by means of recent trade liberalization policies. Similar influences can be detected before World War II. For example, the investment spurt during the "teens" of this century was certainly affected by the bonanza atmosphere of the Japanese economy during World War I. In the same vein, the armaments efforts of the 1930's spearheaded by a free-spending military government also provided vital support for investment activity, especially in industries related to these endeavors.

In spite of the variety of exogenous considerations there are common characteristics in these investment spurts. The most essential condition is a higher-than-average rate of return on capital so that the incentive to invest remains strong.[10] For this to be the case, a number of other conditions must be fulfilled. First, the output effect of investment will be largely due to technological progress. Second, the demand for increased output will be maintained at a high level despite rapidly rising productive capacity. Third, input factors will continue to be available at prices favorable to entrepreneurs. These are some of the most significant common features of the investment spurts, and they suggest reasons both for long-swing expansion and contraction. Of course, the manner in which these similarities affect the economy differs from spurt to spurt. For example, prewar spurts were marked by inflation suggesting some deficit of savings, and this was not the case for 1956–61. Nevertheless, at the present stage of the argument we will continue to place stress on the similarities.

Finally, mention has been made of the relation between specific industries and investment spurts. Each of the three spurts can be labeled in this fashion. The years 1905–19 are particularly associated with increased social overhead investment, the modernization of the cotton textile industry, and especially with the development of the large integrated spinning-weaving establishments. In the 1930's, government-sponsored armaments industries were the leaders in investment. For the postwar period two groups of industries were in the forefront, and this may be one explanatory clue concerning the level of activity. On the one hand, Japan in these years pushed the development of what is sometimes vaguely called "heavy industry": engineering, machinery, iron and steel, chemicals, and so on. These industries had not been solidly established before World War II except in the special sense of a high cost and not particularly efficient armaments industry. Perhaps we can speak of the postwar years as forming part of an orderly technological progression, beginning with consumers' goods industries and moving toward a more balanced industrial base which includes producers' goods, consumers' durables, and heavy industry. But this is not the whole story. The 1950's and 1960's presented Japan with an opportunity outside the "normal" range of technological progression, and this lay in the range of new industries

---

[10] The following figures are available for average annual rates of increase in the rate of capital return (percent)—1922–21: 0.72; 1931–37: 2.15; 1951–54: 1.98; 1954–58: 3.19. All these figures apply only to the nonagricultural sector, and are derived from national income and net capital stock series in constant prices. This may be informative, although the data do not cover the entire period under consideration. See K. Ohkawa, "Bumpairitsu no chōki hendō" (Long-Term Changes in the Share Distribution of Income), *Keizai Kenkyū*, Vol. 16, No. 1 (January, 1965).

developed outside of Japan during and immediately after the war—electronics, television, synthetics, and the like. Japan possessed sufficient trained manpower to take advantage of two simultaneous technological infusions, and this created for it the best investment climate of the last 100 years.

The Flexible Supply of Labor

Relations between the labor supply and growth have up to now been mentioned in three forms. First, it was observed that wages lagged behind increases in productivity. Second, it was noted that wage differentials narrowed toward the end of each upswing. Lastly, we observed that during investment spurts, input factors continued to be available at prices favorable to entrepreneurs, and this must be closely related to the wage lag. Now, we intend to explore the role of wages in somewhat greater detail.

Figure 1–4 shows what happens to wage rates in manufacturing and agriculture during a typical long swing. Wm is the wage rate in manufacturing; Wa is the wage rate in agriculture; and Em/Et is the

FIGURE 1–4.   Wage Rates in Manufacturing and Agriculture.

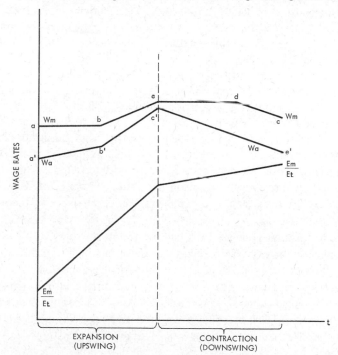

changing ratio of modern to traditional employment. As far as Em/Et is concerned, we assume that during an expansion the ratio of modern to traditional employment increases very sharply. During the contraction, the proportion of modern employment continues to rise, but at a sharply reduced rate. Let us now look at the changing path of absolute and relative wage rates in order to infer certain characteristics about the supply of labor during a long swing.

Wage rates in the modern sector during a typical upswing can be assumed to follow the path traced by line Wm. Here we drew a curve divided into two segments: $a-b$ applies to a period when labor supply is "unlimited"; within a certain range of expansion the wage rate remains unchanged. However, the requirements of the upswing usually go beyond this range, and segment $b-c$ becomes operative, resulting in rising wage rates. Nevertheless, the labor supply remains relatively "flexible" so that wages rise less sharply than productivity increases. Historically, no upswing went beyond the point of flexibility when wage rates would increase more rapidly than, or as rapidly as, productivity. This suggests that cost inflation due to wage increases could not have been a factor in ending a long-swing expansion; other reasons must have been involved.

This description of wage movements in manufacturing is consistent with the pattern of wage differentials described in Section III. Agricultural wages can be assumed to follow the path $a'-b'-c'$ during an upswing. During the entire expansion the number of surplus workers becomes smaller since Em/Et is sharply rising. Until point b' is reached the impact on wage rates is slight, because the number of surplus laborers remains sizable. When point b' is reached, and especially beyond it, the expansion will have continued for some time, and the number of surplus workers will have been reduced by the opportunities of industrial employment. Now, when additional labor is needed in traditional production, and this regularly arises during certain seasons of the year, the relative (short-term) shortage of labor will lead to sharply rising wages in agriculture. As we noted in Section III, Wa/Wm rises during the upswing, and particularly toward the end of the upswing.

Up to this point our analysis has been almost exclusively concerned with periods of expansion. There are two justifications for this. An understanding of postwar growth in historical perspective should concentrate on expansive phases of growth, and furthermore—since 1905 —the Japanese economy has displayed only one genuine contraction, the years from 1919 to 1931. Generalizations concerning contractions must therefore be based on a very limited historical record. We do, however, want to say a word or two about the downswing experience partially in order to achieve a more balanced presentation, but more importantly because the downswing of the 1920's was so crucial to the formation of the differential structure. It also provides a useful comparison with the situation after 1961.

Let us follow the path of wages. It has already been shown that during a typical upswing money wages will rise, and if inflation is moderate real wages should also rise. Of course, wages continue to lag productivity gains in expansion, but this is a pattern which changes in the downswing, when the ratio of wages to labor productivity rises. At the beginning of contraction, the modern entrepreneur will find that a new high has been reached in the level of money wages, and he will also find that these display downward rigidity. Based on the experience of the 1920's, we know that Wm changed only little through 1931, that Wa declined after a short interval, while the general price level declined. For the downswing, wage rates of the modern sector are illustrated by line $c-d-e,$ and for the traditional sector by line $c'-e'$. Wages in agriculture are depicted as relatively elastic in the sense that they tend to fall sharply during downswings when surplus labor becomes more plentiful, and as a result Wa/Wm declines. By contrast, in manufacturing we have drawn segment $c-d$ to account for the period of rigidity, followed by $d-e$ when money wages fall quite gently. The downward rigidity of money wages is an internationally recognized phenomenon, but why does it occur when the supply of labor is flexible? This is a most difficult question. As already mentioned, the available experience with downswings is much too limited for adequate generalizations, and we have serious doubts about the reliability of wage data. But on the whole we tend to believe that manufacturing wages were rigid in a downward direction for some time, and there seems to be some implicit and very partial evidence in the behavior of the modern sectors in the 1920's.

Downward rigidity of wages should affect the investment and production behavior of the modern sectors. For 1919–31, as previously shown, rates of increase of labor productivity in manufacturing were high while increases in employment were very small. Information concerning investment in manufacturing at this time is scarce, but it is fair to assume from partial evidence that there was a considerable amount of capital formation. This concentration of investment, as compared to the more broadly based investment booms associated with expansions, resulted in considerable technological progress and high rates of increases for labor productivity in manufacturing. Technological progress of the laborsaving type in modern sectors may have been in part stimulated by the downward rigidity of wages. It certainly solidified the differential structure, not only by enlarging the productivity "gap," but also by enlarging underemployment in the traditional sectors because of the decreased employment opportunities outside.

Borrowed Technology

Japan is a classic example of industrialization based on borrowed technology—borrowed, of course, by the modern sectors. From the very beginning of its modern economic growth until now, manufacturing depended heavily on technological advances from abroad. This was an economical process and is one of the reasons why Japan could develop so quickly. Reliance and dependence on technology developed by the West and for the West does raise a very interesting question. Considering the factor proportions required by borrowed technology (a comparatively high level of capital intensity), how could it be efficiently adapted in an economy with very flexible (cheap) supplies of labor? In large part, the Japanese had very little choice. Remaining competitive meant keeping up to date, and the modern sectors had to take part in world technological progress. The standards were set by the advanced countries of the West, and reflected their own and not Japanese factor proportions. In modern industry, and especially in those areas where foreign competition had to be faced, a rising rate of capital intensity was an imperative and a simple consequence of reliance on borrowed technology. It is difficult to verify these propositions and to determine the type of technological progress statistically, but some support is provided in Table 1–8. These results for the non-agricultural sector show neither capital shallowing nor capital widening. Capital deepening has been going on continuously since 1885, and seems most rapid of all in recent years, although the postwar values are not strictly comparable to prewar results.

Yet this is only part of the story and it stresses unduly the rigidity of factor proportions. There were possibilities of mitigating the incongruity between required factor proportions and domestic factor prices, and the Japanese explored these paths with great creativity. This subject deserves fuller treatment than we can give it here, but a few suggestions may be helpful. One method of mitigation was the selection of those modern industrial activities relatively most suitable to domestic factor proportions (especially by the private sector). In the postwar period this is best illustrated by the tremendous expansion of the light machinery industry. This industry grew more rapidly than any other, and also absorbed a great deal of labor. Textiles played a similar role

TABLE 1-8

Capital-Labor Ratio: Average Annual Rates of
Growth in Nonprimary Industry

		Gross Capital (%)	*Net Capital* (%)
1.	1885 (T) - 1898 (P)	2.17	2.18
2.	1898 (P) - 1905 (T)	2.01	2.05
3.	1905 (T) - 1919 (P)	4.20	4.22
4.	1919 (P) - 1931 (T)	2.94	2.15
5.	1931 (T) - 1938 (P)	2.52	2.68
6.	1954 (T) - 1961 (P)	4.60	--
7.	1961 (P) - 1964	9.58	--

REMARKS: 1. Prewar data from K. Ohkawa and others, *Shihon stokku* (Capital Stock) (Tokyo, 1966), Part I, chap. iii. These figures exclude residential buildings and include public capital. The series have been smoothed by a seven-year moving average and are given in 1934-36 prices.

2. Postwar data from Economic Planning Agency, Economic Research Institute, *Keizai Bunseki* (Economic Analysis), No. 17 (March, 1966). These series exclude public capital. Growth rates are calculated from crude annual values. Net capital stock series are not available for the postwar period.

during the 1910's and 1920's. Another very well-known method of mitigation is the fuller utilization of capital through the more intensive use of labor. A multishift system is the classic example, and it is valid for any period of modern economic growth in Japan. After World War II, however, a particularly prevalent form has been the use of secondhand machinery by small-scale enterprises. Lastly, there is also the possibility of partially substituting capital by labor even in some technologically advanced industries. Subcontracting performed this role in Japan both before and after the recent war. As a result of these adaptations the absorptive capacity for labor by manufacturing was increased. This tendency was strongest during expansions, especially the one which ended recently, as indicated in Table 1–4.

There remains the task of relating borrowed Western technology to the differential structure. Some of this will by now be familiar ground. Increasingly capital intensive methods of production borrowed from more advanced countries resulted in rising labor productivity in modern sectors. Traditional sectors have also had periods of technological progress since 1905 (the situation before that time is not comparable), and especially after World War II there has been another acceleration in the growth of agricultural productivity. We believe that this progress has been largely induced by the modern sectors, in the form of specific machinery and techniques still applicable within a traditional form of economic organization—in this instance the small peasant farm. However, this induced form of progress has been both late in coming and relatively feeble in its effect. The productivity gap has grown historically, and its evolvement is highly correlated with the sharply differing sectoral levels of capital intensity which first become apparent in 1905–19.

Another aspect of the technology-structure problem pertains to the sectoral allocation of labor. Despite the moderating effects of mitigating devices to offset laborsaving techniques, increased employment opportunities in modern sectors were not sufficient to lower the absolute numbers in traditional employment. Probably the best proxy for the traditionally employed is the total number of workers in the self-employed sectors. As a trend it has risen until very recently, and is only now showing some slight decline. Insofar as international competition required a certain positive rate of capital deepening in the modern economy, and given the rate of population growth, the high levels of traditional employment were unavoidable. Equally unavoidable were the low levels of productivity in the traditional sectors due to the impact of surplus labor.

Sectoral wage differentials are also, as has already been suggested, related to the adoption of highly productive borrowed technology in one of the two sectors. Real wages in modern industry rose (although not as rapidly as productivity) in spite of highly flexible labor supplies. Modern enterprise increasingly needed a reliable, committed, and above all trained labor force, and this suggests why the wage differentials increased despite the validity of a two-sector labor-surplus model. These needs also may be a factor in the downward rigidity of modern wages, which was noted in the previous subsection.

V. A FEW CONCLUDING REMARKS

The Economy after 1961

The purpose of this section is to say something about the immediate past and present and to summarize our findings. The study of postwar growth in historical perspective within a long-swing framework necessarily concentrated on the 1954–61 expansion. For the past five years, however, the Japanese economy has been—in the long-swing sense—experiencing a downswing in terms of the rate of growth of aggregate output. The downswing may still be in process, and it is certainly much too early for any kind of systematic analysis. However, it is tempting to offer a few suppositions.

Our belief is that the downturn which began in 1961 is primarily caused by the fading away of long-run effects associated with war dislocation. This would be mainly the closing of a technological gap created by an isolation before and after the war which lasted some 15 years. Japan eliminated this gap by rapid importation of technology from more advanced countries—mainly the United States. Downswings are characterized by slower rates of aggregate growth and moderate rates of return on capital. This seems to describe Japan's economic situation since 1961, and lends support to the view that downswings are periods in which the industrial sectors adjust to the preceding investment spurt.

It is clear that even a preliminary view of the postwar downswing indicates some unusual features. Compared to prewar downswings, the growth rate of aggregate output since 1961 is very high, and when it will be possible to calculate the rate of growth for the entire postwar long swing, it will certainly be far above any extrapolations based on an accelerating prewar trend. It stands to reason that an explanation of the unprecedented pace of postwar growth cannot be confined to the upswing or the investment spurt period. During the full postwar swing, growth will have been much more rapid than in the past. Many explanations for this are possible. In the "Introduction," we noted the role of certain "new elements" in the postwar economy, and good examples would be the smaller burden of defense expenditures and more effective government policies. We also suggested that certain legacies of war dislocation are still stimulating the Japanese economy, and we pointed to the continued shortage of residential housing and social overhead capital. No doubt all these influences have played a part in maintaining a high rate of growth since 1961.

In spite of what has just been said, one should not lose sight of the elements of historical continuity in the Japanese growth pattern. In prewar downswings the declines of aggregate output growth rates have also been rather moderate, while the proportion of capital formation was generally maintained at the higher level created by the preceding investment spurt. Up to the present, the postwar downswing fits into this historical picture without difficulty. If the downswing is considered to be a period during which the economy adjusts to the effects of the investment spurt, we can say that in Japan investment incentives remain strong at this time—even though the growth rate of investment falls below levels attained during the spurt.

The particular adjustment process differs for each downswing, since it must reflect the specific imbalances created by each upswing. For example, the upswing culminating in 1919 created severe inflation, and this required deflation in the 1920's to bring Japanese price levels more in line with international levels. The postwar expansion, on the other hand, resulted in no general inflation, and no overall deflationary adjustment has been necessary. But the expansion which followed World War II created some highly unusual problems in Japan. Most noteworthy is the spectacular rise of consumer prices, which gathered momentum toward the end of the expansion, *and has continued* unabated during the present contraction. (Consumers' prices rose 7.4 percent during the fiscal year 1965.) Rapid rises of consumers' prices never occurred in the previous downswings, and this alone should underline the significance of this phenomenon. Of equal interest is the observation that consumers' prices have been rising while producers' goods prices have remained stable. We attribute this to the unbalanced growth of output as between these two sectors, that is to say a lag in the output of consumers' goods. Put very loosely in terms of the dualistic structure, one can say that the price movements reflect the unbalanced growth of the modern (producers') and traditional (consumers') sectors.

There is another unusual feature to the postwar downswing: the *continued* narrowing tendency of wage differentials (*Wa/Wm*) which began, as usual, at the end of the postwar expansion. This is a reflection of the much talked about "labor shortages" which are supposed to have afflicted the Japanese economy in the last few years. The ratio indicates that there has been a relative increase in traditional wages as a result of large-scale transfers out of these sectors. For example, the number of workers in agriculture has continued to decline, and labor shortages have been especially noticeable in the traditional occupations: services, crafts, and so forth. As a consequence the price rises have concentrated where the labor shortages exist, particularly in that area of the economy in direct contact with the consumer.

Let us now try to look at the current adjustment process in longer run perspective. The postwar investment boom magnified the gap between modern and traditional sectors, and increased the degree of differential structure. In turn, this has led to two major related structural adjustments in the economy following the boom: a rise in the relative level of traditional wages and a rising level in the prices of consumers' goods. These adjustments, themselves, will in our view lead to fundamental changes in the differential structure, and eventually to its dissolution. The heart of the matter, and the really novel feature of the recent past, is the changed condition of labor supply. At present in Japan the notion of traditional sectors is in the process of becoming meaningless. They are losing their one absolute requirement of existence—cheap labor—and demographic projections indicate that the rate of increase of the labor force will become much smaller, implying that even in an economy growing at a more moderate pace the tendency toward smaller wage differentials will persist. A more unified level of wages means that the traditional techniques will no longer be viable—eventually they will have to be transformed or they will surely disappear. This is what is happening now, and the full elimination of the differential structure is a complex process which may take a long time.

A Summary of Findings

This paper has ranged over a wide variety of subjects and it may be helpful, by way of conclusion, to summarize very briefly the main findings.

1. In examining the growth of the Japanese economy since the 1870's, we have identified long swings in the rate of growth of output and some of its major components, an accelerating trend rate of output growth for successive long swings, and a differential structure defined as a growing gap in productivity and wage differentials between the modern and traditional sectors of the Japanese economy. These three concepts have been employed in analyzing the growth pattern and structure of the economy with particular emphasis on the years 1905 to 1961, and especially for the post–World War II years.

2. Japan's high rate of growth for the past century is seen as depending on two major elements: the capability of absorbing advanced Western technology, and the availability of flexible supplies of comparatively well-trained labor.

3. The long swings in the growth rate of aggregate output have many causes, but in our view the main cause is the investment spurt, which is a common characteristic of all upswings. The investment spurt is considered to be the main factor behind the periodic rises in the growth rate of output, and the decline of growth rates during the downswing is considered a period of adjustment to the previous boom. It should be especially noticed that during each spurt (1905–19, 1931–38, 1954–61) there has been an irreversible rise in the capital formation proportion.

4. The unprecedented rate of output growth following war rehabilitation (which we assume to end around 1954) is considered to

be the result of an unusually vigorous upswing, particularly supported by the opportunities of (short-term) "catching-up." Although it is too early to state a definitive opinion, we believe that the first postwar upswing ended in 1961, and since then the Japanese economy has entered a downswing period in the form of an adjustment process to the post–World War II investment spurt. The continued high rate of growth from 1961 to the present (though let it be noted that the average rate has declined from the level of 1954–61) is due to certain favorable rehabilitation effects which have continued to linger on, and also to the common historical factor that capital formation proportions have continued to maintain high levels.

5. The changing structure of Japan's economy during modern economic growth is analyzed, as mentioned above, in terms of two sectors: a modern sector with technology and organization largely imported from the West, and a traditional sector relying to an overwhelming extent on indigenous techniques and organization. During the period under review, roughly from 1905 to 1961, these sectors assume a relation to one another which is called a differential structure. This is defined as a growing gap in productivity and wage differentials between the modern and traditional sectors due to the effects of borrowed Western technology and organization in the former sector and the lagging progress of traditional technology and organization in the latter, together with the continued existence of "surplus" labor.

6. The postwar upswing enlarged the wage and productivity gap which is the differential structure. However, the downswing which began in 1961 has introduced a very important new dimension into the Japanese economy. A highly flexible supply of labor which had existed ever since the beginnings of Japan's modern economic growth has become less flexible. This situation is expected to continue in the future and will cause profound structural changes in the economy. We postulate that it will eventually mean an end of the traditional sectors and of the differential structure.

2 | Construction Cycles and Their Monetary-Financial Characteristics*

SHOZABURO FUJINO

I. INTRODUCTION

Since the discovery of economic fluctuations lasting from 15 to 25 years, it has been confirmed that the swing has been observed in various aspects of the economy. This has come to be called the Kuznets cycle or the long swing.[1] From J. R. Riggleman's analysis,[2] we know that

* Part of this study was supported by the aid of the Seimeikai Foundation. The author wishes to express his sincere thanks for valuable comments on this paper given by Professor R. C. O. Matthews and other participants in the Conference.

[1] See S. Kuznets, *Secular Movements in Production and Prices: Their Nature and Their Bearing upon Cyclical Fluctuations* (Boston: Houghton Mifflin Co., 1930); and *Capital Formation in the American Economy, Its Formation and Financing* (Princeton, N.J.: Princeton University Press, 1961); C. A. R. Wardwell, *An Investigation of Economic Data for Major Cycles* (Philadelphia: University of Pennsylvania, 1927); A. F. Burns, *Production Trends in the United States since 1870* (New York: National Bureau of Economic Research, 1934); P. J. O'Leary and W. A. Lewis, "Secular Swings in Production and Trade," *The Manchester School*, Vol. 23 (May, 1955), pp. 113–52; M. Abramovitz, "Statement in United States Congress, Joint Economic Committee," *Employment, Growth and Price Levels*, Hearing, 86th Cong., 1st sess., Part II (Washington, D.C.: U.S. Government Printing Office, 1959), pp. 411–66, and "The Nature and Significance of Kuznets Cycles," *Economic Development and Cultural Change*, April, 1961, pp. 225–48; B. Hickman, "The Postwar Retardation: Another Long Swing in the Rate of Growth?" *American Economic Review*, Vol. 53 (May, 1963), pp. 490–507; K. Ohkawa and H. Rosovsky, "Economic Fluctuations in Prewar Japan: A Preliminary Analysis of Cycles and Long Swings," *Hitotsubashi Journal of Economics*, Vol. 3 (October, 1962), pp. 10–33; and M. Shinohara, *Growth and Cycles in the Japanese Economy* (Tokyo: Kinokuniya, 1962), chap. 4.

[2] J. R. Riggleman, "Building Cycles in the United States, 1876–1932," *Journal of the American Statistical Association*, Vol. 28 (June, 1933), pp. 174–83; C. D. Long, "Long Cycles in the Building Industry," *Quarterly Journal of*

long swings appear especially clearly in construction activity. In particular, according to M. Abramovitz's study[3] long swings are observed not only in aggregate construction activity but also in all the main construction fields with a sufficient degree of conformity. This observation suggests that investment in construction plays an important role in causing long swings.[4] Needless to say investment performs an important function in the process of cyclical fluctuations of the economy. Let us divide this into inventory investment, expenditure on producers' durables, and investment in construction, and correspondingly the stock of capital into inventories, the stock of producers' durables, and the stock of construction. Then it seems that the time required to adjust the stock of construction is longer than that required for the stock of producers' durables, and the latter is longer than that required for inventories.[5] Because there are differences in the adjustment time for each stock of capital, we find the Kitchin cycle (or the minor cycle) corresponding to the behavior of inventory investment and the Juglar cycle (or the major cycle) to that of producers' durables. Similarly we think that our long swings are due to the mechanism of capital stock adjustment in construction, having a duration of 15 to 25 years.[6] From this point of view let us call the long swings construction cycles; the mechanism itself will not be dealt with until the last part of this paper. The construction cycle, as defined by us, is thus not confined to the long swings observed in the behavior of expenditure on construction, but covers the long swings in the economy as a whole. That is, it means the long swing itself.

The purpose of this paper is to shed light on various aspects, espe-

---

Economics, Vol. 53 (1939), pp. 371–403; W. Isard, "Neglected Cycle: The Transport-Building Cycle," *Review of Economic Statistics,* Vol. 24 (November, 1942), pp. 149–58; M. Abramovitz, *Evidences of Long Swings in Aggregate Construction since the Civil War* (New York: National Bureau of Economic Research, 1964).

[3] Abramovitz, *Evidences of Long Swings in Aggregate Construction since the Civil War, op. cit.*

[4] Here investment in construction includes all fixed investment except expenditures for producers' durables.

[5] In regard to the capital stock adjustment principle, see R. C. O. Matthews, *The Trade Cycle* (Cambridge, England: Cambridge University Press, 1959), chap. 3.

[6] We analyzed the correspondence between three types of investment and three types of business cycles in S. Fujino, *Business Cycles in Japan, a Theoretical, Statistical and Historical Analysis of the Process of Cyclical Development* (Tokyo: Keiso Shobo, 1965), pp. 5–13 (in Japanese), and "Business Cycles in Japan, 1868–1962," *Hitotsubashi Journal of Economics,* Vol. 7 (June, 1966), pp. 56–79.

cially the monetary-financial aspects, of the construction cycle and to construct tentatively a theoretical model which will explain systematically the construction cycle.

II. THE CONSTRUCTION CYCLE AND TWO TYPES OF EQUIPMENT CYCLE

At first, let us examine what kind of cyclical movements appear in aggregate economic activity. Before examining the long swings, we should like to investigate fluctuations of a shorter period. Economic magnitudes related to the modern sector reveal more sharply cyclical fluctuations than those in the nonmodern sector. Let us take debits to bank deposits estimated by the author as representative of the volume of transactions in the modern sector.[7] We shall approach cyclical fluctuations by means of the ratio of bank debits in one year to those in the previous year. In what follows we shall define the rate of change of a variable X_t by the ratio of X_t to X_{t-1}, where the suffix t denotes time. Therefore our rate of change is greater than the usual rate of change by 100 percent.

In Figure 2–1, the rate of change in bank debits shows cyclical movements with an average duration of about 7.5 years. Notation P expresses peaks and notation T troughs of the movements. The behavior of the rate of change in bank debits corresponds closely to that of monthly series of the business cycle index estimated by the author, which shows on the average a cycle of 7.75 years.[8] The cycle of 7.5 years' duration observed in the rate of change in bank debits corresponds to the Juglar cycle. Figure 2–1 shows that the Juglar cycle appears clearly not only in the rate of change in bank debits but also in the rates of change in prices (wholesale price index) and real bank debits. The cycle is closely related, we think, to the behavior of expenditure on producers' durables; for this reason we shall call it the equipment cycle.

At first sight, long swings do not distinctly appear in the rate of

---

[7] Bank debits cover current deposits, ordinary deposits, deposit bills, deposits to notice, and special deposits, excluding interbank deposits on the one hand, and accounts of the Bank of Japan, Yokohama Specie Bank, Taiwan Bank, Chosen Bank, Nippon Kangyo Bank, Hokkaido Takushoku Bank, Industrial Bank of Japan, national banks, ordinary banks (which include private banks as well as financial companies existing before the Bank Act was put into practice in 1893), savings banks, agricultural and industrial banks and foreign banks on the other. Bank debits estimated are connected with Japan proper which does not include South Saghalien, Korea, and Formosa.

[8] A few monthly series of business cycle index are given in S. Fujino "Business Cycles in Japan, 1868–1962," *op. cit.*

FIGURE 2–1.   Rate of Change in Annual Bank Debits and Prices.

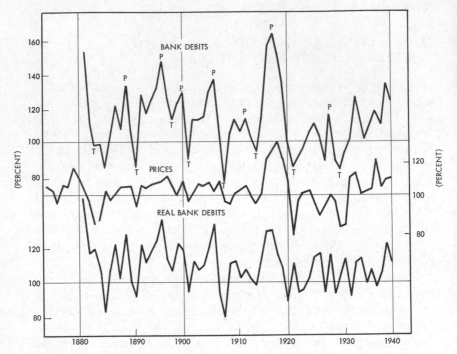

change of annual bank debits in Figure 2–1. But when we connect the peaks or the troughs, we can observe long swings. Or if we calculate the rate of change of bank debits in seven-year moving averages, we can find a clear picture of 3.5 long swings in Figure 2–2. Measuring from trough to trough, the average duration is 15 years. The swing of 1901 through 1911 has a relatively short duration and a low upsurge. However it is judged as an independent construction cycle in the light of movements of funds and the like which will be referred to later. The reason why the downswing in the early period of the 20th century sinks so low will be explained by the special situation at that time in which Japan was still in the period of the so-called takeoff.[9] The rates

---

[9] Regarding the takeoff of the Japanese economy see K. Ohkawa and H. Rosovsky, "A Century of Japanese Economic Growth," *The State and Economic Enterprise in Japan,* ed. W. W. Lockwood (Princeton, N.J.: Princeton University Press, 1965), pp. 66–76; and S. Tsuru, "The Take-off in Japan, 1868–1900," *The Economics of Take-off into Sustained Growth,* ed. W. W. Rostow (London: Macmillan & Co. Ltd., 1963), pp. 139–150. M. Shinohara does not take the period of 1901 to 1911 as an independent cycle, judging the period of 1885 to 1911 as one long swing. M. Shinohara, *A Study of the Japanese Economy* (Tokyo: Seirin Shobo, 1965), pp. 274–78 (in Japanese). We

FIGURE 2–2.   Rate of Change in Seven-Year Moving Averages of Bank Debits, etc.

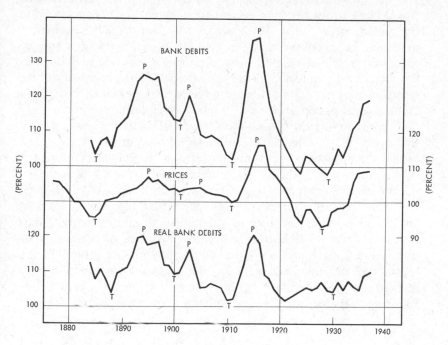

of change in prices as well as real bank debits show similar fluctuations, except that the latter drops more deeply in the early 1920's than in the early 1930's. It seems that the drop occurred because of the Kanto earthquake in 1923.

When comparing Figure 2–1 with Figure 2–2, it is evident that one construction cycle usually contains two equipment cycles. Before 1901, however, there are three medium cycles within one construction cycle. This is because we count the period of 1898 to 1901, which is shorter than the usual equipment cycle, as one independent cycle. An explanation for this cycle has been suggested.[10] But if we suppose that it is part of the equipment cycle starting in 1891, then one construction cycle consists of two equipment cycles in this case, too.[11]

---

can not agree with him in the light of alternative development of various industries and movements of capital or the behavior of the composition of funds demanded by firms.

[10] See Fujino, *Business Cycles in Japan, a Theoretical, Statistical and Historical Analysis of the Process of Cyclical Development, op. cit.,* pp. 54–58, "Business Cycles in Japan, 1868–1962," *op. cit.,* p. 61.

[11] A. H. Hansen thinks also that one building cycle is composed of two Juglar cycles. A. H. Hansen, *Fiscal Policy and Business Cycles* (New York: W. W. Norton & Co., Inc., 1941), pp. 19–23. See also W. Isard, *op. cit.*

Now let us compute the annual rate of growth of real bank debits, and then take an average of them over each equipment cycle measured from trough to trough. It is evident from Table 2–1 that, apart from the period before 1901, there are usually two types of equipment cycles in one construction cycle and that a relatively high rate of economic growth is enjoyed in the first and a low rate of growth in the second type of equipment cycle. Before 1901 technological innovation increased so much as to give rise to a period of takeoff, so that the usual pattern of the construction cycle did not emerge.

There is an interesting fact about the usual pattern of the construction cycle. It is related to the behavior of the change in gross real capital stock by type. According to series of capital stock estimated by K. Ohkawa and others,[12] the rate of growth of stock of real producers' durable equipment in nonprimary industries is relatively high in the first type of equipment cycle, which has a high rate of growth. On the other hand, the stock of structures and nonresidential buildings in nonprimary industries as well as the stock of nonfarm residential buildings enjoys a comparatively high rate of growth in the second type of equipment cycle. In addition, while the former clearly reveals equipment cycles, the latter shows distinctly waves corresponding to the construction cycle.[13] It is clear from Figure 2–3 that

TABLE 2-1

Equipment Cycle	Average Rate of Growth of Real Bank Debits (%)
1883–91.	6.93
1891–98.	15.55
1898–1901.	11.01
1901–08.	6.76
1908–14.	2.61
1914–21.	12.60
1921–30.	4.82
1930–40.	7.55

---

[12] K. Ohkawa, *Capital Stock* (Tokyo: Toyo Keizai Shinposha, 1966), (in Japanese). We have revised the original estimates, using our own method to estimate the stock of nonfarm residential buildings.

[13] Such a tendency is observed not only in Japan but also in the United States. Long swings revealed by movements of the ratio of gross expenditures of producers' durables to gross expenditures of construction estimated by S. Kuznets (Kuznets, *Capital Formation in the American Economy, Its Formation and Financing, op. cit.,* p. 524) lead those of general economic activity. That is, investment in producers' durable equipment occupies a greater portion of total fixed investment in the upswing than in the downswing of the construction cycle. The opposite is true of investment for construction.

FIGURE 2–3. Rate of Change in Gross Capital Stock in the Nonprimary Industries and Nonfarm Residential Buildings.

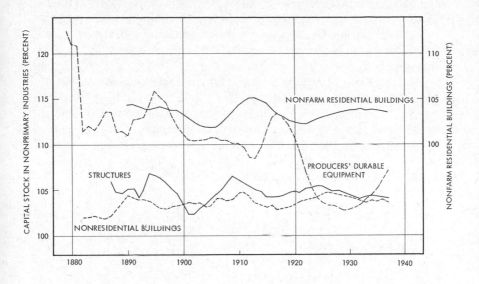

the rate of change in the stock of real producers' durable equipment in nonprimary industries moves in a direction opposite to those of structures, nonresidential buildings and nonfarm residential buildings.

This pattern of two types of fixed investment, however, does not hold before 1901. It seems that investment for railroad construction played a very important role as innovation-type investment in this period and disturbed the usual pattern of fluctuations in investment.

III. CONSTRUCTION CYCLES AND COMPOSITION OF FUNDS (1)

Next let us investigate the relationship between construction cycles and fluctuations in funds for the financing of investment. In this section we shall concentrate our attention on fluctuations in corporate firms' funds. We have available figures of paid-up capital, corporate bonds, and reserves of corporate firms,[14] and we define long-term

---

[14] Sources of data are *Statistical Year Book of the Japanese Empire* for 1883 to 1899, *Statistics of the Ministry of Agriculture and Commerce* for 1900 to 1920 and *Statistics of Corporate Firms* for the period after 1921. The author estimated annual series of the balance of corporate bonds for the period 1891 to 1920 and that of the amount of paid-up capital for the period 1883 to 1888. Since the original industrial classification was changed frequently, we reclassified industries to obtain the following industries in our major classification:

funds of corporate firms as their sum. The rate of change in three-year moving averages of nominal long-term funds in various industries is shown in Figure 2–4 and Figure 2–5. Since only figures of paid-up capital are available in the early period, the rate of change in three-year moving averages of paid-up capital is also shown in all industries including financial institutions and insurance as well as manufacturing.

The two kinds of rate of change move together. In addition paid-up capital covers the overwhelming part of long-term funds in the early period. Therefore we may estimate the behavior of the rate of change in long-term funds by the behavior of paid-up capital.

In spite of the fact that we take only three-year moving averages

FIGURE 2–4.   Rate of Change in Nominal Corporate Funds (1).

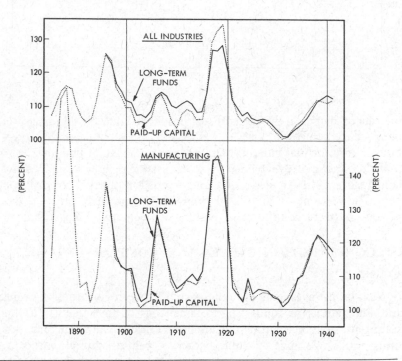

agriculture, fisheries, mining, manufacturing, construction, city gas, electric power, water service, transportation, storage and warehousing, financial institutions, insurance, holding companies, services and commerce. Figures adjusted and estimated by us cover the National Railways and the Yawata Government Factory of Iron and Steel in order to maintain continuity in the data. The government bought up the large private railroad companies in 1906, and the Yawata Government Factory fell into private hands in 1934.

FIGURE 2-5.   Rate of Change in Nominal Corporate Funds (2).

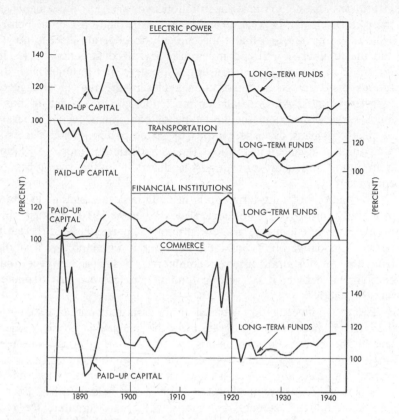

of the original data, construction cycles appear clearly in the movements of the rates of change shown here. In manufacturing, large
waves occur in the above-mentioned first type of equipment cycle,
and extremely small waves in the second type of equipment cycle.
This corresponds well to the behavior noted above of the rate of
growth of the stock of producers' durables. It seems that this is because, compared with other industries, a relatively large part of the
total stock of capital in manufacturing consists of producers' durables.
In the period before 1900, however, movements of the rate of change
in long-term funds (or paid-up capital) are different from those in the
period after 1900. This is further evidence to indicate the special
characteristics of the period before 1900. The behavior of the rate of
change in funds in manufacturing is well reflected in that of all industries. That is, the rate of change of funds in all industries reveals
the construction cycle composed of two types of equipment cycle.

In Figure 2–5 we find that electric power, railroads, and financial institutions distinctly show construction cycles in the movements of the rate of change in long-term funds (or in paid-up capital before 1895). We have found that[15] the capacity to generate electric power and the number of railroad miles also reveal construction cycles in their rate of change. It is interesting to observe that in financial institutions there are clear construction cycles in the rate of change of long-term funds. As we shall see later, the rate of change of bank loans surges upward in the first type of equipment cycle. The rate of change of bank deposits exhibits the same pattern. Thus it is estimated that in financial institutions the composition of sources of long-term funds and short-term funds is different in the two types of equipment cycle.

Fluctuations of long-term funds in commerce are similar to those in manufacturing except for several years before 1910. Because corporate firms in commerce are few in number, particularly in the early period, it is dangerous to infer the behavior of commerce as a whole from that of corporate firms in commerce. It seems, however, that commercial activity has a strong tendency to correspond to manufacturing activity.

The above investigation is based on the nominal value of funds. On the balance sheet of the corporate firm, the increase in physical assets and in financial assets corresponds to the increase in funds. The real stock of capital (physical assets) is the sum of the annual increases of real physical assets, which is equal to the real amount of the difference between funds obtained and financial assets held by firms. Therefore a method to estimate *real* funds will be to cumulate the real increase in funds, i.e., the nominal increase in funds deflated by prices. There remains, however, in this method the question of how to get real magnitudes from the initial nominal funds. To deal with this question we construct a special price index for deflating the initial funds to get real amounts.[16] Figure 2–6 and Figure 2–7 show the rate of change in three-year moving averages of the series of real

---

[15] Fujino, *Business Cycles in Japan, a Theoretical Statistical and Historical Analysis of the Process of Cyclical Development, op. cit.,* pp. 38–41, pp. 368–72 and pp. 437–40; Fujino, "Business Cycles in Japan, 1868–1962," *op. cit.,* pp. 67–69.

[16] The special deflator is constructed as follows: At first we compute the regression of the real increase in funds on time over a certain period having an adequate length for which the data are available. Then by means of this regression we extrapolate annual series of the real increase in funds during some reasonable period. Finally we compute a weighted average of figures of the price index for this period by the real increase in funds estimated. This is our special deflator for converting the initial nominal funds to the real value.

FIGURE 2–6.   Rate of Change in Real Corporate Funds (1).

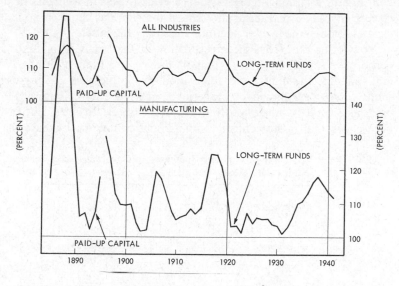

FIGURE 2–7.   Rate of Change in Real Corporate Funds (2).

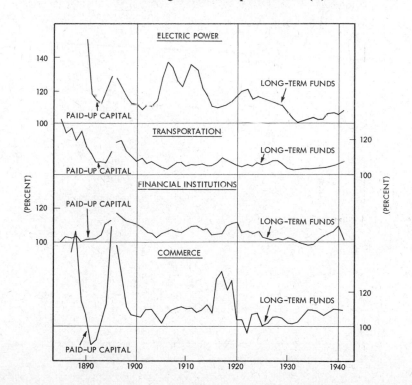

funds thus obtained in various industries. When we compare them with Figure 2–4 and Figure 2–5, it is evident that movements of the rate of change in real terms are almost the same as those in nominal terms, although the former fluctuates less than the latter.

Now let us turn from the investigation of the behavior of funds in corporate firms over time to that of the composition of funds. We first calculate the industrial composition of the increase in long-term funds (three-year moving averages) to get Figure 2–8. Before 1894, paid-up capital is substituted for long-term funds. It is evident from Figure 2–8 that manufacturing, mining, and commerce increase their

FIGURE 2–8.　Share of Amounts Increased in Corporate Long-Term Funds (or Paid-up Capital) by Industry.

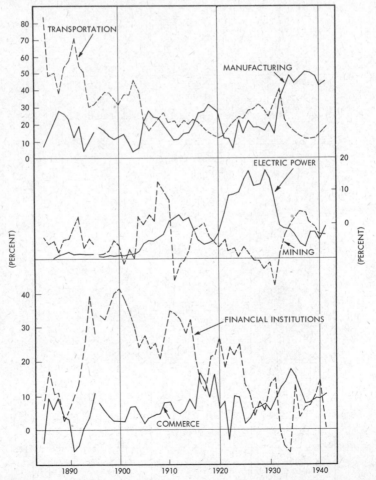

share in the first type of equipment cycle and decrease it in the second type. The opposite tendency is found in transportation, electric power and financial institutions. Although city gas and services are not shown here, they also follow this tendency.

Secondly, let us examine the behavior of the share of paid-up capital, corporate bonds, and reserves in the total increase of long-term funds. Denote the increase in long-term funds by ΔK, that in paid-up capital by ΔK_1, that in corporate bonds by ΔK_2 and that in reserves by ΔK_3. These are all three-year moving averages. Comparing the three marginal ratios $(\Delta K_1/\Delta K)$, $(\Delta K_2/\Delta K)$, and $(\Delta K_3/\Delta K)$, it is clear that the marginal share ratio of reserves $(\Delta K_3/\Delta K)$ lags behind that of paid-up capital $(\Delta K_1/\Delta K)$, moving in a direction opposite to the latter. (See Figure 2–9.) In addition $(\Delta K_1/\Delta K)$ increases

FIGURE 2–9. Share of Paid-up Capital, Corporate Bonds and Reserves in Increase in Corporate Long-Term Funds.

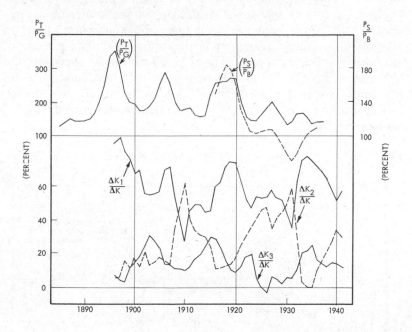

sharply in the first type of equipment cycle and declines in the second type. On the contrary, $(\Delta K_2/\Delta K)$ has a tendency to rise in the second type of equipment cycle. It should be noticed that although we use three-year moving averages of the original figures, all three ratios distinctly reveal long swings.

IV. CONSTRUCTION CYCLES AND COMPOSITION
OF FUNDS (2)

Now let us investigate funds other than the above-defined long-term funds. Apart from internal loans and/or funds within the business firm sector, bank credits are important as sources of funds. We would need, however, a lot of work to obtain a consistent series of bank loans and discounts over the whole period with which we are concerned. Therefore we shall use only figures of national banks' loans in the early period, figures of loans of national banks, saving banks and ordinary banks in the period of transformation of the banking system, and amounts of loans and discounts of ordinary banks and saving banks thereafter. Now let us compare the rate of change in bank loans shown in Figure 2–10, which is computed from three-year moving averages of bank loans, with that of corporate long-term funds (or paid-up capital) in manufacturing as shown in Figure 2–4. It is evident that the behavior of the former closely resembles that of the latter. As mentioned above, corporate firms in manufacturing, mining, and commerce show a similar pattern of movement in their rates of change of long-term funds. Therefore, the behavior of bank loans is similar to that of long-term funds in these industries. That is, the rate of change in bank loans shows an upsurge in the first type and maintains a low value in the second type of equipment cycle.

FIGURE 2–10.   Rate of Change in Bank Loans, National and Local Government Bonds.

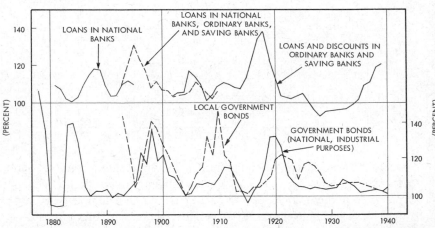

So far we have investigated movements of the main items of funds appearing in the fund market in regard to firms. But in the fund market as a whole, bonds issued by the central government, as well as local governments, occupy an important position. A large part of central government bonds, which we shall simply call government bonds, were issued for the purpose of financing armament and wars. They are entirely autonomous. Therefore we use government bonds issued for industrial purposes to analyze the reaction of the government to the construction cycle.[17]

As shown in Figure 2–10, both the rate of change in the three-year moving averages of government bonds issued for industrial purposes and in the three-year moving averages of local government bonds reveal long swings which lag behind the rate of change in bank loans. Bank loans are congruent with general economic activity (compare Figure 2–10 with Figure 2–2), so that government bonds and local government bonds lag behind general economic activity. This is because manufacturing, mining, and commerce expand relatively in the first type of equipment cycle, so that the economy faces a bottleneck of social overhead capital at the end of the first type of equipment cycle. In the second type of equipment cycle, the government begins to take measures to improve the bottleneck.

Now let us examine the composition of various funds in the trough years of the equipment cycle in order to summarize our observations of funds. As mentioned above, the National Railway is included in the corporate sector, so that bonds issued by the government for railroad construction form a part of the total corporate bond issues. These form a large proportion of total government bonds issued for industrial purposes. We therefore exclude government bonds from our investigation, except for bonds for railroad construction, which are included in corporate bonds. Long-term funds of financial institutions and insurance companies are supplied to meet the demand for funds by nonfinancial business firms, and so are eliminated from our examination to avoid double counting.

According to Table 2–2 loans and discounts from banks (excluding the Bank of Japan) is the largest item in total funds before 1930, with paid-up capital ranking next. The former declines over the whole

---

[17] Government bonds issued for industrial purposes include bonds issued to finance the construction of railroads, harbors, drainages, roads, telephone networks, mining equipment, steel factory equipment, and so forth. They also include bonds issued to nationalize private railroad companies as well as corporate bonds taken over from nationalized private companies. Since these latter bonds were not used to finance construction at the time of issue as government bonds, we exclude them from our calculations.

TABLE 2-2

Composition of Funds In Troughs of the Equipment Cycle
(Unit of Value: Million Yen)

	1898	1901	1908	1914	1921	1930	1940
Loans and discounts by all banks							
Value	497,469	746,789	1,392,550	2,526,345	9,428,179	10,272,929	17,347,751
Percentage	50.21	51.81	47.66	46.09	44.82	31.20	27.34
Loans by other financial institutions							
Value	n.a.	n.a.	n.a.	n.a.	329,214	384,775	1,130,335
Percentage	....	....	....	....	1.56	1.17	1.78
Loans by insurance companies							
Value	n.a.	n.a.	15,505	69,178	139,726	454,239	973,394
Percentage	....	....	0.53	1.26	0.67	1.38	1.53
Paid-up capital							
Value	422,510	530,622	1,139,880	1,645,349	7,658,625	12,775,827	26,936,496
Percentage	42.65	36.82	39.01	30.02	36.41	38.80	42.46
Reserves							
Value	22,441	44,053	126,331	233,000	1,150,195	1,637,732	4,660,446
Percentage	2.27	3.06	4.32	4.25	5.47	4.97	7.35
Corporate bonds							
Value	28,012	76,115	147,642	680,502	1,676,740	5,023,253	8,274,624
Percentage	2.83	5.28	5.05	12.42	7.97	15.26	13.04
Local government bonds							
Value	20,264	43,721	99,824	326,602	654,407	2,374,416	4,121,533
Percentage	2.05	3.03	3.42	5.96	3.11	7.21	6.50
Total							
Value	990,696	1,441,300	2,921,732	5,480,976	21,037,086	32,923,171	63,444,579
Percentage	100.00	100.00	100.00	100.00	100.00	100.00	100.00

NOTE: (1) All banks cover Yokohama Specie Bank, Taiwan Bank, Chosen Bank, Nippon Kangyo Bank, Hokkaido Takushoku Bank, Industrial Bank of Japan, national banks, ordinary banks, saving banks, agricultural and industrial banks, and foreign banks in Japan proper.

(2) Paid-up capital, reserves, and corporate bonds are related to corporate firms (including the National Railway and Yawata Government Factory of Iron and Steel) other than financial institutions and insurance companies.

(3) Figures of part of loans supplied by other financial institutions and local government bonds are at the end of the fiscal year.

(4) The notation n.a. indicates "not available."

period, becoming smaller than the latter after 1930. On the other hand, the shares of reserves and corporate bonds have a rising tendency. Apart from these trends we can observe the following fluctuations. Paid-up capital and reserves increase their proportions in total funds at the end of the first type of equipment cycle, as in 1908, 1921, and 1940. The shares decline relatively in the troughs between these years, i.e., in 1901, 1914, and 1930. The opposite tendency is observed in corporate bonds and local government bonds. Movements of the construction cycle, which is composed of the two types of equipment cycle, are reflected in the composition of funds.

V. THE BALANCE OF PAYMENTS, THE SUPPLY OF MONEY AND INVESTMENT IN CYCLES

We have made clear elsewhere that the rate of change of the supply of money lags behind the balance of payments and leads the rate of change in inventories and/or fixed capital during the equipment cycle and the inventory cycle before and after World War II. The interaction between them is crucial in the mechanism explaining cyclical fluctuations.[18] What relationships are there between them in the course of the construction cycle? Judging from American experience, M. Abramovitz points out that "each general Kuznets cycle was accompanied by an inverse movement in the current balance of payments," and that "this, in turn, reflected chiefly, but not exclusively, a positive wave in merchandise imports," and that "waves in the rate of growth of the money supply and in the rate of change of prices accompanied the general Kuznets cycle."[19] Let us investigate these points. In the following, unless otherwise stated, we shall use a seven-year moving average based on the original data.

As shown in Figure 2–11, the rate of change in imports shows congruent movements with those in bank debits shown in Figure 2–2. This tells us that fluctuations of domestic economic activity are accompanied by corresponding movements in imports. On the other hand the rate of change in exports does not always correspond to domestic economic activity. In particular this is true before 1910. It

---

[18] Fujino, *Business Cycles in Japan, a Theoretical, Statistical and Historical Analysis of the Process of Cyclical Development, op. cit.,* chap. 14 and chap. 24; Fujino "Business Cycles in Japan, 1868–1962," *op. cit.,* pp. 74–77.

[19] See Abramovitz, "The Nature and Significance of Kuznets Cycles," *op. cit.,* pp. 245–46. A. F. Burns also points out the existence of long swings of the supply of money. See Burns, *op. cit.,* pp. 240–41. See also Abramovitz, "Statement in United States Congress, Joint Economic Committee," *op. cit.,* pp. 431–433; Hickman, *op. cit.,* pp. 500–501.

FIGURE 2–11.   Rate of Change in Export and Import, and Ratio of Export to Import.

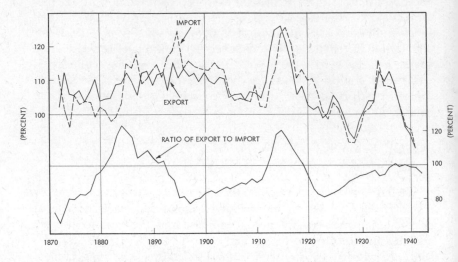

should be also noticed that exports lead imports during the period from 1910 to 1920. This makes clear how much demand for Japanese products came from abroad in this period because of World War I, and what a huge influence it had on domestic activity.

Fluctuations in imports and exports result in changes in the balance of trade. We may express the balance of trade by the ratio of exports to imports. According to figures of the balance of payments since 1902, the current balance of payments behaved as the balance of trade did, and both the balance of long-term capital account and the balance of short-term capital account moved in a direction opposite to that of the current balance of payments. That is, when the balance of trade was in deficit, the inflow of long-term, as well as short-term capital, exceeded the outflow so as to cover the deficit. The situation of the balance of short-term capital in an economy is a signal expressing whether the economy faces difficulty in its balance of payments. That is, we may say that when receipts exceed payments in the short-term capital account, the economy has difficulty in its balance of payments, and vice versa. Thus we can represent the condition of the balance of payments through the balance of trade or the export-import ratio. As shown in Figure 2–11, the export-import ratio behaved countercyclically to domestic long swings, at least until 1910 or 1913. Let us compare the timing of the construction cycle (which will be investigated later) with the peaks and troughs in the export-import ratio. According to Table 2–3, at first glance the export-import ratio lags behind the standard chronology. On estimating movements of the balance of payments from those of the export-import ratio, however, we should take into account the following two points. The first is the fact that until 1887, total imports were calculated as the sum of imports evaluated in gold yen and imports evaluated in silver yen. At the same time exports were evaluated in terms of silver yen. Since silver yen was cheaper than gold yen in that period, the true export-import ratio will show a lower peak in 1884 than Figure 2–11 indicates. But it seems that the behavior of the export-import ratio shown in Figure 2–11 is not essentially modified, even if we adjust our figures. The second point is concerned with the fact that an indemnity from China was obtained as a result of the Sino-Japanese War, and afterward foreign long-term capital flowed into Japan. The export-import ratio reached a trough in 1897, then rose gradually. When taking into consideration the above fact, however, we can say that the ceiling of the balance of payments was reached in spite of the low ratio of exports to imports, in about 1903. Thus it seems that construction cycles are accompanied by congruent countercyclical movements of the balance of payments or positive waves of net lending of short-term capital.

During and after World War I, however, the export-import ratio moved behind general economic activity. This is partly because during World War I, owing to a strong increase in Japanese exports, the high export-import ratio was maintained in spite of a great expansion of domestic economy. Secondly, there was a tendency for imports to exceed exports because of a policy maintaining the foreign exchange rate at its prewar level. After World War I, import requirements were remarkably increased as a result of the abnormal economic expansion during the war. On the other hand, the potential capacity to export

TABLE 2-3

Timing of Export-Import Ratio

	Trough	*Peak*	*Trough*	*Peak*	*Trough*	*Peak*	*Trough*
Standard chronology of construction cycle	1885	1896	1904	1908	1914	1921	1932
Export-import ratio (counter-cycle)	1884	1897	....	....	1915	1923	1937

returned to its prewar condition when the abnormal demand experienced during the war disappeared. As a result the prewar level of foreign exchange under the gold standard system overvalued the Japanese yen in the postwar period. Under such conditions the government pursued a policy of maintaining the foreign exchange rate. This destroyed the negative correspondence between the standard chronology of construction cycles and movements of the export-import ratio. Thirdly and finally, there is the fact that the foreign exchange rate dropped by about 50 percent, owing to Japan's second abolition of the gold standard system in 1932. This brought about an increase in the export-import ratio with increasing economic activity.

Next let us examine the rate of change in the supply of money. It is evident from Figure 2–12 that it moves in conformity with the rate of change in bank loans. This indicates that the part of the money supply which is induced by banking activity, plays an important role in the total. We have analyzed the effect of the money supply on investment by means of the *"money multiplier."*[20] It asserts that the change in the money supply has a positive effect on investment through substitution between holdings of money and holdings of physical assets in economic units, especially firms.[21]

FIGURE 2–12.   Rate of Change in Bank Loans and Stock of Money.

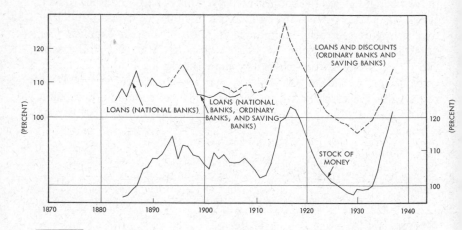

[20] See Fujino, *Business Cycles in Japan, a Theoretical, Statistical and Historical Analysis of the Process of Cyclical Development, op. cit.,* chap. 8–chap. 13.

[21] Roughly speaking this theory will be expressed as follows. The demand for money M_D is a substitute for the amounts of physical assets demanded $p_k K$, and decreases when the expected marginal rate of return on physical assets increases (vice versa). The expected marginal rate of return on physical assets

According to this theory of the money multiplier the first derivative of the money supply in regard to time has some positive connection with the first derivative of holdings of physical assets, i.e., investment. On the other hand, the change in investment is positively related to the change in income in the theory of the investment multiplier. Therefore when we denote the money supply by M_s, investment by I and income by Y, and combine the mechanism of the money multiplier with that of the investment multiplier, we get the following causal relationship:

$$\frac{d^2Ms}{dt^2} \rightarrow \frac{d^2(p_kK)}{dt^2} = \frac{dI}{dt} \rightarrow \frac{dY}{dt} \;.$$

We have shown elsewhere that this relationship is observed during the inventory cycle and the equipment cycle.[22] Can we find again a similar relationship during the construction cycle? For this investigation let us introduce the concept of the second rate of change. We define the second rate of change of a variable X_t by $(X_t/X_{t-1})/(X_{t-1}/X_{t-2})$. That is, it is the rate of change of the rate of change. We may say that it is a concept corresponding to the second derivative of X_t with respect to time t.[23]

Excess receipts in the current balance of payments (or the current balance of payments adjusted by the long-term capital account) bring an increase in the money supply some time later. Thus we should compare *the second rate of change* of the money supply with *the rate of change* in excess receipts in the current balance of payments rather than the level of excess receipts in the current balance of payments. We are using the export-import ratio as an index of the balance of payments. Therefore, we must compare the rate of change of that ratio with the second rate of change of the money supply. In Figure 2–13 we have the rate of change of the export-import ratio, the second rate of change of the money supply, the second rate of change of real gross

---

is defined by the ratio of expected returns brought about by one unit of physical assets to the price of physical assets p_k. It is assumed to be a decreasing function of holdings of physical assets because of diminishing returns. The demand for money is a decreasing function of the expected marginal rate of return on physical assets, so that it is an increasing function of both the price of physical assets p_k and holding of physical assets K. Now suppose that the money supply is increased. For the demand for money to restore equilibrium with the increased supply of money, K should increase with constant p_k. Therefore the demand for physical assets is increased; i.e., investment increases.

[22] Fujino, *ibid.*, chap. 14.

[23] More precisely the second rate of change of X_t corresponds to the second derivative of log X_t with respect to t.

FIGURE 2–13.   Balance of Payments, Money Supply, Investment and Economic Activity.

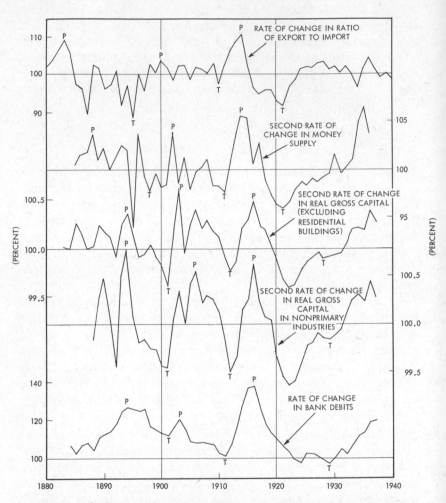

capital (excluding residential buildings) or real gross capital stock in nonprimary industries, and the second rate of change in bank debits.

According to Figure 2–13, the rate of change in the export-import ratio leads the second rate of change of the money supply; both series show a similar pattern of fluctuations. Furthermore, the second rate of change in the money supply leads that of capital stock. Thus we find in Figure 2–13 the phenomena expected by the mechanism of the money multiplier stated above. In addition the second rate of change of capital stock moves well in conformity with the rate of change in economic activity represented by bank debits. Since bank debits seem to lead general economic activity somewhat, our observations correspond well to the waves of the construction cycles which would emerge from the combined mechanisms of the money multiplier and the investment multiplier,

$$\frac{d(E_x - I_m)}{dt} \to \frac{d^2 M_s}{dt^2} \to \frac{dI}{dt} \to \frac{dY}{dt} ,$$

where E_x = exports and I_m = imports.

VI. CHRONOLOGY OF CONSTRUCTION CYCLES AND SUMMARY OF OBSERVED FACTS

Before proceeding to an analysis of the mechanism of the construction cycle, let us fix a tentative chronology of construction cycles and summarize our observations. Table 2–4 shows the timing of peaks and troughs in the rate of change of variables, with exceptions marked with an asterisk (*). (We shall examine the long swing appearing in the number of corporate firms later.) The rate of change is calculated from seven year moving averages of the original data except where there is notation ⊙, which indicates that the rate of change is computed from three-year moving averages. The notation (*) is related to ratios all of which are computed from three-year moving averages.

The share of ΔK in, say, manufacturing means the weight of the increase acquired by manufacturing in the total increase of corporate firms' long-term funds. We classify variables into three groups according to the timing of their peaks and troughs. Table 2–4 gives average dates of peaks or troughs for each group and at the same time shows average dates covering three groups, which we shall call the standard chronology of peaks and troughs of the construction cycle.[24] The standard chronology lags on the average behind the chronology of Group I by 2.8 years, and Group II by 0.8 years. It leads that of

---

[24] As we shall note later, the date of the last trough of the number of corporate firms in Group II seems to be largely influenced by the Kanto earthquake in 1923. We therefore exclude it from our calculation. The share of ΔK in transportation shows the first peak in 1885, an advanced date as a result of the huge innovation that occurred in transportation in this period through the appearance of railroads. The same is true of the first peak and trough of structures and nonresidential buildings in nonprimary industries. Thus we exclude those dates from our computation. Furthermore we assume that the date of first trough of nominal paid-up capital or real paid-up capital is the first year when its rate of change begins.

TABLE 2-4

Chronology of Peaks and Troughs of the Construction Cycle

	Trough	Peak	Trough	Peak	Trough	Peak	Trough
Group I	1884.5	1894.7	1900.8	1903.0	1910.7	1916.0	1929.3
Bank debits	1885	1894	1901	1903	1911	1916	1930
Prices.	1885	1895	1901	1905	1911	1917	1928
Real bank debits.	1888	1894	1900	1903	1910	1915	1930
Imports	1882	1895	(1901)	(1902)	1912	1916	1929
Bank loans.	1883	1894	1901	1903	1910	1916	1930
Stock of money.	1884	1894	1901	1902	1911	1917	1929
*K_3/K				1903	1910	1915	1929
Group II	1885.0	1895.4	1902.6	1907.5	1913.0	1917.8	1930.7
Long-term funds (paid-up capital) . . .	1885	1896	1904	1907	1914	1919	1931
Real long-term funds (real paid-up capital).	1885	1896	1904	1908	1915	1917	1932
Producers' durable equipment		1895	1902	1906	1913	1917	1929
Number of corporate firms		1896	1903	1908	1914	1919	1924
*K_1/K		1897	1903	1907	1914	1919	1931
*Share of K in manufacturing.		1896	1903	1906	1911	1918	1931
*Share of K in mining		1892	1901	1908	1911	1917	1931
*Share of K in commerce		1895	1901	1910	1912	1916	1930
Group III	1887.0	1898.8	1905.8	1910.6	1917.2	1925.9	1935.0
Structures in nonprimary industries.		1894	1901	1909	1916	1924	1937
Nonresidential buildings in nonprimary industries		1890	1897	1911	1917	1926	1937
Nonfarm residential buildings		1896	1905	1913	1922	1932	1937
⊖Government bonds (for industrial purposes). .	1887	1898	1905	1911	1915	1920	1929
⊖Local government bonds .		1898	1904	1910	1915	1921	1931
*K_2/K		1902	1907	1910	1916	1931	1935
*Share of K in electric power.			1912	1917	1927	1937	
*Share of K in transportation.	1885	1906	1909	1920	1932	1938	
*Share of K in financial institutions.	1900	1908	1910	1917	1920	1934	
Standard chronology	1884.9	1895.9	1903.5	1907.5	1913.9	1920.3	1931.9

Group III by 3.2 years. According to it, each duration from trough to trough of the construction cycle is 18.6 years, 10.4 years, and 18.0 years, respectively, so that the average is 15.7 years.

Let us summarize our observations.

1. The construction cycle is usually composed of two equipment cycles. The average duration from trough to trough is 15.4 years.

2. In the first equipment cycle contained in the construction cycle the economy enjoys usually a relatively high rate of growth. On the

other hand in the second equipment cycle the rate of growth declines relatively.

3. The characteristic (2) appears not only in the real magnitude of economic activity but also in prices.

4. In the first type of equipment cycle the stock of producers' durable equipment enjoys a relatively high rate of growth. On the other hand in the second type of equipment cycle the stock of construction shows a relatively high rate of growth.

5. The rate of change in all corporate firms' long-term funds (or long-term funds in manufacturing or commerce) reveals precisely the construction cycle, whether we compute the rate of change in terms of nominal value or in real terms. And in the first (second) type of equipment cycle the rate of change shows an upsurge (a small wave). This corresponds well to the behavior of investment for producers' durable equipment.

6. The rate of change of long-term funds in electric power, transportation, and financial institutions show the construction cycle clearly. It corresponds to the behavior of the rate of change in the stock of construction or investment for construction.

7. In manufacturing, mining, and commerce the industrial composition of the total increase in corporate firms' long-term funds rises (declines) in the first (second) type of equipment cycle. The opposite tendency is observed in electric power, city gas, transportation, services, and financial institutions.

8. Among the shares of paid-up capital, corporate bonds, and reserves in corporate firms' long-term funds, the share of reserves leads others; then comes the share of paid-up capital; and finally the share of corporate bonds. As a result, the share of paid-up capital tends to move in a direction opposite to that of corporate bonds. The former shows a large increase (small wave) in the first (second) type of equipment cycle. In the latter behavior an increase is found in the second type of equipment cycle.

9. The rate of change in bank loans behaves like that of all corporate firms' (or manufacturing corporate firms') long-term funds. That is, it increases greatly (remains low) in the first (second) type of equipment cycle.

10. The balance of government bonds issued for industrial purposes as well as the balance of local government bonds have the construction cycle in their rate of change. They arrive at peaks of the construction cycle in the second type of equipment cycle. Therefore they lag behind general movements of the construction cycle.

11. Among (*a*) loans and discounts of all banks (except the Bank

of Japan), (*b*) loans of other financial institutions, (*c*) loans of insurance companies, (*d*) paid-up capital, reserves, corporate bonds in nonfinancial corporate firms and (*e*) local government bonds, the share of paid-up capital and that of reserves in nonfinancial corporate firms increase (decrease) in the trough of the first (second) type of equipment cycle, apart from their trends. The share of corporate bonds and that of local government bonds reveal the opposite tendencies.

12. The export-import ratio fluctuated countercyclically to domestic economic activity before World War I. Since the outbreak of World War I, the relationship was disturbed (*a*) by the huge increase in exports owing to World War I, (*b*) by the policy of maintaining the foreign exchange rate after World War I at a point near the level of the prewar parity after the interruption of the gold standard system and (*c*) by the decline of the foreign exchange rate resulting from the second prohibition of export of gold (the abolition of the gold standard system) in 1932.[25]

13. Behavior of the rate of change of the money supply corresponds to that of bank loans, showing excellent construction cycles.

14. Among the rate of change of the export-import ratio, the second rate of change in the money supply, the second rate of change of real capital stock (excluding residential buildings) or real capital stock in nonprimary industries, and the rate of change in economic activity, there are lead-lag relationships in the order put down here in the processes of the construction cycle.

VII. AN EXPLANATION OF THE MECHANISM OF THE CONSTRUCTION CYCLE

How can we explain the facts observed above? We may attribute these entirely to historical accidents. It seems, however, that on explaining the long swing as a whole we should take into consideration the fact that investment for construction shows very clear long swings. This suggests that the economic system produces cyclical fluctuations of 15 to 25 years' duration in a stock adjustment process in construction. We shall attempt, from this point of view, to give a tentative picture of the construction cycle. First, we assume that our economic system produces cyclical fluctuations of 15 to 25 years' duration through the mechanism of the investment multiplier combined with

---

[25] Japan stopped the gold standard system in 1917 because of World War I and prohibited the export of gold. It returned to the gold standard system at the beginning of 1930, but abolished it again in 1932.

the capital stock adjustment principle in construction. It seems plausible to suppose that when various shocks, for example wars, exert influence on such a mechanism, cyclical fluctuations are transformed according to their strength and the time of their occurrence. As a result their duration will be varied,

The construction cycle consists in general of two equipment cycles. They will be similar if the construction cycle is produced from the simple combination of the investment multiplier and the capital stock adjustment principle. As observed above, however, in the construction cycle the first type of equipment cycle differs from the second. We could explain this by pointing out that the first type of equipment cycle occurred as a result of wars. But let us attempt here to pursue another possibility in explaining the alternative appearance of the first and second type of equipment cycle. Technological innovations will produce shocks to the economy which result in the construction cycle. Therefore, we assume as an initial condition that there exist sufficient opportunities for technological innovation by which considerable amounts of investment, especially expenditures for producers' durables, are stimulated. After an initial impact, technological progress is assumed to appear with a constant rate over time. In this case we should explain why technological innovations occur in clusters during a certain period, as J. Schumpeter points out, and why they "rest on their oars" in other periods. That is, it is necessary to construct a model in which technological progress does not always mean the utilization of technology. This will be a problem to be solved later.

In order for the upswing of the construction cycle to start and continue during a certain period, there is a constraint in the balance of payments and/or the money supply which should be satisfied. We suppose that in the initial conditions exports continue to exceed imports so that the international liquidity position of the economy being studied is favorable to the upswing. We assume that the money supply is increasing in accordance with this situation.

Let us now start our movement around the construction cycle from the upswing phase. We assume that the starting impulses are autonomous shocks of technological innovation. Opportunities for technological innovation appear as the result of its accumulation; therefore technological innovation subjects the economy to autonomous pressure in the upswing. As pointed out above, however, technological innovation is not technological progress, itself, but the process of utilization of its fruits. We should suppose that whether potential opportunities for technological innovation are utilized or not depends upon internal conditions of the economy. Therefore we must look for a starting impulse of the upswing of the construction cycle in addition to technological innovation. We suppose that it is a monetary factor.

The favorable position of international liquidity in the initial conditions will increase the supply of cash currency to the economy. Part of new cash currency will flow into banks, who will increase the supply of loans to business firms. As a result, the total supply of money, which includes not only cash currency but also deposit currency, will be increased. The increase in the money supply will bring the expansion of investment through the above-mentioned mechanism of the money multiplier. Thus our economic system takes the first step forward in the upswing phase of the construction cycle.

When such increase in investment continues for a while, it will induce further investment. Investment increased through the money multiplier will trigger technological innovation, or become a fuse to expand innovative investment explosively. When the economy starts the upswing as a result of the initial increase in investment, the expected marginal return on physical assets will be raised if there is a sufficient magnitude of potential opportunities for technological innovation. The demand for money will decrease, other things being equal, so that an excess supply of money will occur even if the stock of money remains constant. Equilibrium between the supply of and demand for money will be restored by an increase in the demand for physical assets that increases the demand for money through a diminishing expected marginal rate of return on physical assets. Innovative investment will appear now. It could be investment for producers' durable equipment or investment for construction. The stock of construction will need, however, a longer time to adjust the actual to the optimum value than is the case for the stock of producers' durables. Investment for producers' durable equipment will increase sharply. Mining and manufacturing need equipment in greater proportion than do other industries. The proportion of investment in mining and manufacturing will increase, and at the same time the composition of funds increased will expand there. In addition commercial activity will be raised in accordance with the expansion in mining and manufacturing, so that the demand for funds absorbed by commerce will be increased. Commerce will need working funds rather than fixed funds. Therefore the demand for bank loans will be increased and will be met by the monetary expansion brought about by the initial increase in cash currency through banking activity.

The increase in investment will make economic activity rise and prices increase. As a result, the rate of profits, whether it expresses the rate of profits on capital or on sales, will rise, so that the share of reserves in the increase in long-term funds will grow.

When the rate of profits is improved, it will make the demand for shares of stock increase. The demand for stocks seems to depend on the relationship between the normal level of share price judged by the public and the actual share price. If the normal price exceeds the actual price, then the demand for stocks will be increased. When the rate of profits is raised, the normal price will be increased. Therefore, the demand for stocks will be stimulated by the rise in the rate of profits. The stock price will rise relatively compared with the price of corporate bonds (or that of government bonds) in the security market.

In this situation it will be easier for firms to get long-term funds by issuing stocks instead of corporate bonds. Thus new issues of stocks will be expanded and the composition of paid-up capital in long-term funds will be raised. Let us see the above Figure 2–9. It shows the shares of paid-up capital, of corporate bonds and of reserves in long-term capital increased. It also shows the relative price of stocks issued by the Tokyo Stock Exchange to government bonds yielding 5 percent interest, which we denote by (P_T/P_G). Because there is not available a long series of price indexes of stocks covering the period investigated here, we used the price of stocks issued by the Tokyo Stock Exchange as representative of stock prices. P_G, i.e., the standard price of government bonds yielding 5 percent interest was estimated by the author. The relative price (P_T/P_G) shown in Figure 2–9 is computed from a three-year moving average of P_T and P_G. Since we do not have an index of the corporate bond price over a long period, we use the price of government bonds as a substitute for the price of corporate bonds. To check whether the relative price of stocks to government bonds adequately represents that of stocks to corporate bonds, we compare the former with the latter in a period where both ratios are available. We denote the relative price of stocks to corporate bonds by (P_S/P_B), where the ratio is computed from three-year moving averages of the original data. It is clear from Figure 2–9 that (P_T/P_G) moves in conformity with (P_S/P_B).

Now let us compare the ratio (P_T/P_G) or (P_S/P_B) with the share of paid-up capital of long-term funds $(\Delta K_1/\Delta K)$ in Figure 2–9. Evidently they move similarly. In addition the ratio (P_T/P_G) tends to lead $(\Delta K_1/\Delta K)$. We observe the following sequence of movements;

$$\frac{\Delta K_3}{\Delta K} \to \frac{P_T}{P_G} \left(\text{or } \frac{P_S}{P_B} \right) \to \frac{\Delta K_1}{\Delta K} \to \frac{\Delta K_2}{\Delta K}$$

The sequence indicates that there are causal relationships; the rise in the rate of profits → the rise of ΔK_3 within ΔK → the increase in the demand for stocks → the rise in the relative price of stocks to corporate bonds → the rise of the share of ΔK_1 in ΔK. At the same time we have a decline in the share of ΔK_2 in ΔK.[26]

We must take into consideration one more factor to explain the fact that the share of paid-up capital ($\Delta K_1/\Delta K$) leads that of corporate bonds in long-term capital increased. That is related to the change in the number of corporate firms. As shown in Figure 2–14, its movements correspond clearly to those of the rate of change in long-term funds. An exception is observed in the period from the 1920's to the 1930's. This is perhaps the influence of the Kanto earthquake in 1923. It seems that some corporate firms, especially small-scale enterprises disappeared as a result of the earthquake. Later the number of corporate firms was increased, in the early 1930's. When we compare the behavior of the rate of change in long-term funds or paid-up capital with that of the number of corporate firms, we know that most of the corporate firms established in the early 1930's were small-scale firms. The construction cycle is accompanied by a change

FIGURE 2–14.   Rate of Change in the Number of Corporations.

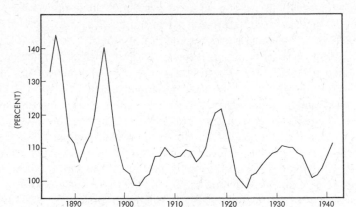

[26] S. Kuznets infers that when the difference between stock yield and corporate bond yield is changed, it is reflected in the change in costs of acquiring funds. He expects that if stock yield rises relatively to bond yield, firms prefer the issue of corporate bonds (vice versa). He observes this relationship in American railroads as well as mining and manufacturing. See Kuznets, *Capital Formation in the American Economy, Its Formation and Financing, op. cit.,* pp. 376–81. His analysis corresponds to our investigations concerning firms' demand for long-term funds, i.e., firms' supply of stocks and corporate bonds. But in his analysis the behavior of the difference between stock yield and corporate bond yield is given and is not explained. We attempt here to take into account not only firms' supply of securities but also the demand for securities, and to explain not only the behavior of $\Delta K_1/\Delta K$ or $\Delta K_2/\Delta K$ but also that of the relative price of stocks and corporate bonds.

in the number of corporate firms, which will, of course, cause a similar change in the increase in paid-up capital. We think that the behavior of $(\Delta K_1 / \Delta K)$ reflects the increase of paid-up capital brought about by the presence of new corporate firms.[27]

When the expected marginal rate of return on physical assets as well as the price of stocks are rising, the attitude of the public in portfolio selection will become more speculative. To make technological innovations is nothing but a kind of speculation. If persons and firms strengthen their propensity to speculate, their demand for money will, other things being equal, be decreased, and the propensity to hold money will decline, where the propensity to hold money is defined by the ratio of money holdings to income or the ratio of the demand for money to the total amounts of assets. In this case an increase in the money supply will produce more investment through the money multiplier or cause more demand for securities than otherwise.

The construction cycle continues its upswing by following the above process, and the economy experiences the first type of equipment cycle. Some time later, difficulties will appear to prevent the continuation of the upswing. The first is the gradual disappearance of opportunities for technological innovation. The second is that the international liquidity position becomes unfavorable, and the increase in the money supply begins to diminish because of the increase in imports brought about by the rise in domestic economic activity. Which of them first appears as the limiting factor to the upswing of the construction cycle depends on individual circumstances. It seems that the disappearance of opportunities for technological innovation usually exerts an important influence on the construction cycle earlier than do the monetary factors. We shall examine this case first. The scale of investment produced by the existence of opportunities for innovation will depend on the backlog of new technology accumulated by technical progress and on the magnitude of potential demand for commodities produced by the innovation. When opportunities for technological innovation disappear, productive capacity in the economy as a whole will catch up with the potential demand for commodi-

---

[27] There is Wardwell's time-series analysis of total liabilities of business failures in relation to the number of firms in the construction cycle. See Wardwell, *op. cit.,* pp. 70–71 and p. 83. Also see Abramovitz, "Statement in United States Congress, Joint Economic Committee," *op. cit.,* p. 418.

The number of firms clearly shows a long swing, because even the rate of change in the three-year moving average of the number of corporate firms reveals a long swing. This fact suggests that the Marshallian long-run adjustment, where the number of firms is changed, occurs in the construction cycle. This is so because the change in the number of firms is related to investment for nonresidential building.

ties. The economy will arrive at a saturation point of productive capacity. Competition among firms will have a tendency to produce excess capacity over the demand for products. Thus the expected marginal rate of return on physical assets will suddenly decline, and investment will decrease. All kinds of investment, however, will not behave uniformly. Investment in construction needs a long time to adjust, and it will not decrease immediately. Some investment in construction is not carried out until a certain amount of savings has been accumulated, and this investment will respond to the past up-swing of the long swing with a considerable lag. Investment in construction will therefore continue to rise, even though it will stagnate for a while in the depression of the first type of equipment cycle. But the behavior of investment in construction does not dominate total investment, so that total investment will decrease.

On the other hand, when the expected marginal rate of return on physical assets declines, and it is expected that the rate of profits will fall, stock prices will suffer a sudden and sharp fall because the sub-stitution of money for stocks will become predominant in the stock exchange market. Stockholders will suffer losses from the sudden and sharp fall of stock prices. As a result the propensity to speculate will diminish, and the safety motives will be strengthened in asset holders' preferences. The propensity to hold money will increase, while the increase in the stock of money diminishes. Therefore the tightness of money will become more severe than otherwise.

Thus the first type of equipment cycle will proceed toward the depression phase. Meanwhile, the economy will start to move upward as a result of the combined mechanism of the investment multiplier and the capital adjustment principle. This upward movement will be different in character from that in the first type of equipment cycle, because opportunities for innovation disappear and because the safety motive will become dominant. Even though investment for construc-tion remains at a high level, the rise in expenditure on producers' durables will be small. There will be few chances for firms to get windfall profits, so that the composition of reserves in long-term funds will increase a little. The relative price of stocks to corporate bonds will be raised a little but maintain a low level compared with the first type of equipment cycle. Thus the share of paid-up capital in long-term funds will remain relatively small. This will result partly from the decline of the rate of change in the number of corporate firms. Since the public will want to substitute corporate bonds, which are rela-tively safe, for stocks, which are relatively risky, the price of corpo-rate bonds will be raised. Thus it will become easier for firms to issue corporate bonds than stocks, and the second type of equipment cycle will appear. It is evident that in various aspects it will be the opposite of the first type.

It is possible to suppose that technological progress occurs in the course of time, so that investment will be stimulated. But fruits of technological progress will not be utilized until they are accumulated to form a backlog. And once firms start to take advantage of them, they will be exhausted during a certain period. Let us quote Matthews' ingenious analogue explanation.

An analogy may be drawn of a bucket into which water flows from a tap at a steady rate. The bucket has a trap-door in the bottom, normally held closed by a ball-catch, with a spring to shut it again once it has been opened. Until a certain amount of water has accumulated in the bucket, the trap-door remains shut, but presently the weight of water forces open the catch. The trap-door opens and all the water in the bucket then flows out. When it has done so, the trap-door is pulled shut by the spring and stays until enough water has accumulated again to force the catch open. And so on.[28]

What matters is the mechanism that plays the role of the bucket. It seems that our version of the construction cycle so far already contains it. It is the change in assetholders' as well as firms' attitude of portfolio selection or choice of asset holdings appearing in the transition from the first type to the second type of equipment cycle. In the first type of equipment cycle innovations taken into practice one after another will stimulate a speculative tendency in assetholders' and firms' choice. Before the second type of equipment cycle starts, the price of stock declines sharply, so that the safety motives are strengthened. In addition excess capacity will appear because innovation fever goes too far, and it becomes a brake to slow down the absorption of inventions, which is accompanied by considerable risk. When the safety motive dominates, fruits or yields brought about by inventions will be underestimated, and they will be accumulated in "the bucket." It is the change in the attitude of choice of asset holdings that will play the role of the above bucket.

Showing the characteristics referred to above, our economy finishes one construction cycle by approaching the trough of the second type of equipment cycle through the working of the investment multiplier and the capital stock adjustment principle. Economic activity stagnates in this equipment cycle, and imports will not increase greatly. Innovation-type investment will need some period before it shows up

---

[28] Matthews, *op. cit.,* p. 71.

in diminishing prices of products. Innovations put into practice during the first type of equipment cycle will bring gradually diminishing prices in the second type of equipment cycle, and exports will be stimulated. Here we have a reason why the current balance of payments will turn favorable in the second type of equipment cycle. This will prepare the ground for monetary expansion.

Thus, when the second type of equipment cycle has arrived at its trough and one construction cycle has been finished, we shall have situations similar to the initial conditions existing at the beginning of this construction cycle, i.e., a backlog of opportunities for technological innovation and a tendency of the money supply to increase. At the same time, although the sharp and sudden fall of stock prices as well as the appearance of excess capacity will be experienced at the peak of the first type of equipment cycle, these hard experiences will be gradually forgotten with the passage of time. There will appear possibilities for the public to strengthen its speculative tendency. Now it is possible for the economy to start the next construction cycle.

In the above, we analyzed the case where the construction cycle starts the downswing because of the disappearance of opportunities for innovation. Let us now examine briefly the case in which a bottleneck appears at first in the balance of payments and/or the monetary condition. It is possible that in this case the economy again enjoys a cycle similar to the first type of equipment cycle if at some future period the balance of payments is improved, and the money supply is allowed to expand. There still exist a considerable number of opportunities for innovation, but perhaps this equipment cycle has intermediate characteristics between the first and second type of equipment cycle.

In the above explanation we attributed an important role to innovation. In actual cases, however, a historical event, for instance, a war, could play this role. Or innovations and shocks caused by such historical events will together produce actual construction cycles. However, the fundamental mechanism for generating the long swing lasting from 15 to 25 years will be the stock adjustment principle in construction combined with the investment multiplier.

3 | Patterns of Industrial Development

YUICHI SHIONOYA

Sustained economic growth is based on favorable changes in demand as well as supply conditions, and patterns of economic growth will be characterized by specific features of these changes. Changes in both demand and supply conditions would be discerned most directly in the structure of output: in the patterns of product use (i.e., consumption, investment, export and intermediate demand), on the one hand, and product origin (i.e., domestic products and imports), on the other. This paper mainly examines the long-term trends of industrial development in prewar Japan by revealing the patterns of use and origin of products. I have confined myself to the growth of manufacturing, which, as the modern sector, played a central role in the industrialization and growth of the economy as a whole. In passing, we compare the prewar pattern of industrial growth with the postwar pattern. However, we do not intend to offer comprehensive analysis of postwar growth; our main purpose is to explore the prewar pattern.

The analysis which follows depends on my own estimates of some basic data for the period 1874–1940: the value of manufacturing output, price and production indexes for manufacturing output, and the value of final (consumption, investment and export) and intermediate demand for manufactured goods.[1] The period covers the initial transition to sustained growth of the Japanese economy and the subsequent expansion up to the eve of World War II. Here I do not enter into detailed estimating procedures, but present a summary of main findings.

---

[1] For the derivation and estimates of the data, see the Appendix.

I. GROWTH AND STRUCTURE OF MANUFACTURING INDUSTRY

Before we describe the general development of manufacturing by production indexes, reference to and comparison with the existing indexes is in order. As estimates of long-term series of industrial output for prewar Japan, we have long had only the production indexes for 1868–1936, prepared at the Nagoya Commercial College.[2] While these indexes, valuable as they are, have frequently been utilized by Japanese and foreign economists to show a strong industrial growth in Japan (e.g., W. W. Lockwood and M. Shinohara),[3] it has been felt that they underestimate output levels for earlier periods and are based on techniques that result in overstatement of the growth rate.[4] Recently Yasuba published new production indexes of manufacturing output for 1905–35.[5] He has used more commodity series in his indexes and the estimates are more carefully worked out in comparison with the Nagoya indexes. In fact, the Yasuba index for all manufacturing combined reveals a slower rate of growth than does the Nagoya index.

The Yasuba indexes start as late as 1905 and are rather short for showing the earlier process of industrialization in Japan. It is often alleged that modern economic growth in Japan had already been

---

[2] Nagoya Commercial College, "Honpō seisan sūryō shisū, Meiji 1—Shōwa 11" (Production Indexes for Japan, 1868–1936), *Shōgyō Keizai Ronsō,* November, 1938. Official statistics of manufacturing production index began with the 1930 figures of the Ministry of Trade and Industry.

[3] W. W. Lockwood, *The Economic Development of Japan: Growth and Structural Change, 1868–1938* (London: Oxford University Press, 1955); M. Shinohara, *Growth and Cycles in the Japanese Economy* (Tokyo: Kinokuniya Bookstore, 1962).

[4] The Nagoya indexes were constructed as weighted geometrical averages of physical output series (sometimes physical material input series or deflated value series), with 1929–33 gross value weights for the indexes of major industries and net value weights for the index of all manufacturing. It is clear that the Nagoya indexes are quite unsatisfactory in revealing actual movements of production, particularly because the selected commodities were only those whose gross value of output exceeded ¥10 millions during 1929–33 and no adjustment for coverage was made.

[5] Y. Yasuba, "Nihon no kōgyō seisan shisū, 1905–1935 nen" (Industrial Production Indexes for Japan, 1905–1935), in K. Inada and T. Uchida (eds.), *Keizai seichō no riron to keisoku* (Theories and Estimates of Economic Growth) (Tokyo: Iwanami Bookstore, 1966). The Yasuba indexes are weighted arithmetic averages of physical output series (sometimes deflated value series) with 1935 as the fixed weight base. The indexes for major industries as well as for all manufacturing combined were calculated by using 1935 value added data as weights.

initiated before 1905. Ohkawa and Rosovsky regard the period 1868–1905 as the first phase of modern Japanese economic growth. This period, in turn, is subdivided into a transition, 1868–85, and a phase of initial modern economic growth, 1886–1905.[6] It is therefore important to know what happened before 1905 in appraising the beginning of economic growth in Japan.

I have attempted to measure production indexes for the earlier missing period. In this case, the method of weighting physical output series that makes up the Nagoya or Yasuba indexes would not be of much help, because data on physical quantities of manufactured commodities are sparse for the earlier period in question. Instead, I deflated values of products by price indexes to obtain production indexes, since the coverage of price indexes for manufacturing output is generally more complete than that of product quantity data for the earlier period in Japan. I used the deflation method consistently throughout the period 1874–1940.[7] This work involved estimation of the value of gross output of manufacturing and a price index for manufacturing output. The production indexes thus obtained relate to gross output of manufacturing.

Annual compound interest rates of growth in the long run computed from the present, Yasuba and Nagoya indexes are compared in Table 3–1. The Nagoya index records a more rapid long-term growth than do the others, and it should be discarded since it appears to overstate the rate of growth. It is surprising to find that the levels of

TABLE 3-1

Comparison of Annual Growth Rates of Manufacturing Output
(Percent)

	Present Index	Yasuba Index	Nagoya Index*
1874-1940.	5.56	----	----
1874-1935.	5.31	----	9.94
1874-1905.	4.53	----	11.68
1905-35.	6.11	6.42	8.17

*The Nagoya index includes gas and electricity.

---

[6] K. Ohkawa and H. Rosovsky, "A Century of Japanese Economic Growth," in W. W. Lockwood (ed.), *The State and Economic Enterprise in Japan* (Princeton, N.J.: Princeton University Press, 1965).

[7] Application of this method even to the later period would not be much inferior to other methods in view of the limited availability of the quantity series used in Yasuba's work.

the present and Yasuba indexes are close to each other, as far as the period 1905–35 is concerned, although we used quite different approaches in constructing the production indexes. Moreover, I found that Yasuba also attempted to deal with the growth rate for the period before 1905, on the basis of estimated output levels of two years, 1874 and 1909.[8] The annual compound interest rates of growth of net output between these two points were calculated as 5.5 percent (Laspeyres) and 4.1 percent (Paasche). According to the present index, the comparable rate of growth of gross output is 4.1 percent between these two years. We therefore conclude that during the 30 years before 1905, there was a fairly high rate of growth of manufacturing, ranging from 4 to 5 percent. This is a little slower than during the 30 years which followed 1905. The present index reveals that over the whole prewar period 1874–1940, the growth rate of gross output per decade was 71.7 percent, and the output level grew to more than 35 times the 1874 level.

Manufacturing output, however, actually did not grow at a steady rate; in fact, we notice changes in the annual growth rates of total manufacturing output. Figure 3–1 illustrates variations in the annual rates of change in total manufacturing output smoothed by three-, five-, and seven-year moving averages, respectively. It shows long-term changes and short fluctuations in the rates of growth of manufacturing output. First of all, we can discern the existence of so-called long swings of about 20 years' duration from the seven-year moving average curve; there are long-swing troughs in 1882–84, 1900–02, 1921–23, and 1940. The last low point is not a proper trough, however, since it is followed by a decline in output as a result of war destruction. We can also see three shorter fluctuations within long swings from the three-year moving average curve; these are not our prime concern here.

On the basis of these findings of long swings in total manufacturing output, we divide the whole period, omitting the short period before 1882/84, into three phases for heuristic purposes: (I) 1882/84–1900/02, (II) 1900/02–1921/23, and (III) 1921/23–1940. Each phase seems to be characterized by a great spurt and its termination: phase I, following the Matsukata deflation, embodied the first spurt of industrial development; phase II had its spurt induced by World War I; and phase III was supported by the drive toward a wartime economy. The comparison of the growth rates of total manufacturing

---

[8] M. Miyamoto, Y. Sakudo, and Y. Yasuba, "Economic Development in Pre-industrial Japan, 1859–1894," *Journal of Economic History,* December, 1965.

FIGURE 3–1. Annual Rates of Changes in All Manufacturing Output.*

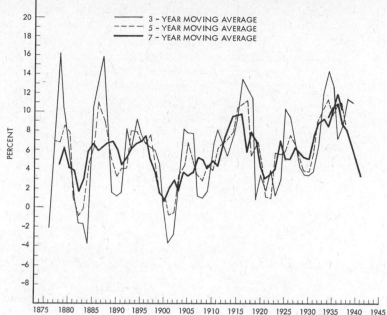

——— 3 – YEAR MOVING AVERAGE
– – – – 5 – YEAR MOVING AVERAGE
———— 7 – YEAR MOVING AVERAGE

* The curve beginning with 1934 is based on the production index of the Ministry of Trade and Industry.

for the three phases shows an acceleration of growth (see Figure 3–1 and Table 3–2), and this suggests an increasing intensity of the spurts underlying the three phases.

Let us now turn to sectoral growth in manufacturing industries. Sectoral growth rates of manufacturing are calculated in Table 3–2 for the whole period and for the three phases, together with the growth rate of agricultural production. In contrast with a decline in the growth rate of agricultural production in phase III, manufacturing growth gathered more momentum in phase III than in previous phases. Of eight major industries distinguished in manufacturing, five major industries (textiles, chemicals, stone, clay and glass, metals and machinery) grew at rates higher than the average of total manufacturing as far as the whole period is concerned. Three other major industries (foods, forest products, and miscellaneous) declined relatively. Major industries, however, did not keep the same relative growth rates throughout the three phases. Let us consider the process of changes in the relative growth rates of the relatively growing industries, with reference to the phases of the long swings in all manufac-

TABLE 3-2

Annual Growth Rates of Gross Output for Major Manufacturing Industries
(Percent)

	1874-78 to 1936-40	(Phase I) 1881-85 to 1900-04	(Phase II) 1900-04 to 1919-23	(Phase III) 1919-23 to 1936-40
Foods.	3.69	4.05	3.84	2.54
Textiles	7.02	8.71	6.90	6.24
Forest products. . . .	2.64	2.70	1.75	3.83
Chemicals.	6.49	4.68	5.70	9.72
Stone, clay, and glass	7.13	4.26	8.43	8.45
Metals	9.08	7.38	10.10	10.35
Machinery.	11.35	9.10	12.74	9.94
Miscellaneous.	4.46	5.15	4.10	6.10
All manufacturing. . .	5.69	5.02	5.74	6.97
Agriculture*	1.69	1.98	1.93	1.02

*Calculated from M. Umemura, *et al.*, *Agriculture and Forestry*, Vol. 9, *Estimates of Long-Term Economic Statistics of Japan since 1868* (Tokyo: Toyo Keizai Shinposha, 1966).

turing output. First, the textile industry grew at a higher rate than the average of total manufacturing in phases I and II, but at a slightly lower rate in phase III. Second, the chemical industry exhibited a rate of growth higher than the average in phase III alone. Third, the stone, clay and glass industry did not grow at a higher rate until phase II. In the earlier period the products of the chemical and stone, clay and glass industries were mostly indigenous types,[9] and it was only in the later period that these industries became producers of modern type products. Finally, the growth rates of the metal and machinery industries greatly exceeded the average throughout all phases.

The divergence of the trends in the output of the major industries resulted in profound changes in the pattern of output of all manufacturing industries. The relative movements in physical output may be checked by changes in the structure of gross value of output in manufacturing (see Table 3–3).

In order to examine more carefully the part played by major industries in each phase of the long swings, we computed the contribu-

---

[9] As defined by H. Rosovsky and K. Ohkawa, "The Indigenous Components in the Modern Japanese Economy," *Economic Development and Cultural Change,* April, 1961.

TABLE 3-3

Structure of Gross Value of Manufacturing Output*
(Percent)

	1874-78	1881-85	1900-04	1919-23	1936-40
Foods.	34.50	32.75	31.26	22.52	11.32
Textiles	24.54	23.13	31.66	35.43	22.64
Forest products. . . .	13.81	17.50	10.91	6.69	4.42
Chemicals.	11.57	11.30	9.56	10.13	16.94
Stone, clay, and glass	2.22	3.49	1.84	2.80	2.52
Metals	4.19	3.94	4.98	6.58	16.61
Machinery.	2.20	3.14	5.07	11.25	20.43
Miscellaneous.	6.97	4.75	4.72	4.60	5.12
All manufacturing. . .	100.00	100.00	100.00	100.00	100.00

*Based on totals in current prices.

tion of each major industry to the growth rate of total manufacturing for each phase, paying explicit attention to the weight each industry receives. Table 3–4 presents the relative contribution of each major industry to overall manufacturing growth.

TABLE 3-4

Relative Contributions of Major Industries to the
Growth Rate of All Manufacturing Output*
(Percent)

	(Phase I) 1881-85 to 1900-04	*(Phase II)* 1900-04 to 1919-23	*(Phase III)* 1919-23 to 1936-40
Foods.	33.2	21.0	6.7
Textiles	29.1	29.9	22.8
Forest products.	8.1	2.5	2.4
Chemicals.	11.0	11.4	20.4
Stone, clay, and glass	1.4	3.0	3.4
Metals	4.6	10.4	16.3
Machinery.	5.3	17.4	23.7
Miscellaneous.	7.3	4.4	4.3
All manufacturing.	100.0	100.0	100.0

*Relative contributions are calculated as the shares of major industries in the increments of real output of all manufacturing industries, the increments being measured between the average output of the initial and terminal period of a phase.

From Table 3–4, it is quite clear that the growth of manufacturing output in phases I and II was sustained primarily by the growth of the food and textile industries whose relative contributions accounted for more than one half of the growth of all manufacturing. Although the relative contributions of chemicals, metals and machinery were increasing, their magnitudes appeared prominent only in phase III because of their minor importance in manufacturing output in the earlier phases. The total of relative contributions of these three industries is 20.9 percent in phase I, 39.2 percent in phase II, and 60.4 percent in phase III.

The growth of the chemical, metal and machinery industries to important positions in phase III is also confirmed by trends in the allocation of capital and labor in favor of these industries. Tables 3–5 and 3–6 indicate the shares of major industries in the increments of owned capital (sum of paid-up capital and reserves of private companies) and labor of total manufacturing, respectively, during selected 10-year periods. The measures of owned capital are not strictly comparable with the output and labor measures; they do not relate to the stock of fixed capital, and they exclude government enterprises as well as private, small firms. It follows that in Table 3–5 the shares in food, textiles and similar industries where small household firms predominate are underestimated in earlier phases. Correspondingly the shares

TABLE 3-5

Shares of Major Industries in Increase
in Owned Capital of All Manufacturing*
(Percent)

	(Phase I) 1894-1904	(Phase II) 1899-1909	(Phase II) 1909-19	(Phase III) 1924-34	(Phase III) 1929-39
Foods.	19.75	16.93	8.72	13.29	4.45
Textiles	41.82	31.61	35.41	11.50	9.45
Forest products. .	1.19	3.88	1.56	-0.33	0.42
Chemicals.	5.32	16.41	20.40	27.57	27.21
Stone, clay, and glass.	5.23	5.17	4.89	6.02	3.08
Metals	0.94	6.89	3.67	27.76	23.68
Machinery.	15.87	10.56	21.31	13.26	29.04
Miscellaneous. . .	9.88	8.55	4.04	0.93	2.67
All manufacturing.	100.00	100.00	100.00	100.00	100.00

*Calculated from Nōshōmushō (Ministry of Agriculture and Commerce), Nōshōmu tōkeihyō (Statistics of Ministry of Agriculture and Commerce); and Shōkōshō (Ministry of Commerce and Industry), Kaisha tōkeihyō (Corporate Statistics).

TABLE 3-6

Shares of Major Industries in Increase
in Labor of All Manufacturing*
(Percent)

	(Phase II)		(Phase III)	
	1899-1909	1909-19	1924-34	1929-39
Foods.	9.64	6.77	0.55	-3.52
Textiles	44.75	44.21	16.45	10.05
Forest products. . . .	5.69	4.19	7.77	3.21
Chemicals.	3.29	9.08	14.66	13.25
Stone, clay, and glass	5.20	5.22	4.90	2.34
Metals	5.62	5.69	13.27	14.33
Machinery.	17.74	16.68	33.07	58.31
Miscellaneous.	8.07	8.16	9.33	2.03
All manufacturing. . .	100.00	100.00	100.00	100.00

*Calculated from K. Akasaka, "Seizōgyō jugyōshasū no suikei, 1899-1918 nen" (Estimates of Labor Force in Manufacturing, 1899-1918), Working Paper C 19 (Tokyo: Institute of Economic Research, Hitotsubashi University, 1965); and K. Akasaka, "Seizōgyō jugyō-shasū no suikei, 1919-1942 nen" (Estimates of Labor Force in Manufacturing, 1919-1942), Working Paper C 15 (Tokyo: Institute of Economic Research, Hitotsubashi University, 1965).

of the metal and machinery industries, where government production is concerned, are too low in the later phases. Nevertheless, it is likely that big changes occurred from phases I and II to phase III in capital and labor allocation among major manufacturing industries. The shares of the food and textile industries declined considerably, while the shares of the chemical, metal and machinery industries increased by a similar magnitude.

After viewing the overall and sectoral growth of manufacturing over the prewar period, we may draw some implications from the findings. First, it is generally agreed that the traditional pattern of industrial growth for capitalist countries in the past was to develop, first of all, the textile and food industries, and then to shift to a more rapid growth of the metal and machinery industries at a fairly advanced stage. Indeed, Japanese industrial growth in the earlier phases was dominated by the textile and food industries, although it was also true that the rate of expansion of the metal and machinery industries was rapid from the beginning. This latter expansion has probably been the basis of the argument that the normal order of industrial development was reversed in Japan; instead of the process of "textiles first" the "metal and machinery first" path was followed.[10] There are certain elements of truth in this argument, but we cannot ignore the strength of early textile expansion in prewar Japan. It would be more meaningful to emphasize the quick succession of the chemical, metal and machinery industries as the new leading sectors. They not only had higher rates of growth, but also showed a substantial capacity to contribute to overall growth; this began to be the case in phase III even before the older textile industry showed a distinct decline in its rate of growth. This close succession of leading sectors in Japan was responsible for the high and accelerating rate of industrial growth. We conclude that Japanese industrial growth never reversed the traditional order of sectoral development, but proceeded more quickly along the traditional course.

A second implication that deserves our attention is a change in the relation between industrial and agricultural development. The textile and food industries were the first-stage manufacturing industries in Japan and accounted for more than half the industrial growth in phases I and II. They depended on the availability of agricultural raw materials, and their growth rates were almost parallel to that of agriculture. Early industrial development was supported by agricultural development through input-output relations, and this pattern was erased in phase III.

Third, when we compare the growth rate of Japanese manufacturing with those of some selected developed countries in Table 3–7, it is observed that the rate of Japanese industrial growth is high on an international scale. This rating is valid despite the crudity of the comparison as a result of differences in weights, coverages, and formulas for industrial production indexes in various countries. Before World War I, the growth rates of industrial production in America, Sweden, Canada, and Italy were as high as, or higher than, in Japan. Thus, the speed of Japanese industrial growth was not unreasonably high when viewed from the experience of other countries, at least before World War I. The most striking characteristic of Japanese growth was its strength after World War I. While most developed countries showed industrial decline and stagnation as a result of war destruction and the Great Depression, Japan continued to grow even more quickly than before, and apparently suffered little from the problems affecting the main industrial nations. During this period Japan advanced very much in the process of catching up with the

---

[10] E. H. Norman, *Japan's Emergence as a Modern State* (New York: Institute of Pacific Relations, 1940), pp. 125–26.

TABLE 3-7

International Comparison of Annual Growth Rates
of Manufacturing Output
(Percent)

	1850-74	1874-1913	1913-37
United Kingdom	3.24	1.79	2.11
Germany.	4.51	3.37	1.79
United States.	----	4.99	2.71
Sweden	----	5.42	3.51
Canada	----	6.34*	2.36
France	----	2.71*	0.90
Italy.	----	3.92†	2.82
Japan.	----	4.43	6.73

*1870-1913.
†1881-1913.
SOURCES: United Kingdom: W. G. Hoffmann, *British Industry, 1700-1950* (New York: Kelley & Millman, 1955), for 1850-99; and K. S. Lomax, "Production and Productivity Movements in the United Kingdom since 1900," *Journal of Royal Statistical Society*, Series A (1959), for 1900-37. Germany: W. G. Hoffmann, *Das Wachstum der Deutschen Wirtschaft seit der Mitte des 19. Jahrhunderts* (Berlin: Springer-Verlag, 1965). United States: E. Frickey, *Production in the United States, 1860-1914* (New York: Harvard University Press, 1947), for 1870-98; and S. Fabricant, *The Output of Manufacturing Industries, 1899-1937* (New York: National Bureau of Economic Research, 1940), for 1899-1937. Italy: A. Gerschenkron, "Description of an Index of Italian Industrial Development, 1881-1913," in *Economic Backwardness in Historical Perspective* (Cambridge, Mass.: Harvard University Press, 1962, for 1881-1913; and F. Hilgerdt, *Industrialization and Foreign Trade* (Geneva: League of Nations, 1945), for 1920-37. Sweden, Canada, and France: F. Hilgerdt, *ibid.*

developed countries. Our point of emphasis is that Japanese growth was particularly strong after World War I and that during this period its industrial structure shifted decisively to new leading sectors, namely the chemical, metal, and machinery industries.

Finally, we point out that manufacturing production increased in Japan at an average rate of 14.5 percent annually after World War II (1955–65), according to the production index compiled by the Ministry of Trade and Industry, and that postwar growth was again led by the chemical, metal, and machinery industries, which were based on new technological foundations.

II. INCREASING INTERMEDIATE DEMAND AND IMPORT SUBSTITUTION

The significance of differences in growth rates of various sectors of manufacturing can be better appreciated if manufacturing output is examined in the light of type of demand absorption and supply source. On the demand side, manufacturing industries are classified into four categories: consumer goods, investment goods, unfinished goods, and export goods. At first glance, this classification seems to be similar to those of Hoffmann[11] and Chenery,[12] but it is essentially different. Hoffmann's categories are consumer goods and investment goods, while Chenery's are consumer goods, investment and related products, and intermediate goods. They adopted classification criteria that might be called the *industry output approach;* they classify total products of an industry without considering the various demand categories for which they were actually destined.[13] Instead, I propose to follow an *economic use approach* by classifying industries according to the economic use made of their output, so that industry output is subdivided into different categories according to the nature of its demand.

An exact classification of manufactured products by economic use needs either input-output statistics or commodity flow statistics. I attempted to classify all manufacturing output in the prewar period into the four categories mentioned above, following the commodity flow method explored by Kuznets[14] and Shaw.[15] In dealing with the

---

11 W. G. Hoffmann, *Studien und Typen der Industrialisierung: Ein Beitrag zur quantitativen Analyse historischer Wirtschaftsprozesse* (Jena: Gustav Fischer, 1931), and *The Growth of Industrial Economies* (Manchester: Manchester University Press, 1958).

12 H. B. Chenery, "Patterns of Industrial Growth," *American Economic Review,* September, 1960.

13 According to Hoffmann, the consumer goods industry includes the food, textile, leather and furniture industries; the investment goods industry includes the metalworking, vehicle building, engineering, and chemical industries. Other mixed sectors (rubber, timber, paper, and printing) are excluded from his scheme. According to Chenery's more sophisticated classification, the consumer goods industry includes wood products, printing, clothing, leather products, foods, beverages, and tobacco. The investment and related products industry includes machinery, transport equipment, metals, nonmetallic minerals. The intermediate industry includes paper, petroleum products, rubber, chemicals and textiles.

14 S. Kuznets, *Commodity Flow and Capital Formation,* Vol. I (New York: National Bureau of Economic Research, 1938).

15 W. H. Shaw, *Value of Commodity Output since 1869* (New York: National Bureau of Economic Research, 1947).

postwar situation, we can make direct use of input-output tables for 1951, 1955, and 1959, thus avoiding the laborious technique of the commodity flow method.

On the supply side, domestic and foreign origins are distinguished for manufactured commodities. We shall use the following notation for the domestic production of manufacturing gross output:

$X =$ Total manufacturing output produced at home, $= C + I + E + U$;

$C =$ Manufactured consumer goods produced at home;

$PD =$ Manufactured producer durables produced at home;

$CM =$ Manufactured construction materials produced at home;

$I =$ Manufactured investment goods produced at home, $= PD + CM$;

$E =$ Manufactured export goods produced at home;

$U =$ Manufactured unfinished (intermediate) goods produced at home;

$Y =$ Manufactured finished goods produced at home, $= C + I + E$.

Except for E, the notation for the imports of manufactured output corresponds to that used above and is as follows: M $(= C_m + I_m + U_m)$, C_m, PD_m, CM_m, I_m $(= PD_m + CM_m)$, U_m and Y_m $(= C_m + I_m)$. Finally, the total of domestic production and imports for each demand category is defined as: $C^* = C + C_m$, $PD^* = PD + PD_m$, $CM^* = CM + CM_m$, $I^* = I + I_m$, $U^* = U + U_m$, and $Y^* = Y + Y_m$.

As in input-output analysis, we have the following accounting identity for total manufacturing:

$$Z = X + M = Y^* + U^* = C^* + I^* + E + U^*, \qquad (1)$$

where Z is the total supply of (and total demand for) manufactured output. This identity holds for each of the major manufacturing industries distinguished in the last section.

Table 3–8 summarizes the composition of total supply and demand for all manufactured commodities based on commodity flow estimates and input-output tables. There are several major changes in the distribution, among major categories, of manufactured output. As far as figures before World War II are concerned, the following observations can be made: On the supply side, the share of imports (M) rises for the period up to the turn of the century (the end of phase I) and declines through phases II and III. On the demand side, the share of consumer goods (C^*) declines strikingly and that of investment goods

TABLE 3-8

Composition of Total Supply and Demand for Manufacturing Output
(Based on Totals in Current Prices)
(Percent)

	X	M	C^*	PD^*	CM^*	$I^* (= PD^* + CM^*)$	E	U^*	Total $(Z = X + M = C^* + I^* + E + U^*)$
1874-83	88.53	11.47	57.75	2.84	8.87	11.71	6.61	23.93	100.00
1877-86	89.26	10.74	56.18	3.42	9.01	12.43	7.50	23.89	100.00
1882-91	88.48	11.52	55.93	6.14	6.80	12.94	10.09	21.04	100.00
1887-96	87.96	12.04	51.66	8.66	5.26	13.92	11.65	22.77	100.00
1892-1901	87.34	12.66	47.77	8.61	6.14	14.75	12.70	24.78	100.00
1897-1906	86.81	13.19	46.15	7.46	6.50	13.96	15.56	24.33	100.00
1902-11	87.24	12.76	44.57	6.95	6.43	13.38	17.38	24.67	100.00
1907-16	88.79	11.21	37.91	8.21	6.32	14.53	19.14	28.42	100.00
1912-21	90.02	9.98	31.75	11.49	6.19	17.68	18.08	32.49	100.00
1917-26	89.25	10.75	33.90	9.41	6.21	15.63	17.48	32.99	100.00
1922-31	89.13	10.87	35.70	6.71	5.79	12.50	18.05	33.75	100.00
1927-36	91.07	9.93	31.35	7.51	4.99	12.50	18.83	32.32	100.00
1931-40	92.65	7.35	25.32	12.64	4.73	17.37	16.04	41.27	100.00
1951-59*	97.62	2.38	22.57	7.56	5.39	12.95	8.85	55.63	100.00

*Average of 1951, 1955, and 1959.

(I^*) remains fairly stable, although both sometimes reflect the effects of spurts and stagnation. Within investment goods, however, there is a noticeable shift of structure. The share of producer durables (PD^*) rises, and the share of construction materials (CM^*) declines. The share of unfinished goods (U^*) remains roughly constant before World War I and then begins to rise rapidly. Finally, the share of export goods (E) trebles by the end of World War I and then remains stable or declines only slightly.

In Table 3–8, post-World War II data show both continuity and interruption of prewar trends. Continuity is observed for the shares of imports, consumption goods, and unfinished goods. The share of investment goods stays roughly at its prewar average, but the export share drops by a large amount.

We shall proceed from the above summary of findings to an inquiry into the causes of the important trends. The discussion will be based on the following analytical framework: The structure of total demand and supply is influenced by the structure of final demand, as the logic of input-output analysis shows. There are two steps by which changes in final demand work their way into domestic production. First, final demand (Y^*) influences total demand (Z) by inducing intermediate demand (U^*) which works through interindustry relations; second, total demand (Z) induces domestic production (X), and a part of total demand not fulfilled by domestic production spills over into imports (M). Therefore, changes in the structure of final demand partly govern changes in the structure of domestic production, but not entirely; we must also take account of intermediate demand and imports as linking factors between them. In the process of industrialization these two links are likely to change the response of domestic production to final demand, and these changes represent the underlying evolution in structure of production which causes industrialization.

We shall now deal with the first step: the relation of final demand (Y^*) to total demand (Z), including intermediate demand (U^*). Since we are not able to get an input-output matrix for the whole period under consideration, we cannot evaluate the detailed interindustry repercussions through which intermediate demand is brought about. We calculate the ratio of intermediate demand to final demand (U^*/Y^*) for each major manufacturing industry as well as for total manufacturing industry. The data in Table 3–8 show that the ratio for total manufacturing increased rapidly after World War I. This ratio for total manufacturing is identically equal to the sum of the products of the shares of major industries in final demand for total manufactures (Y_i^*/Y^*), and their intermediate-final demand ratios, (U_i^*/Y_i^*), where the subscript i relates to the i-th major industry.

In order to test the relative importance of these two factors in influencing changes in the overall ratio of intermediate to final demand, we determine what the overall ratio would have been if the structure of final demand with respect to individual major industries had remained constant, or if the individual intermediate-final demand ratios had remained constant.[16] Table 3–9 provides calculated values of hypothetical ratios of overall intermediate to final demand, together with the actual values, for two periods 1874/83–1902/11 and 1902/11–1931/40. For the former period, there was not a big change in the actual value. Neither the individual ratios nor the structure of final demand changed enough to make the overall ratio diverge much from the actual value at the beginning of the period. For the latter period, however, a substantial increase in the actual overall ratio was mostly explained by changes in the individual ratios on the assumption that the final demand structure was constant at the initial value; changes in the final demand structure had only a small effect on the movement in the overall ratio.

The increase in the intermediate demand for manufactured goods relative to total production for an economy as a whole (and for manufacturing) is regarded as a product of the evolution of the interin-

TABLE 3-9

Comparison of Actual and Hypothetical Overall Intermediate-Final
Demand Ratios for Total Manufacturing
(Percent)

1874-83. . . . . actual	31.46
1902-11. . . . . actual	32.75
hypothetical	
(i) under 1874-83 Y_i^*/Y^*	33.60
(ii) under 1874-83 U_i^*/Y_i^*	34.23
1931-40. . . . . actual	70.27
hypothetical	
(i) under 1902-11 Y_i^*/Y^*	59.75
(ii) under 1902-11 U_i^*/Y_i^*	36.22

[16] Since the individual intermediate-final demand ratio (U_i^*/Y_i^*) is not a pure technical coefficient based solely on input coefficients, but is also affected by the structure of final demand (including Y_i^*/Y^*), this procedure is not fully justified. As technical and demand factors are inseparable in this context, this is not more than an approximation.

dustry structure. This phenomenon is sometimes referred to as a priori evidence of an increase in the degree of interrelatedness among industrial branches and of roundabout production in the process of economic growth, but its causes should be examined more closely.[17]

I propose to emphasize the effect of import substitution on the increase in intermediate demand. Replacement of manufactured imports by domestic production affects not only domestic manufacturing output by the amount of the replaced imports but also the demand for intermediate manufactured goods, whether imported from abroad or produced at home. Suppose that a country imports all cotton fabrics consumed at home and that there is no cotton industry; in this case neither cotton yarn nor raw cotton as an unfinished product is required. Suppose that the country begins to produce cotton fabrics at home. An intermediate demand for cotton yarn will appear, and it will be met by imports for the moment. When the substitution of domestic production for imports of cotton yarn takes place, imports of manufactured cotton products will disappear from the country, and an intermediate demand for (nonmanufactured) raw cotton imports will increase. In this developmental process a given final demand for cotton fabrics is compatible with various patterns of intermediate demand and therefore with various intermediate-final demand ratios, according to the stages of production where import substitution takes place.

The above example assumes a simple relation, i.e., a vertical relation, cotton fabrics–cotton yarn–raw cotton. Actually there are complicated input-output relations in which import substitution proceeds in various lines of production, causing the demand for intermediate goods to expand still more widely.

These considerations suggest a hypothesis that the movement in the overall intermediate-final demand ratio for total manufacturing output (U^*/Y^*) will be associated with the proportion of the total demand for manufactured goods which is met by imports (M/Z). Figure 3–2 indicates the plausibility of this reasoning. The plotted points show the figures for decade averages. The decline in the import ratio after the turn of the century is associated with the increase in the intermediate-final demand ratio. In phase I and the period immedi-

---

[17] H. B. Chenery, "The Use of Interindustry Analysis in Development Programming," in T. Barna (ed.), *Structural Interdependence and Economic Development* (London: Macmillan, 1963), refers to three factors as causes of the relative increase in the intermediate demand for manufactured goods compared with the production of an economy as a whole: (*i*) relative increase in final demand for manufactured goods, (*ii*) replacement of handicraft by factory production, requiring more demand for intermediate goods, and (*iii*) replacement of imports by domestic production of manufactured goods, causing manufacturing output to rise more rapidly than total demand.

FIGURE 3–2.   Intermediate-Final Demand Ratio and Import Ratio for All Manufactures.

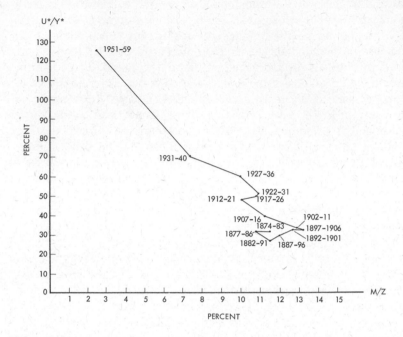

ately after World War I, when the import ratio rises, the intermediate-final demand ratio remains almost constant. This would suggest that there are other factors responsible for the increase in the intermediate-final demand ratio, such as a rise in input coefficients of manufactures or a shift of final demand, and that they work to produce the stable intermediate-final demand ratio by offsetting the effect of the rising import ratio. However, exact analysis of these factors is impossible without an input-output table.

At any rate, after the turn of the century, the intermediate demand for manufactures begins to rise more than proportionally to the final demand for manufactures; more and more total demand for manufactures arises from a given final demand through the changes in intermediate demand.

Let us now turn to the second step. How did the structure of total demand for manufactures (Z) influence the domestic production of manufactures (X)? In this connection, needless to say, import substitution is the crux of the problem. The proportion of imports of manufactures in total supply of manufactures rises until the end of phase I and then declines except during the aftermath of World War I (see Table 3–8). This trend in the import ratio for manufactures is not illuminating by itself because it is a complex result of different movements within manufactures, whether seen from the viewpoint of major sectors or demand categories. Table 3–10 brings out the trend in the import ratio (imports divided by domestic production) for each demand category, together with the proportion of imports of manufactures in all imports, including nonmanufactures. This proportion declines strongly over the whole period, showing that imported manufactures as a whole were quickly replaced by domestic production and that imports of nonmanufactured goods, mostly unfinished, increased rapidly. The very low import ratio for total manufactures in the post–World War II period would suggest that import substitution of manufactures has been carried out almost to its limit, judged from the record of industrial countries, and that there would be little room for further industrialization through import substitution, as far as manufacturing production is concerned.

Import substitution did not take place evenly in different demand categories. The import ratio for consumer goods declined steadily

TABLE 3-10

Import Ratio by Demand Category in Manufacturing
(Based on Imports and Production in Current Prices)
(Percent)

	C	PD	CM	U	X	*Ratio of Imports of Manufactures to All Imports*
1874–83. . . .	10.47	25.11	3.47	27.27	12.95	91.12
1877–86. . . .	8.76	26.93	3.83	27.50	12.03	89.96
1882–91. . . .	7.54	25.56	7.57	38.34	13.02	81.78
1887–96. . . .	8.22	24.24	12.87	34.39	13.69	72.26
1892–1901. . .	7.93	38.89	14.96	31.47	14.49	63.96
1897–06. . . .	7.86	47.24	16.71	36.45	15.19	56.97
1902–11. . . .	6.87	37.29	19.00	39.48	14.63	55.24
1907–16. . . .	4.86	21.77	18.17	32.76	12.62	51.06
1912–21. . . .	3.40	11.34	22.19	25.75	11.09	48.63
1917–26. . . .	4.20	16.66	25.60	25.69	12.05	47.68
1922–31. . . .	4.61	26.79	24.80	24.87	12.19	45.85
1927–36. . . .	3.85	17.28	16.41	18.99	9.80	41.00
1931–40. . . .	2.96	8.06	9.60	14.64	7.94	43.58
1951–59* . . .	1.34	5.24	0.70	27.28	2.34	20.16

*Average of 1951, 1955, and 1959.

during the period before World War I and then remained at a fairly stable level. For other categories, the ratios increased at first and then declined, with different timing of the up-and-down movements, although in the case of producer durables the ratio reflects the investment spurts in the domestic economy. In this way, import substitution took place first in the consumer goods industry and continued during phases I and II, while import dependency increased rapidly in the investment and unfinished goods sectors. The movement in the consumer goods sector reached a limit in phase III, and the tendency toward import substitution began in the investment and unfinished goods sectors. Of course, the decline in the import ratio for investment and unfinished goods was to some extent forced by limited imports during World War I, but, stimulated by this situation, import substitution for these goods was realized.

Figure 3–3 shows the import ratios for major industries. The decline in the import ratio of the consumer goods industry is well represented by that of the textile industry. The import ratios of the chemical, metal, and machinery industries increased quite rapidly at first, but then also declined rapidly. It is interesting to note that these four industries, whose import ratios showed substantial changes, constituted the relatively growing or leading industries of manufacturing. Development in phase III of the new leading industries, namely

FIGURE 3–3.   Import Ratios of Major Manufacturing Industries.

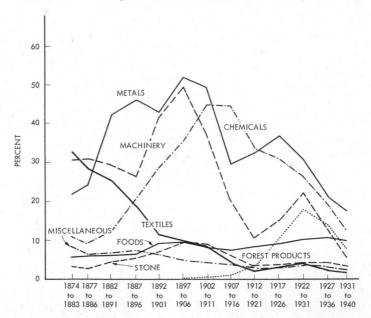

chemical, metal, and machinery industries, which were greatly involved in the production of unfinished goods, was mostly based on the expansion of intermediate demand for manufactures and on import substitution of intermediate goods themselves.

As a consequence of the increasing relative importance of intermediate demand and import substitution, domestic production of manufactures relative to final demand for manufactures changed from 1.16 in 1874–83 to 1.58 in 1931–40; this figure amounted to 2.20 in 1951–59.

III. STRUCTURE OF FINISHED MANUFACTURES

In the previous section we were concerned with the process by which final demand gives rise to domestic production, paying attention to the two links between them: intermediate demand and imports. We may now turn to domestic production of finished manufactures and deal with three trends corresponding to the types of final demand: exports, consumer goods, and investment goods. Table 3–11 shows

TABLE 3-11

Composition of Domestic Production of Finished
Manufactures by Demand Category
(Based on Totals in Current Prices)
(Percent)

	C	PD	CM	$I(= PD + CM)$	*Military Durable Equipment*†	E	$Y(= C + I + E)$
1874–83. . . .	74.96	3.26	12.30	15.56	1.04	9.48	100.00
1877–86. . . .	73.23	3.82	12.30	16.12	0.87	10.65	100.00
1882–91. . . .	70.99	6.62	8.62	15.24	0.85	13.77	100.00
1887–96. . . .	67.23	9.81	6.56	16.37	1.70	16.40	100.00
1892–1901. . .	64.61	9.05	7.80	16.85	2.68	18.54	100.00
1897–1906. . .	62.03	7.34	8.07	15.41	2.98	22.56	100.00
1902–11. . . .	59.95	7.27	7.78	15.05	2.94	25.00	100.00
1907–16. . . .	53.66	10.00	7.95	17.95	2.66	28.39	100.00
1912–21. . . .	47.84	16.09	7.90	23.99	3.40	28.17	100.00
1917–26. . . .	51.60	12.80	7.86	20.66	3.05	27.74	100.00
1922–31. . . .	54.96	8.52	7.46	15.98	2.30	29.06	100.00
1927–36. . . .	50.56	10.72	7.18	17.90	3.23	31.54	100.00
1931–40. . . .	43.40	20.65	7.62	28.27	11.52	28.33	100.00
1951–59* . . .	50.98	16.46	12.21	28.67	---	20.35	100.00

*Average of 1951, 1955, and 1959.

†Value of military durable equipment produced at home was computed from H. Rosovsky, *Capital Formation in Japan, 1868-1940* (New York: The Free Press of Glencoe, 1961).

the composition of domestic production of finished manufactures by demand category.

The share of manufacturing production for exports rose remarkably until the end of World War I and then leveled before World War II. The growing share of exports was met by the expansion of the textile industry. The share of textile exports in total exports of manufactures increased from 48.8 percent in 1874–83 to 69.0 percent in 1922–31, the highest share in the entire period. Exports of manufactures accounted for 57.7 percent of total exports in 1874–83, and this percentage steadily increased to 94.3 percent in 1931–40.

The large and increasing share of exports in the process of industrialization in prewar Japan does not necessarily mean impoverishment of the home market. In view of the unlimited supply of labor then available, it may be argued that the resources employed in the production of textile exports were not diverted from significant alternative uses. They could not have been absorbed in the production of chemicals or metals and machinery. Expansion of industrial production for the home market, except for indigenous production, was more restricted by the supply than by the demand side. As is clearly seen from the increase in the import ratio for chemicals, metals and machinery in the early period, a domestic market for these products was not lacking, but their production was limited by capital and technology. Without international trade, the resources used for textile exports would have been idle in a disguised form. The surplus resources which would have otherwise been idle found use in trade, and exports increased without sacrifice of production for the home market.

Moreover, expansion of textile exports helped to overcome the supply bottleneck of production for the home market. They helped meet the growing need for investment and unfinished goods, manufactured and nonmanufactured, by paying for imports. In fact, the import ratio of the new leading industries, i.e., the chemical, metal, and machinery industries, which occupied prominent places in phase III and served the home market in the prewar period, increased in the earlier phases. In due course, their import ratios began to decline through import substitution.

The textile industry or export sector was properly in the vanguard of the leading industries. Without the rapid expansion of textiles which paid for necessary imports, infant industries, which were constrained by poor resources and techniques rather than by a narrow market, could not have developed as rapidly as they did. The export sector, in a roundabout fashion, overcame the bottleneck on the supply side of the infant, growing industries, which were later to become the real leading sectors and to serve the domestic market.

As a result of the increase in the share of export production, the share of finished manufactures for the home market declined from 90.5 percent in 1874–83 to 71.7 percent in 1931–40 (see Table 3–11). We cannot effectively isolate the relative importance of government purchases in the home market; we have merely isolated the production of military equipment from producer durables (*PD*) in Table 3–11. Except for the latter part of phase III, military demand for investment goods produced at home was not high enough to constrain private investment demand. In what follows we shall deal with the relative growth of consumer goods and investment goods, including those purchased by the government.

It is interesting to see in Table 3–11 that the proportion of investment goods in total production of finished manufactures remained fairly stable if we exclude the periods of investment spurts, when the proportion of investment goods obviously increased. This is the case in spite of the fact that the proportion of so-called heavy industry (the chemical, metal, and machinery industries), which is sometimes classified as investment goods industry under the *industry output approach,* showed a long-term tendency to increase. This apparent contradiction can be explained by noting that the products of heavy industry were mainly absorbed as unfinished goods during the period under consideration. Long-term stability of the proportion of investment goods when the heavy sector is expanding during the process of industrialization is also found in the process of industrial growth of developed countries. This pattern is accounted for by the demand expansion in the form of exports and consumer goods, as well as unfinished goods, in the heavy industry category. Thus, an analysis of the process of industrial growth in some developed countries and an international comparison of the postwar situation, in terms of the *economic use approach,* leads to quite different conclusions about the relative growth of the investment goods sector from those based on the *industry output approach.*[18]

The share of consumption goods in total finished manufactures declined from 75 percent to 43 percent during the whole prewar

---

[18] Y. Shionoya, "Patterns of Industrial Growth in the United States and Sweden: A Critique of Hoffmann's Hypothesis," *Hitotsubashi Journal of Economics,* June, 1964, and "Kōgyōka no nibumon pattern" (Two-sector Patterns of Industrial Growth), in Y. Yamada *et al.* (eds.), *Keizaiseichō to sangyōkōzō* (Economic Growth and Industrial Structure) (Tokyo: Shunjūsha Bookstore, 1965).

period. The ratio of manufactured consumer goods to manufactured investment goods, both defined under the *economic use approach,* is a variant of the so-called Hoffmann ratio.[19] This ratio is calculated in Table 3–12. The long-term trend in the Hoffmann ratio shows a rapid decline for the entire period, although the ratio reflects cyclical expansions and recessions. The trend in the Hoffmann ratio may well reflect a path of "natural austerity" in an economy with unlimited supply of labor. Industrial development in such an economy is likely to be in favor of production of industrial investment goods or exportables rather than production of industrial consumer goods.[20]

In Table 3–12 we show two kinds of relative prices of manufactured consumer to manufactured investment goods. One price relation uses only producer durables (*PD*), but the other uses construction ma-

TABLE 3-12

The Hoffmann Ratio and Relative Prices

	Hoffmann Ratio C/I	Relative Prices (1935 = 100)	
		C to PD	C to (PD + CM)
1874–83.	4.82	49.36	74.70
1877–86.	4.54	58.30	76.90
1882–91.	4.66	60.76	82.88
1887–96.	4.11	63.49	90.90
1892–1901. . . .	3.83	71.19	95.47
1897–1906. . . .	4.03	78.39	102.66
1902–11.	3.98	89.49	114.06
1907–16.	2.99	89.58	114.68
1912–21.	1.99	92.48	108.48
1917–26.	2.50	106.35	108.88
1922–31.	3.44	115.89	110.59
1927–36.	2.82	106.48	105.28
1931–40.	1.51	96.69	94.50
1951–59*	1.78	----	----

*Average of 1951, 1955, and 1959.

[19] In addition to the difference between the *industry output approach* and the *economic use approach* as the basic criterion of classification of the sectors, there are additional differences in that Hoffmann uses net output as the measure of the sectors and includes output due to exports in the production of the two sectors. Here I use gross production and exclude exports as a separate sector. The latter are mainly the results of the differences in the basic criterion for classification.

[20] J. C. H. Fei and G. Ranis, *Development of the Labor Surplus Economy: Theory and Policy* (Homewood, Ill.: Richard D. Irwin, Inc., 1964).

terials (*CM*) in addition to producer durables as investment goods.[21] The two kinds of relative prices move in almost the same way, and it is interesting to note that their long-term trend clearly moves in favor of consumer goods throughout the prewar period. We also observe that in periods of investment expansion in each of the three phases the trend in relative prices in favor of consumer goods is stopped or even reversed. This interruption becomes increasingly larger as we move through the three phases. This means that the investment spurts become increasingly intense. In any event, the long-term tendency is for a rapid increase in the prices of manufactured consumer goods relative to manufactured investment goods. It follows that the trend in the Hoffmann ratio in real terms shows a more rapid decline than in nominal terms.

A distinct feature of the postwar period is an increase in the share of investment goods which exactly corresponds to a decline of similar magnitude in the share of exports. In view of the fact that the production of investment goods in the postwar period no longer includes military equipment, the high postwar percentage for investment goods is indeed striking. This postwar period partly includes the effect of the heavy investment boom, 1955–61. The Hoffmann ratio, therefore, remains at a level as low as that achieved in the period just before World War II, or perhaps declines to an even lower level.

IV. ANALYSIS OF THE CAUSES OF INDUSTRIALIZATION

In order to give a comprehensive review of the preceding two sections, we attempt to evaluate the relative importance of each broad component of total demand and supply in explaining the growth of industrial production. We shall calculate the increase in the real value of total manufacturing production as the difference between adjacent decade averages and consider how the increase in production is caused by five factors: consumption, investment, export, intermediate demand, and import substitution.[22]

---

[21] Prices of manufactured consumer and investment goods relate to the output of the two sectors defined in the *economic use approach*. Their price indexes were constructed by combining the price indexes of the major subsectors which are included in the two sectors.

[22] Analysis of the causes of industrialization was also attempted in H. B. Chenery, "Patterns of Industrial Growth," *op. cit.*, and H. B. Chenery, S. Shishido, and T. Watanabe, "The Pattern of Japanese Growth, 1914–1954," *Econometrica,* January, 1962. But our approach is different in several respects.

We define import ratios, m_c, m_i, and m_u, with respect to demand for consumption, investment and intermediate demand, respectively:

$$C_m = m_c C^*$$
$$I_m = m_i I^* \qquad\qquad (2)$$
$$U_m = m_u U^*.$$

Then, domestic production is expressed as

$$X = C^* + I^* + U^* + E - (C_m + I_m + U_m)$$
$$= (1 - m_c)C^* + (1 - m_i)I^* + (1 - m_u)U^* + E. \qquad (3)$$

For each symbol we have the following definition: the subscripts o and t represent two adjacent decades, and Δ represents the increase during a decade. The increase in domestic production during a decade is given by

$$\Delta X = (1 - m_{co})\Delta C^* + (1 - m_{io})\Delta I^* + (1 - m_{uo})\Delta U^* + \Delta E$$
$$+ (m_{co} - m_{ct})C_t^* + (m_{io} - m_{it})I_t^* + (m_{uo} - m_{ut})U_t^* \qquad (4)$$

where the first four terms on the right side stand for the increase in production caused by increases in demand for consumption, investment, intermediate goods, and exports, respectively; the last three terms stand for increase in production caused by import substitution with respect to consumption, investment and intermediate demand, respectively. In Table 3–13 we evaluate equation (4).

Among the causes of industrial growth distinguished in equation (4), the effect of growth of domestic final demand on industrialization declined from 76 percent to 29 percent over the 60 years of the prewar period. But the effect of the growth of investment remained almost constant at the level of 15–20 percent, except during the depression period after World War I. The declining role of domestic final demand is thus entirely attributed to consumption. The effect of consumption on industrialization declined from 58 percent to 16 percent, while it rose temporarily in the depression period after World War I. On the contrary, the relative importance of the growth of exports, intermediate demand, and import substitution in explaining industrialization increased during the prewar period. The effect of export growth increased from about 10 percent to more than 20 percent, except for the aftermath of World War I; the effect of intermediate demand increased steadily from 14 percent to 37 percent; and the effect of import substitution turned from negative to positive values except for the period immediately after World War I, with a range variation of 20 percentage points.

TABLE 3-13

Causes of Industrialization
(Percent)

	Increase in Output*		Effects of				Import Substitution with Respect to:			
			Consumption	Investment	Intermediate Demand	Exports	Consumption	Investment	Intermediate Demand	Total
1874-83 to 1882-91	(2,758)	100	58.4	17.6	14.1	12.1	4.2	-2.4	-4.0	-2.2
1877-86 to 1887-96	(5,541)	100	55.3	17.6	17.8	10.6	1.4	-1.8	-0.9	-1.3
1882-91 to 1892-1901	(7,888)	100	47.3	18.3	22.6	11.0	-0.1	-1.9	2.8	0.8
1887-96 to 1897-1906	(7,073)	100	43.8	18.0	25.3	17.6	-0.5	-3.3	-0.9	-4.7
1892-1901 to 1902-11	(5,816)	100	35.5	15.8	26.0	27.6	0.2	0.2	-5.3	-4.9
1897-1906 to 1907-16	(10,839)	100	20.5	15.5	29.4	26.1	2.7	3.5	2.2	8.4
1902-11 to 1912-21	(22,315)	100	19.8	19.7	29.9	20.3	2.3	2.9	5.1	10.3
1907-16 to 1917-26	(27,534)	100	33.3	18.4	33.4	14.8	0	-0.9	1.0	0.1
1912-21 to 1922-31	(27,229)	100	46.0	6.8	39.0	16.2	-2.2	-4.1	-1.7	-8.0
1917-26 to 1927-36	(45,240)	100	26.5	6.2	36.8	23.8	0.3	0.6	5.8	6.7
1922-31 to 1930-39	(60,619)	100	16.0	12.6	36.5	20.9	1.3	4.1	8.6	14.0
1951 to 1959	(7,713)	100	23.0	18.5	47.7	11.3	0.5	-0.1	-0.9	-0.5

*Values in parentheses are increases in output in millions of 1935 yen, except 1951-59, when the unit is billions of 1955 yen.

The above analysis shows the structural changes in demand and supply in terms of output, which facilitated industrialization in prewar Japan. Exports as a factor of final demand, on the one hand, and intermediate demand and import substitution as supply factors, on the other, played the leading roles in the prewar process.

If we observe postwar industrial growth measured for 1951–59 in the light of the prewar growth pattern, we find that postwar growth has common characteristics which carry over from the prewar period: first, the ever-increasing importance of intermediate demand; second, the consistently important role of investment; and third, the steady decline of the importance of consumption. The growth of intermediate demand as a cause of industrial growth took place on an unprecedented scale; it accounted for nearly half the growth of all manufacturing. On the other hand, exports and import substitution were of minor importance in the postwar period. Exports played almost the lowest role when compared with the prewar record, except for a recent upturn in the importance of exports. Import substitution of manufactures has reached a limit, and its importance as a source of industrial growth has been exhausted.

In relating the above demand-supply trends to the sectoral analysis, we can say the following:

1. Import substitution is revealed throughout the prewar period in all the leading industries, i.e., in the early growth of textiles and the later expansion of chemicals, metals and machinery. For these industries import substitution is usually followed by the growth of exports with some time lags.

2. Exports supported the growth of the textile industry through the prewar period and contributed to the development of leading industries from an infant stage.

3. Intermediate demand provided the basis for both the pre- and postwar expansion of chemicals, metals, and machinery. The growth of these industries into the place of new leading exporters is probably going to be realized soon.

Finally, we can conclude from the decline of the relative importance of consumption that consumption-led expansion was not a phenomenon present in either pre- or postwar Japanese industrial growth. The past effort of industrialization in Japan was directed toward catching up to the production attainments of advanced countries; consumption-led growth remains to be seen in the future.

Appendix

In this appendix we show the derivation of the data for (1) the value of gross output of manufacturing, (2) the price index for manufacturing output, (3) the production index for manufacturing, and (4) the distribution of gross output of manufacturing and imports of manufactures by use category, for 1874–1940.

1. Value of Output. The basic source of information on manufacturing production is the *Census of Manufactures.* Its records are available for census years only: 1909, 1914, 1919, and then annually through 1940. However, the census does not cover the whole of manufacturing production. First, it covers, in principle, only the production of factories employing more than five workers. In view of the relative importance of small and domestic manufacturing activities for the earlier period, we have to make up for this omission. In order to check the value of output in the census by each commodity, other sources, such as *Statistics of Ministry of Agriculture and Commerce, Statistics of Ministry of Commerce and Industry,* and so forth, were extensively used. In this way compensation was made for the omission of output in the food, textile, forest product, chemical, stone, clay and glass, and miscellaneous industries. As to the other industries, the metal and machinery industries, for which other statistical sources were not comprehensively available, a conventional method was adopted. We made use of the ratio of output produced by firms employing under four persons to output produced by firms employing more than five persons, calculated from the *Census of Manufactures* for 1939–41. Second, since the census records only private production, government production was added by referring to the *Statement of Government Accounts.*

As a source of comprehensive statistics of manufacturing output for the years not covered by the *Census of Manufactures,* we have only the data for 1874, 1889–91 and 1901–03 compiled by M. Umemura from *Statistics of Prefectures.* I drew on his data, adjusting by commodity for possible omissions, including government production. For certain major industries, if not all manufacturing industries, value of product could be obtained for the period covering a part of the still missing years: forest products for 1879–1940 and foods for 1909–40.

We are, however, still not able to obtain the direct estimates of value of manufacturing output for major industries as well as total manufacturing industries for every year during the period under consideration. At this stage of our knowledge we are forced to use a second best procedure, namely to make indirect estimates instead of direct estimates from original data. The procedure involves the following steps:

a) We multiply the Nagoya production indexes for major industries, on a 1935 base, by our 1935 value of product.

b) We multiply the value of product thus expressed in 1935 prices by our price indexes on a 1935 base.

c) We calculate adjustment coefficients by comparing the value of product thus estimated in current prices with our direct estimates of the value of product in current prices for the years when the latter is available.

d) Finally, we interpolate our direct estimates of the current value of product by the value derived from the application of adjustment coefficient to the current value based on the Nagoya indexes to obtain continuous series of current values for the entire period (see Table 3A–1).

2. Price Indexes.   The construction of price indexes is summarized below. The entire prewar period is divided into five subperiods

Period	Number of Price Series	Weight Base	Link Years
1874–89	39	1874	
1887–1902	48	1889–91	1887–89
1900–21	59	1901–03	1900–02
1919–33	54	1919–21	1919–21
1931–40	91	1934–36	1931–33

according to the changing availability of price series. Various wholesale price indexes of manufactured commodities prepared by government and private institutions were used in this study and combined by major industries and all manufacturing, with gross value of product used as weights for each subperiod. The price indexes thus obtained for each subperiod are of the Laspeyres type. They are then linked to produce continuous index series for the entire period, with 1935 as the base (see Table 3A–2).

3. Production Indexes.   We divide the value of output of major industries by corresponding price indexes to obtain the deflated value indexes of major industries, with 1935 = 100. An index of all manufacturing was obtained by converting the current price magnitudes to 1935 prices, using the price index implicit in all manufacturing output (see Table 3A–3).

As explained above, we rely on the Nagoya indexes for interpolation for the years when direct estimates are not available. A justification for the use of the Nagoya indexes is the fact that a comparison of our production indexes based on the direct estimates with those based on the Nagoya indexes shows fairly parallel movements in spite of differences in their levels. At any rate, our indexes for the interpolated period are less reliable than those for other periods and should be used with reservations.

4. Output and Imports by Use.   In order to allocate gross output of manufacturing and imports of manufactures into economic use categories, the data were classified by minor commodity. When commodity items could not be classified as representing a kind of use category, these mixed commodities were further analyzed on the basis of various pieces of information. When the direct estimates of minor commodities were not available and we had only output by major industry, estimated by interpolation, allocation of output was based on an interpolation of percentages of use categories within a major industry. Allocation of output and imports is given in Tables 3A–4 and 3A–5.

TABLE 3A-1
Gross Value of Manufacturing Output
(Millions of Yen)

	Foods	Textiles	Forest Products	Chemicals	Stone, Clay & Glass	Metals	Machinery	Miscellaneous	All Manufacturing
1874.	57.2	38.7	19.4	21.4	3.4	5.6	2.5	9.5	157.7
1875.	51.6	34.3	19.3	17.1	3.3	4.1	2.7	10.9	143.3
1876.	40.3	38.1	19.3	16.6	3.2	6.6	2.7	9.0	135.8
1877.	48.5	34.4	21.7	14.1	3.1	7.3	3.7	12.4	145.2
1878.	66.2	42.1	25.9	19.3	4.0	8.4	5.2	11.5	182.6
1879.	94.5	52.7	32.0	24.1	6.7	10.7	6.2	10.2	237.1
1880.	91.0	61.6	48.3	21.1	9.5	13.0	8.0	9.0	261.5
1881.	112.8	73.4	61.4	20.7	12.9	14.0	8.6	11.5	315.3
1882.	111.8	62.4	51.1	30.9	9.4	10.1	7.4	13.5	296.6
1883.	60.5	56.0	44.0	30.3	7.8	12.4	8.4	12.7	232.1
1884.	73.5	49.0	35.5	29.6	6.6	8.1	7.6	11.0	220.9
1885.	56.6	52.5	29.9	31.8	7.5	5.3	7.8	11.5	202.9
1886.	102.0	63.7	31.6	28.6	8.9	8.3	9.9	14.3	267.3
1887.	134.1	73.8	34.4	27.9	9.4	9.7	15.4	14.3	319.0
1888.	151.4	76.6	33.1	32.1	9.5	12.8	27.4	14.3	357.2
1889.	165.2	83.5	33.7	28.4	7.5	10.0	20.8	16.6	365.7
1890.	165.7	79.7	32.4	31.8	6.8	11.1	28.5	14.7	370.7
1891.	161.0	100.4	36.8	31.2	6.6	11.0	35.8	15.2	398.0
1892.	159.9	133.5	36.0	40.0	10.3	16.2	30.2	17.5	443.6
1893.	202.2	157.7	38.5	46.6	10.6	14.7	40.8	15.0	526.1
1894.	184.1	183.3	46.2	49.4	8.1	23.4	50.2	18.0	562.7
1895.	204.6	253.0	59.2	58.0	12.0	32.8	59.0	28.6	707.2
1896.	245.0	244.2	74.0	61.2	13.0	41.1	84.5	37.0	800.0
1897.	275.9	278.9	92.3	69.2	15.7	46.4	86.7	34.8	899.9
1898.	355.5	349.9	108.5	65.9	14.5	53.3	88.5	42.6	1,078.7
1899.	383.4	455.3	111.3	92.8	17.6	56.0	55.5	43.4	1,215.3
1900.	384.1	368.5	126.9	106.8	22.4	83.2	74.4	54.5	1,220.8
1901.	367.6	353.3	133.7	101.7	22.0	59.9	56.7	51.1	1,146.0
1902.	339.7	377.7	121.8	102.8	22.8	40.6	44.0	54.0	1,103.4
1903.	369.5	375.4	127.2	108.9	22.6	45.5	51.4	53.7	1,154.2
1904.	401.5	411.4	140.2	149.6	19.9	67.4	75.4	68.2	1,333.6
1905.	526.7	521.5	138.6	164.6	25.5	85.6	117.8	98.5	1,678.8

Year									
1906.	552.1	544.0	144.3	165.9	37.6	97.7	111.0	98.8	1,751.4
1907.	656.6	693.4	164.5	156.2	46.2	128.1	135.3	112.4	2,092.7
1908.	664.3	499.3	166.5	141.4	42.9	106.6	121.6	105.0	1,848.6
1909.	604	542	151	154	47	106	97	99	1,800
1910.	611	622	165	165	52	149	133	110	2,002
1911.	683	671	172	197	55	167	167	121	2,230
1912.	737	769	175	197	59	232	239	123	2,527
1913.	784	791	198	198	55	243	223	134	2,630
1914.	732	785	185	278	64	255	192	127	2,610
1915.	717	922	178	322	98	430	272	146	3,051
1916.	849	1,234	202	419	135	706	534	210	4,252
1917.	1,157	1,896	270	594	225	1,203	1,084	199	6,538
1918.	1,472	2,692	393	961	256	1,339	1,474	257	8,813
1919.	2,236	4,265	662	1,089	287	869	1,456	441	11,274
1920.	2,186	3,136	791	1,070	247	741	1,566	435	10,212
1921.	2,164	3,210	614	912	288	469	954	474	9,044
1922.	2,271	3,328	568	924	290	593	921	464	9,357
1923.	2,145	3,370	634	954	304	543	598	435	8,969
1924.	2,388	3,598	552	1,066	311	599	661	508	9,676
1925.	2,452	3,891	599	1,103	325	631	644	531	10,162
1926.	2,454	3,652	549	1,152	305	719	725	535	10,111
1927.	2,357	3,509	552	1,192	311	723	811	592	10,041
1928.	2,400	3,689	507	1,282	325	849	838	574	10,450
1929.	2,352	3,788	484	1,355	248	974	882	577	10,737
1930.	2,019	2,715	393	1,146	223	780	781	500	8,582
1931.	1,774	2,409	345	1,026	254	584	598	455	7,414
1932.	1,794	2,849	359	1,182	329	735	768	507	8,448
1933.	2,042	3,652	443	1,655	373	1,074	1,065	542	10,802
1934.	2,153	4,102	500	1,818	418	1,574	1,392	636	12,548
1935.	2,203	4,323	524	2,188	446	1,912	1,717	707	13,997
1936.	2,316	4,764	579	2,557	523	2,251	1,990	782	15,685
1937.	2,319	5,528	766	3,491	570	3,520	3,174	1,056	20,397
1938.	2,753	5,593	948	4,734	782	4,635	5,206	1,130	25,569
1939.	3,558	6,435	1,412	5,181	920	5,437	7,113	1,668	31,586
1940.	3,580	6,711	1,967	5,781		5,482	8,740	1,942	35,123

TABLE 3A-2

Price Indexes for Manufacturing Industries

(1935 = 100)

	Foods	Textiles	Forest Products	Chemicals	Stone, Clay & Glass	Metals	Machinery	Miscellaneous	All Manufacturing
1874	21.3	60.7	16.5	26.7	39.0	64.2	90.4	20.0	31.6
1875	21.7	56.5	16.0	26.9	39.4	63.6	84.0	19.7	31.0
1876	20.6	60.2	15.7	25.9	43.2	58.8	73.6	18.3	30.6
1877	20.9	54.9	17.3	27.4	47.6	52.9	66.4	18.7	30.3
1878	21.2	56.5	19.8	32.1	48.3	52.1	65.2	19.4	31.9
1879	22.7	60.7	24.2	32.6	57.5	54.0	66.5	20.8	34.4
1880	24.0	65.0	35.1	32.4	82.5	55.6	62.6	22.0	37.9
1881	26.9	80.7	45.2	35.2	96.7	61.5	63.1	24.9	44.5
1882	25.6	74.5	37.8	34.1	79.1	54.5	60.7	23.4	40.9
1883	21.8	59.0	31.6	28.5	63.6	55.2	59.6	21.7	34.4
1884	22.8	55.5	25.8	26.8	48.8	42.6	50.7	20.6	32.3
1885	18.6	59.1	20.2	28.7	42.0	41.4	47.8	19.8	30.0
1886	23.6	58.6	19.5	26.1	35.8	38.8	44.5	18.6	31.4
1887	24.0	59.5	22.2	28.3	41.5	40.9	53.7	19.8	33.0
1888	23.2	60.4	24.0	27.1	44.9	56.6	60.9	20.3	33.5
1889	23.5	63.3	24.3	32.7	42.9	49.4	57.1	20.3	34.3
1890	27.1	60.5	24.5	31.7	41.6	46.2	58.7	19.4	36.0
1891	25.9	55.4	24.5	29.1	44.1	45.2	56.4	19.9	34.2
1892	27.5	62.8	26.9	28.5	41.8	46.1	54.4	19.4	36.2
1893	28.6	69.3	26.3	29.0	42.5	49.9	55.3	20.8	37.9
1894	28.9	65.9	28.9	30.2	41.7	54.9	54.8	22.5	38.3
1895	30.5	73.2	34.2	32.7	43.6	58.6	60.5	26.1	41.7
1896	31.7	69.8	42.4	41.6	46.9	59.1	64.6	30.9	44.4
1897	35.8	75.1	45.7	51.0	60.9	68.0	69.0	34.4	49.7
1898	42.8	78.8	49.8	49.4	62.8	66.1	68.5	36.0	54.7
1899	41.6	90.0	50.2	47.7	64.2	84.8	78.2	37.5	56.3
1900	46.6	84.1	54.6	49.7	74.0	89.1	79.1	40.2	59.7
1901	47.1	83.5	57.0	47.4	73.9	80.9	76.0	40.2	59.5
1902	47.6	85.5	52.5	47.7	68.6	72.7	74.3	38.8	59.2
1903	51.2	88.7	54.5	51.3	69.2	74.3	74.5	39.0	62.0
1904	56.9	90.5	56.7	53.5	68.7	78.1	80.8	39.9	65.6
1905	63.8	98.7	59.4	60.3	71.1	85.8	86.3	41.7	72.0

Year									
1906.	63.5	103.5	58.8	67.4	75.8	91.0	87.5	46.9	74.3
1907.	68.2	113.8	65.3	69.4	87.9	98.4	93.5	53.2	80.6
1908.	72.0	93.9	66.7	67.3	82.2	78.6	82.2	52.4	76.5
1909.	70.9	95.5	61.4	63.9	73.7	73.7	75.9	47.5	74.4
1910.	68.8	97.9	63.8	65.0	72.1	73.3	77.8	48.3	74.6
1911.	71.5	103.7	67.5	67.3	74.8	73.8	77.3	50.3	77.8
1912.	78.6	100.8	67.7	67.3	75.0	88.1	88.7	50.9	81.1
1913.	77.2	102.6	70.0	67.3	78.0	83.1	85.9	51.7	81.1
1914.	73.5	94.4	66.9	67.2	76.8	79.3	82.3	51.1	77.1
1915.	71.2	89.7	65.4	70.9	81.0	116.2	102.5	50.3	77.0
1916.	76.7	118.3	67.9	93.9	98.6	166.7	130.5	59.2	91.9
1917.	87.3	163.1	87.0	103.7	130.6	231.4	175.7	70.3	114.7
1918.	107.6	213.9	114.9	141.6	179.2	261.5	191.6	89.4	145.7
1919.	153.3	299.5	172.4	162.7	193.6	185.1	155.3	125.6	196.3
1920.	174.8	271.2	238.7	200.5	248.0	172.4	162.9	178.0	210.2
1921.	131.7	185.6	202.5	136.3	170.7	114.2	146.6	147.9	155.7
1922.	128.6	190.0	202.2	140.6	178.2	110.1	140.3	155.8	156.3
1923.	137.8	200.6	184.7	129.8	188.0	119.4	143.7	141.0	159.1
1924.	137.5	210.8	183.9	137.6	172.8	112.7	141.0	144.0	161.9
1925.	130.9	208.9	168.9	138.2	142.8	113.6	116.3	133.9	154.5
1926.	123.3	164.0	163.3	127.2	131.3	100.7	108.5	127.3	136.5
1927.	121.2	145.2	152.8	123.1	121.3	95.2	105.4	125.4	128.9
1928.	117.0	143.2	148.8	124.5	122.3	104.1	107.3	131.7	129.4
1929.	117.0	146.3	132.1	120.3	124.1	110.6	109.8	124.7	126.9
1930.	104.1	99.6	99.9	100.2	100.5	83.1	95.1	93.9	100.3
1931.	89.7	81.3	91.7	81.1	90.5	64.0	85.2	80.9	83.2
1932.	94.7	89.9	88.7	86.7	95.4	78.5	92.1	85.8	90.5
1933.	99.7	105.7	105.2	100.4	102.0	108.3	105.5	96.8	106.6
1934.	97.8	100.8	101.5	97.8	102.0	108.0	104.7	101.2	103.9
1935.	100.0	100.0	100.0	100.0	100.0	100.0	100.0	100.0	100.0
1936.	105.3	103.7	105.5	98.4	96.0	103.8	100.9	104.5	104.2
1937.	111.3	120.6	135.0	122.9	105.5	199.2	149.6	127.9	134.1
1938.	117.0	125.5	165.2	142.5	115.1	199.8	153.7	151.8	142.9
1939.	127.1	154.4	204.1	149.3	119.5	178.5	148.9	181.6	154.3
1940.	142.7	173.5	262.9	162.5	131.4	183.9	148.6	209.1	169.8

TABLE 3A-3

Production Indexes for Manufacturing Industries
(1935 = 100)

	Foods	Textiles	Forest Products	Chemicals	Stone, Clay & Glass	Metals	Machinery	Miscellaneous	All Manufacturing
1874	12.16	1.47	22.50	3.67	2.08	0.45	0.15	6.75	4.27
1875	10.78	1.40	23.00	2.90	2.01	0.33	0.19	7.81	3.97
1876	8.88	1.46	23.50	2.93	1.78	0.60	0.22	6.94	3.70
1877	10.53	1.44	24.00	2.34	1.55	0.72	0.32	9.35	4.03
1878	14.15	1.72	25.00	2.74	1.99	0.84	0.46	8.40	4.78
1879	18.90	2.01	25.30	3.37	2.80	1.04	0.54	6.97	5.71
1880	17.21	2.18	26.23	2.99	2.75	1.22	0.75	5.82	5.47
1881	19.03	2.10	25.91	2.70	3.20	1.19	0.79	6.55	5.72
1882	19.80	1.93	28.81	4.13	2.84	0.97	0.71	8.12	6.05
1883	12.61	2.19	26.56	4.84	2.96	1.18	0.82	8.29	5.18
1884	14.65	2.03	26.25	5.04	3.24	0.99	0.87	7.57	5.43
1885	13.82	2.05	28.27	5.05	4.24	0.68	0.94	8.18	5.41
1886	19.62	2.51	30.95	5.02	5.95	1.13	1.30	10.86	6.84
1887	25.38	2.87	29.54	4.52	5.45	1.25	1.68	10.25	7.74
1888	29.61	2.93	26.35	5.42	5.03	1.18	2.61	9.95	8.54
1889	31.91	3.05	26.46	3.98	4.20	1.05	2.12	11.58	8.69
1890	27.75	3.04	25.31	4.60	3.89	1.26	2.83	10.67	8.15
1891	28.22	4.19	28.74	4.91	3.56	1.28	3.69	10.75	8.85
1892	26.40	4.90	25.52	6.42	5.89	1.84	2.28	12.78	9.10
1893	32.10	5.25	27.98	7.34	5.95	1.54	3.06	10.24	10.30
1894	28.93	6.42	30.53	7.48	4.63	2.22	3.83	11.33	10.52
1895	30.46	7.99	33.03	8.10	6.58	2.94	4.12	15.48	11.84
1896	35.08	8.08	33.35	6.73	6.65	3.64	5.59	16.92	12.80
1897	34.97	8.58	38.60	6.20	6.17	3.57	5.46	14.30	12.86
1898	37.71	10.25	41.53	6.09	5.51	4.22	5.70	16.75	14.13
1899	41.83	11.69	42.35	8.89	6.56	3.46	3.21	16.37	15.17
1900	37.40	10.12	44.42	9.82	7.24	4.88	4.37	19.18	14.74
1901	35.44	9.77	44.76	9.81	7.12	3.87	4.34	17.96	13.99
1902	32.39	10.21	44.26	9.85	7.35	2.91	3.46	19.69	13.51
1903	32.75	9.77	44.59	9.71	7.80	3.20	4.03	19.49	13.51
1904	32.02	10.51	47.18	12.79	6.93	4.51	5.43	24.16	14.76
1905	37.48	12.21	44.56	12.47	8.57	5.22	7.95	33.41	16.92

Year									
1906. . . .	39.46	12.17	46.86	11.25	11.87	5.62	7.38	29.79	17.02
1907. . . .	43.70	14.08	46.06	10.29	12.58	6.81	8.41	29.89	18.49
1908. . . .	41.88	12.29	47.62	9.60	12.48	7.10	8.65	28.61	17.52
1909. . . .	38.67	13.11	47.01	11.14	15.21	7.51	7.44	29.48	17.53
1910. . . .	40.29	14.67	49.45	11.80	15.53	10.63	9.96	32.30	19.34
1911. . . .	43.38	14.96	48.52	13.83	16.61	11.82	12.59	34.02	20.81
1912. . . .	42.54	17.62	49.43	13.40	17.55	13.77	15.69	34.03	22.14
1913. . . .	46.06	17.80	53.96	13.45	18.07	15.28	15.12	36.76	23.23
1914. . . .	45.17	19.22	52.94	18.92	17.14	16.82	13.58	35.21	24.26
1915. . . .	45.70	23.74	51.83	20.76	18.94	19.34	15.45	41.11	26.90
1916. . . .	50.26	24.09	56.68	2C.38	23.73	22.15	23.83	50.24	29.86
1917. . . .	60.13	26.85	59.16	26.49	24.73	27.2C	35.93	40.00	34.96
1918. . . .	62.11	29.08	65.32	31.03	30.05	26.78	44.80	40.59	38.17
1919. . . .	66.20	32.90	73.27	30.59	31.64	24.55	54.60	49.67	41.62
1920. . . .	56.76	26.72	63.28	24.39	27.69	22.48	55.99	34.57	35.89
1921. . . .	74.56	39.96	57.75	30.58	34.62	21.48	37.90	45.32	41.95
1922. . . .	80.16	40.47	53.60	33.04	38.66	28.18	38.23	42.12	43.66
1923. . . .	70.65	38.81	65.50	33.59	36.90	23.78	24.24	43.64	40.36
1924. . . .	78.84	39.44	57.27	35.41	42.09	27.80	27.30	49.90	43.21
1925. . . .	85.02	43.03	67.69	36.48	52.10	29.05	32.25	56.09	47.25
1926. . . .	90.32	51.45	64.18	41.39	59.22	37.34	38.91	59.44	53.65
1927. . . .	88.26	55.46	68.94	44.26	60.16	39.72	44.81	66.77	56.62
1928. . . .	93.11	57.12	65.02	47.06	60.83	42.65	45.49	61.65	58.46
1929. . . .	91.23	59.82	69.91	51.48	62.65	46.06	46.79	65.45	60.73
1930. . . .	88.01	62.96	75.08	52.28	59.03	49.08	47.83	75.31	62.45
1931. . . .	89.75	68.50	71.79	57.82	58.95	47.72	40.88	79.55	64.36
1932. . . .	85.98	73.20	77.20	62.31	63.70	48.97	48.57	83.58	67.56
1933. . . .	92.98	79.64	80.35	75.34	77.17	51.87	58.80	79.19	74.71
1934. . . .	99.94	94.00	93.98	84.96	87.49	76.22	77.43	88.89	88.61
1935. . . .	100.00	100.00	100.03	100.00	100.00	100.00	100.00	100.00	100.00
1936. . . .	91.18	106.12	104.74	118.77	111.15	113.42	114.87	105.85	107.90
1937. . . .	94.56	106.31	108.28	129.82	118.60	92.42	123.57	116.78	109.34
1938. . . .	106.80	103.00	109.52	151.83	118.48	121.33	197.27	105.24	126.13
1939. . . .	127.07	96.30	132.03	158.61	156.56	159.31	278.22	129.92	146.64
1940. . . .	113.87	89.35	139.09	162.59	167.5C	155.91	342.55	131.34	151.14

TABLE 3A-4

Value of Manufacturing Output by Use
(Millions of Yen)

	Consumption Goods	Producer Durables	Construction Materials	Unfinished Goods	Exports	Total
1874. . . .	111.7	2.4	12.0	23.3	8.3	157.7
1875. . . .	89.1	2.6	11.2	32.3	8.1	143.3
1876. . . .	78.7	2.6	11.6	26.9	16.0	135.8
1877. . . .	85.5	3.6	12.8	30.0	13.3	145.2
1878. . . .	109.4	5.1	15.4	40.4	12.3	182.6
1879. . . .	144.5	6.1	19.7	51.0	15.8	237.1
1880. . . .	146.8	7.8	28.4	63.0	15.5	261.5
1881. . . .	177.7	8.4	36.4	73.7	19.1	315.3
1882. . . .	177.0	7.3	29.8	58.0	24.5	296.6
1883. . . .	123.9	8.2	26.8	48.9	24.3	232.1
1884. . . .	127.3	7.4	21.5	44.7	20.0	220.9
1885. . . .	114.1	7.6	18.5	39.7	23.0	202.9
1886. . . .	160.3	9.7	20.3	46.3	30.7	267.3
1887. . . .	191.8	15.0	21.9	54.3	36.0	319.0
1888. . . .	212.0	26.8	20.6	53.3	44.5	357.2
1889. . . .	226.5	20.5	19.0	52.8	46.9	365.7
1890. . . .	223.7	28.2	17.0	62.7	39.1	370.7
1891. . . .	225.0	35.4	21.0	60.1	56.5	398.0
1892. . . .	242.0	29.5	21.7	80.7	69.7	443.6
1893. . . .	289.9	39.8	23.5	106.6	66.3	526.1
1894. . . .	283.6	49.0	27.4	115.0	87.7	562.7
1895. . . .	345.1	57.5	37.7	159.9	107.0	707.2
1896. . . .	393.0	82.5	47.2	188.7	88.6	800.0
1897. . . .	438.2	84.7	60.9	182.3	133.8	899.9
1898. . . .	548.4	86.5	67.1	244.3	132.4	1,078.7
1899. . . .	632.4	54.0	70.9	277.9	180.1	1,215.3
1900. . . .	606.7	72.3	85.3	287.2	169.3	1,220.8
1901. . . .	578.3	54.8	84.5	213.1	215.3	1,146.0
1902. . . .	551.1	41.6	78.4	211.2	221.1	1,103.4
1903. . . .	558.0	48.6	79.2	220.2	248.2	1,154.2
1904. . . .	630.1	72.5	91.2	259.3	280.5	1,333.6
1905. . . .	822.4	113.1	93.2	361.1	289.0	1,678.8

Year						
1906	1,751.4	385.9	327.7	95.8	105.9	836.1
1907	2,092.7	383.5	441.3	110.4	124.8	1,032.7
1908	1,848.6	340.9	345.8	108.8	112.9	940.2
1909	1,800	373	363	112	89	863
1910	2,002	418	448	127	123	886
1911	2,230	436	468	157	155	1,014
1912	2,527	524	628	142	219	1,058
1913	2,630	626	582	161	203	1,028
1914	2,610	575	686	154	167	1,031
1915	3,051	669	926	182	243	1,341
1916	4,252	1,042	1,150	255	464	1,749
1917	6,538	1,512	2,013	374	890	2,452
1918	8,813	1,866	2,760	490	1,245	3,971
1919	11,274	2,119	3,321	546	1,317	3,364
1920	10,212	1,970	2,848	632	1,398	3,774
1921	9,044	1,340	2,590	496	844	3,914
1922	9,357	1,685	2,510	470	778	3,762
1923	8,969	1,516	2,647	574	470	3,878
1924	9,676	1,899	2,867	513	519	3,738
1925	10,162	2,377	2,975	568	504	3,715
1926	10,111	2,163	3,126	560	547	3,740
1927	10,041	2,106	3,087	512	596	3,948
1928	10,450	2,155	3,245	495	607	3,700
1929	10,737	2,357	3,488	541	651	3,188
1930	8,582	1,751	2,673	404	566	2,977
1931	7,414	1,333	2,343	331	430	3,039
1932	8,448	1,634	2,854	350	571	3,411
1933	10,802	2,184	3,955	493	759	3,783
1934	12,548	2,587	4,593	612	973	3,925
1935	13,997	3,042	5,210	653	1,167	4,324
1936	15,685	3,321	5,994	724	1,322	4,766
1937	20,397	3,910	8,441	1,039	2,233	5,659
1938	25,569	3,748	11,054	1,200	3,908	7,616
1939	31,586	4,795	12,600	1,382	5,193	8,691
1940	35,123	4,877	13,510	1,672	6,373	

TABLE 3A-5

Imports of Manufactures by Use
(Millions of Yen)

	Consumption Goods	Producer Durables	Construction Materials	Unfinished Goods	Total
1874.	12.1	0.9	0.5	8.3	21.8
1875.	14.6	2.9	0.5	11.2	29.2
1876.	12.3	1.0	0.5	9.1	22.9
1877.	13.0	2.5	0.6	10.3	26.4
1878.	14.6	1.3	0.8	13.7	30.4
1879.	14.8	0.7	0.7	12.7	28.9
1880.	15.7	1.3	1.0	15.4	33.4
1881.	12.9	0.7	0.8	14.3	28.7
1882.	10.5	0.7	0.7	13.7	25.6
1883.	9.7	1.6	0.9	13.4	25.6
1884.	9.5	4.3	0.9	13.4	28.1
1885.	9.4	4.0	1.0	13.4	27.8
1886.	9.7	2.2	1.3	16.0	29.2
1887.	15.2	4.1	1.6	21.1	42.0
1888.	18.9	7.0	2.6	30.7	59.2
1889.	18.1	6.9	2.4	27.8	55.2
1890.	18.8	7.9	2.8	28.0	57.5
1891.	14.6	5.4	2.2	22.1	44.3
1892.	17.3	6.2	1.8	27.1	52.4
1893.	20.2	6.0	2.6	31.0	59.8
1894.	21.5	15.1	4.2	37.3	78.1
1895.	28.3	13.2	5.0	41.9	88.4
1896.	43.5	21.1	8.0	54.2	126.8
1897.	35.2	37.8	9.6	61.9	144.5
1898.	47.3	34.9	10.0	80.4	172.6
1899.	36.6	22.1	8.9	66.5	134.1
1900.	58.9	39.2	17.6	95.7	211.4
1901.	36.9	41.8	11.1	88.0	177.8
1902.	42.7	31.3	11.2	74.4	159.6
1903.	41.3	18.0	12.1	88.0	159.4
1904.	43.3	25.5	13.1	97.4	179.3
1905.	71.4	36.5	21.7	145.5	275.1

Year					
1906	73.9	59.6	19.4	144.2	297.1
1907	63.3	43.6	28.9	161.8	297.6
1908	55.0	49.9	24.7	152.7	282.3
1909	50.9	29.7	17.9	143.5	242.0
1910	55.4	25.2	22.5	162.3	265.4
1911	60.4	48.4	28.5	190.6	327.9
1912	50.8	55.4	37.3	210.2	353.7
1913	52.7	77.9	33.2	236.5	400.3
1914	39.7	36.0	22.2	200.6	298.5
1915	29.5	15.2	16.0	202.6	263.3
1916	37.7	32.4	42.9	317.0	430.0
1917	41.8	45.8	100.8	423.8	612.2
1918	61.3	81.4	132.9	619.7	895.3
1919	95.5	127.5	113.0	779.1	1,115.1
1920	158.7	151.4	149.1	898.1	1,357.3
1921	139.7	169.9	114.1	608.6	1,032.3
1922	179.6	152.2	147.1	699.7	1,178.6
1923	165.9	156.7	135.6	727.8	1,186.0
1924	241.6	210.3	202.2	833.7	1,487.8
1925	195.5	160.5	105.2	740.9	1,202.1
1926	161.4	162.5	137.2	814.9	1,276.0
1927	160.9	134.8	127.9	747.6	1,171.2
1928	168.3	160.5	135.5	787.3	1,251.6
1929	166.7	181.5	120.2	785.7	1,254.1
1930	130.5	121.1	71.5	596.9	920.1
1931	116.5	78.3	49.6	469.6	714.0
1932	114.7	92.0	47.0	477.4	731.1
1933	116.3	105.2	63.5	637.1	922.1
1934	133.5	141.8	71.8	740.7	1,087.8
1935	141.2	155.9	76.4	900.1	1,273.6
1936	139.7	149.5	76.0	967.0	1,332.2
1937	161.4	236.0	119.6	1,581.1	2,098.1
1938	122.5	314.9	85.9	1,254.8	1,778.1
1939	154.7	296.7	99.8	1,598.1	2,149.3
1940	224.7	278.0	122.2	1,701.9	2,326.8

4 | Industrialization, Technological Progress, and Dual Structure*

TSUNEHIKO WATANABE

I. INTRODUCTION

It is clear that the process of Japanese industrialization is often of great interest to those who are concerned with the problems of economic growth. For one thing, Japan entered international relations quite late (i.e., at the end of the 19th century), but has made extraordinarily rapid progress during the last hundred years. Despite this, Japan appears to maintain combined features of both a modern industrialized country and an old tradition-oriented society. This is often termed a dual structure. A straightforward generalization of economic analyses which have been mostly developed in advanced countries, therefore, may not be fully applicable to Japan's case.

It is the purpose of this paper to present a synthetic hypothesis which can explain rapid industrialization based on active technological changes and its impact on the distribution of income in Japan. This hypothesis can be termed "an imitative development of a society," which is an adaptation of what Professor Gerschenkron has proposed in his model for Western countries.[1] There are at least two important aspects to be discussed with regard to imitative development: imitation in industrialization and imitation in consumption

---

* I am grateful to G. Ranis and K. Ohkawa for their constructive criticism of the earlier draft.

[1] See Gerschenkron, "Economic Backwardness in Historical Perspective," *The Progress of Underdeveloped Areas,* ed. B. F. Hoselitz (Chicago: University of Chicago Press, 1952). A good summary of his model with special emphasis on Japanese economic development will also be found in K. Ohkawa and H. Rosovsky, "The Indigenous Components in the Modern Japanese Economy," *Economic Development and Cultural Change,* April, 1961.

structure. The former aspect, however, will be the major topic to be investigated in the present paper.

The first part of the study (Section I) is concerned with the features of technological change, i.e., the extent and bias of technological change, which are to some extent examined in my previous paper.[2] The second part of the present paper (Section II) tries to explain induced elements of dual structure such as wage and profit differentials, by applying the hypotheses derived in the previous section.

In the present study, the problems concerning more basic determinants are not fully explored, such as those dealing with the level of saving, the effects of specific resource endowments, improvements of labor and managerial qualities, and the role and impact of national economic policy. Instead, this paper restricts itself to an analysis of more narrowly selected, preferably quantifiable, features of industrialization. The author wishes to demonstrate the advantages of quantitative economic history in the study of the complex of Japanese economic growth.

II. INDUSTRIALIZATION AND TECHNOLOGICAL PROGRESS

As a point of departure in our discussion, let us briefly examine the overall pattern of industrialization in Japan. Industrialization is so extensively interrelated with the broader variations in the structure of a national economy that it will not be desirable to start our discussion from a partial indicator, e.g., a growing pattern of international trade. It can only be adequately understood in an overall framework that can analyze certain variation in consumers' demand, technology, international trade and sectoral output. The simplest way to handle this requirement is to employ an interindustry model using a statistically or empirically testable framework.

This type of study of Japanese economic growth during the 1914–54 period has already been carried out by Chenery, Shishido and the present author.[3] The addition of the 1955–60 period to this study may give a summary picture of the process of industrialization in Japan.[4] From this approach, the following findings emerged: (*a*) The

---

[2] T. Watanabe, "Economic Aspects of Dualism in the Industrial Development of Japan," *Economic Development and Cultural Change,* April, 1965.

[3] H. B. Chenery, S. Shishido, and T. Watanabe. "The Pattern of Japanese Growth, 1915–1954," *Econometrica,* January, 1962.

[4] The year 1954 with which the previous study ended is not a suitable end-year for the present paper since a big spurt of industrialization occurred after 1958, and also the latest input-output table for 1960 has become available.

dominant feature in the growth pattern is the very rapid rise of industry. (*b*) Despite a common belief that industrialization is usually attributable to changes in demand, more than half of Japan's industrial growth is found to be traceable to changes in supply conditions, including substitution of domestic for imported manufactured goods, substitution of manufactured goods for primary products, and other technological changes. (*c*) In addition to these, the pressure of foreign competition brought about uneven changes in productivity, causing in turn a disparity between the growth of employment and production. (*d*) Finally, the pattern of Japanese growth differs from the earlier Western patterns in several respects, notably in the development of industry at a low-income level, the importance of import substitution, and the unevenness of technological advance.

With these broad conclusions as a background, we shall investigate in the rest of this paper the nature of the technological changes in Japan's economy, and their impact on the distribution of income.

In principle, there are two alternative approaches for investigating the role of technological progress in a process of rapid industrialization. The first approach is a kind of qualitative analysis, which can be carried out by collecting a set of suitable assumptions from those that have already been studied, and organizing them into a new set of hypotheses. This approach may basically be taken as "qualitative." However, to the extent that these hypotheses can also be tested in quantitative terms, for example by sign conditions, it might as well be termed "semiquantitative." The second approach, on the other hand, emphasizes a systematic use of statistical information, based on a theoretical model. In order to follow the latter approach, quantitative information, relevant to the model to be used, must be available (for example, figures of the stock of capital, labor requirement, and relative prices, with a sufficient degree of disaggregation).

From a practical point of view, it is hardly possible to follow the second approach fully, since such statistical information is not always available in Japan, especially for the prewar period.[5] The first type of approach, therefore, will mainly be used in the remaining part of this paper.

Assumptions in explaining the role of technological progress in the industrialization of Japan may be listed as follows:

i) Japan is termed "a latecomer" compared with other industrialized countries.

---

[5] An attempt to collect historical statistics systematically in the prewar period is being carried out by a group at Hitotsubashi University. After completion of this work, the second approach may become feasible.

ii) Almost all the the technological progress achieved during the process of industrialization is derived from imported or borrowed inventions, and the rate of adoption of this imported technology has been quite high.

iii) The range of factor substitution, i.e., substitution between labor and capital, was decidedly limited in the early stage of industrialization.

iv) Labor supply has been abundant.

v) The quality of labor was sufficient to understand and manage the imported techniques.

vi) A high rate of saving has prevailed.

vii) Investment demand created by the government, including military expenditure in the prewar period, has been large.

Some of these assumptions (for example, [*vi*] and [*vii*] have already been tested quantitatively by economists. Before going into the next stage of the discussion, it may be appropriate to make some brief comments here about the assumptions with special reference to the Japanese economy.

Although assumption (*i*) may be observed in all aspects of Japan's society, special attention should be focused on technical progress and the structure of private consumption. In other words, an imitative development with respect to technological process and consumption can be defined as the most crucial content of "a latecomer" concept in the present paper. These features played a significant role in the prewar period but a decreasing one in the postwar period.[6] The former point relates closely to assumption (*ii*), which can be considered a widely recognized phenomenon for any underdeveloped country. On the other hand, the latter point (the structure of private consumption), may be considered as quite different from that encountered in other industrialized countries and also in underdeveloped countries. As a result of a long experience as an isolated economy before the Meiji restoration, a certain type of living structure had been firmly established and continued through the prewar period. (This is often termed the "traditional" pattern or "indigenous components." See for example, A. Bergson.[7]) Furthermore, during the prewar period, this traditional pattern in consumption had been purposely maintained by the Japanese government in order to meet a huge amount of military

---

[6] A decrease in the importance of imitation in the postwar period is found in industrialization but not in consumption, particularly in consumer's asset formation.

[7] A. Bergson, *The Structure of Soviet Wages* (Cambridge, Mass.: Harvard University Press, 1946).

and related expenditures[8] (i.e., nonconsumption goods were heavily emphasized).

Assumption (*iii*), a narrow range of factor substitution in the early stage of industrialization, may be justified for two reasons: the nature of the technological inventions and the size of the market. When almost all technological inventions are imported from advanced countries, they are likely to be capital-intensive compared with the prevailing techniques in Japan, and this will usually imply the technological impossibility of divisible installation of capital equipment. For example, a new type of blast furnace may well be designed to be efficient only for a limited range of factor substitution. Further, even though it may be technologically feasible to adopt a capital-intensive technique, it will not be economically efficient due to the lack of a sufficiently big market. This in turn restricts the scope for factor substitution.

It may not be necessary to add any comment on assumption (*iv*), an abundant labor supply, although the validity of this assumption has become weaker in recent years. Assumption (*v*) may be to some extent supported by the high ratio of pupils in six-year elementary school to all children at the beginning of industrialization (e.g., the year 1910), i.e., around 98 percent.[9]

Under such assumptions, we may set up a broad hypothesis which characterizes Japan's economic growth as an imitative process of growth with a special emphasis on industrialization. That is, although in principle an imitative process could occur jointly in consumption and production, Japan's case has been different in that an imitative process of growth in consumption started rather late compared with that in production. The following two hypotheses can be formulated: (*A*) there are suitable conditions for extensive adoption of imported technological progress; (*B*) the adopted technological progress may well be biased, specifically laborsaving in the Hicksian sense, with a steady level of wage rates in the prewar period and a rising level of wages in the postwar period. With regard to the first hypothesis, the

---

[8] Military expenditure in the general account of the government budget had been around 40 percent of its total in the prewar period. In addition to this, special accounts were established for wartime.

[9] Even in 1868 there is some evidence to indicate a sufficiently high degree of literacy. For example, the first official statistics of the Ministry of Education, Government of Japan (1888) for the three prefectures of Shiga, Okayama and Kagoshima, which are remote from economic, industrial and cultural centers such as Tokyo and Osaka, tell us that of the population above school age, around 40 percent were reported illiterate. This implies a much higher degree of literacy in industrialized areas. (See *Annual Report of Ministry of Education,* No. 16, Ministry of Education, Government of Japan, Tokyo, 1888.)

discussions in the previous section and also assumptions (*iv*), (*v*), (*vi*), and (*vii*) provide sufficient evidence quantitatively and qualitatively. Another quantitative statement can be quoted from the recent work by Ueno and Kinoshita.[10] They fitted a Cobb-Douglas production function with an exponential time-trend to three series of production indices for industry groups, between 1919–36 and 1951–61. The observed rates of "neutral" technological progress in each period were 0.4 percent and 3 percent in agriculture, 4.4 percent and 5.5 percent in the textile industry, and 1.6 percent and 8.4 percent in the metal and machinery industry respectively.[11] Something more can be said about the rate of technological progress for individual industries during the postwar period.[12]

Assuming that all technical progress is disembodied and neutral in the Hicksian sense, the measure of $\dot{A}_i/A_i$ is computed for 14 industries between 1952–61. Here $\dot{A}_i/A_i$ is derived from:

$$\frac{\dot{K}_i}{A_i} = \frac{\dot{X}_i}{X_i} - a_i \frac{\dot{L}_i}{L_i} - (1 - a_i) \frac{\dot{K}_i}{K_i} \tag{1}$$

$$(i = 1, 2, \ldots\ldots\ldots 14),$$

where the assumed neoclassical production function is $X_i = F_i(K_i, L_i)A_i(t)$, and a_i represents the relative share of labor. The estimated average rate of technological progress for 1952–61[13] together with the same type of estimates for the United States by Massel for 1950–57 are given in Table 4–1.[14] From this table some interesting facts emerge which are closely related to the first hypothesis mentioned above.

---

[10] H. Ueno, and S. Kinoshita, "A Simulation Approach with a Modified Long-term Model of Japan," *International Economic Review,* February, 1968.

[11] The relatively higher rate in the postwar textile industry may be due to the inclusion of synthetic products.

[12] With regard to the prewar period, it is almost impossible to investigate this hypothesis for individual industries due to the lack of suitable information.

[13] Capital stock (K_i), labor requirement (L_i), value added (X_i), and the relative share (a_i) for 14 industries were recently compiled by the Economic Planning Agency from the *National Wealth Survey, National Income Account, Census of Manufactures,* and *Interindustry Table.* The details are reported in Economic Research Institute, Economic Planning Agency, "Estimation of Capital Stock in Private Sectors," February, 1966 (mimeographed, in Japanese).

[14] Detail discussions are found in T. Watanabe, "Technological Progress and Economic Growth—The Post-war Manufacturing Industry's Case," mimeographed, 1966 (in Japanese); and C. Kennedy, "Induced Bias in Innovation and the Theory of Distribution," *Economic Journal,* September, 1964.

TABLE 4-1

Measurement of Disembodied Technological Progress 1952-1962

	Expansion of Production (1)	Expansion of Factors			Technological Progress (5)	Contribution (%) (6)	Technological Progress in U.S. (7)
		Capital (2)	Labor (3)	Total (4)			
Food	8.23	5.14	1.68	6.82	1.41	17.1	1.41
Textile	8.04	2.73	0.91	3.64	4.40	54.7	0.86
Wood products	12.84	1.78	1.67	3.45	9.39	73.1	3.77
Paper and pulp. . . .	23.29	8.93	1.63	10.56	12.73	54.6	2.34
Printing and publishing	11.85	7.47	2.36	9.83	2.02	17.0	2.44
Leather products. . .	10.93	4.88	2.34	7.22	3.71	33.9	1.06
Rubber products . . .	17.15	7.66	2.03	9.69	7.46	43.5	0.98
Chemicals	26.65	7.56	0.26	7.82	18.83	70.6	3.46
Coal and petroleum. .	17.43	8.56	0.04	8.60	8.83	50.7	1.89
Nonmetallic mineral products.	12.84	8.48	1.66	10.14	2.70	21.0	2.48
Metal products. . . .	14.14	6.81	2.26	9.07	5.07	35.9	0.25
Machinery	19.86	6.87	4.25	11.12	8.74	44.0	1.97
Transportation equipment.	20.52	6.51	2.22	8.73	11.79	57.4	2.39
Miscellaneous	19.39	13.44	3.63	17.07	2.32	12.0	....
Total	14.43	6.15	1.84	7.99	6.43	44.56	2.80

NOTE: All figures for Japan are compiled from data provided by Economic Planning Agency. See footnote 13. Figures for U.S. are taken from B. F. Massel, "A Disaggregated View of Technical Change," *Journal of Political Economy*, December, 1961.

First, the overall rate of technological progress is high, i.e., around 6 percent, and its contribution to the expansion of production is about 45 percent. This high rate of technological progress may largely reflect an imitative process in the postwar recovery period.[15] Second, the contributions of technological progress and of increases in capital stock to the expansion of production are almost equally important, while the contribution of labor is quite small. Third, although there are quite large differences in the rates of expansion of production among the 14 industries, there are even larger differences in the rates of technological progress in these industries. Fourth, from the last column in this table, which gives the rate of technological progress in the United States for 1950–57, we see that those industries which have higher rates of technological progress in the United States, also have higher rates of technological progress in Japan. Also, except for the printing and the publishing industry, Japanese industries show faster rates of technological progress than the corresponding industries in the United States. These facts can be viewed as evidence for hypothesis (*A*) and also for assumption (*ii*): i.e., the extensive use of imported technology.

Let us turn our discussion to the hypothesis (*B*), i.e., the biasedness of technological progress. Although the extent and bias of technological progress in terms of the classification proposed by Harrod may be asserted as more natural in handling certain problems in growth theory, there are at least two important points to be noted for the present purpose. According to the Harrodian classification, technological progress is neutral if the rate of profit remains constant when the ratio of capital stock to output remains constant. (1) This definition is, however, imprecise when there are more than two factors of production, as stated by Meade.[16] In considering the actual path of economic growth, especially in underdeveloped economies, the exclusion of a third factor of production, say land, is not theoretically appropriate, even though the effect of the third factor becomes negligible in an empirical sense. (2) The Harrodian definition of neutral technological progress is a purely labor-augmenting type of progress, which ascribes to technological progress some element of the improvement of labor which is better ascribed to capital accumulation. As an alternative, the Hicksian definition of technological progress together with the capital-embodiment concept will be discussed here.

---

[15] During this recovery period, there is a sufficient amount of backlog of new technical knowledge, which had been mostly developed during the war and also immediately after the war.

[16] J. E. Meade, *A Neo-classical Theory of Economic Growth* (New York: Oxford University Press, 1961).

In order to clarify hypothesis B quantitatively, we must identify the direction of the change either in the ratio of the marginal product of capital to that of labor or in the ratio of the unit capital requirement to the unit labor requirement.[17] During the prewar period, 1905–33, technological changes in Japan's manufacturing industry were termed laborsaving improvements in my previous paper.[18] Since the criterion used there was derived from an assumption that factor prices were held constant, there might be some overestimation of the bias if the growth of wage rates were much faster than that of capital return. (A Hicksian laborsaving bias will correspond to the positive sign of ρ, where $\rho = \sigma(\dot{r} - \dot{w}) + (k - l)$, and $\dot{r}$, $\dot{w}$, k, and l are the growth rates of capital return, wage rate, unit capital requirement and unit labor requirement respectively, and σ represents the elasticity of substitution.) Although it is not possible to measure quantitatively the growth rate of capital return, $\dot{r}$, for the prewar period, there is available a measure of the growth of wages and it shows a quite stable series.[19] The term $(\dot{r} - \dot{w})$ may therefore be assumed positive or at least zero, since it is safe to assume positive or zero values for $\dot{r}$ in the process of a faster industrialization such as Japan's.

It may be necessary to add some important revisions when the foregoing discussion is applied to the postwar period, since wages have shown a significant upward trend (the average rate of growth of wages in manufacturing industry has been about 8 percent per annum for the last 10 years). Also, during the postwar period, due to faster industrialization, the range of factor substitution may well have become wider. In what follows, therefore, we shall try to shed some light on the features of technological progress in the postwar period.

At the outset, the possibility of biased technological progress using the same procedure as in the prewar period will be examined, under the strong assumption that the wage-rental ratio (w/r) remains constant from year to year. With this assumption, a laborsaving improvement in the Hicksian sense corresponds to a negative sign of S_{Lt}, which is defined as follows: $S_{Lt} = \dfrac{1}{v_L}\dfrac{\delta v_L}{\delta t} + F_t$ where $\dfrac{L}{X} = v_L$, and

---

[17] Detailed discussions about these criteria can be found in T. Watanabe, "Economic Aspects of Dualism in the Industrial Development of Japan," *op. cit.*

[18] See pp. 294–96, especially Table 1 in Watanabe, *ibid.* See also the results derived by J. C. H. Fei, and G. Ranis, "Capital Accumulation and Economic Development," *American Economic Review,* June, 1963.

[19] From 1919 to 1928, the maximum wage rate is 163 sen per day ($= 1/100$ yen) with the minimum rate of 144 sen per day, and from 1929 to 1937, these rates are 44 yen per month and 35.5 yen per month, respectively. More detailed information will be found in Watanabe, "Economic Aspects of Dualism in the Industrial Development of Japan," *op. cit.*

F_t is a partial derivative of the neoclassical production function, $X = F(K, L, t)$ with respect to t.[20] Eight manufacturing industries (food processing, textiles, paper and pulp, chemicals, metal products, machinery, transportation equipment, miscellaneous) and total manufacturing are selected for the present purpose between 1952–63.[21] The sign of S_{Lt} in these nine industries are given in Table 4–2. It is apparent that most values of S_{Lt} are negative, i.e., during 1952–63, laborsaving improvements have prevailed.

As mentioned before, in the case of two factors of production, the negative sign of S_{Lt} corresponds to the sign of $d(K/L)/dt$. If, therefore, there exists a strong correlation between the capital-labor ratio (K/L) and the wage-rental ratio (w/r), the bias identified in the above will include some over- or underestimation. To test this possibility, it is necessary to construct an estimate with regard to r. Data of capital stock at constant (1960) prices, and of labor requirement, wage rates, and value added at constant (1960) prices, are available from independent sources. Thus, assuming competitive imputation of rewards to factors of production, the return to capital can be derived from $r = \dfrac{1}{K}(X - wL)$, although it may still be an approximation.[22] Correlation coefficients between the wage-rental ratio and the capital-labor ratio for the nine industries are shown in Table 4–3.

There are strong positive correlations between the capital-labor ratio and the wage-rental ratio, except in the industries producing machinery and equipment. This result may be interpreted as showing the difficulty of identifying a genuine laborsaving bias, i.e., it may simply indicate that there has been wide scope for factor substitution.[23] If, however, the theory implies that dearer labor stimulates or induces a laborsaving bias in technological development, as is often suggested for the explanation of the history of American prosperity

---

[20] See Watanabe, "Technological Progress and Economic Growth—The Post-war Manufacturing Industry," *op. cit.*

[21] Detailed information about capital stock, labor requirement, value added and other related data are reported by the Economic Planning Agency. See footnote 13.

[22] An alternative measure of the price of capital, i.e., the price index for capital goods has shown stable movement during the last 10 years, e.g., from 93.2 in 1952 to 98.4 in 1963.

[23] In order to make this identification concretely, it is necessary to determine the value of elasticity of substitution. According to Diamond and McFadden, however, it is impossible to identify the bias of technical change and the elasticity of substitution simultaneously. P. A. Diamond, and D. McFadden, "Identification of the Elasticity of Substitution and the Bias of Technical Change: An Impossibility Theorem," Working Paper No. 62, University of California, mimeographed, March, 1965.

TABLE 4-2

Biasedness of Technological Progress in Japan, 1953-1963

	1953	1954	1955	1956	1957	1958	1959	1960	1961	1962	1963
Food.	-0.0094	-0.0143	-0.0015	-0.0138	-0.0155	-0.0865	-0.0516	-0.0196	-0.0340	-0.0846	-0.0483
Textile	-0.0217	-0.0580	-0.0572	-0.0945	-0.0171	-0.0456	-0.1419	-0.0227	-0.308	-0.0067	-0.0153
Paper and pulp. . . .	0.0179	-0.0765	-0.0489	-0.0115	-0.0339	-0.0947	-0.0709	-0.0783	-0.0753	-0.1213	-0.0269
Chemicals	-0.0993	-0.1007	-0.0690	-0.2194	-0.1524	-0.1249	-0.2948	-0.2129	-0.1558	-0.1341	-0.2118
Metal products. . . .	0.0224	-0.0138	-0.0138	0.0752	0.0071	-0.0441	-0.0195	-0.0817	-0.0921	-0.0741	-0.0800
Machineries	-0.0175	-0.0241	-0.0659	0.0643	-0.0105	-0.0714	-0.0376	-0.0829	-0.0259	-0.0822	-0.0529
Transportation equipment	0.0223	-0.0275	-0.0473	0.0332	-0.0011	-0.0962	-0.0672	-0.1032	-0.0847	-0.0938	-0.0719
Miscellaneous	-0.0227	-0.0281	-0.0292	-0.0096	-0.0166	-0.0133	-0.1569	-0.1199	-0.0876	-0.0747	-0.1059
Total	-0.0896	-0.0279	-0.0281	0.0019	-0.0165	-0.0455	-0.0848	-0.0523	-0.0610	-0.0710	-0.0683

NOTE: Computations are made from $S_{Lt} = \frac{1}{\nu_L} \frac{\partial \nu_L}{\partial t} + F_t$ as mentioned in the text. Data sources are found in the report by Economic Planning Agency. See footnote 13.

TABLE 4-3

Correlations between the Capital-Labor
Ratio and the Wage-Rental Ratio

Food processing.	0.97
Textile.	0.89
Paper and pulp	0.91
Chemicals.	0.92
Metal products	0.65
Machineries.	0.34
Transportation equipment	0.05
Miscellaneous.	0.98
Manufacturing total.	0.91

(for example, Habakkuk,[24] Kennedy [25]), then use of laborsaving techniques will be strengthened by high wage-rental rates, especially in the case of Japan's economy where laborsaving techniques or substitution of capital for labor could be easily achieved through the use of borrowed technology.

Finally, with respect to postwar technological progress, the possibility of capital embodiment will now be briefly examined. According to Nelson's formulation,[26] the Cobb-Douglas production function associated with capital embodiment can be approximately rewritten by using the difference of the average ages of capital, i.e.,

$$\frac{\dot{X}}{K} = \frac{A'}{A'} + (1 - a)\lambda_k - (1 - a)\lambda_k\Delta\bar{a} + a\frac{\dot{L}}{L} + (1 - a)\frac{\dot{K}}{K}. \quad (2)$$

Where (apart from the notations which have already been defined) λ_k represents the rate of improvement in the quality of capital per annum (percent), A'/A' is the measure of disembodied technological progress, and $\bar{a}$ is the difference between the average ages of capital. If technological progress is fully embodied, i.e., $A'/A' = 0$, $\dot{A}/A$ in equation (1) should be equal to the sum of the second and the third terms of the above equation, i.e., $\dot{A}/A = (1 - a)\lambda_k - (1 - a)\lambda_k\Delta\bar{a}$, since the other terms are equivalent in both equations. Thus, we can derive the rate of improvement in the quality of capital, i.e., λ_k as follows:

$$\lambda_k = 1/(1 - a)(1 - \Delta\bar{a})\frac{\dot{A}}{A}. \quad (3)$$

---

[24] H. J. Habakkuk, *American and British Technology in the Nineteenth Century* (London: Cambridge University Press, 1962).

[25] C. Kennedy, *op. cit.*

[26] R. Nelson, "Aggregate Production Functions and Medium Range Growth Projections," *American Economic Review,* September, 1964.

Computed values of λ_k for eight industries are shown in Table 4–4.[27] As is easily observed from this table, the rates of improvement in quality of capital defined as in equation (3) are almost comparable with the values of the disembodied rates of technological progress, i.e., the values of λ_k are quite similar to those of $\dot{A}/A$.[28] This can be interpreted to mean that realized technological progress during the postwar period may well be capital embodied, implying that the role of investment has been quite significant. However, this interpretation is still tentative.

It is possible to summarize the present discussions as follows: (1) The process of industrialization in Japan can be termed an imitative development with a special emphasis on the absorption of imported technology. In other words, advantages as a latecomer have been to a considerable extent realized, resulting in faster industrialization. (2) This imitative process of technological change is a labor-saving type of improvement in the early stage of industrialization. This hypothesis is confirmed quantitatively for the prewar period. (2) Due to the rising trend of the wage-rental ratio and also the widening of the range of factor substitution (which can be one of the fruits of industrialization) during the postwar period, a laborsaving bias as observed in the prewar stage has been disappearing. There is substitution of capital for labor, however, although this might be a reflection of adopting imported innovations. (4) Finally, there is a possibility that realized technological progress is capital embodied, although this is quantitatively confirmed for only a specific period, i.e., 1955–61.

III. DUAL STRUCTURE AND INDUSTRIALIZATION

Although the term, "dual structure" or "dualism," appeared only recently in the literature of economics, it can convey significant features of a growing economy. Take Japan as an example. Here, in theory, two elements of dualism may be identified: one that has

---

[27] With the present availability of statistical data, we have the average ages of capital stock only for the years 1955 and 1961. (Both estimates are derived from the corresponding *National Wealth Survey*.) Other estimates, e.g., $\dot{A}/A$ and $(1 - \alpha)$, therefore, are revised to this period, and thus the values of $\dot{A}/A$ are different from those in Table 4–4.

[28] The estimates of $(1 - \alpha)$ may be biased upward since advertising expenses may be included in the figures for capital shares. This makes for a downward bias in the estimation of λ_k. On the other hand, there may be some upward bias in the estimation of $\Delta\bar{a}$ because the sample of firms from which $\bar{a}$ is determined may have too many large firms. This makes for an upward bias in the estimation of λ_k. As a result, errors in $(1 - \alpha)$ and $(1 - \Delta\bar{a})$ may offset each other.

TABLE 4-4

The Rate of Improvement in the Quality of Capital

	Food	Textile	Paper and Pulp	Chemicals	Metals	Machinery	Total
Average ages at 1955	7.35	8.13	8.10	8.01	10.46	9.19	8.40
Average ages at 1961	7.71	9.15	6.80	6.20	8.79	5.99	7.23
$\Delta\bar{a}$	0.06	0.17	-0.22	-0.30	-0.28	-0.53	-0.19
$(1 - \alpha)$	0.72	0.61	0.67	0.73	0.62	0.60	0.65
$\dot{A}/A$	-0.74	2.04	9.65	12.30	3.40	9.05	4.94
λk	---	4.03	11.81	12.96	4.28	9.86	6.39

NOTE: Data sources are found in Economic Planning Agency's report quoted in footnote 13, and National Wealth Survey 1955 and 1960.

emerged from historically inherited sociocultural factors, and another that has been induced through the process of industrialization. In reality, however, these two elements of dualism can easily be combined; thus it might be difficult to determine whether a particular element of dualism is inherited or induced. In the case of Japan, however, it is relatively easy to indicate some elements which should be classified as inherited. For instance, the "indigenous components" of the living pattern in Japan, suggested by Ohkawa and Rosovsky, provide a typical example of the inherited elements of dualism. According to their estimates, about 50 percent of private consumption in 1955 was on indigenous commodities and the weights of such commodities are noticeably larger in food and housing expenditures than others.[29] Although this element of dualism may play a significant role in explaining the pattern of economic growth, in what follows our discussion will mostly concern itself with the induced element of dualism through industrialization,[30] particularly income differentials, i.e., wage and profit-rate differentials.

At the outset, let us present some historical findings on wage differentials. The problem of wage differentials in the Japanese economy became controversial around 1955,[31] when the first systematic survey of wage structure in 1954 was officially published by the Ministry of Labor. That report emphasized that interscale wage differentials have become wider historically and internationally as a result of the rapid recovery in Japan's economy.[32] This widening of wage differentials is illustrated in Table 4–5. There are, however, two questions to be answered: (a) Do the interscale wage differentials have a particular implication with respect to industrial growth as compared with other

---

[29] Bergson, *op. cit.* With respect to this type of dualism in consumption, the habit-formation hypothesis can be one of the most powerful explanations if it is extended historically. As mentioned in the previous section, the long-term experience of Japan as an isolated economy would lead to quite different consumption habits from those in other societies.

[30] This point was first indicated by Bergson, *ibid.*

[31] See, for example, M. Umemura, "Wage Differentials and Labor Market," *Analyses of Japanese Economy,* ed. S. Tsuru and K. Ohkawa (Tokyo: Keiso-shobo, 1955) (in Japanese), and M. Shinohara, "Dual Structure in Japanese Economy," *Industrial Structure,* ed. M. Shinohara (Tokyo: Shunju-sha, 1959) (in Japanese).

[32] The interscale wage differentials are defined with respect to the scale of firms. Although the consistent definition of wage differentials over a long period is certainly difficult (for example, it is almost impossible to make a rigorous and systematic treatment of regular versus nonregular workers given present statistical information), it must be emphasized that the widening of wage differentials is strongly confirmed even after eliminating weighting differences (e.g. in age, sex, occupation).

measures of wage differential, e.g., by industry, age, sex, etc.? (b) Is the Japanese wage structure significantly different from that in other countries?[33]

It is clearly seen in Table 4–5 that the interscale wage differentials have become wider during the postwar period of industrialization. There may be, however, a danger of faulty assessment since the above figures are in terms of aggregates. In order to overcome this objection, Table 4–6 has been compiled, showing interscale wage differentials for 20 industries. From this table we can show the existence of inter-scale wage differentials even in 1909. For example, the interscale wage differential in machinery was about 150. A similar pattern is also found in 1914. Furthermore, in these two years, there were several industries which showed the inverse type of wage differential, i.e., the wage rate in the largest firms was significantly lower than in the smallest.

The inverse type of wage differential can be explained mainly by the proportion of female workers in firms of different size. For ex-ample, in the wood industry in 1909, female workers were 8 percent of the total in the minimum size of firm and 55 percent in the maxi-

TABLE 4-5

Interscale Wage Differentials

| Size (No. of Persons) | Japan | | | | | | U.K. | U.S. |
	1909	1914	1951	1955	1960	1963	1949	1948
5-9	100	100	100	100	100	100	---	100
10-19	97	95	116	108	127	177	100	108
20-29	---	---	127	118	142	184	99	115
30-49	94	89	138	---	152	197	---	---
50-99	94	92	151	133	164	203	100	118
100-199	97	92	173	148	176	216	101	118
200-499	---	---	203	173	194	232	102	121
500-999	94	100	241	198	227	258	106	123
1,000 or more	100	110	270	250	303	323	119	137

NOTE: The wage rate in the firm which employs from five to nine persons engaged is defined as the base, i.e., 100. This table is a corrected version of the table originally included in T. Watanabe, "Economic Aspects of Dualism in the Industrial Development of Japan," *Economic Development and Cultural Change*, April, 1965.

SOURCE: *The Census of Manufactures.*

---

[33] The figures on the interscale wage differentials were available only in 1909 and 1914 for the prewar period.

mum. Assuming that there are wage differentials according to sex, we may find an inversion of wage rates by size of firm. Differences in the proportion of female workers can also partly explain the similarity of wage rates among different sizes of firm with regard to total manufacturing in 1909 as shown in Table 4–5. In 1909, the proportion of female workers in the maximum size of firm was about 73 percent; 97 percent of these female workers belonged to the textile industry. The proportion of female workers in the minimum size of firm was about 40 percent. Similar inferences are also applicable to the 1914 figures. These findings indicate that it may be an overstatement to conclude that there were no interscale wage differentials during the early stages of industrialization.

Although we should not ignore the existence of interscale wage differentials in 1909 and in 1914, it may be true that there are several industries in which interscale wage differentials become larger in the

TABLE 4-6

Interscale Wage Differentials
(Percent)

	1909	1914	1954	1960
Food.	119†	61	310	327
Textile	125	126	228	218
Apparels.	86*	95†	278†	204†
Wood.	79*	58†	188†	196†
Furniture	122*	130*	163*	164†
Paper	151†	148†	560	481
Printing.	116†	129	282	390
Chemicals	119*	117†	239	234
Petroleum	101*	99*	307	332
Rubber.	94*	88*	176	125
Leather	119*	122*	164*	161*
Glass and cement.	96†	108	440	372
Primary metals.	108*	181	234	255
Metal products.	101*	109†	227†	175†
Machinery	147†	133	220	217
Electrical machinery.	78*	83†	214	169
Transportation machinery. . . .	119	118	238	277
Precision machinery	48†	115†	259	225
Others.	132†	77†	237†	201†
Total manufacturing	101	110	305	310

NOTE: The wage rate in the minimum size of firms is defined as the base, i.e., 100. The maximum size includes firms with over 1,000 employees, except the figures with *(= 100-500 employees) and †(=500-1,000 employees). The wage rates in 1909 and 1914 are per day, and others are payroll per number of employees per year.
SOURCE: *The Census of Manufactures.*

postwar period of industrialization. This conjecture can be partly tested by a further breakdown of the industry figures. Figures for 15 narrowly defined industries, using the same measure of interscale wage differentials as defined in Table 4–6, are shown in Table 4–7.

This table suggests an important pattern in interscale wage differentials: the so-called traditional industries, such as sake, tea processing, leather tanning, lacquerware, matches, and broom, show comparatively small change in wage differentials for the last 50 years, while the relatively modern industries, such as sugar refining, petroleum refining, pulp, and medicines, show a considerable widening of wage differentials. Although the size of the above samples may not be sufficiently large to draw a definite conclusion, it is possible to say that the widening of interscale wage differentials could be associated with the growth of modern industries (or changes in structure).

It may be useful to make a simple comparison of sectoral wage rates between different countries. Except for a few countries such as Argentina, Brazil, Chile, and South Africa, fairly similar patterns are observed among the industrialized countries shown in Table 4–8. (1) The lowest wage rates are found mostly in apparels and textiles, which usually employ a large number of female workers. (2) The

TABLE 4-7

Interscale Wage Differentials in Selected Industries
(Percent)

	1909	1954	1960
Japanese wine (sake).	111	154	174
Beer.	121	107	82
Sugar refining.	120	305	297
Tea processing.	137	132	125
Raw silk.	132	159	248
Cotton yarn	184	170	245
Spun silk yarn.	140	214	269
Hard and bast fiber fabrics	245	166	484
Pulp.	198	301	259
Industrial explosives	301	185	219
Medicines	126	232	248
Leather tanning	150	162	188
Petroleum refining.	130	232	379
Lacquerware	155	127	174
Matches	129	157	147
Broom	115	137	148

SOURCE: *The Census of Manufactures.*

TABLE 4-8

International Comparison of Interindustry
Wage Differentials

| | Prewar | | | Postwar | | | Rank |
	Max.	Min.	Max./Min.	Max.	Min.	Max./Min.	Corr.
U.S.	Print.	Tex.	1.85	Chem.	App.	1.74	0.95
Canada	I & S	Tex.	1.60	Paper	App.	1.77	0.89
New Zealand. . .	Food	Oth.	1.89	I & S	App.	1.65	--
Australia. . . .	I & S	App.	1.95	I & S	App.	1.56	0.78
U.K.	---	--	--	I & S	App.	1.70	--
Norway	I & S	App.	1.86	I & S	App.	1.52	0.94
W. Germany . . .	Chem.	App.	1.74	Chem.	App.	1.84	--
Finland.	Print.	Wood	1.77	I & S	App.	1.52	0.84
Argentina. . . .	App.	Wood	1.67	App.	Wood	1.87	0.74
Ireland.	Food	Tex.	2.12	Mach.	Tex.	1.63	0.80
Italy.	I & S	App.	3.46	Rubb.	App.	3.12	0.85
Brazil	Mach.	I & S	3.23	Rubb.	Tex.	1.81	0.64
Chile.	Print.	App.	2.24	Print.	Oth.	2.79	--
U. of So. Africa	Print.	NMM.	3.45	Print.	NMM.	2.84	--
Japan.	I & S	Tex. & App.	2.08	I & S	App.	2.66	--

NOTE: Prewar and postwar classifications correspond to 1938 and 1958, respectively. Abbreviations are: Print. = printing; Tex. = textiles; App. = apparels; Chem. = chemicals; I & S = iron and steel; Oth. = Others Mach. = machinery; Rubb. = rubber; and NMM. = nonmetallic mineral products
SOURCE: The United Nations, *Pattern of Industrial Growth, 1938-1953* (New York: United Nations, 1960).

highest wage rates are found mostly in iron and steel, and chemicals, which could be characterized as modern and capital-intensive industries. (3) The changes in the importance of industries between the prewar and the postwar periods appear to be considerably greater for those industries paying the highest wages than for those paying the lowest. And (4), Japan's wage structure in terms of interindustry wage differentials may not be markedly different from that in other industrialized countries, although the above measures are certainly tentative.[34]

From these historical and international comparisons, we can draw the following tentative conclusion: although it would appear true that Japan's wage differentials in terms of scale and by industry have become wider historically and internationally, the basic determinant

---

[34] The last finding is also suggested in Watanabe's previous paper, "Economic Aspects of Dualism in the Industrial Development of Japan," *op. cit.*

of this phenomenon may well be the process of industrialization. In addition, the nature of wage differentials may be clarified if they are measured for narrowly defined industries.

Now, let us consider another important aspect of dualism: profit-rate differentials. We shall then construct a systematic view of the relationships between industrialization and dual structure. As might be expected, statistical information about profit and related variables, with the necessary coverage and breakdown is available only on a very limited scale, especially for the prewar period. The *Statistical Survey of Business Companies*[35] (started in 1921) compiled and published by the Ministry of Commerce and Industry is the only useful one for the present purpose, since this survey contains data concerning small-scale enterprises.

The profit rate, defined as the ratio (percent) of net profit minus net loss to paid-in capital, is shown in Table 4–9, for 14 aggregated industries, for 1923–39. Almost no systematic trend is found in this table. (The one exception is the general increase of the profit rate after 1936. This may be attributed to the irregularity during the war preparation period.) The more important aspect of the profit rate, namely the differentials among those 75 manufacturing industries, together with the corresponding wage differentials in terms of the coefficient of variation, are summarized in Table 4–10.

Coefficients of variation were computed in a similar fashion for profit rate and for wage differentials in the postwar period. They are shown in Table 4–11.[36] Although the comparability of figures for these two discrete periods may not be perfect, it is still possible to establish a few important points: (*a*) profit-rate differentials tend to

---

[35] This survey, entitled *Kaisha Tokeihyo* in Japanese, contains such items as: number of companies, authorized share capital, paid-up capital, reserves, net profit, dividend, net loss, and debentures outstanding. The samples are classified by about 150 industries, and include about 3,500 companies (covering about 60 percent of all companies in manufacturing industry in 1942). Information is available from 1921 to 1942. An important advantage of this survey is the comparability of the industry classification with that in the *Census of Manufactures* which will provide our information on wage rates. (This is due to the fact that both sets of information were collected by the same government agency, the Ministry of Commerce and Industry, the former name of the present Ministry of International Trade and Industry.) On the other hand, an important disadvantage is its discontinuity with the postwar period. Corresponding information for the postwar period is available from the *Statistical Survey of Incorporated Enterprises* by the Ministry of Finance.

[36] It should be noted that Table 4–10 and Table 4–11 are not comparable in a strict sense, since the classification of enterprises in Table 4–11 is based on a two-way system, i.e., 13 manufacturing industries with six breakdowns of scales. Thus the sample size is roughly comparable with that in the prewar period, 78 and 75, respectively.

TABLE 4-9

Profit Rate, 1923–1939
(Percent)

	Agric.	Fish.	Min-ings	Mfg. Total	Tex-tiles	Metals	Mach.	Nonmetal Minerals	Chem.	Wood	Print-ing	Food	Utili-ties	Misc.
1923. . .	1.31	3.80	4.44	4.24	3.98	1.13	1.04	9.58	2.54	7.14	11.82	5.52	8.64	1.89
1924. . .	1.61	3.39	3.66	6.62	3.51	0.45	7.62	6.56	5.89	4.34	14.55	10.62	10.55	2.58
1925. . .	4.94	7.53	3.58	7.56	7.94	0.80	6.03	5.80	6.35	3.14	21.93	8.13	10.10	2.38
1926. . .	5.60	9.01	3.16	6.64	4.69	1.21	3.80	7.41	6.70	2.00	7.10	5.70	9.80	3.57
1927. . .	3.29	9.98	2.85	6.38	3.64	2.65	6.00	6.76	5.91	1.76	6.31	8.14	8.77	3.54
1928. . .	1.23	15.17	3.09	7.15	8.04	3.10	5.49	6.62	7.18	1.46	7.78	3.72	9.15	3.90
1929. . .	0.20	5.39	4.35	7.38	6.25	4.24	5.23	9.19	7.63	4.00	5.82	7.27	9.26	1.82
1930. . .	0.19	1.47	1.04	4.57	1.34	1.71	4.27	3.43	4.55	4.73	4.27	5.17	8.08	4.64
1931. . .	1.08	0.07	0.44	4.29	4.15	0.29	0.78	1.94	3.03	2.03	2.24	3.43	6.99	2.69
1932. . .	1.54	4.18	1.78	5.02	6.67	1.65	2.99	4.90	4.38	0.19	2.60	4.87	5.68	2.85
1933. . .	0.17	6.47	5.50	6.96	9.47	9.79	6.22	11.12	9.77	1.83	0.93	5.67	4.93	4.66
1934. . .	1.73	9.51	7.85	7.40	7.23	8.81	9.52	10.47	10.17	7.37	3.11	6.69	5.33	6.25
1935. . .	2.55	11.29	8.53	8.93	8.45	12.59	12.46	10.64	9.64	3.24	4.14	7.57	7.04	6.29
1936. . .	3.92	8.99	8.08	8.00	8.29	11.22	11.37	8.97	9.21	3.54	5.54	8.16	7.89	6.24
1937. . .	4.97	7.60	7.37	9.25	8.89	15.04	8.78	10.91	9.41	6.73	6.52	8.67	7.51	7.25
1938. . .	4.29	8.71	8.00	10.13	10.00	14.10	11.84	8.76	9.90	7.81	6.55	8.95	7.63	9.64
1939. . .	5.90	10.37	7.30	10.07	12.21	11.84	12.66	9.69	10.61	8.46	7.38	9.46	7.18	11.22

SOURCE: *Statistical Survey of Business Companies* by the Ministry of Commerce and Industry.

TABLE 4-10

Differentials of Profit Rate and
Wage Rate: 1921-1939

	Profit-Rate Differentials	*Wage-Rate Differentials*
1921.	11.18	0.23
1922.	7.19	0.21
1923.	386.48	0.22
1924.	6.42	0.22
1925.	6.27	0.25
1926.	8.39	0.22
1927.	5.35	0.22
1928.	4.62	0.22
1929.	4.91	0.30
1930.	13.02	0.36
1931.	14.76	0.33
1932.	8.46	0.33
1933.	4.76	0.32
1934.	3.74	0.32
1935.	3.62	0.39
1936.	3.41	0.30
1937.	3.57	0.29
1938.	3.44	0.27
1939.	3.33	0.18

NOTE: The figures on profit and wage differentials were based
on statistics compiled by the *Statistical Survey of Business Companies* and *The Census of Manufactures*, respectively. The maximum
number of comparable industry classifications was 75 except for
1921, 1922, and 1939. (In those three years, the sample sizes
were 59, 59, and 68, respectively.)

be much larger than wage differentials, especially in the prewar
period; (*b*) while during the prewar period year-to-year changes in
the profit-rate differentials may suggest a slight correspondence to a
cyclical phenomenon, changes in wage differentials appear to remain
relatively stable; (*c*) during the postwar period, both profit-rate and
wage differentials have become similar in the sense that neither differential shows stable tendencies, and finally (*d*) when compared with
the prewar figures, profit-rate differentials have become smaller in the
postwar period.[37]

With these facts in mind, the question to be answered can be

---

[37] As mentioned in footnote 36, the comparability of the basic information
is not exact.

TABLE 4-11

Differentials of Profit Rate and
Wage Rate: 1952-1962

	Profit-Rate Differentials	Wage-Rate Differentials
1952.	0.82	0.34
1953.	1.90	0.39
1954.	1.32	0.76
1955.	2.47	0.52
1956.	1.11	0.45
1957.	1.01	0.42
1958.	1.42	0.39
1959.	1.18	0.38
1960.	0.63	0.62
1961.	0.90	0.34
1962.	1.06	0.40

SOURCE: *Statistical Survey of Incorporated Enterprises* by
Ministry of Finance.

phrased as follows: Is it possible to construct a reasonable hypothesis
to explain these facts and relate them to industrialization?

As has already been pointed out in the preceding section of this
paper, the process of industrialization in Japan can be characterized
as imitative. It appears most appropriate, therefore, to assume that
the unevenness of the realized effects has accrued from imported
technological progress, which in turn has increased productivity in
individual industries or firms. This is in fact true in the early stage of
industrialization. Even though there were ample amounts of backlog
in the adoption of technological inventions that had already been
made in advanced foreign countries, the socioeconomic capacity to
integrate those imported technological inventions may have been inadequate, partly because of the limited size of available capital. On
the other hand, as was discussed in previous sections, the imported
technological changes can be regarded as of a laborsaving type in the
Hicksian sense (and most probably capital embodied). The marginal
product of capital will increase faster than that of labor under a laborsaving type of technological improvement. With an abundant and
qualified labor supply and also without interference by powerful trade
unions,[38] firms having a relatively greater capacity to integrate im-

---

[38] These two assumptions may not be necessary and sufficient to maintain
a stable rate of money wages, since the adjustment mechanism of wage deter-

ported technology may have been able to realize a relatively higher rate of return to capital. This in turn would create an unevenness of profit rates among different firms. To the extent that the availability of the backlog of imported technological inventions is high, those firms which have benefited by the use of imported technological inventions could accumulate relatively large amounts of investment funds. They have been in a favorable position to make further profitable expansion by utilizing advantageous imported technology once again.[39] Under such circumstances, some firms could continuously enjoy a spiral of profitable expansions. (Roughly speaking, Zaibatsu firms might be of this type.) Others might find expansion difficult. With a lapse of time, however, some of the weaker firms, too, would be able to grow profitably. Momentum would be provided, for example, by the amount of accumulated national capital together with a relative decline in the prices of investment goods. In accordance with these changes, the profit-rate differentials may become smaller, although it is hardly possible to make any quantitative statement.

The preparation for a war economy by the government in the 1930's brought about some changes in the labor market. In order to make firms' recruitment easier, the lifetime commitment and the seniority system of wage determination were introduced. Entrepreneurs found it to their advantage to make workers stay with the firm, and an army of literally "permanent" employees was formed. The mushrooming of trade unions in the postwar period also added to workers' stability by their opposition to discharges of union mem-

---

mination in a labor market may well be disturbed by some other institutional factors, e.g., the caste system in India. With regard to these obstacles, however, the Japanese labor market has been to a considerable extent competitive. As evidence, an empirical application of the Phillips-Lipsey model for 1929–39 and 1955–63 gives

$$w = 8.73 - 1.82U + 0.57p + 3.42D \qquad R = 0.97,$$

where w, p, U and D represent annual changes in money wage, annual changes in consumer prices, the rate of unemployment, and a dummy variable (zero for the prewar and 1 for the postwar period) respectively. See T. Watanabe, "Wage, Price and Their Policy Implications," *Price Problems in Japan*, ed. H. Kumagaya, and T. Watanabe (Tokyo: Nippon Keizai Shinbun-sha, 1966) (in Japanese) and "Price Changes and the Rate of Change of Money Wage Earnings in Japan, 1955–1962," *Quarterly Journal of Economics*, February, 1966, for further discussion.

[39] In order to make this process of industrialization effective without serious economic and social frictions, it might be necessary to adjust national economic policies. Thus, the relation between national economic policies and the above-stated type of industrialization may be a crucial one. Some discussion of this point will be found in Watanabe's previous paper "Economic Aspects of Dualism in the Industrial Development of Japan," *op. cit.*

bers. Under these new institutional arrangements, profits realized by adopting imported technology have come to accrue not only to entrepreneurs but also to union workers. This in turn may have stimulated factor substitution or induced types of laborsaving techniques in the postwar period. This may correspond to smaller differentials in profit rates and to larger wage differentials as compared with the prewar period.

IV. FINAL REMARKS

The foregoing discussions contain few surprises. For one thing, the data are very crude; one would wish to add inventories to fixed capital stocks in individual industries. For another, even though some of the results generated by an imitative process of industrialization were present, others were not.

It will, therefore, be appropriate as a final remark to indicate briefly some problems to be investigated in the future. The first is the changing patterns of the relative price system during imitative industrialization. This may be especially important for clarifying the imitative development of consumers' behavior and the mechanism of the high-savings ratio in Japan. The second is the relationship between the process of industrialization and national economic policies. Rosovsky[40] contends, for example, that government savings and investments have played a quite important role in promoting Japanese industrialization. Other types of national policies such as price stabilization, the tax system, and promotion of research and education should also be studied, especially those policies which are intended to overcome possible frictions accruing from the induced type of dualism. Finally, the most important problem is the study of those initial conditions which made it possible for Japan to follow the process of industrialization described in this paper. It remains to be answered, for example, how qualified labor and a reasonable amount of capital funds came to be available.

---

[40] H. Rosovsky, *Capital Formation in Japan* (New York: The Free Press of Glencoe, 1961).

5 | Technological Progress in Agriculture

YUJIRO HAYAMI and SABURO YAMADA

Within less than a century, Japan has emerged from being a predominantly rural state to becoming one of the highly industrialized nations in the world. Throughout the process of industrialization, agriculture has been a major source of resources for the nonfarm sector. Especially in the earlier periods when industrial capital had not yet been accumulated, Japan was able to finance industrialization by mobilizing agricultural surpluses.

It is well known that the land tax and landlordism served to siphon off the agricultural surpluses to industry. As a prerequisite, however, agricultural surpluses had to exist. It is through technological progress that the surpluses have been generated.[1] On this account, technological progress in agriculture has been a key to Japan's general economic development. It is the aim of this essay to identify the sources of technological progress.

First, let us draw up a chronology of technological progress for the period 1878–1962 by use of a total productivity index. Second, a hypothesis will be postulated to explain the chronology. Third, the hypothesis will be tested on the basis of average rice yields per unit of area planted in 46 prefectures. Fourth, recent trends in agricultural

---

[1] An alternative hypothesis is that, by the beginning of modern development, agricultural productivity in Japan had reached a high level and that the creation of institutions to exploit the already existing surpluses or the dispossession of unproductive feudal ruling class made it possible to extract funds for industrialization. See I. J. Nakamura, "Growth of Japanese Agriculture, 1875–1920," *The State and Economic Enterprise in Japan,* ed. W. W. Lockwood (Princeton, N.J.: Princeton University Press, 1965), pp. 249–324. We do not share this view. See the authors' "Agricultural Productivity at the Beginning of Industrialization," a paper presented at Agriculture and Economic Development: a Symposia of Japanese Experience, Tokyo, July, 1967.

productivity will be examined in terms of the results of the previous section. Finally, implications of the Japanese experience for today's emerging nations will be discussed.

CHRONOLOGY

Before proceeding to identify factors for technological progress, we have to specify its chronology.

For this purpose we constructed an index of total productivity of inputs, by forming a ratio of gross value produced to a linear aggregate of conventional inputs. This index can be conceived of as a measure of technological progress under the following assumptions: (1) technological progress represents a multiplicative factor of a linear production function and (2) factor markets are operating at equilibrium under perfect competition. As measured by this index, technological progress is the portion of the increase in output, which is left unexplained by the increases in conventional inputs.[2]

The total productivity index we have constructed is compared with the indexes of output and inputs in Figure 5–1, based on the figures in Appendix Tables 5A–1 and 5A–2. Over the whole period, output more than tripled. Land and capital increased much more slowly than output, especially in the prewar years, and labor stayed virtually constant. Only current inputs increased faster than output. Overall, total productivity nearly doubled.

---

[2] We constructed the total productivity index in a conventional fashion. We did not attempt to make refinements, as in Z. Griliches, "The Sources of Measured Productivity Growth: United States Agriculture 1940–1960," *Journal of Political Economy,* Vol. 71 (August, 1963), pp. 331–46, to adjust for the influences of quality changes in input factors or for scale economy. The former influence is included in our index, as it is factor augmenting. The latter influence should have been modest, especially for prewar years, because the average farm scale stayed virtually constant in Japan except Hokkaido. Also, production function studies based on farm records (K. Ohkawa, *Shokuryō Keizai no Riron to Keisoku* [*Theory and Measurement of Food Economy*] [Tokyo: Nihonhyoronsha, 1945], Part 2; Y. Torii, "Nōgyō Bumon no Genkai Seisanryoku Sokutei [Measurement of Agricultural Marginal Productivity]," *Economic Studies Quarterly,* Vol. 16 [June, 1966], pp. 52–66; K. Tsuchiya, *Nōgyō Keizai no Keiryō Bunseki,* [Tokyo: Keisōshobō, 1962], chap. 2) generally support the hypothesis of constant return to scale. It is only Y. Yuize's study "Nōgyō ni Okeru Kyoshiteki Seisankansū no Keisoku (The Aggregate Production Function in Agriculture)," *Nōgyō Sōgō Kenkyū,* Vol. 18 (October, 1964), pp. 1–54, which contradicts the hypothesis of constant returns to scale. There are a number of alternative schemes to evaluate technological progress in terms of the "unexplained output" or "residual," as in R. M. Solow's study, "Technical Change and the Aggregate Production Function," *Review of Economics and Statistics,* Vol. 39 (August, 1957), pp. 317–20. We find it difficult to choose a particular productivity index, but our basic conclusion should not be affected by its choice.

FIGURE 5-1. Movements in Output, Inputs, and Productivity.

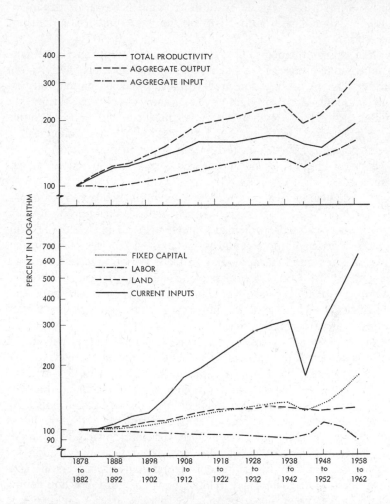

Such movements in output, inputs, and productivity reflect the character of technological progress in Japanese agriculture. As Ohkawa has asserted,[3] since the beginning of modern development until very recently, Japanese agriculture has been the source of an unlimited supply of labor in the sense of Lewis[4] or Ranis and Fei.[5] No major

[3] K. Ohkawa, "Agriculture and Turning Points," *The Developing Economies,* Vol. 3, No. 4 (December, 1965), pp. 471–86.

[4] W. A. Lewis, "Development with Unlimited Supply of Labor," *The Manchester School,* Vol. 22 (May, 1954), pp. 139–92.

[5] G. Ranis, and J. C. H. Fei, "The Theory of Economic Development," *American Economic Review,* Vol. 51 (September, 1961), pp. 533–65.

structural change has ever occurred comparable to the Second Enclosure Movement in England. Traditional small-sized farms dependent on family labor have continued to be the basic units of agricultural production.

While labor remained almost constant, farm output increased considerably. In consequence, a sizable increase in labor productivity was realized. The possibility for area expansion being limited, farmers could increase labor productivity or income only by raising the productivity of land. Rather than investing in machinery and implements which are, by nature, substitutes for the redundant labor, farmers chose to apply more fertilizer in order to raise yields per unit of the scarce land. This, in effect, saved capital and increased current inputs.

Technological innovations, too, have been affected by this emphasis on land improvement. Research efforts have been concentrated on improvements in seeds, which are effective in raising yields per unit of land.[6] A strong complementarity has existed between the improvements in seeds and the input of fertilizer. Varieties have been purposely selected that could withstand heavier application of fertilizer. The improvement in seeds, complemented with the heavier application of fertilizer, has had a major impact on the aggregate production function in Japanese agriculture.[7]

As it is the prime motive of the farmers to raise output per unit of land, technological progress may be better represented by land productivity. In Figure 5–2 (from data in Appendix Table 5A–2), two indices of land productivity are compared with the total productivity index: One is gross value produced divided by cultivated land area, and another is the average rice yield per unit of planted area. Those indexes show a high correlation with the total productivity index (0.95 in both cases). We can also give theoretical justification for using land productivity as an index of technological progress in Japanese agriculture on the basis of relative constancy of labor and capital stock to land.[8] We do not deny that the increase in rice yield is, to a large extent, attributable to the increases in current inputs, especially

---

[6] Another important measure for increasing land productivity was investment in land improvement, including water control. In this paper, however, we do not try to evaluate the contribution of such investment to land productivity.

[7] For this discussion, see Y. Hayami, "Demand for Fertilizer in the Course of Japanese Agricultural Development," *Journal of Farm Economics,* Vol. 46 (November, 1964), pp. 766–79.

[8] On this account, land productivity is likely to overestimate technological progress for the postwar period when labor increased above its normal level for 1948–57 and capital stock rose at an accelerated pace relative to land area.

FIGURE 5–2.   Comparison of the Indexes of Total Productivity, Rice Yield per Unit of Area Planted, and Gross Value Produced per Unit of Cultivated Land Area (1878–82 = 100).

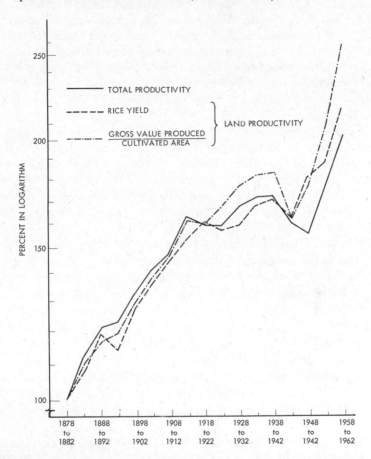

fertilizer. But, considering the complementarity between fertilizer and seed improvements, it would be unrealistic to try to separate the effect of fertilizer application from technological progress.

There is reason to question whether the gross value index might overestimate the rate of technological progress. Gross value produced includes both livestock products and feed. Livestock production, though its weight is not large, has increased faster than total agricultural production. This must have made the double counting of livestock and feed a source of overestimation.[9]

---

[9] The index of value added per unit of land area coincides almost exactly with the total productivity index.

The rice yield index has merit in that it is free from aggregation bias and unrealistic assumptions inherent in the total productivity index. Rice is by far the most important single crop, comprising 50–60 percent of total agricultural production in value terms. Farmers, as well as the government, have placed their major emphasis on the raising of rice yields. Increases in rice yield per hectare have been almost synonymous with technological progress in agriculture. In specifying the chronology of technological progress, we shall consider both the total productivity index and the index of rice yield per unit of planted area.

We now proceed to specify major phases in technological progress in agriculture. In terms both of the total productivity index and of the rice yield index, three major phases are clearly distinguishable, except for the period subject to the disturbances of World War II. They are (1) initial growth ending around 1920,[10] (2) succeeding stagnation until the start of the Sino-Japanese War (1937), and (3) postwar expansion.

This phaseology is applicable not only to technological progress but also to the growth in agricultural output, as may be seen in Figure 5–1. In fact, those who have been engaged in the long-term analysis of Japanese agriculture have not failed to notice the kink in the rate of growth in output at about 1920 (Johnston[11] and Ohkawa and Rosovsky[12]). On comparing the movements in output with the indexes of technological progress, we can explain the kink in the growth in output in terms of the kink in technological progress.[13]

The question now arises: What explains the kink in technological progress? This is one of the major questions we are going to deal with. Another major problem is to find the cause for the postwar spurt.

----

[10] The initial growth phase seems to have ended by 1913–17 according to the total productivity index, but it seems to have ended by 1918–22 according to the rice yield index.

[11] B. F. Johnston, "Agricultural Productivity and Economic Development in Japan," *Journal of Political Economy,* Vol. 59 (December, 1951), pp. 498–513.

[12] K. Ohkawa and H. Rosovsky, "The Role of Agriculture in Modern Japanese Economic Development," *Economic Development and Cultural Change,* Vol. 9 (October, 1960), pp. 43–67.

[13] The weights used in the total productivity index are changed from 1884–86 prices for 1878–1922 to 1934–36 prices for 1923–47. One may wonder if the kink in the index might be attributable to this shift in weight system. But the index using 1884–86 prices as weights and again using 1934–36 prices as weights for 1878–1947 show a kink at about 1920. This shows that the kink in technological progress is not a statistical artifact due to the change in weight system.

HYPOTHESIS

We will now try to postulate a hypothesis which may adequately explain technological progress as measured in the previous section.

The measured technological progress is a gap between the growth in output and the growth in conventional inputs. According to Schultz, factors which close this gap "are represented (1) by new techniques that are adopted in production and (2) by improvements in the labor force, that is, in the quality of the people who engage in production."[14] He has, thus, strongly advocated the inclusion in economic analysis of such nonconventional inputs as investments in research, extension and education.[15]

It was Tang who tried to apply Schultz's theory to the analysis of Japanese agricultural development for the period 1880–1938.[16] He measured technological progress in agriculture analogously to our total productivity index.[17] He tried to explain measured technological progress in terms of government outlays on agricultural research, extension, and rural education by forming a regression of the former on the latter. The government expenditures are considered to represent social cost for technological progress. On the basis of goodness of fit, he claimed that more than 70 percent of the variation in output was explained.

Though his attempt is stimulating, the adequacy of his model must be questioned. We do not deny, of course, the important role of the nonconventional inputs in technological progress in agriculture.[18] However, a crucial defect in Tang's model is that it fails to explain the kink which occurred at about 1920. Measured technological progress had been faster than the government outlays until the end of the

---

[14] T. W. Schultz, "Reflections on Agricultural Production, Output, and Supply," *Journal of Farm Economics,* Vol. 38 (August, 1956), p. 759.

[15] T. W. Schultz, *Transforming Traditional Agriculture,* (New Haven, Conn.: Yale University Press, 1964).

[16] A. M. Tang, "Research and Education in Japanese Agricultural Development, 1880–1938," *Economic Studies Quarterly,* Vol. 13 (February–May, 1963), pp. 27–41 and 91–99.

[17] He measured technological progress as the difference between the growth in output and the growth in a linear aggregate of inputs by assuming that technological progress represents an additive factor in the linear production function.

[18] The role of nonconventional inputs in Japanese agriculture is discussed in detail in S. Yamada "Changes in Output and in Conventional and Nonconventional Inputs in Japanese Agriculture since 1880," *The Food Research Institute Studies* (Stanford, Calif.: Stanford University Press, forthcoming).

1910's when it turned stagnant. In contrast, government outlays began to make a spurt in the 1910's.[19] A picture is drawn in Figure 5–3 (see data in Appendix Tables 5A–1 and 5A–2) which compares our measured technological progress with revised series of nonconventional inputs.[20] While the indexes of technology indicate that tech-

FIGURE 5–3.   Comparison of the Indexes of Total Productivity, Rice Yield per Unit of Area Planted, and Nonconventional Inputs (1933–37 = 100).

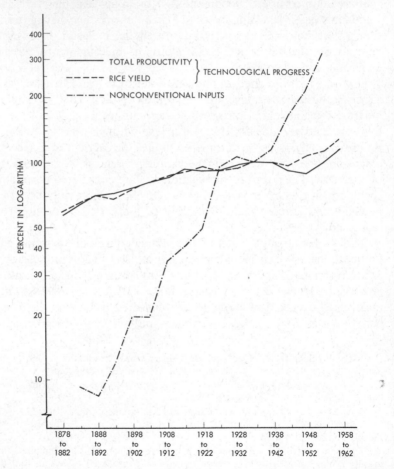

[19] See Figure 2 in Y. Hayami, "A Critical Note on Professor Tang's Model of Japanese Agricultural Development," *Economic Studies Quarterly*, Vol. 15 (August, 1965), pp. 47–54.

[20] While Tang's estimates of nonconventional inputs contain only the outlays of the central government, our estimates contain the outlays of both central and local governments. See the data in Yamada *op. cit.*, which investigated relationships between total productivity and nonconventional inputs.

nological progress decelerated with a kink at about 1920 (1913–17, in the case of total productivity and 1918–22, in the case of rice yield), nonconventional inputs continued to grow linearly (in logarithms) until the 1930's. The rapid technological progress before 1920 contrasted with the stagnation in the succeeding period seems difficult to explain with Tang's variables alone, even if we assume a time lag (as Tang did) in the effects of education and research on output.[21]

What, then, may explain the kink? We should like to identify it by what Ohkawa has called "the backlog inherited from the pre-modern Tokugawa period."[22] Before proceeding to a concrete discussion, we have to theorize about the process of technological improvement.

Technological progress, defined as the upward shifting of the aggregate production function, can be viewed as the combined effect of two processes: invention and diffusion. We define s_t as the actual shift and u_t as the potential shift in the aggregate production function. The latter is the shift which should be realized by year t if all producers have accepted and efficiently practiced all the best techniques currently available. The best techniques will continue to diffuse among producers, and with a lapse of time, s_t will approach u_t if no new techniques are invented on the way. Most simply, we may specify the process as

$$s_{t+1} - s_t = \lambda_t(u_t - s_t), \ 0 \leqq \lambda_t \leqq 1 \qquad (1)$$

where λ_t is the rate of diffusion. The above equation implies that the actual shift in the aggregate production function is a certain proportion of the discrepancy between the potential and actual shifts in a period ahead. If u and λ are constant, s will approach u. In the actual world, however, those values are functions of nonconventional inputs, and will vary as technical, social, and institutional conditions vary.

Over the preceding 300 years of the Tokugawa period, agricultural techniques advanced slowly in raising u. As T. Smith has pointed out,[23] by the end of the Tokugawa period several advanced techniques were already practiced in various districts in the nation. But the restraints of the feudal system had suppressed the diffusion of new techniques so that the actual shift in the aggregate production function was much slower than the potential shift. Under the feudal system,

---

[21] The distributed-lag model which Tang used includes the lagged dependent variable as an independent variable. Hence, even if the model is inappropriate, it fits well to data if the dependent variable is autocorrelated. The fact of the matter is that Tang's dependent variable is significantly autocorrelated.

[22] Ohkawa, *op. cit.,* p. 478.

[23] T. C. Smith, *The Agrarian Origins of Modern Japan* (Stanford, Calif.: Stanford University Press, 1959).

peasants were bound to their land, and were, in general not allowed to leave their villages except for pilgrimages to the Ise Grand Shrine or the Zenkoji Temple.[24] Neither were they free to choose what crops to plant, nor to choose what varieties of seeds to sow. Barriers which divided the nation into feudal territories interrupted nationwide communications. Though feudal lords were anxious to raise agricultural productivity within their territories, in many cases they prohibited the export of the improved techniques from their territorial boundaries. Even within the territory of a lord, diffusion was not quite free. It is recorded that a village called Maesawa in Toyama Prefecture placed a guard at its border to prevent exportation of a variety of rice seeds selected in the village.[25]

It is not difficult to imagine how such institutional restraints suppressed λ. The rate of increase in u had been slow under the feudal regime, but λ had been so low that the discrepancy between u and s had widened cumulatively. Abolition of such feudal restraints at the Meiji restoration and the subsequent modernization measures including the introduction of railway and postal services brought a jump in λ. With the wide gap opened between u and s, the jump in λ resulted in a rapid increase in s.

It is the potential accumulated in the form of $(u - s)$, which is neglected in Tang's model. Government outlays included in Tang's variable certainly contributed to technological progress. Government extension activities as well as the spread of compulsory education should have vast effects on λ. Introduction of Western techniques and the establishment of agricultural experiment stations also helped to raise u. But all those current activities cannot fully explain the increase in s during the phase of initial growth.

The techniques which characterized Japanese agriculture in the Meiji period are generally called *Rōnō Gijutsu* (veteran farmer's techniques). When the imported techniques failed to take root in Japanese soil and research in the agricultural experiment stations was in its infancy, it was the technological potential embodied in the *Rōnō* (veteran farmers), which provided the basis for technological progress. It is generally agreed that the *Rōnō Gijutsu* were replaced by the techniques developed in the experiment stations during the 1910's. By that time the technological potential accumulated under the feudal

---

24 The fact that the varieties of rice originating along the pilgrimage routes were planted widely over the nation shows that such pilgrimages worked as an important medium for the diffusion of technology in the premodern period.

25 S. Yasuda, (ed.), *Meiji Iko ni Okeru Nōgyō Gijutsu no Hatten (Agricultural Development since Meiji)* (Tokyo: Nogyo Gijutsu Kyokai, 1952), p. 3.

regime should have been used up. Without considering this process, the rapid initial growth contrasted with the succeeding stagnation cannot be really understood.

Another question now arises: What explains the postwar spurt? It can partly be explained by the increase in research and extension expenditures by the government, pressed by the keen food shortage immediately after the war. Also, the increased aspiration of farmers due to the land reform must not be ignored. But, a more basic cause must be the backlog of scientific knowledge and technology accumulated during the war as the result of gigantic research investments, domestic and foreign, for military purposes. As is well documented in Nelson,[26] there is a wide spectrum of scientific activity ranging from the applied science end to the basic science end. It is often the latter which produces a major breakthrough for practical problems as is the case with the discovery of hybrid corn in the United States. Most of the researches done during the war were not for agricultural purposes. But, they formed a backlog for the advancements in agricultural techniques. A notable example is the practice of protecting nursery beds by the use of vinyl covers. This has contributed greatly to the stabilization of rice yields in northern Japan. This innovation could not be made without the advancements in synthetic chemistry, which made it possible for farmers to utilize vinyl products.

Our basic hypothesis comes down to an explanation of the major phases of technological progress in Japanese agriculture in terms of the accumulation and diffusion of scientific knowledge and techniques.

ANALYSIS

We will now try to substantiate the hypothesis postulated in the previous section. Materials for the analysis are the average rice yields (paddy rice only)[27] per unit of planted area for 46 prefectures. For the reasons discussed previously, rice yield may be used as a measure for the level of agricultural technology in Japan.

Figure 5–4 (data in Table 5A–3 of the Appendix) includes the series of averages (Y), advanced levels (U), and coefficients of variations (V) of the average rice yields per unit of planted area for (a) all prefectures, (b) 18 eastern prefectures (excluding Hokkaido) and (c) 27 western prefectures. We will use for U the average of the average rice yields of the upper five prefectures in the case of all prefec-

---

[26] R. R. Nelson, "The Simple Economics of Basic Scientific Research," *Journal of Political Economy,* Vol. 67 (June, 1959), pp. 297–306.

[27] The weight of upland rice is negligible.

FIGURE 5–4. Movements in Advanced Levels (U), Averages (Y), and Coefficients of Variations (V) of Rice Yields.

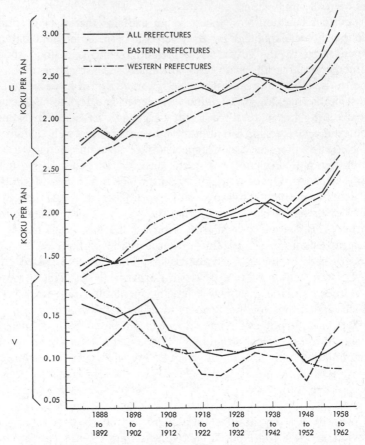

tures, and of the upper three prefectures in the cases of eastern and western prefectures.[28]

Statistically, U, Y, and V are parameters of a distribution.[29] Assuming a form of the distribution, Y will be determined by U and V. It will increase as U increases, for a given V, or as V decreases, for a given U. Economic interpretations may well be possible. Y corresponds to s, U to u and V to $(u - s)$ in equation (1). The national or regional average level of technology will advance as it is led by the progress in the advanced districts or as the backward districts catch

---

[28] The upper five or upper three prefectures varied in the course of agricultural development.

[29] U represents a certain upper centile.

up with the advanced. The former process implies an increase in u and the latter a decrease in $(u - s)$. Naturally, a discrepancy always exists between U and u, as it is inconceivable that all farmers in the advanced prefectures are operating at the very frontiers of current technology. As the potential technology u would diffuse within advanced prefectures, U would rise in closing the gap between U and u.[30] Concurrently, the advanced technology realized in the advanced prefectures would diffuse among less-advanced prefectures in raising Y (which is a proxy of s). In that sense, the decrease in V represents a fraction of the reduction in $(u - s)$.[31]

The relation of Y to U and V may be approximated in the following equation:

$$\dot{Y}_t = {}_a\dot{U}_t + \beta\dot{V}_t + \gamma + \xi_t \tag{2}$$

where

$$\dot{Y}_t = \frac{Y_t - Y_{t-1}}{Y_{t-1}}$$

$$\dot{U}_t = \frac{U_t - U_{t-1}}{U_{t-1}}$$

$$\dot{V}_t = \frac{V_t - V_{t-1}}{V_{t-1}}$$

$$\xi_t = \text{error term}$$

and a, β, and γ are parameters. The above equation is estimated on the basis of quinquennial data in Appendix Table 5A–3 with the results shown in Table 5–1. In this analysis quinquennia were preferred to years as unit observation periods. By taking five-year averages, we aimed at removing weather influences to some extent. Two

---

[30] The following relation is assumed:

$$U_{t+1} - U_t = \gamma_t (u_t - U_t), 0 \leqq \gamma_t \leqq 1$$

Take as an example Osaka prefecture, which belonged to the upper five prefectures continuously for 1883–1947. For the period 1890–1935, the average rice yield per *tan* in Osaka rose by 11 percent from 2.19 *koku* to 2.43 *koku*, while the average of the upper three counties in the prefecture rose by only 4.7 percent from 2.47 *koku* to 2.58 *koku*. For the same period, the coefficient of variation of the county averages declined by 30.5 percent from 0.095 to 0.066. This seems to suggest that the rise in U was affected by the diffusion of u within the advanced prefectures. Again the levels of productivity in the advanced counties in the advanced prefectures would have been affected by the diffusion of u.

[31] Therefore, the analysis in this section will substantiate only a part of the relation specified in general terms in the previous section.

TABLE 5-1

Estimation Results of Equation 2

	Restrictions	Para-meter α	Esti-mates β	Intercept γ	Coef. of Det. R^2	Residual Var. S^2	Durbin-Watson d
All — Y = Weighted average	———	0.9768 (0.0716)	-0.1665 (0.0417)	0.4237 (33.72)	0.9394	2.397	2.13
	Intercept = 0	1.0135 (0.0548)	-0.1775 (0.0390)	———	0.9361	2.333	1.92
Y = Simple average	———	0.9325 (0.0394)	-0.1622 (0.0230)	0.4243 (18.52)	0.9791	0.724	2.56
	Intercept = 0	0.9693 (0.0319)	-0.1733 (0.0227)	———	0.9752	0.791	2.05
East — U = Advanced level of All	———	0.4553 (0.1685)	-0.1726 (0.0779)	3.3578 (71.93)	0.4754	14.595	2.35
	Intercept = 0	0.7279 (0.1673)	-0.1807 (0.0954)	———	0.1449	21.964	1.80
U = Advanced level of East	———	0.7704 (0.1187)	-0.1584 (0.0462)	0.7585 (52.22)	0.8130	5.203	2.81
	Intercept = 0	0.8647 (0.7874)	-0.1584 (0.0464)	———	0.5611	11.272	2.43
West — U = Advanced level of All	———	0.9817 (0.0864)	-0.1599 (0.0616)	-0.5625 (31.45)	0.9462	3.023	1.06
	Intercept = 0	0.9446 (0.0758)	-0.1494 (0.0590)	———	0.9417	3.023	1.24
U = Advanced level of West	———	0.9176 (0.0733)	-0.1900 (0.0711)	0.4498 (35.14)	0.9550	2.529	2.51
	Intercept = 0	0.7599 (0.0535)	-0.3563 (0.0261)	———	0.9159	4.365	2.25

NOTE: The standard errors of the estimates are given in parentheses.

cases were estimated for all prefectures: one used the simple average of prefectural averages for *Y* and another used a weighted average, with the planted areas taken as weights. Hardly any difference can be observed between those cases. Also, two cases were considered for eastern and western prefectures: One used *U* values for all prefectures and another used the *U* values for eastern and western prefectures, respectively. This procedure is designed to test whether it is the nation's *U* or the region's *U* that is relevant as "best practice" technology for farmers in a region. Statistical evidence is not enough, however, to settle this problem.[32]

In all six cases the estimates of *α* and *β* have signs consistent with

---

[32] Probably, the truth lies somewhere between the extremes.

theory and are significant at the 5-percent level. On the other hand, estimates of γ are not significantly different from zero. This indicates there exists no trend in Y, which can not be explained by U and V. The estimates were repeated with the restriction that $\gamma = 0$. The results are very close to the unrestricted estimates.

With the estimates of a and β, we evaluated the contributions of U and V to the growth in Y for five periods, as shown in Table 5–2. Periods I and II correspond to the phase of initial growth, period III to the phase of succeeding stagnation, period IV to the exceptional period subject to the disturbances of the war and period V to the phase of postwar expansion. The first major phase was divided into periods I and II for reasons to be clarified below.

From Table 5–2 and Figure 5–4, we can derive evidence for our hypothesis. First, let us examine the case of all prefectures. Y had grown rapidly until it turned stagnant in 1918–22, the end of period II.[33] The growth path of U seems similar to that of Y, but it differs at a crucial point. While Y rose linearly until the end of period II, U began to decelerate in 1903–07, the end of period I. The linear rise in Y for period II, in spite of the deceleration in U, can be explained in terms of V, which began to fall in 1903–07. The decline in V ended in 1918–22 with the resulting stagnation in Y for the succeeding period. In fact, the contribution of V to the growth in Y increased from I to II, and declined from II to III.

The above observations seem to suggest that, before 1903–07, the prime factor in the rapid progress of technology is a rise in the potential of technology rather than a spread of the existing potential. This is not consistent with our hypothesis postulating that technological progress in the initial growth phase is primarily due to the backlog inherited from the feudal age. This inconsistency can be explained, however, by examining the cases of eastern and western prefectures.

In period I, the Y values of the western prefectures (Y_W) had grown much faster than the Y values of all prefectures. But it began to decelerate in 1903–07. In contrast, the Y values of eastern prefectures (Y_E) rose more rapidly in 1903–07. To a large extent, this difference is attributable to the difference in movements of V. While the V values of western prefectures (V_W) had fallen until 1903–07, when they became stagnant, the V values of eastern prefectures (V_E) had risen until 1903–07 when they began to fall.

This contrast in the ways Y_E and Y_W had grown seems to reflect what agricultural economists have called *"Inasaku gijutsu no tōzen*

---

[33] The drop in the average yield in 1893–97 is due to the severe drought which hit the western part of Japan in 1897.

TABLE 5-2

Contributions of the Changes in U and V to the Growth in Y

	Period	Growth Rates of Y $\dot{Y}$	Contributions of U $\alpha\dot{U}$	V $\beta\dot{V}$	Residual ξ
All					
$Y =$ Weighted average	I	6.0	6.0	-0.1	0
	II	5.9	3.8	2.6	0.5
	III	1.4	2.0	-0.3	-0.3
	IV	-1.6	-3.2	-0.4	2.0
	V	10.3	9.8	-0.2	2.7
$Y =$ Simple average	I	6.3	5.9	-0.1	0.5
	II	6.0	3.7	2.4	-0.1
	III	2.0	2.0	-0.3	0.3
	IV	-2.6	-3.0	-0.4	0.8
	V	8.9	9.4	-0.2	-0.3
East					
$U =$ Advanced level of All	I	4.0	4.4	-1.7	1.3
	II	9.1	2.7	3.4	3.0
	III	2.0	1.5	-1.6	2.1
	IV	1.1	-2.3	0.5	2.9
	V	8.9	7.1	-0.3	2.1
$U =$ Advanced level of East	I	4.0	5.1	-1.5	0.4
	II	9.1	5.2	2.9	1.0
	III	2.0	2.2	-1.4	1.2
	IV	1.2	1.4	0.4	-0.6
	V	8.9	9.4	-0.3	-0.2
West					
$U =$ Advanced level of All	I	7.8	5.7	1.5	0.6
	II	4.3	3.6	0.6	0.1
	III	1.9	1.9	0	0
	IV	-5.0	-3.0	-1.3	-0.7
	V	8.5	9.1	1.6	-2.2
$U =$ Advanced level of West	I	7.8	4.3	3.4	0.1
	II	4.3	3.1	1.5	-0.3
	III	1.9	1.4	0.1	0.4
	IV	-5.0	-3.9	-3.0	1.9
	V	8.5	5.1	3.9	-0.5

NOTE: 1.   Period   I: 1883-87--1903-07   II: 1803-1907--1918-22
          III: 1918-22--1933-37   IV: 1933-37--1943-47
          V: 1943-47--1957-62

2.   Estimates of α and β used here are those obtained under the restriction that $\gamma = 0$ in Table 5-1.

(eastward movement in rice farming technology)." This refers to the process in which the backward districts caught up with and surpassed the traditionally advanced western districts. The backlog of traditional technology had been concentrated among the veteran farmers in such advanced districts as North Kyūshū and Kinki. With the Meiji reforms the accumulated potential started to diffuse among the surrounding districts. This must have reduced V_W and raised Y_W. The diffusion toward the distant eastern districts lagged, however. At the beginning only pioneering farmers in the relatively advanced districts in the east tried to transplant the advanced techniques. In other words, the diffusion of the advanced technology was not uniform among the eastern prefectures in the earlier periods. This must have resulted in the rise in V_E. It was approximately 1903–07 when diffusion among eastern prefectures had reached a stage at which V_E began to fall.

More concrete evidence is available. Figure 5–5 (data in Appendix Table 5A–5) shows the changes in the percentage of total rice area planted in the form of major improved varieties. It clearly indicates that the linear growth in Y for 1890–1920 coincides with the rise in the area planted in what we call *Rōnō* varieties.[34] They are the varieties which were selected by farmers rather than by agronomists in the experiment stations.[35] With the abolition of feudal restraints by the Meiji restoration, a spontaneous movement started among farmers to exchange seed varieties through *Shushi kōkan-kai* (society for exchanging seeds) or *Nōdan-kai* (society for discussing farming matters). This worked, in effect, as a nationwide competition of traditional varieties. From them, the so-called *Zenkoku tōitsu hinshu* (national standard varieties) such as Shinriki and Kameno-o were selected through a trial and error process by the farmers. Those varieties had, in common, characteristics necessary for Japanese agricultural development. Above all, they gave higher yields by absorbing larger quantities of fertilizer.

Regional patterns in the spread of *Rōnō* varieties are also consistent with movements in Y and V. In western prefectures, *Rōnō* varieties

---

[34] *Rōnō* varieties do not include improved varieties which did not spread widely and, hence, did not obtain nationwide recognition. The later the period, the more will be the percentage of area planted in such local improved varieties. For this reason, the growth in area planted in *Rōnō* varieties before 1890 would not adequately represent the rate of diffusion of improved varieties.

[35] This is not to deny that those varieties were improved and publicized by the agronomists in the experiment stations. The later the period, the more was the contribution of the agronomists to the improvement and diffusion of the varieties selected by the *Rōnō*. It is somewhat arbitrary to draw a demarcation between the *Rōnō* varieties and the experiment station varieties.

FIGURE 5–5. Percentages of Total Rice Area Planted in Major Improved Varieties.

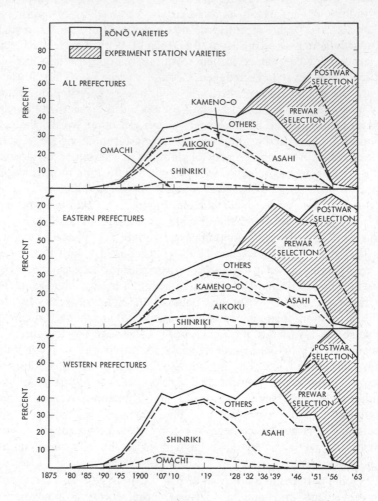

had been selected earlier and spread very rapidly until the end of period I, and then became stagnant. By contrast, in the eastern prefectures their percentage continued to grow until they were replaced by the varieties selected in the experiment stations.

In period III, the area planted in improved varieties (*Rōnō* varieties and experiment station varieties combined) began to show another rapid growth. Nevertheless, *Y* did not show a similar rise. This must be due to the exhaustion of the initial backlog. In order to raise *Y* when the backlog is used up, it is necessary to raise *U* by investing in research and development. The spread of the experiment station varieties represents the fruits of this kind of investment. But, the return to R and D investments, which had seemed very high when the backlog had existed, must have been found rather meager when it disappeared.[36]

We will now turn to the phase of the postwar expansion. The remarkable features of the growth in Y in period V are that it has accompanied a rise in U faster than Y and that V has been rising at the same time as Y rises. This indicates that the leading factors are different between the initial growth and the postwar spurt. While the leading factor in the former period is diffusion, in the latter it is growth in technological potential. This is consistent with the hypothesis postulated in the previous section.

RECENT TRENDS

The faster rise in U and the consequent increase in V during period V represents a slack in agricultural productivity for the years to come. By stretching out this slack, Y is expected to rise. Contrary to expectations, the nation's average rice yield per unit of planted area has turned out to be declining somewhat since its peak in 1962.

Year	Metric tons per hectare
1962	4.07
1963	4.00
1964	3.96
1965	3.90

This is partly due to the unfavorable weather. But, more important as a cause must be the structural change taking place.

Industrial development since 1955 has been so great that the Japanese economy is now coming up to what Ohkawa has called "the first Lewis turning-point."[37] The unlimited supply of labor has ceased to exist, or labor has become a limiting factor in agriculture for the first time in modern history. Data from the *1965 Census of Agriculture* given in Table 5–3, show a dramatic reduction in the agricultural labor force. Within the past five years, the number of workers gain-

---

[36] The initial backlog included such practices as the increased application of fertilizer and the selection of seeds in salt water, besides the use of improved seeds. When the backlog was used up, the improvement in seeds (which was the product of current research expenditures) did not assure as fast a rise in productivity as it did when the backlog existed.

[37] K. Ohkawa, "Agriculture and Turning Points," *op. cit.,* p. 484.

TABLE 5-3

Changes in the Number of Workers Gainfully Occupied in Agriculture

	Age Bracket (Years)	Number in Thousands 1960 A	1965 B	$\frac{B-A}{A} \times 100$
All Workers:	16 - 59	12,003	8,982	-25.2
	Over 60	2,538	2,532	- 0.2
	Total	14,541	14,514	-20.8
Male Workers:	16 - 59	4,645	3,276	-29.5
	Over 60	1,350	1,290	- 4.4
	Total	5,995	4,566	-23.8
Female Workers:	16 - 59	7,358	5,707	-22.4
	Over 60	1,188	1,242	4.5
	Total	8,546	6,949	-18.7

SOURCE: *1965 Chūkan Nōgyō census Kekka Gaiyō (Summary of the 1965 Intermediate Census of Agriculture)*, Statistics and Research Division, Ministry of Agriculture and Forestry, December, 1965.

fully occupied in agriculture decreased by as much as 3 million. Equally serious is the deterioration in the quality of the labor force. Almost all the 3 million are workers from 18 to 59 years old. Male workers are leaving agriculture more rapidly than female workers. Consequently percentages of female workers and of workers over 60 years old are increasing.

The decline in the absolute number and deterioration in the quality of workers have been shaking the very basis of agricultural productivity in Japan, namely the labor-intensive and land-productivity-increasing technology. Still, a new system of technology oriented for laborsaving has not been established yet. In this transitory period it must be the slack in productivity in the form of the gap between Y and U which is protecting Y from its sharp decline. In order to maintain agricultural productivity, it will be necessary to establish a new system of technology before the gap will be closed.

CONCLUSION

In this study, the chronology of technological progress in Japanese agriculture was explained in terms of the accumulation and diffusion of knowledge and techniques. An important source of technique for initial growth was identified as the backlog inherited from the pre-modern period, and that for the postwar spurt was identified as the accumulation of scientific knowledge during the war. This is not to deny the importance of investment in agricultural research, extension, and rural education. Without them, the potential might, to a large extent, have remained as mere potential. But, without the potential, those investments would have turned out to be far less fruitful.

Does this imply a dark prospect for agricultural development in the underdeveloped nations which may not seem to possess such potential? On the contrary, those nations can utilize as their backlog the vast amount of knowledge and techniques accumulated in the advanced nations. In many cases, however, social and institutional reforms which release the suppressed energy of the people will be a prerequisite. Unless this prerequisite is met, current outlays in education and research will merely produce frustrated intellectuals who do not contribute much to economic growth. Japan made such reforms at the Meiji restoration. They were successful in setting Japanese agriculture for the takeoff, which came through the exploitation of the backlog inherited from the premodern period. This implication of social and institutional reforms must be kept in mind when we try to derive lessons from the Japanese experience.

Appendix

TABLE 5A-1

Movements in Output and Inputs, 1878-1962
(Million Yen at 1934-36 Price, Except as Otherwise Indicated)

Periods	Gross Output	Labor (Million Persons)	Land (Million Chos)	Fixed Capital	Current Inputs	Nonconventional Input
1878-82. . . .	1,413	14.66	4.78	4,617	224	
1883-87. . . .	1,587	14.48	4.86	4,640	225	22
1888-92. . . .	1,725	14.30	4.97	4,691	237	19
1893-97. . . .	1,793	14.20	5.07	4,808	258	23
1898-1902. . .	1,985	14.20	5.24	4,912	289	45
1903-07. . . .	2,166	14.08	5.35	5,034	313	45
1908-12. . . .	2,421	14.00	5.62	5,303	388	81
1913-17. . . .	2,771	13.95	5.83	5,473	433	94
1918-22. . . .	2,863	13.94	6.03	5,597	497	115
1923-27. . . .	2,918	13.94	5.98	5,728	560	215
1928-32. . . .	3,147	13.92	6.03	5,984	635	244
1933-37. . . .	3,300	13.75	6.16	6,107	679	230
1938-42. . . .	3,329	13.54	6.16	6,099	714	263
1943-47. . . .	2,768	13.93	5.91	5,648	405	378
1948-52. . . .	3,083	15.88	5.91	6,064	714	489
1953-57. . . .	3,722	15.17	6.03	6,910	995	735
1958-62. . . .	4,582	13.38	6.13	8,308	1,449	

NOTES: 1.   All series except nonconventional input will be compiled in K. Ohkawa *et al.* (eds.), *Estimates of Long-Term Economic
Statistics of Japan since 1868*, Vol. 9 (Tokyo: Toyokeizaishinposha,
1966).   For details and basic data of estimations, see Section II
of Ohkawa, *et al.*, *ibid.*
   2.   Gross output is gross value produced.   Output series at 1934-
36 price was obtained by deflating current values by a price index in
Ohkawa, *et al.*, *ibid.*
   3.   Labor series are the number of gainfully occupied.
   4.   Land area consists of paddy field and upland field.   I Cho =
0.99174 hectares.
   5.   Fixed capital is the real net capital stock employed on farms.
It consists of machinery and implements, trees and shrubs, livestock,
and farm buildings.
   6.   Current inputs consist of fertilizer, seeds, feed, agricultural chemicals, etc.
   7.   Nonconventional input data from S. Yamada, "Changes in Output
and in Conventional and Nonconventional Inputs in Japanese Agriculture
since 1880," *The Food Research Institute Studies* (Stanford, Calif.:
Stanford University, forthcoming).   The series contain the outlay by both
central and local governments for agricultural research, extension,
public service, infrastructure, and rural education.   Periods 1878-
82 and 1958-62 were not estimated.   For details of estimations, see
Yamada, *ibid.*

TABLE 5A-2

Indices of Output, Aggregate Input, and
Productivity, 1879-1962
(1878-82 = 100)

Periods	Gross Output	Aggregate Input	Total Productivity	Land Productivity	Rice Yield per Tan
1878-82. . . .	100.0	100.0	100.0	100.0	100.0
1883-87. . . .	112.3	100.2	112.1	110.3	108.3
1888-92. . . .	122.1	101.1	120.7	117.5	119.2
1893-97. . . .	126.9	103.3	122.8	119.5	114.2
1898-1902. . .	140.5	106.7	131.7	128.2	126.7
1903-07. . . .	153.3	109.0	140.6	136.8	135.8
1908-12. . . .	171.3	116.5	147.1	145.6	144.2
1913-17. . . .	196.1	121.3	161.7	160.6	153.3
1918-22. . . .	202.6	127.4	159.1	160.4	160.8
1923-27. . . .	206.5	130.2	158.6	165.0	156.7
1928-32. . . .	222.7	134.1	166.1	176.6	159.2
1933-37. . . .	233.6	136.0	171.7	181.2	167.5
1938-42. . . .	235.6	136.5	172.7	182.7	170.0
1943-47. . . .	195.9	124.3	157.7	158.3	162.5
1948-52. . . .	218.2	142.3	153.4	176.5	180.0
1953-57. . . .	263.4	152.3	173.0	208.8	187.5
1958-62. . . .	324.3	164.8	196.7	252.9	216.7

NOTES: 1. Gross output index is the index of gross output series in Table 5A-1 taking 1878-82 as the base.
2. Aggregate input index is the linear aggregate of conventional inputs such as labor, land, fixed capital, and current inputs, weighted by 1884-86 factor prices for 1878-1922, 1934-36 factor prices for 1923-47, 1955 factor prices for 1948-62. For details of computation, see Ohkawa *et al.* (eds.), *Estimates of Long-Term Economic Statistics of Japan since 1868*, Vol. 9 (Tokyo: Toyokeizaishinposha, 1966).
3. Total productivity index is the index of the ratio of gross output to aggregate input.
4. Land productivity index is the index of gross value produced divided by cultivated land area.
5. Rice yield data from Table 5A-3 of this paper. It is the official series of the government statistics, while rice yield used for the construction of gross output index are revised for the period 1878-90. The difference is, however, slight and does not affect our conclusion.

TABLE 5A-3

Averages and Variations of Rice Yields among Prefectures

Periods	Averages Y (Koku/Tan)				Advanced Levels U (Koku/Tan)			Coefficient of Variation V		
	All Prefectures		East Prefec-tures Simple	West Prefec-tures Simple	All Prefec-tures	East Prefec-tures	West Prefec-tures	All Prefec-tures	East Prefec-tures	West Prefec-tures
	Weighted	Simple								
1883-87. . . .	1.30	1.30	1.23	1.34	1.68	1.42	1.74	0.163	0.109	0.180
1888-92. . . .	1.43	1.43	1.36	1.48	1.85	1.58	1.89	0.155	0.111	0.165
1893-97. . . .	1.37	1.39	1.39	1.39	1.75	1.67	1.77	0.147	0.129	0.158
1898-1902. . .	1.52	1.53	1.42	1.59	1.94	1.80	1.99	0.156	0.151	0.143
1903-07. . . .	1.63	1.65	1.44	1.79	2.11	1.77	2.15	0.168	0.155	0.121
1908-12. . . .	1.73	1.76	1.57	1.89	2.20	1.86	2.26	0.143	0.112	0.111
1913-17. . . .	1.84	1.88	1.71	1.99	2.31	2.00	2.37	0.128	0.108	0.105
1918-22. . . .	1.93	1.96	1.87	2.02	2.35	2.11	2.42	0.106	0.081	0.107
1923-27. . . .	1.88	1.91	1.87	1.94	2.27	2.14	2.29	0.101	0.079	0.109
1928-32. . . .	1.91	1.98	1.93	2.02	2.37	2.19	2.44	0.104	0.092	0.106
1933-37. . . .	2.01	2.08	1.98	2.14	2.49	2.27	2.55	0.111	0.104	0.105
1938-42. . . .	2.04	2.09	2.12	2.06	2.45	2.45	2.42	0.111	0.101	0.117
1943-47. . . .	1.95	1.97	2.02	1.93	2.34	2.34	2.29	0.116	0.099	0.124
1948-52. . . .	2.16	2.15	2.26	2.08	2.47	2.52	2.35	0.093	0.069	0.094
1953-57. . . .	2.25	2.24	2.31	2.18	2.65	2.73	2.42	0.103	0.112	0.087
1958-62. . . .	2.60	2.53	2.64	2.46	3.07	3.18	2.77	0.116	0.136	0.086

NOTES: 1. Eastern prefectures: Aomori, Iwate, Miyagi, Akita, Yamagata, Fukushima, Ibaragi, Tochigi, Gunma, Chiba, Saitama, Tokyo, Kanagawa, Niigata, Nagano, Yamanashi, Shizuoka, Aichi. Western prefectures: Toyama, Ishikawa, Fukui, Gifu, Mie, Shiga, Kyoto, Osaka, Hyogo, Nara, Wakayama, Tottori, Shimane, Okayama, Hiroshima, Yamaguchi, Tokushima, Kagawa, Ehime, Kochi, Fukuoka, Saga, Nagasaki, Kumamoto, Oita, Miyazaki, Kagoshima.

2. All prefectures include Hokkaido.

3. Advanced level: All prefectures = Simple average of upper five prefectures. Eastern prefectures = Simple average of upper three prefectures. Western prefectures = Simple average of upper three prefectures.

4. Coefficient of variation is the unweighted standard deviation divided by the unweighted mean.

5. 1 Koku ≡ 150 Kilograms, 1 Tan = 0.099174 hectare.

SOURCE: Data are from Statistical Year Book of Ministry of Agriculture and Forestry (formerly Ministry of Agriculture and Commerce).

TABLE 5A-4

Areas Planted in Rice by Varieties: Eastern Prefectures
(1,000 Cho)

	1875	1880	1885	1890	1895	1900	1907	1910	1919	1928	1932	1936	1939	1946	1951	1956	1963
Rōnō varieties																	
Aikoku					4	23	143	142	176	253	249	221	197	97	149		
Asahi									1	38	73	95	111	152	123	276	55
Kameno-o . . .							17	52	133	121	70	21	12	6	3		
Omachi							1	3									
Shinriki					2	27	80	82	110	63	34	28	22	7			
Others																	
Bozu					3	22	67	66	61	131	203	209	148	28	31		
Gin-bozu . . .										35	72	92	81	29	37		
Ishiziro . . .					1	5	15	17	25	15	12	3	2	17	14		
Ōba							4	4	5	4	3						
Takenari . . .			1	3	7	19	37	29	5								
Experiment station varieties																	
Prewar selection																	
Norin numbers .											11	73	179	370	383	276	55
Rikuu-132 . .											121	212	210	62	63	19	
Others.											5	15	55	54	47	222	64
Postwar selection																	
Norin numbers .														18	157	462	740
Others															28	217	274
Major improved varieties total. .			1	3	17	96	364	395	516	660	853	969	1,017	840	1,035	1,213	1,133
Traditional varieties.	1,150	1,187	1,192	1,228	1,224	1,152	922	923	858	826	696	558	436	547	451	389	556
Total	1,150	1,187	1,193	1,231	1,241	1,248	1,286	1,318	1,374	1,486	1,549	1,527	1,453	1,387	1,486	1,602	1,689

TABLE 5A-4 (Continued)

Areas Planted in Rice by Varieties: Western Prefectures
(1,000 Cho)

	1875	1880	1885	1890	1895	1900	1907	1910	1919	1928	1932	1936	1939	1946	1951	1956	1963
Rōno varieties																	
Aikoku									21	54	86	86	79	38	62		
Asahi									12	81	296	435	481	285	296	40	
Omachi		3	5	7	12	41	122	113	96	40	28	17	9		3		
Shinriki	1	1	10	28	72	211	440	441	500	318	171	68	49	28	30		
Others																	
Gin-Bōzu . . .									6	28	62	80	57	29	23		
Ishiziro. . . .			1	4	7	14	25	19	13	15	16	14	15	10			
Kameji								3	21	26	37	29	24	7	9		
Ōba					2	18	45	51	52	29	22	5	2				
Takenari . . .					1	3	14	7	8								
Experiment station varieties																	
Prewar selection																	
Norin numbers .												42	79	330	394	320	125
Rikuu-132 . . .													1	1	8		
Others.														5	46	321	142
Postwar selection																	
Norin numbers .														1	104	338	475
Others.															14	144	176
Major improved varieties total	1	4	16	39	94	287	646	634	729	591	718	776	796	734	989	1,163	918
Traditional varieties	1,338	1,378	1,364	1,442	1,390	1,213	888	918	836	953	824	734	679	598	426	320	552
Total	1,339	1,382	1,380	1,481	1,484	1,500	1,534	1,552	1,565	1,544	1,542	1,510	1,475	1,332	1,415	1,483	1,470

TABLE 5A-4 (Concluded)

NOTES: 1. The classification of prefectures between Eastern and Western regions is the same as in Table 5A-3.
2. Areas planted in individual varieties in original data are grouped into the specified varieties by prefectures, which are aggregated into Eastern and Western regions.
3. Areas planted in respective varieties are assumed to increase linearly from the years of their selection to 1907 by prefectures._ _
4. Rono varieties include varieties which were_improved by experiment stations after their selections by the Rono (veteran farmers).
5. Traditional varieties include improved varieties which cannot be specified here.

SOURCES: Ministry of agriculture and forestry, *Suito-hinshu no hensen to ikusei-hinshu no tokusei narabini fukyu-jokyo no Gaiyo (Summary Report on Changes in Rice Varieties and the Characteristics and Diffusions of Improved Varieties)*, 1953.

_____, *Suito-hinshu betsu Sakuzuke Menseki Chosasho — 1951 — (Survey Report on Area Planted in Respective Rice Varieties in 1951)*, 1952.

_____, *Ine Mugi Hinshu no Tokuseihyo (Tables of Characteristics of Rice, Wheat, Barley and Naked Barley)*, 1955.

_____, *Suirikuto Mugirui Shorethinshu Tokuseihyo (Tables of Characteristics of Selected Rice, Wheat, Barley and Naked Barley)*, 1964.

Nogyo Hattatsushi Chosakai, Meiji-iko ni okeru Suito-hinshu no Hensen (Changes in Rice Varieties since Meiji Era), 1955.

6 | Foreign Trade and Economic Growth in Japan: 1858–1937*

MASAO BABA and MASAHIRO TATEMOTO

> . . . *the resources of Japan, when developed by the action of free trade, would show a vast amount of exchangeable values . . .*
>
> —*Townsend Harris*

INTRODUCTION

No nation could compare with Japan before and after July 4, 1859, when it eventually opened its door to the rest of the world after 200 years' national seclusion. Japan is an excellent example of a sharp contrast between a closed economy of stagnation and an open economy of rapid growth. If the Japanese economy flew like a wild bird from an opened cage after the opening of the country, it is not unreasonable to expect Japan's foreign trade to have been one of the propelling engines. This paper attempts to evaluate the contribution of foreign trade to the rapid growth of the Japanese economy.

In Section I we shall examine the initial conditions in existence prior to the Meiji Restoration. We will be concerned in Section II with the economic growth process in the period 1868–96. This process is considered to be growth through export of traditional semimanufactured products[1] and through import substituting industrialization.

---

* This study has been financed by a grant from the Harvard-Yenching Institute through the Japan Council for East Asian Studies. The authors wish to express their gratitude to the Institute and the Council. Grateful acknowledgment is due to Mr. Michael Birch for correcting the English; to the Misses Misako Tsuji, Tomoko Matsumoto, and Kyōko Motoda for research and clerical services; and last but not least, to Professor Hideo Aoyama, the director, Kyoto Institute of Economic Research, for organizing this study.

[1] See Section II (*a*) (*ii*).

In Section III, we will be concerned with economic growth in the period 1897–1937, especially as a pattern of growth through export of manufactured consumer goods (cotton textiles in the case of Japan).

As there are no official published statistics of Japan's balance of payments for the period 1868–1901, we have made our own estimates for this period after having corrected the valuation of import statistics for the period prior to 1881. The results are listed and explained by one of the authors in the *Statistical Appendix* (p. 183).

I. TRADE PRIOR TO THE MEIJI RESTORATION: 1858–67

A. *Initial Conditions: 1858*

The conditions under which Japanese trade was started had been provided in the 1858 treaties of commerce signed in succession between the Shogunate and five powers; namely, United States, Holland, Russia, England, and France. Our main concern with these treaties is in their treatment of exchange rate, extraterritoriality, and lack of tariff autonomy.

1. Exchange Rate. At the time the treaties were signed, both gold and silver *ryo* were in circulation, and it was agreed that "the equivalent content of the equivalent metal" should have been at par. In other words, the exchange rate between "gold dollar" and "gold *ryo*" and that between "silver dollar" and "silver *ryo*" were determined. One "silver dollar" was equivalent in content to ¾ "silver *ryo*," while one "gold dollar" was equivalent to one "gold *ryo*." This inconsistent system of exchange rates was a consequence of the disparity between the domestic ratio of exchange (1 gold to 6 silver in weight) and the international ratio (1 gold to 15 silver). The domestic ratio was higher as a result of the Shogunate policy of seclusion. Well-informed foreigners "rushed" to bring in "silver dollars," to exchange for "silver *ryos*" and then convert "silver *ryos*" into "gold *ryos*" to make arbitrage profits.[2] The actual situation favored the dollar which was exchanged at a premium of 311 *quarter ryos* for $100, i.e., 77.75 *ryos* for $100. These 77.75 *ryos* in silver were exchanged for the same amount of gold *ryos* which were worth from $230 to $344 (!), depending upon the specific gold *ryo* coins to be exchanged.[3] By the time

---

[2] The U.S. Consul-General Townsend Harris cheerfully wrote, in his diary on that date when this agreement was made in 1855, that the United States would pay only $34.5 for things that had previously cost $100.

[3] K. Yamaguchi, *Bakumatsu Boeki Shi* (A History of Foreign Trade at the End of Tokugawa Era) (Tokyo: Chuo Koron Sha, 1943), pp. 123 ff.

the Shogunate devalued the gold content of the *ryo* to be equivalent to the international ratio in early 1860, approximately one million *ryos* of gold are said to have been taken out of the country, and a substantial portion of accumulated gold reserves were exhausted.

2. *Extraterritoriality.* The second factor resulting from the same imprudence and ignorance of Shogunate officials was the establishment of extraterritoriality or consular jurisdiction. It was only in 1899 after 41 years of negotiation by Meiji diplomats that these unequal treaties were abolished. It was this struggle for the abolition of extraterritoriality that became a force behind Japanese modernization. There followed the establishment of a modern legislative system and modernized industry, business practice, education, and armed forces.

3. *Lack of Tariff Autonomy.* The treaties in 1858 deprived Japan of tariff autonomy. The treaty in 1866 fixed most duties unilaterally at the low rate of 5 percent *ad valorem* until the general tariff was revised in 1911, following the recovery of autonomy in 1899. Even in 1858, the import duties on cotton and woolen textile goods were as low as 5 percent at a time when England had a comparative advantage in world trade.

The Meiji government had to rely more heavily on a land tax than might otherwise have been necessary, but a more important consequence of these low duties was that Japan had to participate in the international division of labor with little protective measures, and specialized in the lines of production in which it had comparative advantage in textbook fashion.

B. Trade before the Restoration: 1859–67

There have been a number of attempts to estimate the export and import figures for the nine years subsequent to the opening of three ports in 1859. Table 6–1 shows Ishii's estimate[4] which we consider to be the most reliable among the estimates. Table 6–1 also shows the main items of exports and imports at the port of Yokohama, after 1860, together with their percentage shares. As this port handled nearly 80 percent of the total trade, these shares approximately represent the composition of Japanese total exports and imports at that time.

1. According to Table 6–1, trade grew rapidly in these nine years, the rates of growth of exports and imports being about 15 percent per

---

[4] T. Ishii, *Bakumatsu Boeki Shi no Kenkyu* (Studies in the History of Foreign Trade at the End of Tokugawa Era) (Tokyo: Nippon Hyoron Sha, 1944), pp. 50–54.

TABLE 6-1

Foreign Trade of Japan: 1859-1867

Year	Total Export ($000)	Percentage Silk (%)	Share Tea (%)	Total Import ($000)	Percentage Share Cotton Textile (%)	Woolen Textile (%)	Trade Balance ($000)
1859.	891			603			288
1860.	4,713	56	8	1,659	53	40	3,054
1861.	3,787	62	17	2,365	56	23	1,422
1862.	7,279	81	14	3,882	50	30	3,397
1863.	12,208	83	5	6,199	--	--	6,009
1864.	10,572	69	5	8,102	--	--	2,470
1865.	18,490	84	10	15,144	36	44	3,346
1866.	16,617	--	--	15,771	--	--	846
1867.	12,124	54	17	21,673	25	22	Δ9,550

SOURCE: T. Ishii, *Bakumatsu Boeki Shi no Kenkyu* (Studies in the History of Foreign Trade at the end of Tokugawa Era) (Tokyo: Nippon Hyoron Sha, 1944), pp. 50-54.

annum. In spite of the Shogunate's policy of discouraging silk exports from 1860 until 1864, and of prohibiting silkworm egg exports until 1865, total exports increased throughout this period. This somewhat strange policy of export discouragement was based on the absurd but firmly held belief that exports would decrease the total quantity of commodities available for home use. The exports were considered to be the cause of severe inflation which was experienced in the Japanese economy at the end of the Tokugawa era. The same belief made lower class samurai join the "expel the Western barbarians" movement and threaten or exert physical pressure against foreign and Japanese merchants engaged in foreign trade.

2. According to Table 6–1, exports consist of such traditional semimanufactured products as silk and tea; the percentage share of these two items taken together amounts to about 80 percent, on average, of total exports.

Imports consist of manufactured goods such as cotton and woolen textiles, the percentage share of these two items taken together amounts to 70 percent, on average.

3. The trade balance, according to Table 6–1, has been in favor of Japan, until 1865. In 1867, however, sizable import deficits are observed.

II. GROWTH THROUGH IMPORT SUBSTITUTION: 1868–96

A. *Import Deficit: 1868–81*

To gain a clear understanding of the import deficit, it must be realized that there is a problem in the valuation of imports in the official trade statistics. Prior to 1887, imports were valued by the prices in the exporting countries converted into yen. Silver yen or dollars were, however, widely used in international transactions, and it can be said that Japan was, in reality, on a bimetallic standard. After 1873, when Germany and other Western countries changed to the gold standard, silver currencies, including the yen, continued to depreciate against gold currencies. Thus, it is necessary to correct the official import statistics (in terms of gold yen) from gold standard countries for the depreciation of the silver yen. One of us has made this correction for the period 1874–87, according to the procedures explained in the *Statistical Appendix, Section I.*

Two facts that characterize trade in the period 1868–81 are an import deficit and the pattern of trading traditional semimanufactured goods for imported manufactures.

1. Import Deficit.   Table 6–2 represents the movement in exports and imports (before and after the correction) during the period 1868–96. Political and economic confusion (caused by a civil war to restore a young emperor to power) and the crop failure in 1869 and 1870 resulted in a sharp increase in imports just after the Restoration. During the subsequent 11 years, exports increased more slowly than imports. As a result, the overall trade balance for the first 14 years after the Restoration showed a big import deficit. In view of the fact that imports were valued at f.o.b. prices in the exporting countries, we might suspect that the balance-of-payments gap would have been even greater if we could take freight, insurance, and other invisible

TABLE 6-2

Foreign Trade of Japan: 1868-1896
(In Thousands of Yen)

Year	Export	Import (Official)	Import (Corrected)	Trade Balance (Official)	Trade Balance (Corrected)	Volume Index (1913 = 100) Export	Volume Index (1913 = 100) Import
1868.	15,553	10,6,93		4,860		(4)	(4)
1869.	12,909	20,784		Δ 7,875		(3)	(6)
1870.	14,543	33,742		Δ19,199		(3)	(9)
1871.	17,969	21,917		Δ 3,948		(4)	(5)
1872.	17,027	26,175		Δ 9,148		(4)	(6)
1873.	21,635	28,107		Λ 6,472		5	6
1874.	19,317	23,462	(24,487)	Δ 4,145	(Δ 5,170)	6	6
1875.	18,611	29,976	(31,899)	Δ11,365	(Δ13,288)	6	7
1876.	27,712	23,965	(26,544)	3,747	(1,168)	8	7
1877.	23,349	27,421	(29,979)	Δ 4,072	(Δ 6,630)	8	7
1870.	25,988	32,874	(37,722)	Δ 6,887	(Δ11,365)	9	9
1879.	28,176	32,953	(38,015)	Δ 4,777	(Δ 9,839)	8	10
1880.	28,395	36,627	(42,240)	Λ 8,231	(Δ13,850)	8	11
1881.	31,059	31,191	(35,767)	Δ 132	(Δ 4,708)	9	10
1882.	37,722	29,447	(33,354)	8,275	(4,367)	11	10
1883.	36,268	28,445	(32,449)	7,823	(3,819)	12	10
1884.	33,871	29,673	(33,617)	4,199	(254)	11	10
1885.	37,147	29,357	(33,499)	7,790	(3,648)	11	10
1886.	48,876	32,168	(37,364)	16,708	(11,512)	14	11
1887.	52,408	44,304	(53,153)	8,103	(Δ 745)	15	15
1888.	65,706	65,455		205		20	19
1889.	70,061	66,104		3,957		20	19
1890.	56,604	81,729		Δ25,125		15	24
1891.	79,527	62,927		16,600		23	19
1892.	91,103	71,326		19,777		22	22
1893.	89,713	88,257		1,456		21	24
1894.	113,246	117,482		Δ 4,236		25	26
1895.	136,112	129,261		6,851		27	29
1896.	117,843	171,674		Δ53,831		24	38

SOURCE: The Oriental Economist, *Foreign Trade of Japan, A Statistical Survey* (Tokyo: The Oriental Economist, 1935). The figures in parentheses are our own estimates and Δ stands for negative magnitudes. The corrections of import statistics are based on the method suggested by Y. Horie, *Meiji Ishin to Keizai Kindaika* (The Meiji Restoration and the Modernization of Japanese Economy) (Tokyo: Shibundo, 1964). See Statistical Appendix, Section I.

items into consideration. Moreover, government imports of such items as weapons, ships, railroad equipment, and general plant and equipments were not included in customs statistics. In addition to these balance-of-payments items on current account, two kinds of government bond issues in the London market in the early years are well known. The above-mentioned facts have led one of the authors to carry out a study in econometric history in order to secure annual estimates of individual items in the balance of payments of Japan for the period 1868–1902. The results are listed in a standardized accounting form in Table 6A–2 in the *Statistical Appendix*. Items in Table 6–3 were computed from Table 6A–2. A cursory glance at Table 6–3 will reveal a greater payment gap on current account and also on basic balance (i.e., current transactions *plus* long-term capital movements) for the first five years. How were these deficits financed? Our conjecture for the first five years is that they were financed by the outflow of old gold and silver coins. Unfortunately, there is no statistical information on gold and silver movements in the earliest four years of the Meiji era, but information on the stock of old gold and silver coins at the end of 1868 is available. The difference between this amount (140,276,000 yen) and the peak in 1872 of the new gold and silver coin stock (54,812,000 yen) reprocessed by the mint in accordance with the New Currency Act, 1870, is equal to

TABLE 6-3

External Balances: 1868–1881
(In Thousands of Yen)

Year	Trade Balance	Balance on Current Account	Basic Balance	Gold and Silver Movement
1868.	4,860	3,474	3,823	n.a.
1869.	Δ 7,875	Δ 12,659	Δ 13,083	n.a.
1870.	Δ 19,199	Δ 28,533	Δ 24,549	n.a.
1871.	Δ 3,948	Δ 9,735	Δ 9,914	n.a.
1872.	Δ 9,148	Δ 17,153	Δ 20,233	789
1873.	Δ 6,472	Δ 15,867	Δ 4,783	2,042
1874.	Δ 5,170	Δ 20,220	Δ 20,735	12,923
1875.	Δ 13,288	Δ 24,487	Δ 25,231	15,222
1876.	1,168	Δ 7,523	Δ 8,271	3,258
1877.	Δ 6,630	Δ 15,601	Δ 16,375	8,007
1878.	Δ 11,734	Δ 21,141	Δ 21,970	6,917
1879.	Δ 9,839	Δ 18,926	Δ 19,849	10,444
1880.	Δ 13,850	Δ 23,237	Δ 24,225	10,723
1881.	Δ 4,708	Δ 12,255	Δ 13,514	6,075
Total	Δ105,833	Δ223,863	Δ218,909	76,402

85,464,000 yen. This amount corresponds to the accumulated balance-of-payments deficits: 1869–72 (△ 67,779,000). Assuming the validity of our conjecture, we might say that Japan in the initial phase of development was more fortunate than contemporary underdeveloped countries, in the sense that it inherited a substantial amount of international reserves from the pre-Meiji era.

2. *Pattern of Trade.* Table 6–4 shows the percentage shares of the main commodities exported and imported. The share of the two largest items (silk and tea) amounts to 33–64 percent of total imports. Thus, we observe here the pattern of trading traditional semimanufactured products for manufactured goods. By *traditional semimanufactured products,* we mean handicraft products from farm households. As shown in Table 6–5, the predominance of hand-reeled over machine-reeled silk was present until 1893. The first machine to manufacture tea was not introduced until 1898.

B. Industrialization through Import Substitution: 1876–96

The Meiji government which had to depend for most of its revenue on the issue of inconvertible paper money and land tax, with no protective duty to shelter its infant industry, initiated industrialization by venturing into state enterprises in a large variety of industrial activities. It should be noted that this venture of government was done in the face of a great flood of imported manufactured goods, mostly cotton and woolen textiles, with the consequent result that sizable import deficits persisted, as we have observed in the previous section. Not all the government enterprises were started for the purpose of import substitution. "Wealthy country, military strength" was the slogan of the Meiji government. It established several arsenals, shipyards, and powder mills under the second part of the slogan. Some social overhead investments including railway, telegraph, telephone, postal services, and the opening of mines were made under the slogan as a whole. It is evident, however, that the government's investments and loans in cotton spinning, silk reeling, and other consumer goods industries were made under the first part of the slogan. "Wealthy country" in the eyes of mercantilistic bureaucrats in the Meiji government, meant the prevention of a gold and silver drain by replacing imports with homemade manufactured goods, and by stimulating the export of traditional semimanufactured products.

1. *Import Substitution.* For the largest item in imports, cotton textiles, import substitution was advanced by establishing two model factories using British technology, by selling government imported

TABLE 6-4

Composition of Imports and Exports: 1868-1881
(Percent)

Year	Imports				Exports		
	Cotton Yarn Fabrics	Woolen Textiles	Rice and Sugar	Machine and Metal Products	Raw Silk	Silkworm Egg	Tea
1868	35.38	18.22	12.37	12.03	40.40	23.87	23.02
1869	29.07	11.33	29.12	4.98	44.31	19.37	16.28
1870	22.24	7.99	52.29	1.57	29.42	17.67	31.02
1871	41.27	17.73	19.59	3.56	44.54	7.15	26.00
1872	39.05	27.57	6.46	3.18	30.57	13.20	24.82
1873	32.06	25.12	7.85	5.28	33.32	14.16	21.53
1874	38.27	13.34	11.16	8.54	27.45	3.79	37.54
1875	30.37	19.27	11.50	11.51	29.15	2.55	36.88
1876	37.81	17.09	11.60	7.61	47.62	6.86	19.68
1877	30.20	17.67	10.18	12.87	41.23	1.49	18.74
1878	37.15	16.49	8.79	8.56	30.36	2.50	16.48
1879	36.22	16.08	10.92	7.85	34.55	2.07	26.22
1880	36.10	15.81	10.83	10.74	30.31	3.49	26.41
1881	39.46	13.92	12.39	8.99	34.28	1.00	22.61

SOURCE: The Oriental Economist, *Foreign Trade of Japan, A Statistical Survey* (Tokyo: The Oriental Economist, 1935).

TABLE 6-5

Percentage Share
of Hand-Reeled Silk in Total Silk Production

```
1890. . . . . . . . . . . . . . . . . . 59
1891. . . . . . . . . . . . . . . . . . 61
1892. . . . . . . . . . . . . . . . . . 55
1893. . . . . . . . . . . . . . . . . . 52
1894. . . . . . . . . . . . . . . . . . 43
```

SOURCE: *The 14th Statistical Yearbook
of the Empire of Japan* (Tokyo: Government
Statistical Office, 1895) Reprint (Tokyo:
Tokyo Reprint Sha, 1965).

spinning machinery to 10 private enterprises for 10 years, and by making favorable government loans to finance the import of spinning machinery by private spinners in the period 1878–84. For the second largest item, woolen textiles, import substitution was advanced by establishing a government mill using German technology to provide army and navy uniforms as early as 1876. An attempt was made at manufacturing spinning machinery at a government factory, but it failed. Machinery for making cement and glass at home were planned and succeeded in replacing imports.

2. *Export Stimulation.*   Two model silk reeling factories based on French technology were established in 1871 and 1874 to accustom workers and engineers to newly imported Western technology and to raise productivity in that industry.[5]

These factories mentioned above failed to make profits in subsequent years, and Count Matsukata, when he as Finance Minister engaged in a deflationary policy to retire inconvertible government paper at the end of 1881, decided to dispose of these assets (except a navy shipyard, a wool mill, a machine shop, and arsenals). They were, in fact, disposed of in the period 1882–93 at very low prices compared with their original costs. They went to private capitalists, who later formed the well-known Zaibatsu. In spite of the business failures among the early state enterprises, we might describe this episode as a glorious defeat of a reconnaissance force, which eventu-

---

[5] For these state enterprises which are called "Shokusan Kogyo," a good account is given in Yasuzo Horie, "Government Industries in the Early Years of the Meiji Era," *Kyoto University Economic Review,* Vol. XIV, No. 1 (January, 1939).

ally led to victory in war. As Lockwood wrote, "the State shouldered the early risks, reconnoitered the path of technological advance, and patronized many private ventures which followed on its heels."[6] In fact, after 1883, when the Osaka Spinning Company was established without any government aid, the subsequent decade witnessed the mushrooming of many purely private spinning companies which prospered. In 1885, the domestic production of cotton cloth exceeded its import, and its export exceeded its imports in 1910. In the case of cotton yarn, the first milestone was reached in 1890 when domestic production exceeded imports, and the second milestone was reached in 1897 when export exceeded imports. This successive pattern of import, domestic production, and export of an industry was plotted by Akamatsu in an impressionistic way, in his chart of "Wild-Geese-Flying Pattern of Economic Growth," shown in Figure 6–1. It is

FIGURE 6–1.   Akamatsu's Wild-Geese-Flying Pattern of Economic Growth.

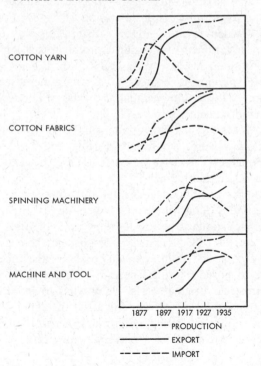

COTTON YARN

COTTON FABRICS

SPINNING MACHINERY

MACHINE AND TOOL

1877   1897   1917 1927 1935

·—·—·—· PRODUCTION

———— EXPORT

————— IMPORT

[6] W. W. Lockwood, *The Economic Development of Japan, Growth and Structural Change, 1868–1938* (Princeton, N.J.: Princeton University Press, 1955), p. 507.

reproduced by his kind permission for cotton yarn, cotton fabrics, and spinning machinery.[7]

For the nation as a whole, the above process of economic growth through the development of import substitution at home, may be evidenced by the lowering of the share of manufactured goods in total imports. This is shown in our Figure 6–2 for the period 1872–97.

FIGURE 6–2. Share of Manufactured Goods in Total Imports: 1872–1897.

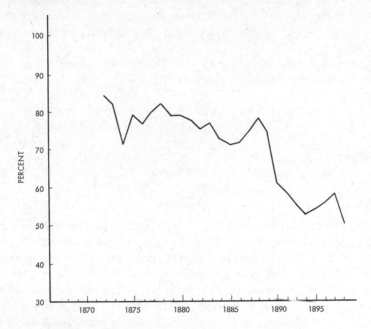

C. *Export Surplus: 1882–96*

What then is the role played by the exports of traditional semimanufactured goods (silk, tea, and other) in the process of economic growth? No doubt, they were very important because they soon found a growing world market and succeeded in financing imports of manufactured consumer goods until home infant industries developed, and also in financing imports of capital goods that were used to start such industries. In other words, traditional semimanufactured exports

---

[7] K. Akamatsu, "A Theory of Unbalanced Growth in the World Economy," *Weltwirtschaftliches Archiv,* Band 86, Heft 2 (1961), p. 196 ff. Figure 6–1 has been reproduced from his Japanese book, *Keizai Seisaku Ron,* (Economic Policy) (Tokyo: Seirin Shoin, 1959), p. 123. His idea of this pattern appeared in a Japanese article in 1935.

contributed greatly to the early development period of infant industry. They were strategic for industrialization.

Let us turn back to our trade statistics in the period 1882–96 which are shown in Table 6–2. Import figures before 1887 are again corrected for the depreciation of silver, as in Section II (c); consequently, there is not as large an export surplus as is shown in official statistics. Except in 1890 (the world panic year), 1894 (outbreak of the Sino-Japanese War) and 1896, there is an export surplus in this period. The favorable balance is due partly to currency stabilization, partly to import substitution, and to the exports of traditional products (mainly silk) that were finding a growing demand in the world market.

The export and import functions of the type which follow have been fitted to the data for the period 1879–96:

$$\log x = -5.61 + 0.882 \log \frac{rP_x}{P_w} + 2.953 \log T_w \quad (1)$$
$$\underset{(0.482)}{} \qquad \underset{(0.697)}{}$$
$$\bar{R} = 0.842$$

$$\log m = -2.907 - 0.586 \log \frac{P_m}{P_d} + 1.852 \log Y \quad (2)$$
$$\underset{(0.347)}{} \qquad \underset{(0.225)}{}$$
$$\bar{R} = 0.911$$

where x = export volume index (1913 = 100 for this and the other index values to follow); r = index of Japanese exchange rates of yen in terms of dollars; P_x = Japanese export price index; P_w = world export price index; T_w = an index of world trade; m = Japanese import volume index; P_m = Japanese import price index; P_d = Japanese domestic price index; Y = Japanese GNP in 1913 yen; $\bar{R}$ = corrected coefficient of multiple correlation; and figures in parentheses show the sampling errors of estimated parameters.

Although the estimated price elasticity of exports has a wrong sign, the estimated world trade elasticity of demand for exports is very high at 2.9 and is greater than the estimated income elasticity of demand for imports. This indicates that the export demand for Japanese traditional semimanufactured products was very elastic, and contributed to export expansion. Exports grew hand in hand with imports and had a "balancing" effect; i.e., "Exports did not lead economic growth in Japan, but provided close support."[8]

---

[8] C. P. Kindleberger, *Foreign Trade and the National Economy* (New Haven, Conn.: Yale University Press, 1962), p. 206.
Ragnar Nurkse distinguished three patterns of growth and trade.
Pattern I.   Growth through exports of primary commodities.
Pattern II.   Growth through exports of manufactured consumer goods.
Pattern III. Expansion of output for domestic markets which includes

D. Reparation and Its Influence

Reparations of 37 million pounds (365 million yen) in seven installments were received in London during the period 1895–98. Compared with the expenditures for the Sino-Japanese War (200 million yen), this was a large amount to the Japanese economy at that time. In fact, the above amount of reparations was comparable with total import deficits in the decade 1894–1903 (352 million yen). As a result, the postwar investment boom which embodied new technology, took place both in the government and private sectors. Government embarked upon the "seven-year program" of modernization of army and navy weapons, railroads, universities, government banks, and a steel mill in Yawata. The number of private enterprises established in the period 1894–1902 created a new record in the annals of business enterprises. In fact, 85 percent of the total enterprises established during the 30-year post-restoration period occurred during these 9 years. The most important effect of Chinese reparations was that they enabled Japan to change to the gold standard in 1897. This was a landmark in the monetary history of this country. In the same year, as we have seen in Section II(*b*), Japanese exports of cotton yarn exceeded its imports of the same commodity. It is on these landmarks in our economic history that we base our assumption that 1897 witnessed a new era in trade and development.

III. GROWTH THROUGH INDUSTRIAL EXPORTS: 1897–1937

A. Industrialization and Exports: 1897–1914

Table 6–6 represents the movement of Japan's foreign trade in the period 1897–1937. The prewar period 1897–1914 with which we will be concerned here (Tables 6–7 and 6–8) is characterized as follows:

1. During 1897–1914, the export contribution to the growth of GNP was especially large in comparison with the previous period. Table 6–7 shows the percentage contribution of exports to the growth in GNP. These figures have been computed as the ratio of the in-

---

(*a*) purely domestic goods, (*b*) the substitution of home-produced goods for imported goods, (*c*) the substitution of capital goods imports for consumer goods imports. (R. Nurkse, *Equilibrium and Growth in the World Economy*, ed. G. Haberler and R. M. Stern, Harvard Economic Studies, Vol. CXVIII [Cambridge, Mass.: Harvard University Press, 1961], p. 282 ff.) Japan's case, in his classification, would be a combination of patterns III and I.

TABLE 6-6

Foreign Trade of Japan: 1897-1937
(In Thousands of Yen)

Year	Export	Import	Trade Balance	Volume Index Export	Volume Index Import
1897.	163,135	219,301	Δ 56,166	32	45
1898.	165,754	277,502	Δ111,748	30	58
1899.	214,930	220,402	Δ 5,472	37	45
1900.	204,430	287,262	Δ 82,832	32	48
1901.	252,350	255,817	Δ 3,467	44	43
1902.	258,303	271,731	Δ 13,428	45	51
1903.	289,502	317,136	Δ 27,634	49	57
1904.	319,261	371,361	Δ 52,100	53	60
1905.	321,534	488,538	Δ167,004	49	82
1906.	423,755	418,784	4,971	57	67
1907.	432,413	494,467	Δ 62,054	54	76
1908.	378,246	436,257	Δ 58,011	54	66
1909.	413,113	394,199	18,914	65	67
1910.	458,429	464,234	Δ 5,805	77	74
1911.	447,434	513,806	Δ 66,372	71	74
1912.	526,982	618,992	Δ 92,010	85	88
1913.	632,460	729,432	Δ 96,972	100	100
1914.	591,101	595,736	Δ 4,634	101	84
1915.	708,307	532,450	175,857	113	82
1916.	1,127,468	756,427	371,041	131	91
1917.	1,603,005	1,035,811	567,194	147	89
1918.	1,962,101	1,668,144	293,957	147	105
1919.	2,098,873	2,173,460	Δ 74,587	127	126
1920.	1,948,395	2,336,175	Δ387,780	108	124
1921.	1,252,838	1,614,155	Δ361,317	102	131
1922.	1,637,452	1,890,308	Δ252,856	124	162
1923.	1,447,751	1,982,231	Δ534,480	102	160
1924.	1,807,035	2,453,402	Δ646,367	131	176
1925.	2,305,590	2,572,658	Δ267,068	159	174
1926.	2,044,728	2,377,484	Δ332,756	161	190
1927.	1,992,317	2,179,154	Δ186,837	175	201
1928.	1,971,955	2,196,315	Δ224,360	184	190
192⌐.	2,148,619	2,216,238	Δ 67,619	205	196
193u.	1,469,852	1,546,071	Δ 76,219	182	171
1931.	1,146,981	1,235,673	Δ 88,691	188	193
1932.	1,409,992	1,431,461	Δ 21,469	217	189
1933.	1,861,046	1,917,220	Δ 56,174	229	201
1934.	2,171,925	2,282,602	Δ110,677	268	217
1935.	2,499,073	2,472,236	26,837	305	227
1936.	2,692,976	2,763,681	Δ 70,705	333	250
1937.	3,175,418	3,783,177	Δ607,759	345	265

SOURCE: The Oriental Economist, *Foreign Trade of Japan, A Statistical Survey* (Tokyo: The Oriental Economist, 1935).

TABLE 6-7

Percentage Contribution of
Export to Economic Growth

I.   From 1876-80* to 1894-98. . . . . 8%
II.   From 1895-99   to 1911-15. . . . . 29%
III.   From 1921-25   to 1934-38. . . . . 39%

*Five-year average.

TABLE 6-8

Percentage Composition of Japanese
Trade and Its Intertemporal Change

		Food	*Material*	*Semi-manu-factured*	*Manu-factured*	*Misc.*	*Total*
A.	EXPORTS						
	1876-80	38.1	11.1	41.6	4.7	3.9	100.0
I:	1894-98	15.1	10.7	44.3	26.5	3.3	100.0
	change	-22.9	-0.4	+2.7	+21.8	-0.6	48.4†
	1895-99	14.3	10.7	45.9	26.0	3.1	100.0
II:	1911-15	10.8	7.9	49.5	30.4	1.4	100.0
	change	-3.5	-2.8	+3.6	+4.4	-1.7	16.0
	1921-25	6.4	6.0	47.8	38.6	1.3	100.0
III:	1936-40	9.9	4.3	26.0	57.4	2.4	100.0
	change	+3.5	-1.7	-21.8	+18.8	+1.1	46.9
B.	IMPORTS						
	1876-80	13.5	3.7	27.2	52.1	3.4	100.0
I:	1894-98	23.2	22.5	18.2	34.1	2.0	100.0
	change	+9.7	+18.8	-9.0	-18.0	-1.4	56.9
	1895-99	22.5	25.9	17.8	32.0	1.9	100.0
II:	1911-15	11.7	52.2	18.3	17.1	0.7	100.0
	change	-10.8	+26.3	+0.5	-14.9	-1.2	53.7
	1921-25	14.1	49.3	18.0	17.9	0.7	100.0
III:	1936-40	8.7	51.1	25.7	13.0	0.7	100.0
	change	-5.4	+1.8	+7.7	-4.9	0	19.8

*Five-year average.
†An index of change as the sum of the absolute values of the
changes in percentage shares of each item during the period.

crease in exports in 1913 prices to the increases in real GNP in 1913 price; i.e., $100(x_t - x_{t-1})/(y_t - y_{t-1})$. According to these percentages, we find that there was a sharp change in the role played by exports in the process of economic growth after 1897.

2. According to Table 6–8, however, there seems to have been less change in the commodity composition of exports in this period in comparison with the preceding and subsequent period. Silk was still a leading item in exports, although the ratio of the machine-reeled to hand-reeled silk yarn was steadily increasing.

3. In contrast with the commodity composition of exports, the composition of imports shows as drastic a change in this period as in the preceding period. This is due to the substitution of producers' goods (i.e., raw cotton) for manufactured consumer goods.

B. Role of Foreign Capital: 1897–1914

Foreign capital of 194 million yen was imported into Japan in the period before the Russo-Japanese War (1897–1903); and the amount increased to the recorded value of 1,857 million yen (including indemnities) in the subsequent decade before World War I (1904–14). The sizable inflow of foreign capital must have accelerated the industrialization of Japan in this period, although a portion was directed to defense purposes.

C. Export and Import Functions: 1897–1913

The export and import functions of the same type as in Section II(c), were fitted to the data in the period 1897–1913, and are given as follows:

$$\log x = -1.156 - 0.858 \log \frac{rP_x}{P_w} + 1.421 \log T_w, \qquad (3)$$
$$\qquad\quad (0.125) \qquad\quad (0.123)$$
$$\bar{R} = 0.981,$$

$$\log m = -0.659 - 1.144 \log \frac{P_m}{P_d} + 0.977 \log Y, \qquad (4)$$
$$\qquad\quad (0.419) \qquad\quad (0.200)$$
$$\bar{R} = 0.825.$$

Here, all the price and income elasticities are statistically significant. The price elasticity of the demand for imports is higher in value than that of the demand for exports. The world demand for exports is found to be more income elastic, than is the home demand for imports.

D. Wartime Export Boom: 1914–19

According to Table 6–6, exports increased, hand in hand with invisible exports, such as shipping, during World War I, on account of decreased production and exports in European countries. The result was an export surplus, which was large enough to make Japan a creditor nation in its balance of international indebtedness. Before World War I, it was a debtor nation, due to the foreign capital inflow observed in Section III(*b*).

E. Export-Led Growth: 1920–37

Returning to Table 6–7, we find that the percentage contribution of exports to economic growth in the third period 1921–38 is even greater than in the second period. The index of the changes in the commodity composition of exports shown in Table 6–8 is found to be higher in the third period in comparison with the second. This is due to the shift of weight from traditional semimanufactured goods (silk) to cotton textile and other manufactured goods.

1. Export Behavior. In Table 6–9, we represent the interwar movements of the index of Japanese exports (in 1930 prices), the relative export price index and three indexes taken as representative of world economic activity (The League of Nation's index of world industrial production and world trade and an index of world incomes compiled from Colin Clark's individual country estimates in "international units"). A cursory glance at Table 6–9 shows that all three world series change in the same direction in textbook type cycles, with an expansion phase up to 1929, a contraction phase in 1929–32, and a second expansion after 1932. This, however, is not so in the case of Japanese exports, which showed a steady growth apart from one exceptional disturbance: i.e., Japan's return to the gold standard in the midst of world panic in 1930. The export price series, on the other hand, shows a steady decline throughout the period under review.

These features lead us to expect a relatively strong price and a relatively weak income effect. The same type log-linear regression equation as in Section II(*c*) has been fitted covering the period 1924–37 with the result,

$$\log x = 0.754 - 1.029 \log \frac{rP_x}{P_w} + 0.690 \log T_w. \qquad (5)$$
$$(0.528) \quad (0.103) \qquad \quad (0.255)$$
$$\bar{R} = 0.939.$$

TABLE 6-9

Indices in the Interwar Period: 1924-37

(1930 = 100)

Year	World Trade	World Income	World Industrial Production	Japan's Export Volume	Japan's Export Price	World Export Price	Japan's Real GNP	Japan's Import Volume	Japan's Import Price	Japan's Domestic Price
1924	82	87	81	72	153	126	94	103	154	151
1925	90	92	88	87	158	130	60	102	172	148
1926	92	97	92	88	157	122	107	111	144	131
1927	99	100	98	96	140	119	96	117	126	124
1928	102	103	103	101	130	118	101	111	131	125
1929	108	107	112	113	127	115	104	115	127	122
1930	100	100	100	100	100	100	100	100	100	100
1931	92	93	89	103	75	78	102	113	71	85
1932	80	84	79	119	43	60	114	111	86	94
1933	81	86	89	125	39	54	128	117	111	108
1934	84	93	99	147	33	50	128	127	122	110
1935	88	101	112	167	33	49	136	130	126	112
1936	92	114	130	182	33	50	147	143	128	117
1937	104	121	142	189	37	55	167	152	165	142

As expected, the results show high-price elasticity and low-income (world trade) elasticity (contrary to the results obtained by the elasticity pessimists in recent years).[9]

A demand function of this type presumes the direct dependence of a country's exports on world trade. We can make an alternative assumption that a country's share in exports depends on its competitive position as reflected in the ratio of its export prices to those of its competitors. If this assumption is adopted, we are, in effect, estimating the elasticity of substitution between a country's exports and those of its competitors, rather than measuring the price elasticity of demand for its exports. Using as a first approximation the ratio of Japanese to world export prices, we obtained the following regression equation (covering 1924–37):

$$\log (x/x_w) = 2.138 - 1.040 \log (p_x/p_w) \qquad (6)$$
$$(0.081)$$
$$\bar{R} = 0.98$$

where x_w represents world exports. Here again we have an elasticity of substitution between Japanese exports and world exports, which exceeds unity, although the sampling error is so large that we cannot exclude the possibility that this parameter is less than unity.

2. Import Behavior. Let us now turn to the import side. Table 6–9 also gives the index of Japanese imports and import price, and the index of real national income constructed by Shinohara,[10] based on the estimates of Hitotsubashi Institute of Economic Research. Using these data, we have fitted the same type of log-linear regression equation as in Section II(c), obtaining

$$\log m = 1.557 + 0.445 \log \frac{P_m}{P_d} + 0.367 \log Y \qquad (7)$$
$$(0.177) \quad (0.225) \qquad (0.086)$$
$$\bar{R} = 0.855.$$

Here the price elasticity has a wrong sign, and a relatively low-income elasticity is observed.

The above estimates of export functions give some support to Shinohara's arguments on the significance of the price effect in the process of Japanese economic growth.[11]

---

[9] This type of export function also fits very well to the postwar years. According to our studies for the period 1954–66, the estimated values of the price—and income—elasticities are approximately 1.4 and 1.8, respectively.

[10] M. Shinohara, *Growth and Cycles in the Japanese Economy* (Tokyo: Kinokuniya Bookstore, 1963).

[11] *Ibid.*

SUMMARY

This paper has discussed the role played by foreign trade in the process of long-term economic growth of Japan. In doing so, it has attempted to explain why this nation has become one of the biggest exporters of industrial products in the world.

As we observed in Section I, the initial conditions of Japan's trade were unfavorable as a result of extraterritoriality and treaty-determined tariffs. Japan was to specialize in the production of primary goods. This was a static adjustment to an external environment, in accordance with the doctrine of comparative advantage.

Japan was dissatisfied with this pattern of trade and used traditional semimanufactured exports as a springboard for growth. As shown in Section II, the Meiji government ventured into state enterprise in a variety of industrial activities in which Japan at that time had a comparative disadvantage. This governmental venture of import substitution was followed by mushrooming of private industrial enterprises.

Chinese reparations and large inflows of foreign capital enabled Japan to accumulate capital to transform its industrial structure. By 1887, domestic infant industries had grown sufficiently to have a comparative advantage in the world market. This pattern of trade and growth, as shown in Section III, became effective and superseded earlier patterns.

Japanese exports of textiles found a growing demand in the world market. In addition, its competitive strength in exports enabled Japan to increase its share in the world market. As a result, the export contribution to the growth in GNP was accelerated as shown in Section III. When Japan had the first contact with the outside world in 1858, and extraterritoriality and tariff treaties had to be signed, the country was in a poor position in import-competing industries.

There were other factors which on balance may have been favorable, such as the winning of two great wars. Also its exports of traditional semimanufactured product were able, at an early stage, to find a growing market in the rest of the world. A nation's response, however, to external pressure may be positive or negative. Japan's attitude was positive. The dynamics of these changes shown in our report brought about dramatic increases in production and income, in a way that is unparalleled in world economic history.

Statistical Appendix
by Masahiro Tatemoto

I. THE CORRECTION OF OFFICIAL IMPORT STATISTICS, 1874–1887, FOR THE DEPRECIATION OF SILVER

As mentioned in the text [Section II(a)] there is a problem in the valuation of imports in the official trade statistics for the period 1874–87. This problem relates to the monetary system in the early Meiji period. The New Currency Act in May, 1871 provided that legal tender was yen, the net content of which was 23.14 grains of gold. In addition to this "gold yen," "silver yen" (374.4 grains of silver, equivalent in content to the "Mexican dollar" which was widely accepted in Far Eastern trade) was issued as subsidiary coin to be used for international trade settlement. As 101 gold yen were exchanged for 100 silver yen, the legal rate of exchange between gold yen and silver was 16.01.[1] The ratio was changed to 1:16.17 in 1875, 1:16.33 in 1876, and restored to 1:16.17 in 1878. The last ratio was maintained nominally until 1897 when Japan went off the bimetallic standard. After 1874 when Germany, other European countries and the United States changed to the gold standard, silver continued to depreciate against gold in the international market. In fact, the price of gold in terms of silver witnessed a drastic decrease of 30 percent in the period 1874–87. In spite of this depreciation, Japanese monetary authorities pegged the legal price of gold in terms of silver at the 1878 level (1:16.17) for two decades.

This system caused a rather complicated method of valuation in customs statistics before 1887. On the one hand, imports from silver currency countries and exports to all countries were valued in terms of (depreciated) silver yen. On the other hand, imports from gold currency countries were valued *in terms of gold yen.* In other words, the fixed legal ratio of exchange between gold yen and silver (1:16.17) was maintained in customs valuation in the face of depreciation of silver yen.

After 1887, when government statisticians came to recognize the mistake, imports to all countries were valued in terms of silver yen. Hence, in order to secure comparability of statistics before and after

---

[1] $(374.4 \times 100)/(23.14 \times 101) = 16.17 - 0.1617 = 16.01.$

1887, it is necessary to correct the import statistics from gold currency countries for the appreciation of gold. Table 6A–1 shows the result of this correction. The imports from gold currency countries [U.K, Germany, France, Italy, Belgium, Switzerland, the Netherlands, Spain, Portugal, Sweden, Denmark, Turkey, U.S., Canada, Hawaii, and Australia] were separated from those from silver currency countries [China, Hongkong, East Indies, Korea, Siam, the Philippines, Austria, Russia, and Peru] by using the data published by the Monetary System Investigation Committee in 1895,[2] (column (a) and (b) in Table 6A–1). Next, each figure in column (a) was multiplied by the corresponding price of gold yen in terms of silver yen in column (c) [after 1879 data were obtained from the *Statistical Yearbook of the Empire of Japan,* No. 6, 1887 to No. 8, 1889; before 1878 the data are our estimates] to get the import value from gold currency countries *in terms of silver yen,* entered in column (d). The sum of the figures in column (b), (d), and (f) is entered in column (g) to give the final result of correction. These are to be compared with the figures in column (h).

II. ANNUAL ESTIMATES OF JAPAN'S INTERNATIONAL BALANCE OF PAYMENTS: 1868–1901

In spite of increasing concern by foreign economists about the international aspect of Japan's economic development in the early Meiji years, there have been no statistics available on its balance of payments for the last 34 years in the 19th century: namely, for the period 1868–1901.

This was the reason why Mrs. Gordon,[3] in discussing annual balances of payments, had to confine herself to the period 1904–31. Moulton[4] in appraising Japanese economic performance made a sort of guesswork on the balance of payments in two long periods, 1881–95 and 1896–1903. Reubens,[5] recently, in discussing the role of foreign capital, based his analysis on Mrs. Gordon and Moulton.

[2] The Ministry of Finance, *Meiji Zenki Zaisei Keizai Shiryo Shusei* (The Collections of Historical Materials on Financial and Economic Conditions in Early Meiji Era) (Tokyo: Kaizo Sha, 1931), Vol. 12. Reprint (Tokyo: Meiji Bunken Shiryo Kanko Kai, 1961).

[3] M. S. Gordon, "Japan's Balance of International Payments: 1904–1931," in E. B. Schumpeter, *The Industrialization of Japan and Manchukuo, 1930–40* (New York: Macmillan, 1940).

[4] H. G. Moulton, *Japan: Economic and Financial Appraisal* (Washington, D.C.: Brookings Institution, 1931).

[5] E. P. Reubens, "Foreign Capital and Domestic Development in Japan," in S. Kuznets, W. E. Moor, and J. J. Spengler (eds.), *Economic Growth: Brazil, India, Japan* (Durham, N.C.: Duke University Press, 1955).

TABLE 6A-1

Correction of the Value of Imports for the Depreciation
of Silver Yen: 1874-1887

Year	(a) Import from Gold Currency Countries (Gold Yen)	(b) Import from Silver Currency Countries (Silver Yen)	(c) Price of Gold Yen in Terms of Silver Yen	(d) Import from Gold Currency Countries in Terms of Silver Yen	(e) (d) + (b)	(f) From Unknown Countries	(g) (d)+(b)+(f) Corrected Value of Imports	(h) Value of Imports before Correction	(i) Difference (g) - (h)
1874	14,041,726	8,665,716	1.037	15,006,772	23,732,488	754,372	24,486,860	23,461,814	1,025,046
1875	21,375,690	8,200,382	1.090	23,299,502	31,499,884	399,556	31,899,440	29,975,628	1,923,812
1876	15,827,024	7,472,055	1.163	18,406,829	25,878,884	665,600	26,544,484	23,964,679	2,579,805
1877	21,316,338	5,865,068	1.120	23,874,299	29,739,367	239,497	29,978,864	27,420,903	2,557,961
1878	27,233,324	5,653,169	1.178	32,080,856	37,714,025	8,341	37,722,366	32,874,834	4,847,532
1879	25,437,956	7,479,827	1.199	30,500,109	37,979,936	35,219	38,015,155	32,953,002	5,062,153
1880	28,963,708	7,614,321	1.194	34,582,667	42,196,988	48,573	42,245,561	36,626,601	5,618,960
1881	23,343,174	7,796,349	1.196	27,918,436	35,714,785	51,723	35,766,508	31,191,246	4,575,262
1882	20,460,131	8,904,384	1.191	24,363,016	33,272,400	82,079	33,354,479	29,446,594	3,907,885
1883	20,121,970	8,257,827	1.199	24,126,242	32,384,069	65,045	32,449,114	28,444,842	4,004,272
1884	19,821,954	9,804,140	1.199	23,766,523	33,570,663	46,554	33,617,217	29,672,647	3,944,570
1885	19,087,802	10,232,343	1.217	23,229,855	33,462,198	36,824	33,499,022	29,356,968	4,142,054
1886	20,798,646	11,376,905	1.245	25,894,314	37,271,219	72,881	37,364,100	32,168,432	5,195,668
1887	29,794,156	14,466,209	1.297	38,643,020	53,109,229	43,887	53,153,116	44,304,252	8,848,864

Professor Horie[6] is the only economic historian who attempted to estimate the balance of payments in the early 26 years of Meiji, but his careful study did not result in annual estimates. Thus, our study purports to be the first attempt to venture to give annual estimates of Japan's balance of payments, 1868–1901. (In the following, the number of each section corresponds to the classification number of each item in Table 6A–2).

Current Transaction

1. Merchandise
    1.1. Merchandise (f.o.b.)
    The import figures for 1874–87 are taken from Table 6A–1. Prior to 1898, import valuation was based on f.o.b. prices (converted into yen) at the port of embarkation; thus, import values do not include freight and insurance charges. This fact makes it necessary for us to estimate these charges, as explained later in 4.1 and 5. In accordance with the strict f.o.b. definition, we have added to the reported export values the packing and lighterage costs which were estimated by the Ministry of Finance[7] to be about 2 percent of total exports.
    1.2. Other
    Government import of ships, weapons, munitions, railroad equipment and various types of machinery were not included in customs statistics. After 1888, these are listed as "special imports," but before 1887, information has been collected and reclassified from various individual items in the annual statements of government revenues and expenditures since 1867.[8] After 1878, we have included the import of books by international mail in 1.2.
    2. Nonmonetary Gold (or Silver)
    In accordance with the International Monetary Fund (IMF) standard form, gold production which increases the specie reserve

---

[6] Y. Horie, *Meiji Ishin to Keizai Kindaika* (Meiji Restoration and Modernization of Economy) (Tokyo: Shibun Do, 1963), chap. 5 (in Japanese).

[7] The Ministry of Finance, *Seika Shushi Shirabe* (Survey of Specie Inflow and Outflow) (Tokyo: Government Printing Office, 1902) (in Japanese), (referred to as the *Survey for 1901*).

[8] The Ministry of Finance, *Sai Nyu Shutsu Kessan Hokokusho* (referred to as the *Report of Revenues and Expenditures*) (in Japanese) since 1867 in *Meiji Zenki Zaisei Keizai Shiryo Shusei* cited in footnote 2, Vol. 4–6. The author wishes to acknowledge Miss Tomoko Matsumoto for her patience in computational assistance.

TABLE 6A-2

Balance of Payments of Japan: 1868-1901
(Unit: Yen)

	1868 Cr.	1868 Dr.	1869 Cr.	1869 Dr.	1870 Cr.	1870 Dr.
Current Transaction						
1. Merchandise						
1.1 Merchandise (f.o.b.)	15,873,875	10,693,072	13,174,903	20,783,633	14,842,599	33,741,637
1.2 Other.		106,267		333,457		1,552,153
2. Nonmonetary gold.	---	---	---	---	---	---
3. Foreign travel.	388,837	4,943	328,138	56,365	369,674	214,734
4. Transportation.	---		---		---	
4.1 Freight.		1,532,317		2,978,295		4,980,266
4.2 Other.	---	---	---	---	---	---
5. Insurance	---	381,743	---	741,975	---	1,261,937
6. International investment income						
6.1 Direct investment.	---	423,488	---	823,114	---	1,336,302
6.2 Interest	---	28,973	---	71,967	---	275,746
7. Government transaction. . . .	568,725	82,369	501,089	262,048	580,716	401,244
8. Miscellaneous services. . . .	---	---	---	---	---	---
9. Donations						
9.1 Private.	---	---	---	561,928	---	561,928
9.2 Reparation	---	103,654	---	50,500	---	---
9.3 Government	---	---	---	---	---	---
10. Total	16,831,437	13,356,826	14,004,130	26,663,282	15,792,989	44,325,947
Capital Transaction						
11. Long-term capital (private) . .	---	---	---	---	---	---
12. Short-term capital (private). .	---	---	---	---	---	---
13. Long-term capital (official). .	894,750	545,936	---	425,000	4,880,000	894,750
14. Short-term capital (official) .	---	---	100,500	100,125	---	---
15. Monetary gold	---	---	---	---	---	---
16. Total (1-14).	17,726,187	13,902,762	14,104,630	27,188,407	20,672,989	45,220,697
17. Total (1-15).	17,726,187	13,902,762	14,104,630	27,188,407	20,672,989	45,220,697
18. Errors and omissions.	---	3,823,425	13,083,777	---	24,547,708	---

TABLE 6A-2 (Continued)

	1871 Cr.	1871 Dr.	1872 Cr.	1872 Dr.	1873 Cr.	1873 Dr.
Current Transaction						
1. Merchandise						
1.1 Merchandise (f.o.b.)	18,338,762	21,916,728	17,377,396	20,174,815	22,681,131	28,107,390
1.2 Other.	---	24,600	---	113,549	---	---
2. Nonmonetary gold.	---	---	---	---	---	---
3. Foreign travel.	456,751	568,884	432,807	961,150	549,983	146,019
4. Transportation						
4.1 Freight.	---	3,204,226	---	3,863,403	---	4,710,799
4.2 Other.	---	---	---	---	---	---
5. Insurance	---	806,535	---	978,938	---	1,191,753
6. International investment income						
6.1 Direct investment.	---	867,989	---	1,036,626	---	1,138,741
6.2 Interest	---	441,235	---	439,330	---	852,077
7. Government transaction. . . .	760,755	899,017	644,073	1,432,410	827,862	2,611,663
8. Miscellaneous services. . . .	---	---	---	---	---	---
9. Donations						
9.1 Private.	---	561,928	---	561,928	---	561,928
9.2 Reparation	---	---	---	44,826	---	5,469
9.3 Government	---	---	---	---	---	---
10. Total (1-9)	19,556,268	29,291,142	18,454,276	35,606,975	23,458,976	39,325,839
Capital Transaction						
11. Long-term capital (private) . .	---	---	---	---	---	---
12. Short-term capital (private). .	---	---	---	---	---	---
13. Long-term capital (official). .	---	178,990	---	3,080,392	11,712,000	628,304
14. Short-term capital (official) .	---	---	---	---	---	---
15. Monetary gold	---	---	4,480,896	3,691,510	5,122,927	3,080,542
16. Total (1-14).	19,556,268	29,470,132	18,454,276	38,687,367	35,170,976	39,954,143
17. Total (1-15).	19,556,268	29,470,132	22,935,172	42,378,877	40,293,903	43,034,685
18. Errors and omissions.	9,913,864	---	19,443,705	---	2,740,782	---

TABLE 6A-2 (Continued)

	1874 Cr.	1874 Dr.	1875 Cr.	1875 Dr.	1876 Cr.	1876 Dr.
Current Transaction						
1. Merchandise						
1.1 Merchandise (f.o.b.)	19,715,243	24,486,860	18,994,500	31,899,440	28,282,386	26,544,484
1.2 Other............	---	5,237,441	---	3,823,135	---	1,993,222
2. Nonmonetary gold.......	180,122	---	412,758	---	529,986	---
3. Foreign travel........	584,357	73,864	685,761	81,531	677,511	299,445
4. Transportation						
4.1 Freight...........	---	3,790,566	86,388	4,523,341	97,880	3,724,191
4.2 Other...........	---	---	---	---	---	---
5. Insurance..........	---	959,885	---	1,122,860	---	921,094
6. International investment income						
6.1 Direct investment......	---	959,211	---	1,255,725	---	1,052,364
6.2 Interest..........	---	1,227,346	---	1,175,680	---	1,135,849
7. Government transaction.....	820,270	2,698,990	849,057	1,857,775	885,556	1,763,371
8. Miscellaneous services.....	---	---	---	---	---	---
9. Donations						
9.1 Private...........	---	561,928	---	561,928	---	561,928
9.2 Reparation.........	---	1,524,340	785,245	---	---	---
9.3 Government........	---	---	---	---	---	---
10. Total (1-9)...........	21,299,992	41,520,431	21,813,709	46,301,415	30,473,319	37,995,948
Capital Transaction						
11. Long-term capital (private)..	---	---	---	---	---	---
12. Short-term capital (private)..	---	---	---	---	---	---
13. Long-term capital (official)..	---	514,663	---	743,390	---	748,394
14. Short-term capital (official).	---	---	---	---	---	---
15. Monetary gold.........	13,995,202	1,071,731	15,522,842	300,470	11,644,640	8,386,283
16. Total (1-14)..........	21,299,992	42,035,094	21,813,709	47,044,805	30,473,319	38,744,342
17. Total (1-15)..........	35,295,194	43,106,825	37,336,551	47,345,275	42,117,959	47,130,625
18. Errors and omissions......	7,811,631	---	10,008,724	---	5,012,666	---

TABLE 6A-2 (Continued)

	1877 Cr.	1877 Dr.	1878 Cr.	1878 Dr.	1879 Cr.	1879 Dr.
Current Transaction						
1. Merchandise						
1.1 Merchandise (f.o.b.)	23,829,502	29,978,864	26,523,496	37,722,366	28,756,191	38,015,155
1.2 Other............	---	1,815,439	---	1,417,715	---	1,321,063
2. Nonmonetary gold.......	713,175	---	622,905	---	584,431	---
3. Foreign travel........	533,140	261,607	575,764	235,620	563,045	274,356
4. Transportation						
4.1 Freight...........	188,281	4,251,003	204,037	4,918,997	299,260	4,626,444
4.2 Other...........	---	---	---	---	---	---
5. Insurance..........	---	1,055,256	---	1,229,749	20,000	1,151,860
6. International investment income						
6.1 Direct investment......	---	1,208,016	---	1,355,940	---	1,696,800
6.2 Interest..........	---	1,083,678	---	1,064,854	---	1,081,647
7. Government transaction.....	911,771	1,605,179	900,663	1,441,220	1,025,496	1,279,274
8. Miscellaneous services.....	---	---	---	---	---	---
9. Donations						
9.1 Private...........	---	518,161	---	581,611	---	727,818
9.2 Reparation.........	---	---	---	---	---	---
9.3 Government........	---	---	---	---	---	---
10. Total (1-9)...........	26,175,869	41,777,203	28,826,865	49,968,072	31,248,423	50,174,417
Capital Transaction						
11. Long-term capital (private)..	---	---	---	---	---	---
12. Short-term capital (private)..	---	---	---	---	---	---
13. Long-term capital (official)..	---	773,911	---	828,483	---	922,402
14. Short-term capital (official).	---	---	---	---	---	---
15. Monetary gold.........	10,200,328	2,193,297	9,106,236	2,189,142	13,724,041	3,280,406
16. Total (1-14)..........	26,175,869	42,551,114	28,826,865	50,796,555	31,248,423	51,096,819
17. Total (1-15)..........	36,376,197	44,744,411	37,933,101	52,985,697	44,972,464	54,377,225
18. Errors and omossions......	8,368,214	---	15,052,596	---	9,404,761	---

TABLE 6A-2 (Continued)

	1880 Cr.	1880 Dr.	1881 Cr.	1881 Dr.	1882 Cr.	1882 Dr.
Current Transaction						
1. Merchandise						
1.1 Merchandise (f.o.b.)	28,980,332	42,245,561	31,698,701	35,766,508	38,498,819	33,354,479
1.2 Other.	---	1,545,581	---	1,287,162	---	1,075,470
2. Nonmonetary gold.	676,029	---	980,753	---	933,794	---
3. Foreign travel.	863,130	346,222	1,044,453	319,872	1,102,889	339,035
4. Transportation						
4.1 Freight.	431,184	5,263,797	524,484	4,456,507	642,050	3,872,455
4.2 Other.	---	---	---	---	---	---
5. Insurance	103,000	1,326,511	112,000	1,123,068	114,000	963,944
6. International investment income						
6.1 Direct investment.	83,646	2,034,185	156,722	2,568,175	154,625	2,383,287
6.2 Interest	---	1,049,068	---	1,198,759	---	800,476
7. Government transaction. . . .	1,051,886	1,584,486	1,122,515	1,145,197	1,402,132	990,177
8. Miscellaneous services. . . .	---	---	---	---	---	---
9. Donations						
9.1 Private.	842,591	872,534	1,071,956	1,101,585	1,808,844	1,022,276
9.2 Reparation	---	---	---	---	---	---
9.3 Government	---	---	---	---	---	---
10. Total (1-9)	33,031,798	56,267,945	36,711,584	48,966,833	44,657,153	44,801,599
Capital Transaction						
11. Long-term capital (private) . .	---	---	---	---	---	---
12. Short-term capital (private). .	---	---	---	---	---	---
13. Long-term capital (official). .	---	988,674	---	1,258,930	---	952,470
14. Short-term capital (official) .	---	---	---	---	---	---
15. Monetary gold	14,365,299	3,642,230	7,930,937	1,856,176	4,669,146	6,160,820
16. Total (1-14).	33,031,798	57,256,619	36,711,584	50,225,765	44,657,153	45,754,069
17. Total (1-15).	47,397,097	60,898,849	44,642,521	52,081,939	49,326,299	51,914,889
18. Errors and omissions.	13,501,752	---	7,439,418	---	2,588,590	---

TABLE 6A-2 (Continued)

	1883 Cr.	1883 Dr.	1884 Cr.	1884 Dr.	1885 Cr.	1885 Dr.
Current Transaction						
1. Merchandise						
1.1 Merchandise (f.o.b.)	37,015,141	32,449,114	34,569,218	33,617,217	37,911,913	33,499,022
1.2 Other.	---	2,714,031	---	4,545,410	---	4,165,913
2. Nonmonetary gold.	1,237,199	---	1,165,507	---	1,206,912	---
3. Foreign travel.	915,895	327,730	884,442	685,761	1,000,970	590,040
4. Transportation						
4.1 Freight.	669,626	3,488,280	792,141	3,082,699	1,099,647	3,021,612
4.2 Other.	---	---	---	---	---	---
5. Insurance	122,000	859,901	102,000	783,281	101,000	763,777
6. International investment income						
6.1 Direct investment.	189,602	2,200,110	275,622	1,592,662	669,696	1,567,577
6.2 Interest	---	730,190	---	706,425	---	680,775
7. Government transaction. . . .	1,455,246	937,838	1,268,342	1,149,220	1,427,168	1,145,703
8. Miscellaneous services. . . .	---	---	---	---	---	---
9. Donations						
9.1 Private.	964,685	943,705	900,432	683,150	1,206,237	672,390
9.2 Reparation	---	---	---	---	---	---
9.3 Government	907,515	---	---	---	---	---
10. Total (1-9)	43,476,909	44,650,899	39,957,704	46,845,825	44,623,543	46,106,809
Capital Transaction						
11. Long-term capital (private) . .	---	---	---	---	---	---
12. Short-term capital (private). .	---	---	---	---	---	---
13. Long-term capital (official). .	---	452,571	---	481,090	---	526,159
14. Short-term capital (official) .	---	---	---	---	---	---
15. Monetary gold	3,357,469	5,451,612	5,288,379	5,671,300	4,363,348	7,678,953
16. Total (1-14).	43,476,909	45,103,470	39,957,704	47,326,915	44,623,543	46,632,968
17. Total (1-15).	46,834,378	50,555,082	45,246,083	52,998,215	48,986,891	54,311,921
18. Errors and omissions.	3,720,704	---	7,752,132	---	5,325,030	---

TABLE 6A-2 (Continued)

	1886 Cr.	1886 Dr.	1887 Cr.	1887 Dr.	1888 Cr.	1888 Dr.
Current Transaction						
1. Merchandise						
1.1 Merchandise (f.o.b.)	49,883,165	37,364,100	53,487,279	53,153,116	67,059,043	65,455,234
1.2 Other	---	3,573,900	---	3,604,677	---	465,264
2. Nonmonetary gold	1,777,201	---	1,921,637	---	2,331,984	---
3. Foreign travel	1,074,874	622,482	1,247,775	678,660	1,523,798	788,095
4. Transportation						
4.1 Freight	1,728,795	3,161,003	2,069,621	4,948,555	2,150,969	7,121,529
4.2 Other	---	---	---	---	92,074	---
5. Insurance	129,000	799,592	121,000	1,217,206	126,000	1,780,383
6. International investment income						
6.1 Direct investment	476,509	1,500,478	632,181	1,637,224	682,610	1,927,665
6.2 Interest	---	684,925	---	683,379	---	658,472
7. Government transaction	1,546,329	1,101,938	1,647,379	1,172,406	2,100,171	1,232,020
8. Miscellaneous services	---	---	---	---	---	---
9. Donations						
9.1 Private	1,299,040	643,609	1,678,315	702,263	2,282,206	826,844
9.2 Reparation	---	---	---	---	---	---
9.3 Government	---	---	---	---	---	---
10. Total (1-9)	57,914,913	49,452,027	62,805,187	67,797,486	78,348,855	80,255,506
Capital Transaction						
11. Long-term capital (private)	---	---	---	---	---	---
12. Short-term capital (private)	---	---	---	---	---	---
13. Long-term capital (official)	---	598,800	---	665,125	---	743,431
14. Short-term capital (official)	---	---	---	---	---	---
15. Monetary gold	9,700,571	9,455,944	11,061,100	9,245,346	7,833,444	8,732,492
16. Total (1-14)	57,914,913	50,050,827	62,805,189	68,462,611	78,348,855	80,998,937
17. Total (1-15)	67,615,484	59,506,771	73,866,287	77,707,957	86,182,299	89,731,429
18. Errors and omissions	---	8,108,713	3,841,670	---	3,549,130	---

TABLE 6A-2 (Continued)

	1889 Cr.	1889 Dr.	1890 Cr.	1890 Dr.	1891 Cr.	1891 Dr.
Current Transaction						
1. Merchandise						
1.1 Merchandise (f.o.b.)	71,503,957	66,103,767	57,769,538	81,728,581	81,165,534	62,927,268
1.2 Other	---	217,512	---	191,720	---	981,198
2. Nonmonetary gold	2,456,767	---	2,774,010	---	3,039,739	---
3. Foreign travel	1,656,138	834,673	2,196,840	700,386	2,159,888	915,355
4. Transportation						
4.1 Freight	2,284,323	5,851,479	2,464,512	7,727,790	2,240,021	5,406,248
4.2 Other	142,945	---	100,070	---	94,094	---
5. Insurance	125,000	1,486,039	152,000	1,914,183	418,000	1,326,970
6. International investment income						
6.1 Direct investment	472,760	2,158,753	374,315	2,697,807	543,236	2,447,354
6.2 Interest	---	606,487	---	527,067	---	470,446
7. Government transaction	1,857,173	1,211,166	1,555,748	1,159,448	2,322,336	1,037,254
8. Miscellaneous services	---	---	---	---	---	---
9. Donations						
9.1 Private	2,103,880	925,966	3,239,539	1,157,185	4,110,992	1,049,757
9.2 Reparation	---	---	---	---	---	---
9.3 Government	---	---	---	---	---	---
10. Total (1-9)	82,602,943	79,395,842	70,626,572	97,804,167	96,093,840	76,561,850
Capital Transaction						
11. Long-term capital (private)	---	---	---	---	---	---
12. Short-term capital (private)	---	---	---	---	---	---
13. Long-term capital (official)	---	804,597	---	832,120	---	819,718
14. Short-term capital (official)	---	---	---	---	---	---
15. Monetary gold	5,188,529	14,173,246	13,778,531	1,200,607	1,452,964	13,888,526
16. Total (1-14)	82,602,952	80,200,439	70,626,572	98,636,287	96,093,840	77,381,568
17. Total (1-15)	87,791,472	94,373,685	84,405,103	99,836,894	97,546,804	91,270,094
18. Errors and omissions	6,582,213	---	15,431,791	---	---	6,276,710

TABLE 6A-2 (Continued)

	1892		1893	
	Cr.	Dr.	Cr.	Dr.
Current Transaction				
1. Merchandise				
1.1 Merchandise (f.o.b.)	92,979,471	71,326,080	91,560,950	88,257,172
1.2 Other.	---	4,690,975	---	1,133,960
2. Nonmonetary gold.	3,156,188	---	3,651,516	---
3. Foreign travel.	2,521,846	787,104	3,120,469	856,394
4. Transportation				
4.1 Freight.	2,441,929	5,619,998	2,031,251	8,280,497
4.2 Other.	96,712	---	721,362	---
5. Insurance	746,000	1,441,284	480,000	2,045,592
6. International investment income				
6.1 Direct investment.	671,745	2,582,955	500,704	2,364,316
6.2 Interest	----	444,882	---	408,409
7. Government transaction. . . .	2,326,674	892,207	1,907,909	811,019
8. Miscellaneous services.	---	---	---	---
9. Donations				
9.1 Private.	5,201,158	1,107,922	5,120,808	1,014,139
9.2 Reparation	---	---	---	---
9.3 Government	---	---	---	---
10. Total (1-9)	110,141,723	88,893,407	109,094,969	105,171,498
Capital Transaction				
11. Long-term capital (private) . .	---	---	---	---
12. Short-term capital (private). .	---	---	---	---
13. Long-term capital (official). .	---	1,030,574	---	1,196,984
14. Short-term capital (official) .	---	---	---	---
15. Monetary gold	9,729,753	22,883,757	12,289,188	11,186,487
16. Total (1-14).	110,141,723	89,923,981	109,094,969	106,368,482
17. Total (1-15).	119,871,476	112,807,738	121,384,157	117,554,969
18. Errors and omissions.	7,063,738	---	3,829,188	---

TABLE 6A-2 (Continued)

	1894		1895	
	Cr.	Dr.	Cr.	Dr.
Current Transaction				
1. Merchandise				
1.1 Merchandise (f.o.b.)	115,578,955	117,481,955	138,916,089	129,260,578
1.2 Other.	---	4,245,573	---	9,454,884
2. Nonmonetary gold.	4,008,108	---	4,151,589	---
3. Foreign travel.	3,892,680	880,765	4,962,742	1,282,740
4. Transportation				
4.1 Freight.	1,934,937	12,153,449	1,226,516	10,379,624
4.2 Other.	462,501	---	1,382,439	---
5. Insurance	184,000	3,001,723	187,000	2,546,434
6. International investment income				
6.1 Direct investment.	552,066	1,505,571	585,314	2,291,759
6.2 Interest	---	377,525	---	297,336
7. Government transaction. . . .	2,374,561	815,543	2,447,959	1,137,253
8. Miscellaneous services.	---	---	---	---
9. Donations				
9.1 Private.	5,365,552	645,793	6,544,982	983,017
9.2 Reparation	---	---	119,050,553	---
9.3 Government	---	---	---	---
10. Total (1-9)	134,353,360	141,107,897	279,455,183	157,633,625
Capital Transaction				
11. Long-term capital (private) . .	---	---	---	---
12. Short-term capital (private). .	---	---	---	---
13. Long-term capital (official). .	---	1,585,057	---	1,928,794
14. Short-term capital (official) .	---	---	---	119,000,000
15. Monetary gold	34,379,111	26,783,653	27,301,699	5,874,164
16. Total (1-14).	134,353,360	142,692,954	279,455,183	278,562,419
17. Total (1-15).	168,732,471	169,476,607	306,756,882	284,436,583
18. Errors and omissions.	744,136	---	---	22,320,299

TABLE 6A-2 (Continued)

	1896 Cr.	1896 Dr.	1897 Cr.	1897 Dr.	1898 Cr.	1898 Dr.
Current Transaction						
1. Merchandise						
1.1 Merchandise (f.o.b.)	120,270,322	171,674,474	166,495,660	219,300,772	169,168,280	277,502,157
1.2 Other.	---	8,422,141	---	42,157,069	---	47,261,555
2. Nonmonetary gold.	3,877,180	---	1,382,273	---	1,545,880	---
3. Foreign travel.	6,150,191	1,610,030	6,514,555	1,774,625	5,468,211	2,519,646
4. Transportation						
4.1 Freight.	3,511,259	13,785,460	6,832,265	17,609,852	11,995,987	27,028,710
4.2 Other.	1,881,664	---	1,981,126	---	2,486,780	---
5. Insurance	170,000	3,381,987	565,000	4,320,225	317,000	6,826,553
6. International investment income						
6.1 Direct investment.	828,799	2,800,866	2,092,413	3,496,974	1,550,995	4,057,446
6.2 Interest	114,580	171,000	495,693	33,482	2,802,544	5
7. Government transaction.	1,988,910	1,431,480	2,799,573	1,580,629	2,400,400	1,790,731
8. Miscellaneous services.	---	---	---	---	---	---
9. Donations						
9.1 Private.	8,410,198	1,201,391	9,973,311	1,499,976	13,057,085	1,740,383
9.2 Reparation	84,460,540	---	35,006,278	---	119,157,659	---
9.3 Government	---	---	---	---	---	---
10. Total (1-9)	231,663,643	204,478,829	234,138,147	291,773,604	329,950,821	368,727,186
Capital Transaction						
11. Long-term capital (private) . .	---	---	---	---	---	---
12. Short-term capital (private). .	---	---	---	---	---	---
13. Long-term capital (official). .	---	1,792,273	43,000,000	474,577	---	---
14. Short-term capital (official) .	---	---	70,000,000	---	---	---
15. Monetary gold	11,598,884	39,142,208	19,219,164	81,466,713	86,987,481	42,563,781
16. Total (1-14).	231,663,643	206,271,102	347,138,147	292,248,181	329,950,821	368,727,186
17. Total (1-15).	243,262,527	245,413,310	366,357,311	373,714,894	416,938,302	411,290,967
18. Errors and omissions.	2,150,783	---	7,357,583	---	---	5,647,335

TABLE 6A-2 (Concluded)

	1899 Cr.	1899 Dr.	1900 Cr.	1900 Dr.	1901 Cr.	1901 Dr.
Current Transaction						
1. Merchandise						
1.1 Merchandise (f.o.b.)	219,357,450	195,937,313	208,641,252	250,865,770	257,547,944	230,362,889
1.2 Other.	---	8,696,136	---	26,151,550	---	26,460,811
2. Nonmonetary gold.	2,233,803	---	2,832,958	---	3,301,095	---
3. Foreign travel.	5,184,797	3,764,725	15,747,403	3,477,851	17,015,116	2,886,214
4. Transportation						
4.1 Freight.	14,631,003	20,519,419	18,925,236	31,254,089	17,979,647	20,874,638
4.2 Other.	3,452,076	---	5,132,912	---	5,402,816	---
5. Insurance	443,000	3,945,194	79,000	5,141,987	764,000	4,579,118
6. International investment income						
6.1 Direct investment.	3,158,680	4,090,706	1,516,592	4,753,782	1,905,620	4,894,346
6.2 Interest	918,129	1,960,025	734,746	3,931,081	503,756	3,924,937
7. Government transaction.	1,241,087	2,134,241	255,814	2,514,024	14,706	2,345,485
8. Miscellaneous services.	---	---	---	---	---	---
9. Donations						
9.1 Private.	18,318,347	1,754,650	24,616,159	2,039,067	12,190,507	2,099,359
9.2 Reparation	---	---	---	---	---	---
9.3 Government	---	---	---	---	---	---
10. Total (1-9)	268,938,372	242,802,409	278,482,072	330,129,201	316,625,207	298,427,797
Capital Transaction						
11. Long-term capital (private) . .	---	---	---	---	---	---
12. Short-term capital (private). .	---	---	---	---	---	---
13. Long-term capital (official). .	97,880,000	15,522	---	---	---	---
14. Short-term capital (official) .	50,000,000	---	---	---	---	---
15. Monetary gold	11,178,247	20,163,501	56,707,063	11,517,835	14,049,099	10,960,750
16. Total (1-14).	416,818,372	242,817,931	278,482,072	330,129,201	316,625,207	298,427,797
17. Total (1-15).	427,996,619	262,981,432	335,189,135	341,647,036	330,674,306	309,388,547
18. Errors and omissions.	---	165,015,187	6,457,901	---	---	21,285,759

position, has been entered as a credit item. Since Japan was on a bimetallic standard before 1896, silver production was also included before that year. Specie is valued in terms of silver yen.

3. Foreign Travel

Government travel expenditures have been obtained from the *Report of Revenues and Expenditures*[9] as in 2.1. Private expenditures have been estimated from number of outgoing passengers in the *Statistical Yearbook,* and average travel expenditure per passenger can be obtained from *The Survey for 1901.* Foreign tourists' expenditures have been estimated from the number of incoming vessels and average expenditure per tourist in the same *Survey.* Both series have been corrected for price changes.

4. Transportation

4.1. Freight

There are annual statistics on freight costs for both exports and imports for the period 1889–94 in *Statistical Yearbook, 1895.* These have been carefully examined and the year 1892 has been chosen as a bench mark year to estimate freight costs in the period before 1888 and after 1895. First, the ratio of freight to total exports and imports (both in f.o.b. prices) has been computed for the year 1892. It has turned out to be 5.85 percent for exports and 7.89 percent for imports. This constant ratio has been corrected for overtime charges in freight rates by using L. Isserlis' index of tramp shipping freight rates[10] (1892 base) to obtain the freight ratios in other years. This ratio in each year has been multiplied by the total value of exports and imports of that year to obtain total freight cost. (Total freight costs for imports are to be entered as debit item in 4.1 so that the sum of debit items in 1.1 and 4.1 gives the value of imports in c.i.f. The next step is to divide these total costs into two parts: freights due to Japanese vessels and those due to foreign vessels. This has been done by using the statistics on shares of Japanese and foreign freighters in value terms.[11] Both export and import freights received by Japanese vessels have been entered as credit items in 4.1, together with charges received on passengers.

---

[9] See footnote 8.

[10] L. Isserlis, "Tramp Shipping Cargoes and Freights," *The Journal of the Royal Statistical Society,* 1938 (reproduced in B. R. Mitchell, *Abstract of British Historical Statistics* (Cambridge: Cambridge University Press, 1962), p. 224.
Owing to Professor Tsuru's helpful comment on the underestimation of freight and the overestimation of insurance cost, the author has been able to revise his estimates of these two items.

[11] Oriental Economist, *Foreign Trade of Japan, A Statistical Survey,* (Tokyo: Oriental Economist, 1935).

4.2. Other

It is to be noted that purchases made by vessels in port usually entered in this item are already included in the case of Japanese custom statistics before 1900, in the value of exports or imports. Thus, the remaining transactions are canal tolls, rentals or chartered vessels, etc.

5. Insurance

There have been two attempts to estimate the c.i.f./f.o.b. ratio. Rathgen, in 1891[12] estimated the ratio in early Meiji years at 112–118 percent. The late Professor Ishibashi of Kyoto Imperial University, in 1924[13] estimated the ratios as 118 percent in 1868, 115 percent in 1877, 112 percent in 1887, and 110 percent in 1897. We have assumed the ratio as 110 percent in 1897.[14] As explained in 4.1, the ratio, f/f.o.b. in 1897 was estimated as 8 percent, thus, the share of insurance charges in total f.o.b. imports becomes 2 percent in that year. Assuming this proportion of freight to insurance to be constant (8:2) throughout the whole period, we have estimated the insurance cost for each year. The credit item in 5, on the other hand, was estimated from the records of Japanese insurance companies.

6. International Investment Income

6.1. Direct Investment Income

Direct investment by foreigners was limited within the area of extraterritorial settlement, mostly in Yokohama and Kobe. The *Survey for 1901* gives an estimate of profit earnings by foreigners in 1901. This has been used as a bench mark, and annual estimates of the profit on direct investment have been obtained by using the population statistics of foreign merchants in the settlements. These have been corrected for price changes. The credit entries of this account are the overseas profit earnings of the Yokohama Specie Bank and others.

6.2. Interest

Interest payments on government bonds, which will be explained in 13, are entered.

7. Government Transactions

Government overseas expenditures on diplomatic agencies,

---

[12] K. Rathgen, *Japan's Volkswirtschaft und Staatshaushalt, Staats und Socialwissenschaftliche* Forschungen hrg. von G. Schmoller, Bd. 10 (Leipzig: Duncker, 1891).

[13] G. Ishibashi, "On the Valuation of Foreign Trade in Meiji Era," *Kokumin Keizai Zasshi,* Vol. 36, No. 6 (1924) (in Japanese).

[14] This is the same assumption which IMF usually makes at present to convert f.o.b. statistics into c.i.f.

expositions and trade fairs, etc. have been obtained from the *Report of Revenues and Expenditures.*

8. Miscellaneous Services

No attempt has been made to estimate this item, on the assumption that it might have not been important.

9. Donations

9.1. Private

After making the figures in the *Survey for 1901,* private remittances have been estimated on the bases of the number of Japanese abroad and foreigners in Japan in the *Statistical Yearbook.*

9.2. Reparations

The reparation payments at the beginning of the Meiji era: 1868–74 were those due to the old Shogunate government. These figures have been obtained from the *Report of Revenues and Expenditures.* Large amounts were received from China in the period 1895–98, and very detailed information on these can be found in the *Financial History in the Meiji Era,* Vol. 5.[15]

9.3. Government

Only one entry in 1883 represents the donation of the U.S. government in order to cancel American receipt of reparations at the end of the Tokugawa era.[16]

Capital Transaction

11. Long-Term Capital (Private)
12. Short-Term Capital (Private)

Although there should have been a direct investment in the settlement, no attempt has been made to estimate it. There is no sizable private portfolio investment recorded in the whole period.

13. Long-Term Capital (Official)

Two kinds of government bond were issued in London in the early years: a 9 percent bond in 1870 and a 7 percent bond in 1873. The very detailed records of the receipt and repayment of principal and the payment of interest, commissions, etc. are given in the *Financial History in the Meiji Era,* Vol. 9. The former has been entered in 13; the latter in 6.2. There was no government loan made until 1897.

---

[15] The Ministry of Finance, *Meiji Zaisei Shi* (referred to as *Financial History in the Meiji Era*) (Tokyo: Maruzen & Co., 1904) Vol. 5.

[16] These were for bombardment of an American ship in Shimonoseki in 1862.

14. Short-Term Capital (Official)

One small loan from the Oriental Bank in 1869 is the only one recorded.

15. Monetary Gold

There are no statistics of specie inflow and outflow for the first four years of the Meiji era, 1868–71. Both gold and silver movements are entered in 15 in terms of silver yen before 1896.

7 | Trends in Level and Structure of Consumption

SIMON KUZNETS

In this paper we summarize the trends in private consumption suggested by the available long-term estimates of product and its distribution by use.[1] These estimates are currently being revised and some of the details of the tables and discussion below will be changed; but the major findings, if cautiously formulated, should remain valid even after revision. Since the role of consumption in the mechanism of economic growth is too important to be neglected, and the approximate orders of magnitude are implied by aggregates already being used in analyzing other aspects of economic growth, the explicit formulation of these implications may help in the revisions and may provide better balance in the analysis.

I. LONG-TERM TRENDS

Per capita consumer expenditures rose to over six times their initial level from 1879–83 to 1962–64 (Table 7–1, col. 3, lines 1 and 19), and the average rate of growth over the entire period of more than eight decades was about 25 percent per decade (line 24, col. 3),

---

[1] I am indebted to Professors Kazushi Ohkawa and Henry Rosovsky for permission to use the basic estimates of product and labor force and their components, prepared from the files of the Institute of Economic Research of Hitotsubashi University; and to Professor Alan H. Gleason for the unpublished extension of Appendix Table 2, pp. 438–41 in his paper, "Economic Growth and Consumption in Japan," in William W. Lockwood (ed.), *The State and Economic Enterprise in Japan* (Princeton, N.J.: Princeton University Press, 1965), a paper that was of much help in the preparation of this manuscript. I am also grateful to Professor Miyohei Shinohara and Professors Ohkawa and Gleason for their valuable comments on a preliminary version presented at the Conference.

TABLE 7-1

Movements and Rates of Growth of Population, and of Gross Domestic Product (GDP), Personal Consumption Expenditures (PCE), and Other Expenditures per Capita, 1879-83 to 1962-64
(Based on Volumes in Constant Prices, Mostly to the 1934-36 Base)

A. INDEXES (1924-28 = 100) AND SHARE OF PCE

			Per Capita			
		Popu- lation (1)	Gross Domestic Product (2)	Personal Consumption Expenditure (3)	Residual (Govt. Cons., Gross Cap. Form., Balances of Exports and Imports) (4)	Share of PCE in GDP (%) (5)
1.	1879-83. . .	61.3	31.9	(34.3)	(25.3)	(79.0)
2.	1884-88. . .	63.8	34.2	(36.7)	(27.2)	(79.0)
3.	1889-93. . .	66.6	40.0	40.3	39.0	74.2
4.	1894-98. . .	69.7	48.5	52.5	37.5	79.6
5.	1899-1903. .	73.6	53.2	55.3	47.2	76.5
6.	1904-08. . .	78.1	56.3	54.4	61.6	71.1
7.	1909-13. . .	83.0	64.6	64.2	65.8	73.1
8.	1914-18. . .	88.7	74.9	74.0	77.6	72.6
9.	1919-23. . .	93.4	85.7	81.6	97.1	70.0
10.	1924-28. . .	100.0	100.0	100.0	100.0	73.6
11.	1929-33. . .	107.8	105.2	99.5	121.0	69.6
12.	1934-38. . .	115.1	134.3	107.8	207.9	59.1
13.	1939-44. . .	120.0	146.8	84.2	324.0	42.2
14.	1946-48* . .	129.6	82.0	64.7	130.1	58.1
15.	1949-51* . .	138.5	97.5	81.5	141.8	61.5
16.	1952-54* . .	144.9	123.0	106.8	167.1	63.9
17.	1955-58* . .	150.7	156.3	131.8	222.0	62.1
18.	1959-61* . .	155.6	216.1	168.1	342.3	57.3
19.	1962-64* . .	160.1	279.7	211.6	457.8	55.7

B. RATES OF GROWTH PER DECADE (%)

20.	1879-83 to 1899-1903 (20 years)	9.6	29.1	27.0	36.6
21.	1899-1903 to 1924-28 (25 years)	13.0	28.7	26.7	35.0
22.	1879-83 to 1924-28 (45 years)	11.5	28.9	26.8	35.7
23.	1924-28 to 1962-64 (37.25 years)	13.5	31.8	22.3	50.4
24.	1879-83 to 1962-64 (82.25 years)	12.4	30.2	24.8	42.2

*Fiscal years beginning April 1.

TABLE 7-1 (Continued)

NOTES: *Lines 1-12*--From the basic tables for Kazushi Ohkawa and Henry Rosovsky, *Century of Japanese Growth* (in preparation), derived from the Hitotsubashi series made available in 1964. For the first two quinquennia (lines 1-2) the share of PCE in GDP was assumed to be 79 percent--suggested by the shares for the later quinquennia (column 5, lines 3-10). The entries for population (column 1) are based on arithmetic means of annual population estimates; those in columns 2-4 are indexes of ratios of arithmetic means of GDP and its components to the arithmetic means of population. All product series relate to volumes in 1934-36 prices.

Lines 13-16--Population was extrapolated from 1934-38 by the annual series given in the United Nations, *Demographic Yearbook*, various issues. The product series were extrapolated by estimates shown in the Bank of Japan, *Hundred-Year Statistics of the Japanese Economy* (Tokyo, 1966), Series 9, p. 51. Since GDP in constant prices is not available, GNP is used as extrapolator.

Lines 17-19--Extrapolated from 1952-54. For population the series is from the sources cited in the notes to lines 13-16. For the product series, extrapolators are from the *Supplement* to *Hundred-Year Statistics of the Japanese Economy, ibid.*, containing revised statistics for 1951-64.

despite depression and war. This is an impressive record, a greater relative rise in per capita consumer expenditures than, I suspect, in any developed country over the period except possibly Sweden.

Since the rate of growth of gross domestic product per capita was high and the long-run fraction representing diversion of current product from consumption is limited, such a high rate of growth of consumer expenditures per capita should have been expected. Per capita GDP rose to almost nine times its initial level from 1879-83 to 1962-64. If we assume that the minimum diversion fraction (i.e., government consumption, gross domestic capital formation, and the balance of current foreign transactions excluding factor payments) is 15 percent, and the long-run maximum is not above 50 percent (both figures are suggested by cross-section and long-term data for a variety of national economies), the growth in per capita GDP shown in column 2 should produce, *at the minimum,* a rise in per capita consumer expenditures from 85 (i.e., 100×0.85) to 438 (i.e., 877×0.50), or by a factor of 5.2. The actual growth factor in column 3 is 6.2—not much above the implicit minimum. In view of this close relationship of the observed rise in per capita consumption to the minimum suggested by the growth in per capita total product and the limits on the diversion fraction, any substantial downward revision in the growth rate of consumption would require an equally sizable downward revision in the growth rate of total product.

The great rise in per capita consumption, despite its positive association with the higher rate of growth of per capita gross product, is still meaningful. If Professor Gleason's conversion to purchasing power comparable to the U.S. dollar is acceptable, the extrapolation back to the early 1880's suggests a per capita consumption of $80 (in 1958 prices), compared with $495 in 1962–64.[2]

Such changes usually mean great shifts in the pattern of life. And, indeed, evidence on urbanization, structure of consumption, and so forth confirms this statement. Thus if we use the old census definition (recently changed) of urban population in Japan, viz, "shi" most of which are agglomerations of 30,000 or more inhabitants, the urban proportion was about (and not more than) 10 percent in the early 1880's; 18 percent in 1920; 56 percent in 1955; and 63 percent in 1960.[3] And the data on industrialization are no less impressive. Table 7–2 below shows that the share of the labor force in the A sector

---

[2] Calculated by applying the index implicit in consumer expenditures in the United States for 1958 to the 1955 price volumes given in Gleason, Appendix Table 2, pp. 438–41, and the mimeographed extension to 1964 (the ratio of 1958 to 1955 prices is 1.065, see e.g., *Economic Report of the President, January, 1965* [Washington, D.C.: U.S. Government Printing Office], Tables B–1 and B–2, pp. 189–90). The revised estimate for 1962–64, $465 in 1955 prices, became $495 in 1958 prices. It was extrapolated back to 1879–83 by column 3 of Table 7–1.

The conversion to 1958 prices was intended to facilitate comparison with per capita GDP at factor cost given for 1958 in United Nations, *Yearbook of National Accounts Statistics, 1965* (New York, 1966), Tables 9A and 9B, pp. 493–503, where the figures are shown in 1958 U.S. dollars. With the ratio of consumer expenditures to GDP at factor cost in Japan in 1958 of 0.665, per capita GDP for 1958 works out to $504—which may be compared with $285 given in the *Yearbook,* Table 9A and with $339 in Table 9B. Professor Gleason's adjustment for price differences was much more thorough than that involved in the UN conversion, even in Table 9B.

The approximation to GDP per capita at factor cost in 1879–83 would work out to $80 divided by perhaps 0.84, five points above the ratio of 0.79 used in Table 7–1 in relating PCE to GDP in market prices, or $95 in 1958 U.S. prices. This estimate of the per capita product of Japan in 1881 is appreciably above those shown for 1958 in the *Yearbook,* Table 9B for the populous countries of Asia (e.g., India—70; Pakistan—66; Indonesia—73; and a total for East and Southeast Asia, excluding Japan—78). But further adjustments are required, which may put per capita product of Japan in those days not much above that of the Asian underdeveloped countries today.

[3] The data for 1920, 1955, and 1960 are from United Nations, *Demographic Yearbook, 1952 and 1963* (New York, 1953 and 1964), Table 6, p. 177 in the former, and Table 5, p. 200 in the latter. Extrapolation to the 1880's is based on the distribution of population by communities of different size in Irene B. Taeuber, *The Population of Japan* (Princeton, N.J.: Princeton University Press, 1958), Table 13, p. 49 and the table on p. 71. The Taeuber monograph shows that the proportion in communities of more than 50,000 was 12.4 percent in 1888 and about 16 percent in 1920.

(agriculture, forestry, fisheries) declined from 81.6 percent in 1879–83 to 34.6 percent in 1959–61, whereas the share attached to non-agricultural, urban pursuits rose from 18.4 to 65.4 percent.

And yet these shifts in pattern of residence and industry attachment, and other related shifts, can account for only part of the rise in per capita consumer expenditures. While the analysis would require more evidence than is now easily available, some discussion may be worthwhile.

Consider the implications of the shift in the distribution of the labor force between the agricultural (A) and the nonagricultural sector (N); assume that we can distinguish between population dependent upon the product (or income) of the A sector and that dependent upon the product (or income) of the N sector, the two groups within total population being proportional to the A and N groups within the labor force; and assume further that the consumer expenditures per capita of the A- and N-dependent populations are closely related to the total product per worker in the A and N sectors. With these reasonable assumptions, or some modifications thereof, we can translate the existing estimates of product originating in and labor force attached to the A and N sectors into inferences concerning trends in consumption per capita for the A- and N-dependent population respectively.

Table 7–2 presents two variants of the trends in per capita consumption of the A- and N-dependent groups based on these assumptions. Variant I assumes a proportional relation between total product per worker (or per capita, assuming the same number of dependents per worker in the A and N sectors) and consumption per capita, which implies that the nonconsumption parts of the product -the allowance for capital consumption, taxes to cover government outlays that do not enter ultimate consumption, savings (personal or corporate) to finance capital formation, and so forth—are combined in the same proportions to total product in the A and the N sectors. This assumption is simple, but unrealistic. In recent years, the proportion of capital consumption charges, savings, and taxes to total product was much greater for the N sector than for the A sector; whereas in earlier years with the greater burden of the land tax, lesser importance of capital consumption charges, and smaller share of corporate savings, the proportions of the "residual" in total product for the A sector may have been as high as, or even higher than, the corresponding proportion for the N sector. While the matter is of some importance, no ready data are at hand, and Variant II is based on the assumption that at the beginning of the period, the proportion of

TABLE 7-2

Illustrative Calculation of Personal Consumption Expenditures (PCE) per Capita of Population Dependent upon the Agricultural (A) and Nonagricultural (N) Sectors, Selected Dates, 1879-1961
(Based on Volumes in 1934-36 Prices)

	Variant I (Proportions of Residual to PCE Assumed the Same for the A- and N-Dependent Populations)				Variant II (Proportions of Residual in PCE Assumed the Same for the A and N Sectors in 1879-83, Twice as High for the N Sector in 1924-28, and Four Times as High for the N Sector in 1959-61)		
	1879-83	1899-1903	1924-28	1959-61	1879-83	1924-28	1959-61
	(1)	(2)	(3)	(4)	(5)	(6)	(7)
1. PCE per capita, countrywide, 1924-28 = 100 . .	34.3	55.3	100.0	168.1	34.3	100.0	168.1
Percentage shares in GDP (assumed to represent shares of A-dependent and N-dependent population in PCE, unadjusted in Variant I and adjusted in Variant II in accordance with assumptions stated)							
2. A sector.	62.5	44.3	25.1	12.2	62.5	28.9	18.8
3. N sector.	37.5	55.7	74.9	87.8	37.5	71.1	81.2
Percentage shares in labor force (assumed to represent shares of A-dependent and N-dependent population in total population)							
4. A sector.	81.6	69.3	51.5	34.6	81.6	51.5	34.6
5. N Sector.	18.4	30.7	48.5	65.4	18.4	48.5	65.4
Ratio of sector product per worker (unadjusted in Variant I, and adjusted in Variant II) to countrywide product per worker (assumed to represent ratios of sectoral PCE per capita to countrywide PCE per capita)							
6. A sector (line 2/line 4)	0.765	0.640	0.487	0.353	0.765	0.561	0.543
7. N sector (line 3/line 5)	2.042	1.812	1.545	1.342	2.042	1.466	1.242
8. Intersectoral spread (line 7/line 6)	2.67	2.83	3.17	3.80	2.67	2.61	2.29

Sectoral PCE per capita as percent of countrywide PCE per capita in 1924–28							
9. A (line 1 × line 6) . .	26.24	35.39	48.70	59.13	26.24	56.10	91.28
10. N (line 1 × line 7) . .	70.04	100.20	154.50	224.79	70.04	146.60	208.78
Sectoral PCE per capita, 1924–28. = 100							
11. A (based on line 9) . .	53.88	72.67	100.0	121.42	46.77	100.0	162.71
12. N (based on line 10). .	45.33	64.85	100.0	145.50	47.78	100.0	142.41

NOTES: *Columns 5–7*--The proportions of the residuals in total product are derived from Table 7-1, column 5. Given these percentage shares (21.0 in 1879-83, 26.4 in 1924-28, and 42.7 percent in 1959-61, see lines 1, 10, and 18 in Table 7-1), the percentage shares of the A and N sectors in GDP given in lines 2-3, columns 1-4 of this table, and the assumptions made for Variant II, we allocated the residual to the A and N sectors in each of the three periods and adjusted the shares in GDP to represent shares in PCE.

Line 1--See Table 7-1, Panel A, column 3.

Lines 2-5--From the Ohkawa-Rosovsky basic tables in *Century of Japanese Growth* (in preparation). The shares are derived from quinquennial or three-year totals.

"residual" to total income is the same in both the N and A sectors; but that by 1924–28 the proportion in the N sector is twice that in the A sector, and by 1959–61 the former is four times the latter. While this assumption may be extreme in that the proportion for the N sector may be too high relative to that for the A sector, it does yield a reasonable estimate of the *change* over time in the relative share of the "residual" in the total income of the two sectors—and it is this change over time that is crucial for our purposes. The assumption underlying Variant *II* stresses a major trend that is important in the interpretation of the "dual structure," viz, that the sectoral product per worker may represent a changing fraction of both consumption and income per worker or per capita of the sector-dependent populations, in which case the widening of the intersectoral disparities in product per worker may not be accompanied by widening intersectoral disparities in consumption (and possibly income) per capita and per worker.

The calculations in Table 7–2 are subject to several qualifications. And after summarizing the findings we shall consider those qualifications that are likely to modify them.

a) In both variants, the long-term rise in consumer expenditures per capita is substantial for both population groups—while their relative proportions shift markedly. In Variant *I,* consumption per capita for the A-dependent population rises by a factor of 2.25 from 1879–83 to 1959–61; in Variant *II* the rise is by a factor of 3.48 (line 11). For the N-dependent population, the rise in consumption per capita over the same period is by a factor of 3.21 in Variant *I* and one of 2.98 in Variant *II* (line 12).

b) While the detail is not provided, it is clear that the rate of rise in consumption per capita is high in both the earlier and later periods —even though the growth rate from 1924–28 to 1959–61 is somewhat lower than before the 1920's, presumably reflecting the effects of depression and particularly war in the later period.

c) In Variant *I* the intersectoral difference in product per worker and hence consumption per capita widens in the course of time (lines 6–8). But if we assume that Variant *II* reflects realistically trends in the proportions of the "residual" in the total product of the two sectors, the intersectoral difference in consumption per capita (and those possibly in income per worker) becomes narrower over the period.

d) We noted under (*a*) that over the period as a whole, per capita consumption of the A-dependent population increased by a factor of 2.25 or 3.48, depending upon the variant used; that of the N-dependent population increased by a factor of 3.21 or 2.98, depending upon the variant. Yet according to Table 7–1, the countrywide per capita consumption expenditures rose over the same period by a factor of 4.9—much larger than the growth factor for either population component. The difference is due, of course, to the fact that *countrywide* per capita consumption is affected not only by increases in per capita consumption *within* each sector but also by the shift of population (and labor force) from the low per capita consumption (and product) *A* sector to the high per capita consumption (and product) *N* sector. We could calculate the separate contributions of the intrasectoral rise in consumption per capita and of the intersectoral shift, but it seems best not to complicate discussion by statistical detail. Obviously the contribution of the intersectoral shift in numbers would be substantial; and it would be proportionately greater for Variant *I*, in which the intersectoral differences in consumption per capita (which are used as weights in establishing the contribution of intersectoral shifts) widen, than for Variant *II*, in which these intersectoral differences narrow.

If we accept, as we must, the estimates of sectoral product and labor force, as well as the general order of magnitude of the assumptions underlying Variant *II*, what are the qualifications that attach to the other assumptions underlying Table 7–2? These qualifications concern us particularly because they might cast some doubt upon the identification of the *A*-dependent group with the agricultural, rural population, and of the *N*-dependent group with the nonagricultural, largely urban population; and invalidate the inference that the per capita consumption of both the *A*- and *N*-dependent population groups rose markedly in the course of Japan's economic growth.

Three relevant, and possibly significant, qualifications may be noted. The first bears directly upon the identification of the *A*-dependent and *N*-dependent categories with two distinguishable groups within the population, the former primarily with agriculturists living in the countryside and the latter with nonagriculturists, a dominant proportion of whom are urban residents. Product originating in the *A* sector may flow to landlords living either in the countryside or in the cities; and both they and the farmers and farm workers may also be engaged in nonagricultural pursuits, thus being both *A*- and *N*-dependent. Second, we may question the validity of assuming that the movement of the ratio of dependents to workers was the same for both groups of the population. Third, the ratios of sectoral products per worker are based on volumes in *current* prices; and differential price trends may affect the comparative trends in consumption per capita in *constant* prices.

The last two qualifications are unlikely to affect the findings much.

The second, which emphasizes ratios of dependents to workers, relates to *differences* in trends between the two broad sectors, and such differences can hardly be significant compared with the trend in per capita consumption.[4] The third requires some knowledge of the trends in prices of goods consumed (whether purchased or retained from own production) by the A-dependent and N-dependent population groups. The crude comparison possible with the few available price indexes does not reveal significant differences in long-term trends, particularly for the mixtures of agricultural and nonagricultural product prices that the two composite price indexes should represent.[5]

It is the first qualification that is most relevant, and if pushed to the extreme may modify our inferences significantly. Thus if we were to assume that in the early periods nonagricultural activity by farmers, foresters, and fishermen was substantial and contributed significantly to their total product, the group whom we call the A-dependent population, still identified by the A symbol and still 81.6 percent of total labor force in 1879–83, would be assigned some of the product now assigned to the N group in line 3 of Table 7–2. If we then assumed that such engagement in non-A activities is reduced in the course of economic growth, the upward trend in the product per worker and in consumption per capita in the A sector would be reduced, while the long-term rise in the product per worker and consumption per capita in the N sector would be further enhanced. But, in view of the widening rather than narrowing over time of opportunities for nonagricultural employment and income to the A-dependent population, the assumption should probably not be given much weight.

We may conclude that even with the qualifications considered, per capita consumption of both the agricultural rural and nonagricultural

---

[4] The emphasis is on trends in the ratios, not on their levels at a given point of time. With the wide inclusion of women and family labor in Japanese labor force data, the ratio of dependents to workers may be significantly lower in the A than in the N sector. But there is no ground for assuming that the trends in the ratios were significantly different in the two sectors.

[5] The comparison should cover prices of all commodities and services consumed by the A-dependent and N-dependent groups, including both agricultural and nonagricultural commodities and services for each group, even though with different weights. Any observable differences in price trends between say agricultural and industrial consumer goods would, therefore, have to be reduced to allow for the consumption of both types of goods by both population groups.

The easily available data show no great differences in trend between prices for commodity classes of the type noted above, although this may be due to the crudity of the data. See the sector specific deflators in Kazushi Ohkawa and others, *The Growth Rate of the Japanese Economy since 1878* (Tokyo, 1957), Figure 1, p. 33 and Table 16, p. 29 compared with Table 1, p. 17; and also the price ratio used in Table 7–5 below.

urban population in Japan rose markedly, not only in the years before 1924–28 but also over the long period as a whole; and implicitly, therefore, real total income per head in both sectors rose similarly. Although the duality of the economy, in the sense of the contrast in per worker product and per capita income (and consumption) has persisted, both parts of the duality have risen at quite high rates. And the finding obviously bears upon the common assumption of the existence of surplus labor, and of the presumptive effect of the latter on the long-term real rates for labor.[6] This assumption and the inferences drawn from it may not prove incompatible with the rising trends revealed by Table 7–2, but additional analysis should be undertaken in an attempt to reconcile presumptive stability over time in the real wage rate of industrial labor with rising real income and consumption per capita in both the A and the N sectors.

The findings in Tables 7–1 and 7–2 are only *implications* of the familiar data on sectoral labor force and output—the data from which countrywide product and consumer expenditures, total and per capita, were derived. In this sense we are not using any new independent

---

[6] See, for example, John C. H. Fei and Gustav Ranis, *The Development of the Labor Surplus Economy: Theory and Policy,* Economic Growth Center, Yale University (Homewood, Ill.: Richard D. Irwin, Inc., 1964), pp. 263–64.

The evidence on the movement of real wages (in manufacturing) is puzzling. In this monograph, the authors refer to Umemura's data for 1902–30, and, using a five-year moving average, find that "The virtual constancy before and rapid rise of the real wage after approximately 1918 is rather startling" (p. 264). In Appendix Table 3, pp. 442–43 of "Economic Growth and Consumption in Japan," *op. cit.,* Professor Gleason gives an index of real wages in manufacturing starting in 1879. The five-year moving average shows fair stability (although with a perceptible swing to a peak in 1885) to about 1903 or 1904 (midyear for the moving average). The average, 80 at that point, then rises to 107 for the period centered in 1918, an increase of 34 percent in about a decade and a half. The rise to 158 centered in 1930 is even more rapid, but it is part of another swing in which the index drops sharply to an average of 134 centered in 1938; or, if we exclude years of war participation, to an average of 143 centered in 1935. Thus the percentage rise from 1903–04 to 1918 is no smaller than that between 1918 and 1935—also about 34 percent for a somewhat longer period.

Moreover, the five-year averages for per capita GDP and PCE in Table 7–1 suggest fair stability from 1894–98 through 1904–08, and a rise thereafter—a movement similar to that in the Gleason real wage five-year moving averages; and the similarity in the movement continues into the 1930's. Hence the stability of real wages in manufacturing before the end of the 19th century, which differs from the upward movement of the aggregative measures in Table 7–1, is suspect; and should be checked to see whether the discrepancy is due to the data for money wages or for the consumer price indexes.

Whether the relevant real wages are averages or for new entrants only, the evidence must be examined much more carefully before tenable conclusions concerning trends of real wages in manufacturing in Japan can be reached.

information. We are merely expounding—after making a few reasonable assumptions—the implications of the output estimates for per capita consumption in the broad sectors of the economy and society. But the implications are important because they stress an impressive rise in per capita consumption of the "traditional labor surplus" A sector that has dominated, quantitatively, the Japanese economy through much of the period.

A related finding is of some interest. In a paper published seven years ago, Ohkawa and Rosovsky discussed the relative importance of the traditional or indigenous component in the nationwide output and consumption of Japan. Their calculation of the 1955 consumer expenditure pattern, based on the revised consumer price index, shows that urban indigenous consumption accounted for about 49 percent of the total, if *ampan* and housing are excluded.[7] Since this was *urban* consumption, one may conjecture that the share of indigenous product in *total* consumption was more than a half. This share is, of course, applicable to both total and per capita consumption.

But let us take the low figure of 50 percent for 1955 to represent 1955–58 and make the extreme assumption that the share of indigenous products in consumption in 1879–83 was 100 percent, i.e., that no modern products were consumed then. If per capita consumer expenditures rose from 34.3 in 1879–83 to 131.8 in 1955–58 (see Table 7–1, col. 3), per capita consumption of indigenous products rose from 34.3 in 1879–83 to (131.8 × 0.5), or 65.9, in 1955–58, i.e., almost doubled. But since some "modern" goods were being produced and imports were relatively substantial in the early 1880's, some allowance should be made for nonindigenous consumption. If the latter was a moderate fraction of the total, say 10 percent, per capita use of indigenous consumer goods rose from 30.9 to 65.9, more than doubling between the early 1880's and 1955–58.

This again is an inference from the known production data. It is related to the earlier findings in two ways. First, since most of the indigenous products come from the A sector, the high rate of growth of the output of the A sector, particularly before 1909–13, would contribute to a high rate of growth in indigenous consumer goods. Second and perhaps more important, the retention of the taste for indigenous goods, by both the rural and the urban population, has contributed to a high rate of growth of both product and consumption per capita. Given the resources of the country, particularly in the

---

[7] See "The Indigenous Components in the Modern Japanese Economy," *Economic Development and Cultural Change,* Vol. 9, No. 3 (April, 1961), Table 7, p. 489.

early periods, the growth potential of indigenous goods may have been higher than the potential for increasing consumption of nonindigenous, Western types of consumer goods.

II. PATTERNS OF TRENDS

Table 7–1 suggests that there is a distinct break after the 1920's in the upward trend in consumption per capita. From 100 in 1924–28 the index drops to 99.5 in 1929–33 and then recovers to 107.8 in 1934–38 (col. 3, lines 10–12). But the rise of 8 percent over the decade is low compared with an average of more than 25 percent per decade from 1879–83 to 1924–28, even though there was an equally low rise from 1894–98 to 1904–08 (col. 3, lines 4 and 6). With World War II, per capita consumption declined sharply and did not regain the prewar levels until about 1952–54. The pattern of movement in the 1930's in Table 7–1 is based on the Hitotsubashi data and differs somewhat from that in the official series, which shows a drop in per capita consumption expenditures from 1930–33 to 1934–38 of about 3 percent, suggesting a pre–World War II peak in 1924–28 rather than in 1934–38.[8] If we had spliced the Hitotsubashi and the official series in 1930, as Professor Gleason did in his paper (instead of using the overlap in 1934–38, when the absolute values of the two series are close), the break in the rate of growth of per capita consumption would have been sharper than it is now in Table 7–1, and would have dated back to a peak in 1924–28. A better reconciliation of the Hitotsubashi and the official series for the 1930's than is available now would greatly facilitate the analysis of the long-term record.

Whether we characterize the 1930's as a break in the trend or a phase in a long swing, there is little doubt that World War II and its immediate aftermath did constitute sharp breaks from which recovery to prewar levels was not attained until the early 1950's. We shall discuss two aspects of this time pattern of growth in per capita consumption—a high sustained rate of rise from the early 1880's to the late 1920's, stagnation in the 1930's, a sharp decline during the war and the immediate postwar years, and explosive growth since the

---

[8] The official data appeared (in English) originally in Economic Planning Board, *National Income and National Economic Accounts of Japan, 1930–1954* (Tokyo, December, 1955), and were recently reprinted and extended in Bank of Japan, *Hundred-Year Statistics of the Japanese Economy* (Tokyo, 1966), Series 9, p. 51.

For the same span, from 1930–33 to 1934–38, the Hitotsubashi series shows a rise of 8.4 percent. Both series are in 1934–36 prices.

early 1950's—(a) one suggested by the behavior of the other components of product, which we treated as a residual in Table 7–1; (b) the other bearing directly upon the meaning for recent growth of the stagnation and long-term decline in per capita consumption from the 1930's to the early 1950's.

a) The trends in the components of product other than private consumption expenditures are indicated by the summary data in Table 7–3 and we list the findings *seriatim*.

(i) Until the late 1920's or mid-1930's, the shares of these components rose, but only slightly. The shares based on current price volumes rose about 4 percentage points from the 1880's to the 1920's, and those based on volumes in constant prices rose about 5 percentage points (lines 1–4 and 15–18). It is only in the 1930's that the shares of other components rose sharply, and that of private consumer expenditures declined.

The rise in the share of gross capital formation was moderate. In terms of constant prices, it rose from about 13.5 to about 17 percent over the whole period from the 1880's to the 1920's or even the 1930's (lines 15–20, col. 4); and the addition of changes in claims against foreign countries, in shifting from gross domestic capital formation to gross national capital formation, would not change the picture. Thus, before the 1930's, consumption per head could rise at a high rate—almost equal to that of gross product per capita—because the high rate of growth of gross product could be attained with only moderately rising proportions of either government consumption or gross capital formation. In other words, a persistently low marginal capital-output ratio was characteristic of Japan's economic growth in the earlier decades.

This is hardly the place to discuss the reasons for this combination of persistently low capital-output ratios and high rates of growth of per capita product. But it is relevant to note that this combination was not limited to Japan. In several other "follower" countries, particularly the three Scandinavian countries and possibly Canada, high aggregate rates of growth were combined with fairly low and stable capital formation proportions that did not rise significantly until several decades after modern economic growth began.[9] But whether common or unique, the fact is that the first four or five decades of modern growth in Japan were characterized by the absorption of a constant and dominant share of the rise in GDP into consumption—with

---

[9] See S. Kuznets, "Quantitative Aspects of the Economic Growth of Nations: VI. Long-Term Trends in Capital Formation Proportions," *Economic Development and Cultural Change,* Vol. 9, No. 4, Part II (July, 1961).

considerable delay in shifting a significantly higher share of the product into either government consumption or capital formation. The investment, so to speak, was largely in consumption, not in material capital.

(*ii*) Whatever the reasons for the turn from the 1920's to the 1930's, which could best be discussed by those more familiar with the country's social and political history, GDP per capita still grew 34.3 percent in the decade from 1924–28 to 1934–38, i.e., at a *higher* rate than in the preceding 45 years when GDP per capita grew 28.9 percent per decade (Table 7–1, col. 2, lines 10, 12, and 22). If a 28.9 percent rate of growth could have been attained with the usual allocation of product among consumer expenditures, government consumption, gross domestic capital formation, and the net foreign balance residual, the stagnation or decline in per capita consumer expenditures that actually occurred in the 1930's would have been surprising. But it occurred because the share of government consumption, including military investment, rose sharply—while the share of gross domestic capital formation remained unaffected (although its orientation probably shifted away from consumer expenditures to government consumption including military needs). Since this shift was similar to the experience during the war years proper, when the share of government consumption increased further and that of gross domestic capital formation (even private) also rose slightly, one could say that the second half of the 1930's saw, in fact, the beginning of the war period—which then continued to the mid-1940's, with the immediate recovery lasting to the early 1950's.

This statement may seem to dismiss too easily the role of the world depression in the decline or stagnation of per capita consumer expenditures in Japan in the 1930's. It does deny the *direct* effects of the depression as manifested in most other free market countries—a decline in both per capita product and per capita consumption, but a rise in the share of consumer expenditures in the total.[10] But it does not deny that the depression did affect the balance of forces within the country, favoring those that eventually led to intensification of aggression abroad and to the rise in the share of government consumption.

---

[10] In the United States, gross national product (in 1964 prices) was $218 billion in 1929 and $220 billion in 1937, whereas personal consumption expenditures were $147 and $152 billion, respectively; and the share of the latter in GNP rose from 67 to 69 percent. Of course, with population increasing about 6 percent over the interval, per capita GNP and PCE both declined, the latter somewhat less than the former. For these data see *The Economic Report of the President, January 1965, op. cit.,* Tables B–2 and B–16, pp. 190 and 209.

TABLE 7-3

Use Structure of Gross Domestic Product, 1889 to 1964

A.   PERCENTAGE SHARES BASED ON VOLUMES IN CURRENT PRICES

	Personal Consumption Expenditures (1)	Government Consumption (including Military Investment) (2)	Military Investment (3)	Gross Domestic Capital Formation (4)	Remainder (Balance on C/A, Errors) (5)
Hitotsubashi Series, 1889-1938					
1. 1889-98. . 76.0	9.5	1.8	15.3	-0.8
2. 1899-1908. 72.7	14.6	2.3	13.4	-0.7
3. 1909-18. . 71.2	9.7	2.0	15.0	4.1
4. 1919-28. . 72.4	10.3	2.0	19.2	-1.9
5. 1929-33. . 67.9	14.5	1.8	16.8	0.8
6. 1934-38. . 58.1	18.8	6.8	18.1	5.0
Official Series, 1934-54					
7. 1934-38. . 59.3	19.1	n.a.	21.6	0
8. 1939-44. . 38.9	35.0	n.a.	26.6	-0.5
9. 1946-51 (F) 59.6	11.3	n.a.	29.0	0.1
10. 1952-54 (F) 61.6	11.1	n.a.	26.1	1.2
Official Series, Revised, 1952-64					
11. 1952-54 (F) 65.4	11.1	n.a.	24.5	-1.0
12. 1955-58 (F) 60.8	9.7	n.a.	29.5	0
13. 1959-61 (F) 54.8	8.7	n.a.	36.9	-0.4
14. 1962-64 (F) 54.4	9.1	n.a.	36.6	-0.1

B.   PERCENTAGE SHARES BASED ON CONSTANT PRICE VOLUMES

Hitotsubashi Series, 1889-1938, 1934-36 Prices					
15. 1889-98. . 76.9	9.1	1.0	13.6	0.4
16. 1899-1908. 73.8	14.3	1.5	11.5	0.4
17. 1909-18. . 72.8	9.5	1.4	13.3	4.4
18. 1919-28. . 71.8	10.4	1.9	16.7	1.1
19. 1929-33. . 69.6	16.7	1.9	15.9	-2.2
20. 1934-38. . 59.1	23.9	5.5	17.3	-0.3
Official Series, Shares in GNP, 1934-54 (1934-36 Prices)					
21. 1934-38. . 59.7	18.7	n.a.	20.3	1.3
22. 1939-44. . 42.7	29.0	n.a.	29.0	-0.7
23. 1946-51 (F) 60.8	10.0	n.a.	30.5	-1.3
24. 1952-54 (F) 64.7	11.6	n.a.	23.9	-0.2
Official Series, Revised, Shares in GNP, 1952-64 (1960 Calendar Year Prices)					
25. 1952-54 (F) 61.4	12.9	n.a.	24.5	1.2
26. 1955-58 (F) 59.6	10.3	n.a.	28.7	1.4
27. 1959-61 (F) 54.9	8.5	n.a.	36.8	-0.2
28. 1962-64 (F) 53.5	7.8	n.a.	38.7	0

TABLE 7-3 (Continued)

NOTES: F--Fiscal years beginning April I.

Since the underlying totals in lines 21-28 are gross national product, the balance on current account in the remainder includes net income from abroad.

All percentages are based on cumulative totals for the period, except in lines 1-4 and 15-18 where the percentages were calculated for each quinquennium and averaged for the decade.

Lines 1-6 and 15-20--Calculated from the Ohkawa-Rosovsky basic tables in *Century of Japanese Growth* (in preparation).

Lines 7-10 and 21-24--From the Bank of Japan, *Hundred-Year Statistics of the Japanese Economy* (Tokyo, 1966), Series 7, pp. 48-49 (for most current price items), Series 6, pp. 46-47 (for net factor income from abroad, needed to derive GDP and the proper remainder); and Series 9, p. 51 (for gross national product in constant prices).

Lines 11-14 and 25-28--From *Supplement* to *Hundred-Year Statistics of the Japanese Economy*, *ibid*.

(*iii*) With the much sharper contraction in per capita consumer expenditures during the war than in either private capital formation or government uses of resources, following the 1930's when the share of consumer expenditures in total product also declined, one would expect that *after* the war consumer expenditures would account for a large share of total product and rise at higher rates than the other components of national product. Yet Table 7–3 shows that even with the recent upward revision of private consumer expenditures, the share was lower in 1952–54 than in 1929–33, in volumes in current prices and particularly in volumes in constant prices (col. 1, lines 5 and 11, and 19 and 25). After 1952–54, it dropped sharply and in 1959–64 it was lower than in any other nonwar period since the 1880's.

If one asks why the shares of government consumption and gross domestic capital formation were still much higher after the diversion into armaments and the war were over than before the 1930's, the answer lies in factors and forces not revealed in our tables, or indeed, in any of the usual economic accounts. One explanation may be that the destruction during the war of the material capital stock, private or public, affected the postwar needs for capital formation (and government consumption) more than it did the need for household consumption (except for the stocks of *durable* consumer commodities which may also have been partly destroyed during the war). Another may be the cumulative effects of urbanization, which is demanding of both material capital and government consumption; with such demands starved during wartime and a return flow of people after the war from the countryside to the cities, the need for government consumption and overhead capital formation may have been too acute to be post-poned, despite pressure for a greater rate of rise in per capita household consumption. Some components of capital formation, such as residential housing (and others not distinguishable in the easily available data), are closely related to household consumption, and will tend to rise at least *pari passu* with the latter (or at higher rates if more of their stock has been destroyed than of the stocks and flows of perishable and semidurable consumer goods). Finally, a variety of economic and social mechanisms may have generated a large flow of internal savings into capital formation; and the decisions to limit household consumption may have been made by the human agents themselves in allocating resources between consumption and investment along the lines revealed in Table 7–3. This interpretation is suggested by the data on the structure of savings given in Table 7–4.

The change in the share of consumer expenditures from 1919–28 to 1962–64 is associated primarily with a rise in the share of capital formation, that of government consumption either remaining about the same (despite wide fluctuations in the 1930's and 1940's) or declining (Table 7–3, lines 4 and 14 and 18 and 28). The share of capital formation rose from between 17 and 19 to between 37 and 39 percent of gross national product. A detailed breakdown of the capital formation totals for the 1920's and for recent years, both by type of goods and by industrial destination, would be particularly illuminating; but it is not at hand.

However, we do have data on the structure of financing of gross capital formation back to the 1930's; and, despite the discontinuity introduced by the recent revision of the national accounts, these show some clearly significant trends (Table 7–4).

The increase in savings that financed the striking rise in the gross capital formation proportion in Japan to the high levels in the late 1950's and early 1960's can be observed in all the distinguishable major sources: provision for capital consumption, net corporate savings, government savings, and personal savings. Unfortunately, the records do not extend back of the disturbed 1930's into the more normal 1920's. However, the fixed capital consumption charges (as a proportion of GNP) could not have been much larger in the 1920's than in the 1930's; and neither net corporate savings nor government savings, while probably positive, could have been large percentages of GNP in the 1920's. One may reasonably surmise that the major contributions to finance the much higher capital formation proportion in recent years compared with the 1920's and early 1930's came from a rise in the share of capital consumption charges (about 6 percentage points, as a percent of GNP), government savings (another 6 percentage points), and particularly, personal savings (at least another 6 percentage points). As a result of this latter rise, the ratio of personal savings to disposable personal income was almost 18 percent in the late 1950's and early 1960's, much higher than the ratio in any other free market country.

While decisions concerning government savings are collective, and those on provision for fixed capital consumption may be largely business and corporate, those on personal savings are individual. These high personal savings ratios are a recent phenomenon in Japan, if one may judge by the relatively moderate capital formation proportions even in the 1920's, let alone earlier periods. Low-capital formation proportions signify equally low-personal savings ratios, if neither corporate nor government savings are large and negative—an unlikely contingency for any long period. An explanation of the extremely high-savings propensity of individuals in Japan since the 1950's and the emergence of the propensity rather late in the economic development of the country would add immeasurably to our understanding of the high growth rates in Japan.[11]

b) We turn now to the possible implications of the stagnation or decline in per capita consumption that extended from the 1930's to the early 1950's. We can calculate the *total* gap between actual consumption per head and that attained in 1929–38 by using the estimates in column 3 of Table 7–1, lines 12–16. If we set prewar per capita consumption at the average for 1929–38, i.e., 103.6 (1924–28 = 100), we can deduct the actual consumption for 1939–52 from that level (fiscal 1952 being the year in which per capita consumption returned to the prewar level).[12] For this period of some 13 years (from 1939 through 1951 inclusive, and disregarding the shift from the calendar to fiscal year base), the cumulated gap is 323.4 points (1924–28 = 100). If we assume that this gap has to be worked off by an *extra* increase of the 1952 base (103.6) of say 5 percent per year, it would take some 23 years to eliminate the backlog; and presumably after that there would be no need for "extra" growth.

---

[11] A suggestive discussion of this aspect of Japan's economy may be found in Miyohei Shinohara, *Growth and Cycles in the Japanese Economy* (Tokyo: Kinokuniya Bookstore, 1962), chap. 9 and 10, pp. 205–83; and in a pamphlet entitled *The Role of Savings in the Japanese Economy* (Tokyo, 1965).

[12] Consumption for 1945, a year missing in the table, was assumed to be as low as in fiscal 1946 (which was 60.2 percent of 1924–28). The calculation involved subtracting each of the entries in col. 3, lines 13, 14, 15 (and the estimate for 1945) from 103.6, multiplying the differences by the number of years in each period, and adding.

TABLE 7-4

Level and Structure of Gross National Savings, 1930-1964 (Omitting War Years), Based on Volumes in Current Prices

A. SHARES IN GROSS NATIONAL PRODUCT (%)

	Capital Consumption (1)	Personal Savings (2)	Corporate Savings (3)	Government Savings (4)	Net Balance, Current Transactions (5)	Statistical Discrepancy (6)
Official Series, 1930-54						
1. 1930-33. . . .	6.5	8.0	-0.4	-2.4	0.7	-0.9
2. 1934-38. . . .	7.1	12.9	2.3	-4.0	0.4	4.0
3. 1949-51 (F). . .	5.1	8.5	3.5	10.6	3.2	3.0
4. 1952-54 (F). . .	6.7	8.6	3.5	5.0	-0.2	2.2
Official Series, Revised, 1952-64						
5. 1952-54 (F). . .	8.8	5.9	3.4	5.6	-0.3	0.4
6. 1955-58 (F). . .	10.4	10.0	3.8	5.7	-0.1	-0.5
7. 1959-61 (F). . .	11.1	11.8	5.7	8.1	-0.6	-0.3
8. 1962-64 (F). . .	12.6	11.6	4.3	7.9	-0.5	-0.2

B. SAVINGS RATIOS

	Shares in GNP (%)		Savings Ratios (%)		
	NNP (100 minus Col. 1 above) (1)	Personal Disposable Income (2)	GNCF/GNP (3)	NNCF/NNP (4)	Personal Savings / Personal Disposable Income (5)
Official Series, 1930-54					
9. 1930-33..............	93.5	81.0	11.5	5.4	9.9
10. 1934-38.............	92.9	71.8	22.7	16.8	18.0
11. 1949-51 (F).........	94.9	68.4	33.8	30.2	12.4
12. 1952-54 (F).........	93.3	70.2	25.8	20.5	12.2
Official Series, Revised, 1952-64					
13. 1952-54 (F).........	91.2	70.9	23.8	16.4	8.2
14. 1955-58 (F).........	89.6	70.8	29.3	21.1	14.2
15. 1959-61 (F).........	88.9	66.6	35.8	27.7	17.7
16. 1962-64 (F).........	87.4	66.2	35.7	26.4	17.5

NOTES: *Lines 1-4, Columns 1-6 and Lines 9-12, Column 2*--Derived from Bank of Japan, *Hundred-Year Statistics of the Japanese Economy* (Tokyo, 1966), Series 8, p. 50 and Series 7, pp. 48-49. The shares for 1946-48 were omitted because the statistical discrepancy (column 6) was far too large, amounting to almost half of total national capital formation. *Lines 5-8, Columns 1-6 and Lines 13-16, Column 2*--From the *Supplement* to *Hundred-Year Statistics of the Japanese Economy*, *ibid.*

All percentages were derived from the cumulated totals for the periods indicated.

The carryover effects of a long stagnation or decline in per capita consumption can be considered here only briefly. Four points seem relevant.

(*i*) The first has to do with the effect on the structure of consumer population of urbanization and other aspects of economic and social growth that influence consumption standards. If per capita consumption has been steadily 2 to 3 times as high in one sector of the population as in another, and if aggregate per capita consumption has remained stable, a rise in the population share of the higher consumption sector would imply a *decline* in per capita consumption in at least one of the sectors, if not in both. In that sense, stagnation of per capita consumption implies a greater shortfall when accompanied by a marked shift in the distribution of the population toward urban or generally higher consumption sectors than when the structure of population is unchanged.

The share of urban population (Census definition) rose markedly between the mid-1920's and mid-1950's despite the absence of a rise in the war decade. As already indicated in the discussion of Table 7–1, this share was 21.7 percent in 1925, rose to 37.9 percent in 1940, declined to 1945, rose to 37.5 percent in 1950, and then jumped to 56.3 percent in 1955 (to rise further to 63.5 percent in 1960). The shift in the distribution of the labor force was not as marked: the share of the nonagricultural sectors rose from 48.5 percent in 1924–28 to 65.4 percent in 1959–61 (see Table 7–2, line 5). These sets of shares in population and in the labor force indicate that much of the nonagricultural labor force resided in rural areas even in the 1920's, and was defined as rural population—a point emphasized by Irene Taeuber.[13] Hence, for our purposes it may be preferable to stress the distribution of population by residence rather than by industrial attachment. If so, Table 7–2 should have been based on the rural-urban distribution of population rather than on the *A* and *N* distribution of the labor force—but that would have required data on per capita consumption in the rural and urban sectors for the long period covered. But to return to the point here, it is clear that urbanization and industrialization proceeded apace between 1924–28 and the 1950's; and consequently the decline and stagnation in per capita consumption expenditures meant an even greater shortfall and accumulated backlog than the simple calculation above suggests.

(*ii*) The second point has to do with differences among consumer goods with respect to the "cumulatability" of unsatisfied needs.

---

[13] See Taeuber, *op. cit.*, pp. 90–91.

Granted that during the 13-year period per capita consumption fell far short of levels attained in the 1930's, this need not mean that the failure to achieve the levels of the 1930's can be cumulated into a realistic backlog of unsatisfied demand in the late 1950's or 1960's. If people had to limit their food consumption in 1945, they would not make it up by eating more in the 1950's than the normal amount of the 1920's or the 1930's. And even a depleted store of clothing and other semidurables does not mean a backlog that can be carried along for many years.

In other words, the durability of consumer goods is as important a factor in the "cumulatability" of their shortfall as it is in current consumption, with any stagnation of overall per capita consumption. In general, goods of daily necessity—foods, for example—will be less affected by a reduction of per capita outlays, since the needs that such goods satisfy (at fairly high levels) cannot be ignored for long. Consequently, persistent food shortfalls cannot be cumulated into a lasting backlog of food needs in excess of a rather limited "normal." By contrast, the services of a consumers' durable commodity can be prolonged and replacement of the commodity can be delayed for a long time without injurious effects; and for that reason a cumulative shortage in the supply of passenger cars, refrigerators, and television sets can be carried forward for many years—even disregarding the rising standards associated with continuing technological improvements of what are in essence recent innovations in consumers' goods.

Hence, in terms of our simple calculation, we would need to know the proportions of the various categories of consumer goods within the changing total over the years between 1929–38 and 1952, the extent of the shortfall for each category, and the length of the period for which an unsatisfied backlog is a real incentive in the markets. We may find that only a relatively small fraction of the large total of consumer goods is durable and therefore *postponable* for substantial periods. In that case the total backlog is much smaller. Thus if we assume that durable goods were only 15 percent of the total, even if their shortfall was triple that assumed above, the cumulated backlog is cut to 0.45 of the one originally calculated; and while this suggests some seven to eight years before the backlog is eliminated, at an annual rate of extra growth of 5 percent, the period may in fact be shorter, partly because of the mortality of the human agents involved, and partly because of the possible obsolescence of the backlog.

(*iii*) The third relevant point is that in modern economic growth innovations are constantly being introduced into the supply and the patterns of use of both consumer and producer goods. Hence if a given country becomes less preoccupied for a time with increasing per capita consumption and then returns, as it were, to the comity of nations with the usual drive toward learning, imitation, and adaptation, the gap between it and the others, particularly the leaders, will have widened; and the backlog of *new* consumer goods to adopt and enjoy will have increased. Thus while per capita consumer expenditures in Japan were at about the same level in 1952 as they were in the 1930's (although perhaps with a different composition), in the United States they were more than 50 percent higher in 1952 than in the 1930's.

The shortfall must therefore be calculated not from a constant level attained in the past to be "recovered" to, but from a changing level set by worldwide progress, particularly by the leading countries, to be "caught up with." And here again the distinction among consumer goods is important. Since technological change is highly selective, some categories of consumer goods are favored at any given time, and grow more rapidly than others; and the changing pattern of life itself yields choices with respect to consumer goods that are also highly specific, if only indirectly connected with the technological change. Thus, the increased use of certain types of urban goods, e.g., professional sports, is not a result of any technological changes in sport "production" but is a consequence of greater urbanization (itself largely a result of scale of production effects of technological changes).

The "lagging" country, whose lag has widened by concentration on other activities, upon resuming its contact and competition with the rest of the world, is open to the demonstration effect even if its own consumer population still has to learn about the new goods. The effect is enhanced by the possibility of an export market for the new products; and the given country may discover comparative advantages with respect to some new goods that were not evident in the preceding years of relative isolation. Thus, if Japan found that it could profit from a wider export market for its transistors, the very availability of transistors within the country would make for a speedier demonstration effect, stimulating domestic demand for them. The return to world markets necessarily involves acquaintance with new products and rising consumer aspirations—particularly if the return promises significant comparative advantages in the production of these new consumer goods.

While the above discussion is necessarily limited, enough has been said to suggest the problems involved in assessing the extent of past unsatisfied demand under conditions of decline or stagnation in per capita consumer expenditures associated with war preparations or actual conflict: the distinction between the single set of per capita consumption levels and the sectoral standards; the gauging of the cumulative shortfall from a past static level, involved in defining recovery; and the shift to rising levels, and the formulation of the "catching up" drive as a realistic force in postwar development.

(*iv*) One final point, partly covered under (*ii*), deserves specific formulation and emphasis. In theory, consumption can be viewed as a flow of services, and consumer expenditures as the acquisition of *stocks* to produce such services (or of rights to those). Where the distinction between the stocks and current flow is important, as in housing and consumer durables, the shortfall can be measured in terms either of current services or of available stocks. For the period under discussion this is important because of the war-inflicted damages on material stocks (and to some extent on stocks embodied in human beings, who provide services). Clearly in such cases the shortfall may be far larger than that reflected in estimates of per capita expenditures (a point already made in the discussion of capital formation above); its "cumulatability" may be much greater; and the period over which it extends may be much longer. Thus, many prosperous countries of Europe are still suffering from a cumulative shortage of residential housing, despite the passage of more than 20 years since the end of the war, and despite the fact that some of these countries (e.g., Sweden) were not active participants in, or physically affected by, World War II.

The whole problem of recovery and catching up after a long period of isolation from world markets and some years of physical destruction merits further discussion. The time pattern of the rates at which an accumulated backlog is "worked off" has not been mentioned at all. Yet the interpretation of the postwar growth record, the distinction between the growth rate representing an "extra" component associated with the pressure of an accumulated backlog, and the growth rate reflecting more "normal" and persisting postwar factors, depends not only upon how long the backlog lasts but also upon the time pattern of the "extra" growth that it induces. But such analysis requires examination of specific consumer goods and wants, which is beyond our scope here. The rather general comments made above are intended largely to emphasize the problems involved in the interpretation of the postwar growth process—given the combination of the long period of isolation and massive destruction in Japan with the continuing high rate of technological and economic progress in other countries.

III. TRENDS IN STRUCTURE OF CONSUMER EXPENDITURES

The estimates of consumer expenditures in the long-term records for Japan are a residual, obtained by subtracting from aggregate product, directly estimated, the non-PCE components (government consumption, capital formation, and so forth) also directly estimated. This procedure implies a lack of direct information on consumption, at least for the entire period; and we cannot draw upon easily available long-term data on the structure of consumption.

Table 7–5 represents an attempt to use the detailed estimates in the Hitotsubashi studies, particularly those published in 1957, to derive an approximation to the share of food in consumer expenditures over a long period. The procedure is fairly similar to that apparently used in the preparation of official estimates of the distribution of private consumer expenditures for recent years.[14] It distinguishes the food items within the gross value output of agriculture (including livestock) and fisheries; allows for *internal* costs (e.g., use of fishery products as fertilizer in agriculture) to avoid duplication; adds the *net* value originating in food and drink manufacturing (both factory and other); allows for exports and imports of food; adds the transportation and distributive margins—to pass from flow into domestic use and inventories at producers' prices to the same flow at cost to ultimate consumers; and then relates the estimated final value of food flow to the countrywide total of private consumption expenditures.

The procedure itself is subject to biases. The totals of food flow may be *too small* because in shifting from factory to total manufacturing we raised the net value of factory output of food products by the ratio for all manufacturing, and *domestic* manufactures (relative to factory) probably were more important for food than for other branches of manufacturing. Another source of downward bias is that no allowance was made for the indirect taxes on food and drink that enter the final prices and are part of the food share as it should be measured in the distribution of consumer expenditures. Offsetting these downward biases in the procedure is the implicit inclusion of changes in inventories in the derived totals: net additions to inventories of food products, finished or unfinished, are part of capital formation, not of consumer expenditures. And the markup assumed to

---

[14] See a brief description in United Nations, *National Accounting Practices in Sixty Countries, Studies in Methods, Series F, No. 11,* provisional issue (New York, 1964), p. 126.

cover transportation and distribution margins may be too high for the earlier periods—although I do not know enough to form a useful judgment.

But all these biases in the *procedure* are relatively limited and cannot affect the estimated food totals and food share by a large fraction. The total in line 4 of Table 7–5, which rests completely upon the output data for agriculture and fisheries, dominates the total in line 12—so that even relatively sizable proportional errors in line 5 or line 11 cannot affect the result significantly. And inventory change can reduce the food total by 3 percent at most, lowering the ratios by similarly small fractions.[15]

The possible deficiencies in the underlying basic estimates may affect the results in Table 7–5 far more than any biases in the procedure. Discussion of a preliminary version of this paper at the Conference emphasized possible underestimation of the food flow because domestic production of sugar, tobacco, tofu, miso and shoyu sauce, and the like was not included. On the other hand, the *share* of food in total consumer expenditures may have been exaggerated because the underestimation of other consumer goods, such as textiles, may have been even greater. These and other deficiencies of the underlying data are now being corrected, but the results are still to come. Under the circumstances, it seems best to discuss the series as given in Table 7–5, to see what results they yield and what questions they raise. This, as already suggested, should be helpful in the revision itself, as well as in the interpretation of the new series when they become available.

In this discussion we emphasize the shares based on volumes in current prices. The adjustment for price change differentials (lines 15 and 16), based on the ratio of the wholesale price of rice to the consumer price index, is rough; and is made only to suggest that the differences between price trends of foods and all consumer goods are not likely to modify the trends or levels substantially.

As could have been expected, the food share in consumer expenditures declined markedly, from 75 percent in 1879–83 to less than 40 percent in 1934–38 (line 14). Indeed, given the limited proportion of the foreign trade balance to domestic food output, and the dominant role of agriculture in the latter, the sharp contraction of the share of

---

[15] This estimate can be justified by deriving the ratio of the proportion of GNP or GDP accounted for by changes in inventories to the annual rate of growth of GNP or GDP (the marginal ratio of inventory-change to output). This ratio for the recent decade is about 0.6; and applied to an annual growth rate of food output of say 5 percent, yields a 3 percent estimate.

TABLE 7-5

A Commodity Flow Approximation to the Share of Foods in Private Consumption Expenditures, Selected Dates, 1879-1938

(Absolute Entries in Millions of Yen per Year, Current Prices)

	1879-83 (1)	1889-93 (2)	1899-1903 (3)	1909-13 (4)	1924-28 (5)	1934-38 (6)
1. Agricultural gross product, including livestock products	398	456	941	1,601	3,866	3,527
2. Agricultural gross product, excluding nonfoods	360	412	817	1,386	3,073	3,008
3. Agricultural gross product, also excluding internal costs	331	379	751	1,275	2,827	2,767
4. Agricultural gross product, including gross value of fisheries	360	417	833	1,422	3,436	3,362
5. Net value of food manufacturing (factory and domestic)	49	53	136	160	491	504
6. Domestic production of food (line 4 + line 5)	409	470	969	1,582	3,927	3,866
7. Net balance of exports and imports of foodstuffs	-6	0	33	14	199	-15
8. Flow of food into domestic use and inventories, at producers' prices (line 6 + line 7)	403	470	1,002	1,596	4,126	3,851
9. Proportion of total labor force outside of A sector (%)	18.4	24.5	30.7	37.7	48.5	53.1
10. Flow of marketed food (line 8 x line 9)	74	115	308	602	2,001	2,045
11. Transportation and distribution markup (0.4 x line 10)	30	46	123	241	800	818
12. Flow of food into domestic use, at cost to consumers (line 8 + line 11)	433	516	1,125	1,837	4,926	4,669
13. Total personal consumer expenditures	577	668	1,631	2,876	10,897	11,895
14. Percent share of food in PCE (line 12 ÷ line 13)	75.0	77.2	69.0	63.9	45.2	39.3
15. Ratio of index of price of rice to consumer price index	0.99	0.94	0.97	1.01	1.08	1.01
16. Percent share of food in PCE, adjusted for differential price changes (line 14 ÷ line 15)	75.8	82.1	71.1	63.3	41.9	38.9

TABLE 7-5 (Continued)

NOTES: *Line 1*--From Kazushi Ohkawa and others, *The Growth Rate of the Japanese Economy since 1878* (referred to below as O-G),Tables 3, 4, and 5, pp. 55-57.

Line 2--The deductions, from *ibid.*, are the gross value of industrial crops (set at 10 percent of the agricultural total, excluding livestock, for columns 1 and 2; and at 7 percent for 1899 in the calculation of column 3); cocoons; seedlings; and straw-made goods.

Line 3--Agricultural gross product after allowance for consumption of inputs derived from food output in agriculture and fisheries. In accordance with O-G, Table 9, p. 61 and discussion on pp. 61-62, we allowed for seeds and for about half of the gross value of fisheries (to cover herring fertilizer). The two were roughly 8 percent of gross value (line 2) between 1890 and 1910; and we used this percentage throughout, assuming that increased cost proportions were due exclusively to purchases from other sectors.

Line 4--The gross value of fisheries is given for 1878-1919 in O-G, Tables 3 and 4, pp. 55-56. For years after 1919 only the *net* product of fisheries is given in O-G, Table 13, pp. 72-73. We raised it to gross value by multiplying by 1.84, the ratio of gross to net for 1917-19.

Line 5--The basic data up to 1930 are in O-G, Table 7, pp. 88-89, which shows the net product of factory manufactures by industry, and Table 11, p. 95, which shows total net product of manufacturing including domestic production, for quinquennia from 1878-82 to 1938-42. For columns 1-5 we raised the net value of food and beverage factory manufactures by the ratio of total to factory production, for all manufactures, using the 8-2 quinquennia for the 9-3. For 1934-38 (column 6) detailed data on net product of manufacturing by industry are not available and we assumed that the ratio of line 5 to line 4 was 15 percent (it was 14.3 percent for 1924-28).

Line 7--Annual data on exports and imports of foodstuffs are from the Bank of Japan, *Hundred-Year Statistics of the Japanese Economy* (Tokyo, 1966), Series 115, pp. 280-81. A minus sign indicates an excess of exports.

Line 9--See Table 7-2 above, line 5, and the original source.

Line 10--The transportation and distribution markup was based on O-G, Table 4, pp. 105-6, which shows data from ESB on the components of product of the tertiary sector. We assumed that all of commerce and one half of transport and communication are relevant to the commodity-producing sectors (i.e., the A sector and Industry). The ratio of commerce plus half of transport to commodity product other than food assumed *not* to enter trade and transport channels (i.e., line 8 multiplied by the share of labor force in the A sector), works out to over 60 percent for 1930-33 and over 50 percent for 1934-38. Since the markup should be somewhat lower for foods than for all commodity product, we set it at 40 percent. Alternative calculations, with a lower or higher (or changing) transportation and distribution markup can easily be made.

TABLE 7-5 (Concluded)

Line 13--Columns 2-6 are from the Ohkawa-Rosovsky basic tables in *Century of Japanese Growth* (in preparation). For column I PCE was estimated to be 79 percent of GDP (see notes to Table 7-I).

Line 15--The price of rice is from the Bank of Japan, *Hundred-Year Statistics of the Japanese Economy*, *op. cit.*, Series 28, p. 90; and the consumer price index is from the Ohkawa-Rosovsky basic tables. The price of rice was shifted to the 1934-36 base, the base of the consumer price index; quinquennial averages were calculated for both price indexes; and then the ratio of the price index for rice to the consumer price index was computed.

Line 16--Dividing line 14 by line 15 is equivalent to adjusting the numerator by the price index for rice and the denominator by the index for all consumer goods.

agriculture in total product would suggest a marked decline in the share of food in total consumption—despite the bolstering effects of greater relative costs of manufacturing, transportation, and distribution, with increasing urbanization.

But three interrelated aspects of the trend in the food share are distinctive, and call for further scrutiny and explanation. The first is the extremely high share before World War I (columns 1–4). A share of 65 percent for food allows little room for other indispensable consumption components. In the 1926–27 family expenditures study for Japan, tenant farmers had the *lowest* per capita expenditures, 12.7 yen per month (about a seventh below the countrywide average), and their share for food, the highest shown, was 53.4 percent, that for clothing was 6.5 percent, for housing, etc. 20 percent, with a residual category of 20 percent.[16]

In recent years, in countries with low per capita income—as low as or much lower than in Japan in the late 19th and early 20th centuries—the food share ranged between 55 and 63 percent: in Ghana in 1955–59 it was 62.2 percent, in Ceylon in 1950–59 it was 61 percent, and in China-Taiwan in 1953 it was 61 percent.[17] And even the Desai estimate for India for 1938 allows 66.3 percent for

---

[16] See Taijiro Matsuda, "The Family Budget Enquiry in Japan, 1926–1927," *Bulletin de l'Institut International de Statistique, Tome XXV, 2me livraison* (Tokyo, 1931), Tables I–IV, pp. 284–301. The survey covered the year September 1, 1926–August 31, 1927.

[17] See S. Kuznets, "Quantitative Aspects of the Economic Growth of Nations: VII. The Share and Structure of Consumption," *Economic Development and Cultural Change*, Vol. 10, No. 2; Part II (January, 1962), Appendix Table 5, pp. 76–79, or United Nations, *Yearbook of National Accounts Statistics, 1965, op. cit.*

food, beverages, and tobacco (which may be an overestimate, since coverage is usually better for food than for other items).[18] The food share of close to 70 percent as late as about 1900 and about 75 percent in 1880 is a finding that warrants further examination.[19]

Second, the food share, which was large before World War I, declined sharply by the 1930's or even the 1920's. The drop over some 50 years of more than 35 percentage points is much wider than any found in the Western developed countries over an equally long or longer period. However, even with such a sharp drop, food use per capita could have risen substantially. Allowing roughly for differential price trends, the tripling of per capita expenditures between the early 1880's and the 1930's (see Table 7–1) would, with a decline in the food share from 75 to 40 percent, still mean a rise of more than 50 percent in per capita food consumption. It is harder to explain the explosive rise in per capita expenditures on nonfood items, a multiplication of more than seven times.

Finally there is the sharp break between 1909–13 and 1924–28. From 1879–83 to 1909–13, the food share dropped some 13 percentage points (lines 14 and 16), but over the next 15 years, it declined close to 20 percentage points. Of course, World War I and the possibly wide discrepancies in differential price trends may contribute to an explanation, but it is an intriguing finding.

In concluding these comments on the findings in Table 7–5, one may ask whether the high proportions of food in total consumption before World War I reflect a genuine phenomenon, or are due to deficiencies in the basic estimates. It is extremely unlikely that the food consumption totals are overestimated. But it may well be that the flow of nonfoods into consumption in the earlier periods is substantially underestimated. However, if such underestimation is the *only* source of the exaggeration of the food proportions, and if the "true" proportion is say 65 percent, the implied shortage is more than 60

---

[18] The Desai estimate is quoted in William W. Lockwood, *The Economic Development of Japan* (Princeton, N.J.: Princeton University Press, 1954), footnote 40, p. 433.

[19] In the United States in 1839 all *perishable* commodities were no more than 57 percent of total flow of goods to consumers (see Robert E. Gallman, "Gross National Product in the United States, 1834–1909," in Dorothy S. Brady (ed.), *Studies in Income and Wealth*, Volume 30 [New York: National Bureau of Economic Research, 1966], Table 5, pp. 18–19). Since perishables include drugs, paper, etc., the share of food must have been significantly lower. Of course, per capita income and expenditures in the United States even at that early date were higher than in Japan in 1880; yet the former was in 1839 still an overwhelmingly agricultural country.

percent of the present estimate of nonfoods.[20] It will be interesting to see whether the current revisions will introduce marked changes in the shares for the pre-World War I periods in Table 7–5.

We may end the review of trends in the structure of private consumer expenditures by observing the distributions available since the late 1930's (Table 7–6). As in Table 7–5, food includes not only basic sustenance but also "luxuries" such as beverages and tobacco. While light and fuel, and rent and furnishings, are shown separately, they may be more conveniently combined; and although this combined category includes purchases of furniture, household equipment, and other related consumer durables, it is not clear how much of other consumer durables (e.g., radios and television sets) is included here, and how much in the miscellaneous category. More detailed analysis is presumably possible, particularly for the post–World War II years for which additional sample data on consumer expenditures have become available; but we are interested here in a longer perspective.

The recent revisions introduced marked discontinuity into the structure of consumer expenditures (see lines 4 and 5). But the changes, particularly striking in the shares of clothing and of the miscellaneous category, appear to be due largely to changes in categories—clothing including "other personal effects" in the revised series. If we concentrate discussion on the share of foods, and consider only the marked movements in the shares of other categories, the effects of discontinuity are reduced.

The food proportion for 1934–38 shown here is quite close to that in Table 7–5, i.e., about 40 percent—confirmation, in a way, of the validity of the procedure used in Table 7–5, at least for that quinquennium. The trend in the food share following 1934–38 might have been expected: the contraction of production and consumption during the war led to much higher shares of food in the late 1940's and early 1950's. Then with the marked rise in per capita product and consumption, the food proportion declined, while those of housing (including furnishings) and miscellaneous, including services and such durable consumer goods as automobiles, rose.

Two aspects of the food proportion in recent years should be mentioned explicitly. The first depends upon our view of the com-

---

[20] The conclusion is derived from the equation:

$$0.65(100 + x) + 25 + x = 100 + x$$

where 25 is the percentage share of nonfoods (100 being total consumption *before* the addition of more nonfoods), and x is the required addition (in percentages of the unrevised consumption total). The value of x is 15.4, i.e., more than six-tenths of 25, the share of nonfoods before revision.

TABLE 7-6

Structure of Personal Consumption Expenditures, 1934-1964
(Omitting War Years)

	Food, Beverages, and Tobacco (1)	Cloth- ing* (2)	Fuel and Light (3)	Housing (including Furniture) (4)	Miscel- laneous (5)
Shares Based on Volumes in Current Prices (%)					
1. 1934-38	40.9	9.7	4.7	10.9	33.8
2. 1946-48 (F)	66.0	6.0	4.0	4.9	19.1
3. 1949-51 (F)	62.0	8.1	4.0	6.0	19.9
4. 1952-54 (F)	55.7	8.9	3.9	7.6	23.9
5. 1952-54 (F)	53.0	14.8	4.7	9.0	18.5
6. 1955-58 (F)	49.4	13.7	4.2	11.0	21.7
7. 1959-61 (F)	43.9	13.3	3.9	15.0	23.9
8. 1962-64 (F)	39.9	13.0	3.7	15.7	27.7
Shares Based on Volumes in 1960 (Calendar) Prices (%)					
9. 1934-38	41.7	n.a.	n.a.	n.a.	n.a.
10. 1952-54 (F)	54.1	n.a.	n.a.	n.a.	n.a.
11. 1952-54 (F)	50.7	12.7	4.8	12.3	19.5
12. 1955-58 (F)	48.6	12.9	4.1	12.4	22.0
13. 1959-61 (F)	43.9	13.3	3.9	15.0	23.9
14. 1962-64 (F)	38.9	13.4	4.1	15.6	28.0

*"Clothing" in lines 1-4; "clothing and other personal effects" in lines 5-8 and 11-14.

NOTES: *Lines 1-4*--Based on the Bank of Japan, *Hundred-Year Statistics of the Japanese Economy* (Tokyo, 1966), Series 7, p. 48.

Lines 5-8 and 11-14--Based on the *Supplement* to *Hundred-Year Statistics of the Japanese Economy, ibid.*

Lines 9-10--Lines 1 and 4 adjusted by the ratio of prices of food to all consumer prices, approximated from consumer price indexes for cities from 1946 on, and for villages from 1952 on (in Bank of Japan, *Hundred-Year Statistics of the Japanese Economy, ibid.*, Series 22 and 23, pp. 81-83) and from wholesale price indexes back to 1934-38 (in Bank of Japan, *Hundred-Year Statistics of the Japanese Economy, ibid.*, Series 8, p. 77).

parability of the share in 1934–38, derived from the old estimates, with that in 1962–64 shown in the revised estimate. If they are assumed to be comparable, implying that the old estimates only for the postwar years needed revision, we find that over the 27 years (from 1936, the midpoint of 1934–38, to 1963, the midpoint of 1962–64) the food proportion based on current price volumes declined only 1 percentage point and that based on constant price volumes declined about 3 percentage points. Over the same period the index for total consumer expenditures per capita grew from 107.8 to 211.6 (see Table 7–1, col. 3, lines 12 and 19), or 96 percent. This is a surprising but not necessarily improbable result: historical records show several cases of a constant (or rising) share of food, even with a perceptible secular rise in real per capita income or expenditures;[21] but in no case is a doubling of per capita consumption accompanied by as slight a decline in the food proportion as shown in Table 7–6.

The second comment relates to the food proportion in Japan in recent years compared with that in other developed countries. For 1962–64, the share in Japan, about 40 percent, is distinctly higher than those in the United States (25.4 percent), Canada (29.8 percent), Australia (32 percent), and the Scandinavian countries and Netherlands (which range from 32.7 to about 37 percent). But it is not significantly above those for France (38.6 percent) and the United Kingdom (39.3 percent); and is distinctly lower than those for Austria (44.7 percent) and Italy (52.7 percent). Since the comparable per capita consumption in Japan, which with generous assumptions we estimated to be $528 per capita in 1963,[22] is significantly lower than that in all the countries listed above, we can conclude that the food proportion in Japan is moderate.

If this observation is valid for the food share in Japan in 1962–64, it is all the more defensible for the share in the 1930's, when it was about 41 percent. In the 1930's, Japan was even further down in the array of developed countries ranked by per capita consumer expenditures. Yet in the United Kingdom the share of food, beverages, and tobacco in 1930–39 was 41 percent; in Norway in 1930, 38.5 percent; in Sweden in 1926 and 1938, over 40 percent (if we distribute the unallocated commerce and transport services proportionately to

---

[21] See Appendix Table 6 in S. Kuznets, "Quantitative Aspects of the Economic Growth of Nations: VII. The Share and Structure of Consumption," *op. cit.*, in footnote 17.

[22] This estimate was derived by assuming that the difference between the Gleason and United Nations estimates of per capita product in Japan in 1958 (see footnote 2 above) in U.S. prices (about 50 percent of the lower figure) could be applied to the 1963 estimate given in the *Yearbook of National Accounts Statistics, 1965, op. cit.*, Table 9B, p. 500 (the *Yearbook* was also the source for the food shares in consumer expenditures for the other countries cited in the text). The figure given for 1963 was $640; we raised it to $960; and applied the proportion of consumer expenditures given in Table 7–3 above (about 55 percent for 1962–64). Per capita consumption by this procedure was $528.

commodity output in various categories); and in Italy in 1931–40, 57 percent. Real per capita expenditures at that time in all these countries, probably including Italy, greatly exceeded those of Japan; yet the food share in Japan was no higher. It was distinctly higher, however, than the shares in the United States (29 percent in 1929–38) and Canada (30 percent in 1931–40).[23]

If the food proportions in the 1930's and in the 1960's, relative to per capita consumption, were moderate in Japan, compared with other industrialized countries, then the very high shares of food in the early periods are all the more intriguing. More careful scrutiny of the estimates between the 1930's and the 1960's would probably provide information germane to the explanation of Japan's economic growth.

IV. CONCLUDING COMMENTS

The findings suggested in the preceding discussion may be briefly summarized.

a) Economic growth in Japan since the 1880's has been accompanied by a rate of growth in per capita consumer expenditures of 25 percent per decade. This rate was quite high, particularly for the period before the 1930's. The rate of growth of household consumption per capita was a function of the high rate of growth of total product per capita, since the rise of the proportion of total product that could be diverted to government consumption and capital formation was limited.

b) Per capita consumer expenditures of the population attached to and dependent upon the *A* sector (agriculture and related industries) and of that attached to and dependent upon the *N* sector (non-agricultural industries and pursuits) both rose markedly. The increase in the per capita product and consumption of the *A* sector, the traditional and labor surplus sector, is particularly significant. Furthermore, the impressive rise of consumption per capita meant a marked rise in per capita consumption of *indigenous* products, since the latter accounted for over 50 percent of total household consumption as late as the mid-1950's.

c) Per capita consumption expenditures grew steadily from the early 1880's until the 1930's, and were sharply reduced during World War II and the immediate postwar years. Yet the rapid recovery after

---

[23] For these shares see S. Kuznets, "Quantitative Aspects of the Economic Growth of Nations: VII. The Share and Structure of Consumption," *op. cit.*, in footnote 17.

the war restored per capita consumption to the prewar levels by 1952 or 1953; and with the rapid rise continuing, the 1930's level was almost doubled by 1962–64.

d) The share of private consumer expenditures in total product remained high until the late 1930's, despite the rise in the share of capital formation after World War I. It dropped sharply in the late 1930's, when the share of government consumption rose significantly; and, of course, World War II brought with it a further drop in the share of private consumption, a marked rise in the share of government consumption, and a lesser rise in capital formation. After the war the private consumption share rose and then declined, this time accompanied by a marked rise in the share of gross capital formation, the share of government consumption declining somewhat.

e) Because of the shift in the distribution of product, suggested under (*d*), by the 1960's the share of private consumption expenditures was lower and the share of capital formation was higher than in any other free market economy. The ratio of personal savings to personal disposable income was also higher than elsewhere.

f) The proportion of food in total consumer expenditures, extrapolated by rough procedures back to the 1880's, was quite high in the early decades: about 75 percent in the 1880's and almost 65 percent just before World War I. The possibility that this finding is due to major deficiencies in the estimates, particularly to relatively large underestimates of the flows of nonfoods, is still to be investigated.

g) For recent decades, the proportion of food in total consumer expenditures, about 40 percent, was relatively moderate in Japan— compared with other industrialized countries with higher real per capita household consumption. Between 1934–38 and 1962–64 the share of food in total private consumer expenditures barely changed, although per capita expenditures almost doubled.

The findings are subject to qualifications which, we hope, have been adequately set forth in the discussion. But except as indicated above, the qualifications do not modify the findings substantially, and the issues raised by these findings are clearly important. They are sufficiently relevant to our understanding of the economic growth process to warrant urging that in further analysis of Japan's economic growth more attention be paid to trends in level and structure of consumption (and related uses of national product), supplementing models that emphasize duality of production structure, foreign trade dependence, unlimited labor supplies, etc. The consumption aspects are a key in any analysis connecting one level of production performance with the next. Furthermore, in any attempt to measure economic growth by the system of national product accounts, findings concerning sectoral outputs, employment, trade, etc., have clear implications for consumption levels and structure; and these implications must be made explicit and studied. Their study may reveal some peculiarities of a real nature, i.e., of testably observed reality—in which case analysis must explain them, i.e., attempt to connect these findings with the broader framework of our knowledge; or it may cast doubt upon the reliability of the underlying data—in which case revision of the underlying statistical quantities, and of any findings based on them, must be undertaken. In general, if a set of empirical data yields implications that are too "peculiar" to be reconciled with other existing knowledge, either the latter has to be revised (or enriched) to explain the peculiarity or the empirical data that yielded the implications must be revised—to remove the peculiarity.

Appendix: Comparison with the New Estimates of Personal Consumption Expenditures by Professor Shinohara

After this paper had been completed, a new set of long-term estimates of personal consumption expenditures covering the period from 1874 to the late 1930's was published in *Estimates of Long-Term Economic Statistics of Japan since 1868*.[24] These new estimates, which differ significantly and in several respects from the series used in the paper, have not yet been integrated into a complete national accounts framework or tested in their relation to other components of the aggregate product. Therefore, they cannot be used now in revising the statistical analysis in the paper. However, it seemed advisable to add brief comments on the differences between the new estimates and those used in the paper, and indicate the qualifications and questions that seem appropriate.

Table 7A–1 provides the first set of comparisons for the period that extends to 1924–28 or 1934–38. After stating the findings, we consider the effect for the longer period through the early 1960's.

1. While the Shinohara estimates of consumer expenditures in current prices are distinctly larger, by percentages ranging from 20 to 50 (lines 1–3), the effect on the *trend,* or the growth rate, is moderate (lines 9–11). (We limit the comparison of growth rates to

---

[24] See detailed reference in the notes to Table 7A–1.

TABLE 7A-1

Personal Consumption Expenditures, Residual Estimate in the Paper and the New Shinohara Estimates, 1879-83 to 1934-38

I. ABSOLUTE VOLUMES (MILLIONS OF YEN PER YEAR)

	1879-83 (1)	1889-93 (2)	1899-1903 (3)	1909-13 (4)	1924-28 (5)	1934-38 (6)
Volumes, Current Prices						
1. Paper	577	668	1,631	2,876	10,897	11,895
2. Shinohara	792	1,014	2,227	3,772	12,852	14,467
3. Ratio, line 2 to line 1	1.37	1.52	1.37	1.31	1.18	1.22
Implicit Price Indexes, 1934-36 = 100						
4. Paper	30.7	27.7	44.7	60.2	121.6	107.0
5. Shinohara	23.5	23.0	40.4	57.8	118.5	107.1
Volumes, 1934-36 Prices						
6. Paper	1,880	2,408	3,647	4,774	8,959	11,113
7. Shinohara	3,374	4,407	5,519	6,525	10,848	13,506
8. Ratio, line 7 to line 6	1.79	1.83	1.51	1.37	1.21	1.22

II. RATES OF GROWTH PER DECADE (%)

	1879-83 to 1899-1903 (1)	1899-1903 to 1924-28 (2)	1879-93 to 1924-28 (3)
Volumes, Current Prices			
9. Paper	68.1	113.8	92.1
10. Shinohara	67.7	101.6	85.8
11. Ratio (100 + line 10) to (100 + line 9)	0.998	0.943	0.967

Implicit Price Indexes

12. Paper.	20.7	49.2	35.8
13. Shinohara.	31.0	53.8	43.3
14. Ratio (100 + line 12) to (100 + line 13)	0.921	0.970	0.948

Volumes, 1934-36 Prices

15. Paper (from lines 9 and 12).	39.3	43.2	41.5
16. Shinohara (from lines 10 and 13) . . .	27.9	31.1	29.7
17. Ratio (line 11 × line 14, or directly from lines 15 and 16 in parentheses) .	0.919 (0.918)	0.915 (0.916)	0.917 (0.917)

Population

18. Paper and Shinohara.	9.57	13.04	11.49

PCE per Capita, 1934-36 Prices

19. Paper (lines 15 and 18, or directly in parentheses)	27.1 (27.0)	26.7 (26.7)	26.9 (26.8)
20. Shinohara (lines 16 and 18, or directly in parentheses).	16.7 (16.1)	16.0 (16.3)	16.3 (16.2)

NOTES: *Lines 1, 4, and 6*--Based on the Ohkawa-Rosovsky series in *Century of Japanese Growth* (in preparation), used for Tables 7-1 and 7-5.

Lines 2, 5, and 7--See *Estimates of Long-Term Economic Statistics of Japan since 1868*, Vol. 6, Miyohei Shinohara, *Personal Consumption Expenditures* (Tokyo, 1967), Tables 1 and 3, pp. 132-35 and 138-39.

In both series the entries are arithmetic means for the quinquennia indicated, and the implicit price indexes were obtained by dividing the current price average volumes by the constant price average.

Line 18--Taken from Table 7-1.

Line 20--The entries in parentheses are calculated directly from Shinohara, Table 4, pp. 140-41, showing per capita PCE in 1934-36 prices. The implicit movement of population in the Shinohara series is the same as in Table 7-1 for the full period 1879-83 to 1924-28, but there are slight differences in the movement over the two subperiods.

the period ending in 1924–28, since the movements from 1924–28 to 1934–38 are identical; and the 1920's provide a better dividing line). Indeed, if we were to assume that the *price* movements in the two sets of estimates were the same (and were for both as given in line 12), the derived rate of growth in Shinohara's series on consumer expenditures per capita in constant prices for the same period would be 22.7 percent per decade (instead of 16.3 percent per decade now shown in line 20, col. 3)—compared with the rate of 26.9 percent per decade shown by the residual estimates used in Table 7–1.

2. The difference in the movement of the price indexes is the major factor underlying the difference in the growth rates in constant price volumes (see lines 12–14). This is particularly true of the subperiod 1879–83 to 1899–1903. In the later subperiod the difference in price trends is smaller; but it is offset by the larger difference in the movement of the volumes in current prices.

3. The combination of moderate differences in the trends in volumes in current prices with larger differences in the trends in the price indexes produces substantial differences in the rates of growth of the volumes in constant prices. As lines 15 and 16, column 3, indicate, the rate of growth per decade of aggregate consumer expenditures is 41.5 percent in the estimates in the paper, and 29.7 percent in the Shinohara estimates, and the latter is about seven tenths of the former. Then the division by the rate of population growth, to yield rates of growth in per capita expenditures, while reducing the absolute difference, widens the relative spread. Thus, on a per capita basis, the growth rates are 26.9 and 16.3 percent, with the latter about six tenths of the former.

4. Whereas in the series in the paper, PCE per capita almost triples from 1879–83 to 1924–28, moving from 34.3 to 100, according to the Shinohara series it only doubles, moving from 50.9 to 100. But even the *reduced* growth rate, about 16 percent per decade, is higher than that in most developed countries over a comparable historical span.

To study the effects on the growth rates over the full period to 1962–64, one simple procedure would be to use the rate of growth in PCE per capita for 1924–28 to 1962–64 shown in Table 7–1— which is based on the Ohkawa-Rosovsky series from 1924–28 to 1934–38 (over which decade the residual and the Shinohara series move in a parallel fashion) and on the official series from 1934–38 to 1962–64. This would mean an index of 50.9 in 1879–83 and 100 in 1924–28 (from the Shinohara series) and 211.6 in fiscal 1962–64 (from Table 7–1, line 19, col. 3), or a growth rate of 18.9 percent per decade for the full period. This quadrupling of PCE per capita, while a reduction from the sextupling in the residual series, still leaves a markedly high rate of growth, in comparison with other developed countries.

The difficulty with the procedure just used is that the Shinohara estimate of consumer expenditures in 1934–38 is 21.5 percent above the old official estimate (in current prices), whereas the estimate used in the paper is at the same level; and it may be argued that the Shinohara estimates should be compared directly with the current official series rather than linked to a growth rate from a lower level (in 1934–38). Since the current official series of personal consumer expenditures is 9.1 percent above the old official series (in fiscal 1952–54, the most relevant overlap) the net excess in the Shinohara series over the current official is 11.4 percent in 1934–38. Using this datum, we can derive the comparable 1962–64 (*F*) value for per capita consumer expenditures in 1934–36 prices of 190 (instead of 211.6). The results yield a growth rate for 1924–28 to 1962–64 (*F*) of 18.8 percent per decade (instead of 22.3 percent) and an average of 17.4 percent per decade for the full period. This maximum allowance for the effect of the Shinohara series still leaves a high rate of growth in PCE per capita, with an index that almost quadruples over the period (from 50.9 to 190).

In Table 7A–2 we repeat the analysis developed in the paper to approximate trends in per capita consumption for the *A*- and *N*-dependent populations separately; but this time we base the approximations on the movement of countrywide PCE per capita suggested by the Shinohara series (line 2) which allows for the *maximum* effect of the new series on the full period.

In the less realistic Variant *I,* the reduction in the growth rate of countrywide PCE per capita suggested by the new series yields a particularly low rate of growth for per capita consumption of the *A*-dependent population (line 5)—only about 4 percent per decade or a total rise over some eight decades of somewhat over a third. But even for the *N*-dependent population in Variant *I,* the growth rate in per capita consumption is moderate—less than 9 percent per decade (line 6, col. 6). The reason is that the effects of *inter*-group shifts, which are quite large in Variant *I,* remain roughly the same whether we use the residual or the Shinohara series, so that the reduction primarily affects the *intra*-group trends. This can be seen from Table 7A–2 if the unweighted average of the growth rates for the *A*- and *N*-dependent populations is taken as a rough approximation to the *intra*-trend and the difference between this average and the country-wide growth rate as the *inter*-group shift. For the full period the

TABLE 7A-2

Trends in PCE per Capita of the A- and N-Dependent Populations,
Based on Table 7-1 and on the Shinohara Estimates

	Indices of PCE per Capita, 1924-28 = 100		Change, 1879-83 to 1924-28		Change, 1879-83 to 1959-61 (F)	
	1879-83 (1)	1959-61 (F) (2)	Ratio, 1924-28 to 1879-83 (3)	Growth per Decade (%) (4)	Ratio, 1959-61 to 1879-83 (5)	Growth per Decade (%) (6)
Countrywide per Capita PCE						
1. Based on Table 7-1	34.3	168.1	2.92	26.8	4.90	22.3
2. Based on Shinohara, assuming direct comparability with the 1960's	50.9	150.9	1.96	16.3	2.96	14.7
VARIANT I						
Based on Table 7-1 (from Table 7-2)						
3. A-dependent	53.9	121.4	1.86	14.7	2.25	10.8
4. N-dependent	45.3	145.5	2.21	19.2	3.21	15.9
Based on Shinohara						
5. A-dependent	80.0	109.4	1.25	5.1	1.37	4.0
6. N-dependent	67.3	131.1	1.49	9.2	1.95	8.8
VARIANT II						
Based on Table 7-1 (from Table 7-2)						
7. A-dependent	46.8	162.7	2.14	18.4	3.48	17.0
8. N-dependent	47.8	142.4	2.09	17.8	2.98	14.8
Based on Shinohara						
9. A-dependent	69.4	146.1	1.44	8.5	2.11	9.9
10. N-dependent	70.9	127.8	1.41	7.9	1.80	7.7

NOTE: For sources and derivation of the estimates of PCE per capita for the two population groups see
Table 7-2 and the accompanying discussion. For the Shinohara series see reference in note to Table 7A-1.

results for Variant *I* based on the residual series would show an *intra*-component of 13.35, which compared with 22.3 would leave an *inter*-component of 8.95 (col. 6, lines 3 and 4 and 1). In Variant *I* based on the Shinohara series, the *intra*-component, would be 6.4 which, compared with 14.7, would leave an *inter*-component of 8.3 (lines 5 and 6 and 2). Thus, while the reduction in the countrywide rate is 7.6 percentage points (from 22.3 to 14.7), 6.95 of these points are reflected in the reduction of the *intra*-group trends (from 13.35 to 6.4).

In the more realistic Variant *II,* where the weight of *inter*-group shifts is reduced, the average of the growth rates for the *A*- and *N*-dependent populations based on the Shinohara series is 8.8 percent per decade (lines 9 and 10) compared with 15.9 percent per decade for the residual series (lines 7 and 8). Even here the reduction is marked, because again the large *inter*-group shift remains unaffected, and the full impact of the reduction in the countrywide growth rate falls upon the trends within each population group.

One major conclusion stands out in Table 7A–2—the importance of proper estimates of the *differences* in PCE per capita between the *A*- and *N*-dependent populations, or among any similar groups within the population. The wider the *inter*-group differences and the greater the shift in numbers among them, the greater the weight of *inter*-group shifts in the countrywide movement of per capita PCE, and the lesser the weight of trends *within* each distinct population group. The interpretation of the impact of economic growth upon economic welfare and the analysis of the mechanism of response of the human factors depend upon greater knowledge of the structure represented by the different economic groups within labor force and population.

The final comparison emphasizes the distribution between food and other goods within personal consumption expenditures (Table 7A–3). This comparison is of particular interest following our discussion of the large share of food in total consumption suggested for the period before World War I by the estimates and their analysis in Table 7–5. The major results and questions can best be listed *seriatim.*

a) The Shinohara series suggests a smaller share of food in total expenditures in the earlier periods—65 to 66 percent in 1879–83, instead of 75 to 76 percent according to the estimates in Table 7–5. Nor does the food share drop as sharply from 1909–13 to 1924–28 in the Shinohara series as in the series in Table 7–5. In both respects, the Shinohara estimates raise fewer questions concerning the food share than the estimates in Table 7–5.

b) Nevertheless, the Shinohara series only weakens—it does not

TABLE 7A-3

Share of Food in Total Consumer Expenditures,
Table 7-5 and the Shinohara Estimates

	1879-83 (1)	1889-93 (2)	1899-1903 (3)	1909-13 (4)	1924-28 (5)	1934-38 (6)
SHARE OF FOOD IN PCE (%)						
1934-36 Prices						
1. Table 7-5	75.8	82.1	71.1	63.3	41.9	38.9
2. Shinohara	65.1	62.9	60.3	60.7	56.2	48.8
Current Prices						
3. Table 7-5	75.0	77.2	69.0	63.9	45.2	39.3
4. Shinohara	65.9	64.1	63.3	63.3	57.0	48.8
VOLUMES IN CURRENT PRICES (MILLIONS OF YEN PER YEAR)						
Food Expenditures						
5. Table 7-5	433	516	1,125	1,837	4,926	4,669
6. Shinohara	522	650	1,409	2,389	7,327	7,065
7. Ratio, line 6 to line 5	1.21	1.26	1.25	1.30	1.49	1.51
Nonfood Expenditures						
8. Table 7-5	144	152	506	1,039	5,971	7,226
9. Shinohara	270	364	818	1,383	5,525	7,402
10. Ratio, line 9 to line 8	1.87	2.39	1.62	1.33	0.93	1.02
Total Expenditures						
11. Ratio, Shinohara estimates to those in Table 7-5	1.37	1.52	1.37	1.31	1.18	1.22

NOTES: Percentage shares are based on quinquennial totals. For the Shinohara series see volume cited in notes to Table 7A-1.

negate—the basic finding of Table 7–5, that the food share in Japan in the early periods is unusually high. Ranging from 60 to 66 percent between 1879–83 and 1909–13 it is still higher than that in many underdeveloped countries today with their much lower income—and most probably higher than that in the developed countries in their early development phases.

c) The effect of the new series on the movement of the food share after 1934–38 is still to be established. In 1934–38, the food share in the new series, 49 percent (line 4, col. 6) is markedly above that shown by the old official series, 41 percent (see line 1, col. 1 of Table 7–6). The volume of food consumption expenditures for 1934–38, in current prices, shown by Shinohara, is 45 percent above the old official series; and the new official estimates suggest only a slight upward adjustment in the old series (judging by the overlap for fiscal 1952–54). Thus, if the Shinohara estimates are taken to be comparable with the current official estimates, the implication is that the rate of growth in per capita food consumption suggested in the residual and official series for 1924–28 to 1962–64 is too high. If we set the food share in 1924–28 at 56 percent, on the basis of Table 7A–3, lines 2 and 4, and take 40 percent for 1962–64 (*F*) from the official series in Table 7–6, the implicit rate of growth of food consumption per capita (derived from the growth rate of 18.9 percent per decade for total PCE per capita in the Shinohara series; see page 236 above) for the period is 8.54 percent per decade—not more than 17 percent as implied by the food shares in Tables 7–5 and 7–6.

d) While this downward movement of the food share from 1924–28 to 1962–64 suggested by the new series looks more reasonable · than the virtual stability of the share in the estimates presented and discussed in connection with Table 7–6 (and would resolve the puzzle raised), it still leaves a question as to why the decline in the food share was so slight over the earlier period. From 1879–83 to 1924–28, while per capita PCE in constant prices practically doubled (from 50.9 to 100), the Shinohara series suggests a decline in the food share of barely 9 percentage points—from 65 to 56 or from 66 to 57 percent (see lines 2 and 4). This implies an expenditure elasticity of demand for food over the earlier period as high as 0.78 (using annual growth rates) compared with a similar measure of 0.48 for the period from 1924–28 to 1962–64 (*F*). This break in the response of the demand for food to higher per capita expenditures (and it would be more conspicuous in the response to higher per capita income), if confirmed, would warrant a more searching examination than the usual explanation of declining elasticity of demand for food with rising per capita income.

e) Finally, Table 7A–3 indicates that the new series involves a drastic revision of the estimates of nonfood consumer expenditures, particularly in the early periods (see line 10, columns 1–3). The revisions are proportionately far greater than those for foods. If these revisions are confirmed, it follows that the current estimates of GDP or GNP for the early periods are particularly short in sectors that generate nonfood consumption goods—possibly manufacturing, but probably services. Since these shortages are conspicuous in the earlier periods, and, judging by the new series, diminish or vanish by the 1920's, the trends in industrial structure of aggregate product would clearly be affected—whatever the change in the overall growth rate.

While the major findings of the paper will still remain valid for the most part and some of the puzzles raised in the paper will be answered if the new estimates prove acceptable, important effects on the level of per capita consumption and product in the early years, on the growth rates, and on the trends in industrial structure will have to be carefully analyzed.

Since the new series just discussed are the first set of long-term estimates of consumption derived directly from commodity and service flow data, rather than as a residual from national product totals based on output, they are most welcome as a base for more detailed and valuable analysis of consumption than has been possible heretofore. But the potential value of such analytical use makes it all the more important to have the new estimates scrutinized and tested—both by a direct critical review, and by incorporating them into a broader national accounts framework and testing them in the light of the relationships indicated.

PART II

Postwar Economic Growth

8 | Factors for Rapid Economic Growth: A Social Accounting Approach*

SHINICHI ICHIMURA

INTRODUCTION

This paper deals with the development of the Japanese economy from 1951 to 1961, a period during which per capita national income grew from $179 to $523. The annual average rate of growth in real national income over these 11 years was about 9.5 percent and was considerably faster than that of West Germany or the Soviet Union. Since, however, it is only in 1955 or 1956 that Japanese per capita income reached the prewar maximum, the beginning half of the period under investigation covers the years of predominantly postwar recovery, and only the latter half shows significantly the true development of Japanese economic life beyond the prewar standard. This paper, therefore, deals with an interesting transitional period from recovery to development.

This paper purports to offer an anatomical analysis of rapid Japanese economic growth in terms of social accounting of national income and related statistical aggregates. The social accounting scheme we adopt here is the one which we have constructed for the *Osaka Econometric Model of Postwar Japan*. It is basically the national income accounts supplemented by simplified input-output tables and accounts of labor force, capital stocks by industrial sectors and the money flow table. As we explain immediately, it is essential for the analysis of a

* The research was supported by a grant from the Ford Foundation to the Graduate School of Business Administration and administered through the Center for Research in Management Science, University of California. The computation was carried out by Mr. Hans Tjian at the above-mentioned center. I would like to express my gratitude for his careful and time-consuming work.

national economy not only to have a consistent overall social accounting system for economic time series in current value but also to define
price indexes and wage rates appropriately so that the basic identities
hold, even in real terms.

After constructing consistent time series in real terms within the
framework of social accounts—or, in other words, in a way that
satisfies basic identities—we take selected ratios of important variables
and use them to test simple but important hypotheses used in explaining the rapid Japanese economic growth. This kind of simple anatomy
of social accounts is admittedly inferior to an elaborate econometric
analysis, but if it is wisely done it can effectively reveal some important aspects of economic growth and supplement or check more
high-powered analysis of econometric models or equations. It can
draw attention to a few important points of interest so that it can be
free from rigid hypotheses. It is the method which Professor Simon
Kuznets often adopts in his international comparison of long time
series of different countries' national incomes or similar to the model
which Professor Lawrence R. Klein constructed to describe the long-
term growth of the U.S. economy in terms of "great ratios," of economic growth. (See Kuznets[1] and Klein.[2]) In Japan, too, a number of
economists including Dr. Osamu Shimomura, Professor Miyohei
Shinohara and the authors of *White Papers* of government have skill-
fully made use of a few crucial ratios like "marginal capital coefficient"
and "incremental export-capital ratio" and have given very sensible
analyses and even predictions of postwar economic growth.

It does not seem appropriate to lump these analyses together under
what Professor R. Stone called "casual empiricism,"[3] but more properly they are parts of social accounting analysis of a national economy.
What we attempt here is nothing but an anatomy of the social accounts
of the Japanese economy from 1951 to 1961.[4] Section I gives an

---

[1] S. Kuznets, *Modern Economic Growth* (New Haven, Conn.: Yale University Press, 1966).

[2] L. R. Klein, *An Introduction to Econometrics* (Englewood Cliffs, N.J.:
Prentice-Hall, Inc., 1962), pp. 180–201.

[3] R. Stone, and others, *The Measurement of Consumers' Expenditure and
Behaviour in the United Kingdom, 1920–1938, Vol. I* (Cambridge: Cambridge
University Press, 1954).

[4] As for anatomical analyses of social accounts, see, for instance, G. Stuvel,
Systems of Social Accounts (Oxford: Oxford University Press, 1965); and
M. Yanovsky, *Anatomy of Social Accounting Systems* (London: Chapman &
Hall, 1967). Professor R. Stone's Transaction Model and its applications in
R. Stone, *Mathematics in the Social Sciences and Other Essays* (London: Chap-
man & Hall, 1966) are also similar studies.

exposition of the use of this method and its limitations. Section II explains a system of social accounts adopted in this paper. Section III discusses the sectorial breakdowns of Japanese economic growth and sectorial characteristics of technological progress. Section IV takes up the problems of supply of labor and capital. Section V discusses their allocations among sectors through the market mechanism of free enterprise. The appraisal of Japanese growth under free enterprise is examined to some extent. Section VI analyzes the characteristic composition of national expenditure in postwar Japan.

I. EXPOSITION OF A SIMPLE SOCIAL ACCOUNTING MODEL

Suppose that a simple system of social accounts is given for a closed economy as in Table 8–1, where notations are:

C = Consumption
I = Investment
M = Material input
X = Total national production
Y = National income
W = Wage payments
P = Profits
N = Labor employed

K = Capital stock
w = wage rate
π = profit rate
p_x = output price index
p_c = consumer's price index
p_k = investment price index
p_m = materials price index
p = national income deflator

TABLE 8-1

National Income Accounts

	Industry	Capital Formation	Consumption	Output
Industry	M	I	C	X
Wages.	W			Y
Profit	P			
Expenditure.	X	I	C	$X + Y$

These symbols with primes denote money values, and those without primes denote values in constant yen. It should be obvious that the following identities hold:

$$X' = M' + C' + I' \tag{1.1}$$
$$X' = M' + W' + P' \tag{1.2}$$
$$Y' = W' + P' \tag{1.3}$$
$$W' = wN \tag{1.4}$$
$$P' = \pi K \tag{1.5}$$
$$X' = p_x X \tag{1.6}$$
$$I' = p_k I \tag{1.7}$$
$$C' = p_c C \tag{1.8}$$
$$M = X - C - I \tag{1.9}$$
$$Y = C + I \tag{1.10}$$
$$Y' = pY \tag{1.11}$$
$$M' = p_m M. \tag{1.12}$$

Notice here that p and p_m are implicit deflators defined for given values of p_x, p_c, and p_k. Notice also that by defining wage incomes and profits in real terms, we have:

$$W = W'/p = \frac{w}{p} \cdot N, \tag{1.13}$$

$$P = P'/p = \frac{\pi}{p} \cdot K. \tag{1.14}$$

Three basic identities for national income hold also in real terms; namely,

$$Y = X - M, \tag{1.15}$$
$$Y = C + I, \tag{1.16}$$
$$Y = W + P. \tag{1.17}$$

They represent production, expenditure and distribution sides of national product and offer the bases for analyzing various factors in economic growth. They can be rewritten in terms of growth rates:

$$\frac{\Delta Y}{Y} = \frac{\Delta(1 - M/X)}{(1 - M/X)} + \frac{\Delta X}{X} \tag{1.18}$$

$$\frac{\Delta Y}{Y} = \frac{\Delta C}{C} \frac{C}{Y} + \frac{\Delta I}{I} \frac{I}{Y} \tag{1.19}$$

$$\frac{\Delta Y}{Y} = \frac{\Delta(W/P)}{(W/P)} \frac{W}{Y} + \frac{\Delta P}{P} \tag{1.20}$$

where ΔY denotes the increase of Y in one period, and the same interpretation holds for other similar magnitudes. Equation (1.18) breaks down the growth rate of national product into the change in the ratio of value added to output and the change in total output. If, therefore, M/X becomes smaller, the growth rate of national product can exceed that of total industrial output.[5]

It would not be unusual to associate X with labor and capital so that we may define:

$$X = \rho N, \tag{1.21}$$
$$X = \sigma K, \tag{1.22}$$

where ρ and σ stand for the observed average productivities of labor and capital. Needless to say,

$$\frac{\Delta X}{X} = \frac{\Delta \rho}{\rho} + \frac{\Delta N}{N}, \tag{1.23}$$

$$\frac{\Delta X}{X} = \frac{\Delta \sigma}{\sigma} + \frac{\Delta K}{K}. \tag{1.24}$$

We have always $\Delta \rho > 0$, but $\Delta \sigma$ may be positive or negative. Since

$$\frac{\Delta \rho}{\rho} = \frac{\Delta \sigma}{\sigma} + \frac{\Delta(K/N)}{K/N}, \tag{1.25}$$

$\Delta \rho / \rho$ can exceed $\Delta \sigma / \sigma$ by the growth rate of the capital-labor ratio. If $\Delta \sigma = 0$, $\Delta \rho / \rho$ is precisely equal to the rate of growth in K/N. These equations are nothing but the identities which give the relations among related variables. No simple rules of causation can be deduced from them. But careful observation of these variables often reveal interesting aspects of economic growth.

The changes of ρ and σ in equations (1.23) to (1.25) may or may not be related to a change in production function. It is not possible to make any inference about technical progress without explicit introduction of hypotheses on production function. Let us assume that production in this system is of the Cobb-Douglas type, and that the theory of marginal productivity of labor holds approximately. Then,

$$X = AN^\alpha K^\beta, \tag{1.26}$$

and

$$\alpha \frac{X}{N} = \gamma \frac{w}{p_x}, \tag{1.27}$$

---

[5] Technical progress with respect to M/X will be analyzed analogously as labor-capital substitution is in the following discussion.

where γ is an index that shows the degree of approximation of marginal productivity of labor to real wage. Then,

$$\frac{\Delta a}{a} - \frac{\Delta \gamma}{\gamma} = \frac{\Delta(w/p_x)}{w/p_x} - \frac{\Delta \rho}{\rho} = \frac{\Delta(W'/Y')}{W'/Y'} + \frac{\Delta(Y'/X')}{Y'/X'} \quad (1.28)$$

where a and γ are not observables. By comparing the growth rate of ρ with that of w/p_x, we can make an inference about the change of a, provided we can tell something about $\Delta\gamma/\gamma$. If, for instance, it is safe to assume that the degree of competition in the Japanese economy did not increase so that $\Delta\gamma/\gamma \leqq 0$, and the growth rate of labor productivity exceeds that of real wage, then we may infer that $\Delta a/a < 0$; namely, technical progress was of the laborsaving type in the Hicksian sense.[6]

Similar inferences can be made from the conditions for the marginal productivity of capital. From equation (1.26), we obtain

$$\beta \frac{X}{K} = \delta \frac{\pi}{p_x}, \quad (1.29)$$

where δ is an index that shows the degree of approximation of marginal productivity of capital to real rate of profit, π/p_x. From this and equation (1.27) we have

$$\frac{a}{\beta} \frac{K}{N} = \frac{\gamma}{\delta} \frac{w}{\pi}. \quad (1.30)$$

Equations (1.29) and (1.30) give

$$\frac{\Delta \beta}{\beta} - \frac{\Delta \delta}{\delta} = \frac{\Delta(\pi/p_x)}{\pi/p_x} - \frac{\Delta \sigma}{\sigma} = \frac{\Delta(P'/Y')}{P'/Y'} + \frac{\Delta(Y'/X')}{Y'/X'}, \quad (1.31)$$

$$\left(\frac{\Delta a}{a} - \frac{\Delta \beta}{\beta}\right) - \left(\frac{\Delta \gamma}{\gamma} - \frac{\Delta \delta}{\delta}\right)$$
$$= \left(\frac{\Delta w}{w} - \frac{\Delta \pi}{\pi}\right) - \frac{\Delta(K/N)}{K/N} = \frac{\Delta(W'/P')}{W'/P'} \quad (1.32)$$

---

[6] For classification of technical change, see, for instance, J. Fei, and G. Ranis, *Development of the Labor Surplus Economy: Theory and Policy* (Homewood, Ill.: Richard D. Irwin, Inc., 1964). It seems important to keep in mind that rapid technical progress tends to be concentrated in some leading firms in the industry and thereby increases the degree of imperfect competition. Hence, one should always suspect that $\Delta\gamma$ or $\Delta\delta$ may be positive rather than negative in a fast-growing economy.

If $\Delta\gamma/\gamma = \Delta\delta/\delta$, then the sign of the right-hand terms in (1.32) can determine the bias of technical progress; namely, if $\Delta a/a - \Delta\beta/\beta <$ 0, $= 0$ or > 0, then technical progress is respectively "laborsaving," "neutral," or "capital-saving." If, however, it is not always possible to know the sign of $\Delta\gamma/\gamma - \Delta\delta/\delta$, it is desirable to pay attention to all of equations (1.28), (1.31), and (1.32) and make our inference.

It is of some use to summarize the supply side of national product by the following equation which can be derived from the equations presented above:

$$\frac{\Delta Y}{Y} = \frac{\Delta A}{A} + \frac{\Delta(Y/X)}{Y/X}$$

$$+ a\frac{\Delta N}{N} + \beta\frac{\Delta K}{K} + \Delta a \log N + \Delta\beta \log K. \qquad (1.33)$$

Especially if $a + \beta = 1$, then

$$\frac{\Delta Y}{Y} = \frac{\Delta A}{A} + \frac{\Delta(Y/X)}{Y/X}$$

$$+ \frac{\Delta N}{N} + \beta\left(\frac{\Delta K}{K} - \frac{\Delta N}{N}\right) + \Delta\beta \log \frac{K}{N}, \qquad (1.34)$$

where each term on the right-hand side shows a different factor which contributes to the growth rate of national product. $\Delta A/A$ is the growth rate of overall efficiency; $\Delta(Y/X)/(Y/X)$ is the growth rate of the value-added to output ratio; $\Delta N/N$ is the growth rate of employment; $\Delta(K/N)/(K/N)$ is the growth rate of the capital-labor ratio; and the last term is the contribution of biased technical progress. If $\Delta\beta > 0$, laborsaving technical progress contributes to $\Delta Y/Y$ more as K/N increases.

Now we turn to national expenditure represented by (1.16) and (1.19). Rapid economic growth requires not only that the various factors on the supply side, like those in (1.33) or (1.34), be large but also that the level and growth rate of effective demand remain large. Moreover, the composition of national expenditure must be consistent with requirements from the supply side. This is particularly important with respect to investment. Take for instance the simplest case in which C is proportional to Y:

$$C = (1 - s)Y. \qquad (1.35)$$

From (1.19), we know that

$$\Delta Y/Y = \Delta I/I. \qquad (1.36)$$

Given I, and comparing it with K and assuming also that all the other terms in (1.34) are given, we can obtain the growth rate of supply of Y. If supply should be equal to demand, this would have to equal (1.36). Hence, we can establish

$$\frac{\Delta I}{I} - \frac{\Delta K}{K} = \frac{\Delta A}{A} + \frac{\Delta(Y/X)}{Y/X} + \Delta\beta \log \frac{K}{N} - \alpha \frac{\Delta(K/N)}{K/N} . \quad (1.37)$$

Unless this equality holds from one period to another, effective demand is not equal to the supply of national product. Finally (1.20) shows the relation between $\Delta Y/Y$ and the functional distribution of income. From this and (1.32) we know that if technical progress is laborsaving and $\Delta\gamma/\gamma - \Delta\delta/\delta = 0$, then labor's share of national income must decline so that $\Delta P/P$ must be greater than $\Delta Y/Y$. Furthermore it is of some interest to notice that we can derive from (1.16) and (1.17) the following identity:

$$\frac{W}{P} = \left(\frac{1}{1 - C/Y}\right)\frac{I}{P} - 1. \quad (1.38)$$

This implies that if the average propensity to consume does not change, W/P must change in the same direction as I/P. (See Kaldor.[7]) Hence, under the same assumptions above, $\Delta I/I < \Delta P/P > \Delta Y/Y > \Delta W/W$. If, therefore, $\Delta I/I$ exceeds $\Delta P/P$ when W/P is falling, C/Y must be declining considerably.

II. OUR SOCIAL ACCOUNTING SYSTEM AND STATISTICAL DATA

The social accounting system adopted here has five industrial sectors: (1) agriculture, (2) heavy industry, (3) textile industry, (4) other manufacturing industry, and (5) tertiary industry. (2), (3), and (4) are further divided into large- and small-scale enterprise. The dividing line between large and small is placed at corporate paid capital of 50 million yen. The basic scheme of social accounts is summarized in Table 8–2. (See also Ichimura *et al.*[8])

---

[7] N. Kaldor, "Alternative Theories of Distribution," *The Review of Economic Studies,* February, 1960.

[8] S. Ichimura, L. R. Klein, S. Koizumi, K. Sato, and Y. Shinkai, "A Quarterly Econometric Model of Japan, 1952–1959," *Osaka Economic Papers,* March, 1964.

The notations are:

$X_{ij} =$ Total production of industry i of scale j, where $i = a$, h, M, E; $j = L$, S; a denotes agriculture, h, heavy, M, other manufacturing and E, tertiary; L, large scale and S, small scale.

$M_{ij} =$ Materials input for industry i of scale j,

$T_{ij} =$ Indirect tax *minus* subsidies for industry i of scale j,

$W_{ij} =$ Wage payments by industry i of scale j,

$D_{ij} =$ Depreciation in industry i of scale j,

$P_{ij} =$ Profits in industry i of scale j,

$Y_o =$ Rental income,

$D_r =$ Depreciation of residential houses,

$D_g =$ Depreciation of government-owned buildings,

$I_{ij} =$ Fixed capital formation in industry i of scale j,

$I_r =$ Residential capital formation,

$G_I =$ Government capital formation,

$J_a =$ Inventory investment of agriculture,

$J_d =$ Dealers' inventory investment,

$J_m =$ Producers' inventory investment of raw materials,

$J_p =$ Producers' inventory investment of goods in process,

$J_{fi} =$ Industry i's inventory investment of finished products,

$C_f =$ Consumption of food,

$C_t =$ Consumption of textiles,

$C_o =$ Consumption of other goods,

$W_g =$ Government wage payments,

$G_c =$ Government nonwage consumption,

$E_a =$ Exports of agricultural products,

$E_h =$ Exports of heavy industry products,

$E_M =$ Exports of other manufactured products,

$B_m =$ Imports of raw materials,

$B_f =$ Imports of food,

$B_h =$ Imports of heavy industry products,

$B_c =$ Imports of consumption goods,

$Y_G =$ Gross national product,

ζ, η, $d_s =$ Some statistical adjustments.

Here it is to be noted that heavy industry includes mining besides metal, machinery and armament industries. The M sector covers all the rest of manufacturing industries. Textiles are included in the M sector for this presentation. Agriculture includes forestry and fishery. All other industries are included in the E sector.

TABLE 8-2

Social Accounts and Interindustrial Relations in the Osaka Model

		Current Material Input						Adjusted Items	Inventory Investment					
		A	hL	hS	ML	MS	E		A	h	M	d	m	p
Agriculture:	A	*	*	*	*	*	*	J_A						
Heavy industry, large:	hL	*	*	*	*	*	*			J_{fh}		*	*	*
Heavy industry, small:	hS	M_A	M_{hL}	M_{hS}	M_{ML}	M_{MS}	M_E			*		J_d	J_m	J_p
Other manufacturing industry, large:	ML	*	*	*	*	*	*				J_{fM}	*	*	*
Other manufacturing industry, small:	MS	*	*	*	*	*	*				*	*	*	*
Tertiary industry:	E	*	*	*	*	*	*							
Indirect tax		T_A	T_{hL}	T_{hS}	T_{ML}	T_{MS}	T_E							
Wages			W_{hL}	W_{hS}	W_{ML}	W_{MS}	W_E	Y_o ξ						
Profits		Y_A	P_{hL}	P_{hS}	P_{ML}	P_{MS}	P_E							
Depreciation		D_A	D_{hL}	D_{hS}	D_{ML}	D_{MS}	D_E	D_r D_g						
								d_s						
Total expenditure									(*	*	J	*	*	*)

The following identities must hold in money values:

$$Y'_G = Y'_a + Y'_{hL} + Y'_{hS} + Y'_{ML} + Y'_{MS} + Y'_E + Y'_o + W'_g + \zeta', \quad (2.1)$$

$$Y'_G = C' + I' + J' + G' + E' - B' + \eta', \quad (2.2)$$

$$Y'_G = W' + P' + Y'_a + Y'_o + T' + D' + d'_s, \quad (2.3)$$

$$C' = C'_f + C'_t + C'_o, \quad (2.4)$$

$$I' = I'_{hL} + I'_{hS} + I'_{ML} + I'_{MS} + I'_E + I'_a, \quad (2.5)$$

$$J' = J'_a + J'_d + J'_p + J'_m + J'_{fh} + J'_{fM}, \quad (2.6)$$

$$G' = G'_c + G'_I + W'_g, \quad (2.7)$$

$$D' = D'_{hL} + D'_{hS} + D'_{ML} + D'_{MS} + D'_E + D'_r + D'_g, \quad (2.8)$$

$$T' = T'_{hL} + T'_{hS} + T'_{ML} + T'_{MS} + T'_E + T'_a, \quad (2.9)$$

$$E' = E'_a + E'_h + E'_M, \quad (2.10)$$

$$B' = B'_m + B'_h + B'_c + B'_f, \quad (2.11)$$

Private Capital Formation							Government Exp.		Consumption			Export	Imports	Total
A	hL	hS	ML	MS	E	Res.	Capital	Other	Food	Textiles	Other			
							(*)					E_a	$-B_f$	X_A
*	*	*	*	*	*	*	*	*		*	*	*	*	X_{hL}
I_a	I_{hL}	I_{hS}	I_{ML}	I_{MS}	I_E	I_R	G_I	G_c			*	E_h	B_h	X_{hS}
*	*	*	*	*	*	*	*	*		*	*	*	$-B_m$	X_{ML}
*	*	*	*	*	*	*	*	*	C_f	C_t	C_o	E_M	B_c	X_{MS}
*	*	*	*	*	*	*	*	*	*	*	*	*	*	X_E
								W_g						(*)
														Y_G
														*
														(*)

$$(* \quad * \quad * \quad * \quad I_p \quad * \quad * \quad *) \quad (\quad G \quad *) \quad (* \quad C \quad *) \quad E \quad (* \quad -B)$$

$$W' = W'_{hL} + W'_{hS} + W'_{ML} + W'_{MS} + W'_{E}, \tag{2.12}$$

$$P' = P'_{hL} + P'_{hS} + P'_{ML} + P'_{MS} + P'_{E}, \tag{2.13}$$

$$P'_{ij} = X'_{ij} - M'_{ij} - W'_{ij} - D'_{ij} - T'_{ij} \quad (i = h, M, E;\ j = L, S), \tag{2.14}$$

As we discussed in the preceding section, we can define similar identities in real terms by appropriate use of price indexes. Real GNP (Y_G) can be defined as:

$$Y_G = C + I + J + G + E - B + \eta, \tag{2.15}$$

where

$$C = C'_f/p^c_f + C'_t/p^c_t + C'_o/p^c_o,$$

$$I = I'/p_k$$

$$J = J'_d/p^J_d + J'_m/p^J_m + J'_p/p^J_p + J'_{fh}/p_h + J'_{fM}/p_M + J'_a/p_a,$$

$$G = G'_c/p^c + W'_g/p^g_w + G'_I/p_k,$$

$$E = E'_a/p^e_a + E'_h/p^e_h + E'_M/p^e_M,$$

$$B = B'_m/p^b_m + B'_h/p^b_h + B'_c/p^b_c + B'_f/p^b_f,$$

and the new notations denote:

p_f^c = consumers' price index of food,

p_t^c = consumers' price index of textiles,

p_o^c = consumers' price index of other goods,

p_k = price index of investment goods,

p_d^J = price index for dealers' inventory investment,

p_m^J = price index for raw materials,

p_p^J = price index for goods in process,

p_h = price index of heavy industry products,

p_M = price index of other manufacturing products,

p_a = price index of agricultural output,

$p^c = C'/C$ = implicit deflator for total consumption,

p_w^g = index of wages,

p_a^e = export price index for agricultural products,

p_h^e = export price index for heavy industry products,

p_M^e = export price index for other manufacturing products,

p_m^b = import price index for raw materials,

p_h^b = import price index for heavy industry products,

p_c^b = import price index for consumption goods,

p_f^b = import price index for food.

Needless to say, the implicit deflator for GNP can be obtained by

$$\frac{Y'_G}{Y_G} = p. \qquad (2.16)$$

It is easy to see that the value added of each sector, say, Y_{ij} in real terms, can be obtained by

$$Y_{ij} = (X'_{ij} - M'_{ij})/p = \frac{p_i}{p}\left(1 - \frac{p_i^m}{p_i}\frac{M'_{ij}/p_i^m}{X'_{ij}/p_i}\right)\frac{X'_{ij}}{p_i} \qquad (2.17)$$

where p_i^m = the price index of raw materials for industry i.

From (2.14) and (2.17) it can be seen that

$$Y_{ij} = \frac{w_{ij}}{p} N_{ij} + \frac{\pi_{ij}}{p} K_{ij} + \frac{T'_{ij}}{p} + \frac{D'_{ij}}{p}, \qquad (2.18)$$

where w_{ij}, π_{ij}, N_{ij} and K_{ij} are defined for each sector in the same way that w, π, N, K were for the entire system.

Thus the identities similar to (2.1), (2.2) and (2.3) can be established and they can be used to analyze various aspects of economic growth in the same way as in the preceding section.

The statistical data are compiled according to the scheme of Table 8–2 for 44 quarters from the beginning of 1951 to the end of 1961. The time series used are published in *Osaka Economic Papers*,[9] except for some additional data prepared for this paper and listed in the Appendix. Price indexes are mostly components of the wholesale price index published by the Bank of Japan. The detailed explanation of statistical data will be made available later.

III. RAPID INDUSTRIALIZATION, DUAL STRUCTURE AND TECHNICAL PROGRESS

Let us observe first the industries that grew most rapidly. The rate of growth in, say, X_{hL} is computed by estimating

$$\log X_{hL}(t) = \log A_{hL} + a_{hL} t + \log U_t. \qquad (3.1)$$

We then compare a's in different sectors. The same method is applied to the computation of growth rates in any other variables or their ratios. Needless to say, if the growth rates computed in this way for X, Y, Z, are a, β, γ and $Z = XY$, then $a + \beta = \gamma$. To simplify the presentation, $\Delta X/X$ will be denoted by $g(X)$.

Table 8–3 shows annual growth rates in total production of the six sectors of the Japanese economy, 1951–61, and the growth rates of raw material input coefficients M/X.[10]

---

[9] S. Ichimura, L. R. Klein, S. Koizumi, K. Sato, and Y. Shinkai, "A Quarterly Econometric Model of Japan, 1952–1959: Data Appendix," *Osaka Economic Papers*, July, 1964.

[10] Here as well as in the following discussion we do not consider the so-called "vertical integration" of firms, particularly among different scales of firms, but treat large and small scales of industries as if they were producing the same industrial product-mix, only in different scales. Needless to say, to the extent that this is inadequate, our discussion in this paper must be reconsidered.

TABLE 8-3

Growth Rates of Industrial Production and
Raw Material Input Coefficients

		g(X)	g(M/X)
Heavy:	Large	18.5	0.6
Other:	Large	15.7	0.9
Heavy:	Small	14.1	0.3
Other:	Small	11.0	-1.2
Tertiary.		6.4	-0.6
Agriculture		4.8	1.4

Since the raw materials input coefficients did not change significantly, except for agriculture and tertiary industries, and also the relative prices of raw materials and outputs changed very little, we can compute the contribution of each sector to the growth rate of GNP according to (2.1) and (2.17). It is clear that the leading industry was heavy industry in this simple classification.

There is no doubt that there was an avalanche of new technologies in postwar Japan and that this was one of the major factors in its rapid growth. In order to assess their importance, we follow the method explained in Section I. Table 8–4 shows the means and the growth rates of capital coefficients and labor productivities in six sectors; Table 8–5 the rates of change in factor and output prices and factor shares. These tables reveal, first of all, the surprisingly large differentials in productivities among different scales of same industry as well as among different industries. For instance, labor productivity in the *ML* sector is three times as large as that in the *MS* sector, and

TABLE 8-4

Capital Coefficient, Labor Productivity,
Capital-Labor Ratio and Their Rates of Growth

	K/X	X/N	K/N	$g(X/K)$	$g(X/N)$	$g(K/N)$
hL.	1.73	4.46	7.10	5.6	11.8	6.2
ML.	1.40	6.50	8.55	4.0	10.1	6.1
hS.	0.75	2.44	1.78	3.1	7.1	4.0
MS.	0.80	2.14	1.56	9.1	6.4	-3.1
E.	1.62	1.77	2.87	-3.0	0.4	3.4
A.	1.08	1.15	1.22	7.3	5.6	2.5

TABLE 8-5

The Growth Rates of Output, Labor, and Capital, and Their Prices

	$g(X)$	$g(N)$	$g(K)$	$g(p)$	$g(w)$	$g(\pi)$
hL.	18.5	6.7	12.9	0.5	8.9	6.9
ML.	15.7	5.6	11.7	-0.4	8.7	2.6
hS.	14.1	6.9	10.9	0.5	7.3	8.0
MS.	11.0	5.0	1.9	-0.4	7.2	10.9
E.	6.4	6.0	9.3	4.2	8.4	1.6
A.	4.1	-1.5	0.4	0.8	(7.0)	

almost 1.5 times as big as that in the *HL* sector. Since there is no significant difference in M/X; for instance, $M_{hL}/X_{hL} = 0.68$, $M_{ML}/X_{ML} = 0.68$, these differentials can be compensated only by the differentials in factor prices. This is nothing but the problems of what are often referred to as "dual structure" of Japanese economy. By observing the growth rates of these productivities we can see also that the productivity differentials widened rather than narrowed among industries as well as between scales throughout the period under investigation.

The widening differentials in productivities did not accompany a similar movement in money wages. $g(w)$ shows a remarkably uniform movement upward. As a result, the rates of profit π widened, particularly among industries.

The direct cause of the productivity gap is, as we can see in Tables 8–4 and 8–5, the large difference in capital-labor ratio. What is more significant, however, is the fact that the difference in this ratio became larger in spite of little difference in $g(w)$ among the different scales of same industries as well as different industries. Especially the difference between the *ML* sector and the *MS* sector was widened by an opposite movement in K/N. This may be explained partly by the growth of some better quality firms from small- to large-scale sectors. But it can hardly be the whole story, because $g(X)$ and $g(\pi)$ are as high as 11.0 percent and 10.9 percent for the *MS* sector.

These sectoral differences in observed technical relations and their changes must be related to the differences in technical progress among sectors. By an argument similar to those explained in connection with (1.28), (1.31), and (1.32) we seem to be able to infer the types of technical progress which prevailed in different sectors during this period. Since it does not seem that there was any noticeable change in the degree of competition in the *hL, hS,* and *ML* sectors, the rates of change in the indexes of the degree of competition can safely be suppressed for these sectors. The hL sector shows in Table 8–6 that its technical progress was "laborsaving" and in Table 8–3 slightly "material-using." The ML sectors shows that its change was "neutral" and slightly "material-using." The hS sector was slightly "laborsaving" and "material-saving." In the case of the MS sector, the same sign for wN/pX and $\pi K/pX$ does not permit the straightforward classification of this sector's technical progress. If, however, the degree of competition in the capital market may be assumed, to have increased in this sector, then $g(\delta) < 0$ so that 2.2 percent may very well have been negative. Hence we seem to be able to infer that this sector's technical progress was "capital-saving" and "material-saving."[11] Similar arguments seem to hold for tertiary industry as well, because this is the sector dominated by small-scale unincorporated firms. Thus, it may be assumed that $g(\delta) < 0$ in this sector, and that technical progress was "capital-saving" and "material-saving." Technical progress in agriculture requires similar but converse arguments. Assume that $g(w)$ in agriculture is equal to the average of $g(w)$ in the industrial sectors. It is well known that the price of rice is not a competitive price but is fixed by political as well as economic considerations. If $p \cdot aX/N = \gamma w$ holds, as Table 8–6 shows, $g(a) - g(\gamma) = -0.7$. Since, the logic in determining w here involves determination of p_a first and

TABLE 8-6

Factor Shares and Biases of Technical Progress

	$g\left(\dfrac{wN}{pX}\right)$	$g\left(\dfrac{\pi K}{pX}\right)$	$g\left(\dfrac{wN}{\pi K}\right)$	$g\left(\dfrac{M}{X}\right)$	Class I	Class II
hL. . . .	−3.4	0.8	−4.2	0.6	laborsaving	mat.-using
ML. . . .	−1.0	−1.0	0	0.9	neutral	mat.-using
hS. . . .	−0.4	4.3	−4.7	0.3	laborsaving	mat.-using
MS. . . .	1.6	2.2	−0.6	−1.2	cap.-saving	mat.-saving
E. . . .	3.8	0.3	3.5	−0.6	cap.-saving	mat.-saving
A. . . .	(−0.6)			1.4	laborsaving	mat.-using
	$g(\alpha)$ $- g(\gamma)$	$g(\beta)$ $- g(\delta)$	$g(\alpha/\beta)$ $-g(\gamma/\delta)$			

----

[11] Hugh Patrick cast some doubt in his comment on the reliability of capital stock data for the MS sector. Since, however, K_{MS} is computed by adding to the base year's value I_{MS}, which is obtained by subtracting I_{ML} from the investment of the whole industry, and I_{ML} is reliable, his conjecture can only concern underestimation of industrial investment. It may be that small-scale firms often purchase inexpensive used capital equipment, which would make our price deflator too high for I_{MS}. The author does not believe that these factors can be decisive in upsetting the reasoning in the text.

then of farmer's mixed income, and since there is no reason to believe that the supply price of farmers' labor does not increase nearly as fast as the industrial wage, $g(p_a) = 0.8$, $g(w) = 7.0$ can only be explained by the decline of the bargaining power of farm relative to industrial labor. This implies $g(\gamma) < 0$, $g(a) < -0.7$. Thus, we may conclude that agricultural technical progress is "laborsaving." Unlike the other sectors $g(p_a^m)$ and $g(p_a)$ showed different rates: $g(p_a^m) = 1.7$ and $g(p_a) = 0.8$; therefore we need to compare them with $g(M/X)$. But we know from Table 8–3, Table 8–6 and these figures that $g(p_a^m M_a/p_a X_a) = 1.7 - 0.8 + 1.4 = 3.3$ and $g(p_a^m M_a/w_a N_a) = 1.7 - 7.0 + 6.2 + 2.1 = 3.0$, we can conclude that agriculture's technical change is not only "laborsaving" but also "material-using." The postwar introduction of chemical weeding and fertilizers must have been the major source of increase in agricultural productivity.

These various types of technical progress in six sectors may be summarized by a triangle. The relative position of each point marked by sectoral designation to the central point indicates the change of factor proportions per unit of output according to the distance to each corner. If, for instance, a point A is located as it is in the triangle, Figure 8–1, it shows that the amounts of three factors per unit of output in 1961 compared with those in 1951 for the same set of relative prices are less labor, more capital, and more materials. On the whole it is quite clear that technical progress was primarily "laborsaving." This is very significant in view of the high rate of unemployment prevailing during this period. According to (1.33) or (1.34), this type of technical progress was an additional factor giving rise to rapid growth on the supply side along with additional factors represented by other terms in (1.33) or (1.34).

FIGURE 8–1.   Types of Technical Progress.

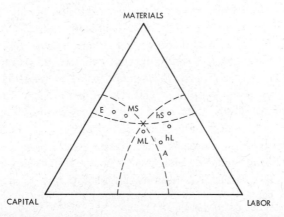

IV. SUPPLY OF PRODUCTIVE FACTORS, TECHNICAL PROGRESS

Let us proceed further in showing how the various productive factors contributed to Japanese economic growth on the supply side. Table 8–5 gives an unusually high rate of growth in nonagricultural employment, which accounts for a very high percentage of growth in industrial production of each sector, as the first column of Table 8–7 shows. Since the following identity must hold for the employment of industrial labor:

$$N_f = N_I + N_a + U + N_{s+g} \qquad (3.1)$$

where N_f, labor force; N_a, agricultural employment; N_I, industrial employment; and N_{s+g}, employers and government employees; we can write

$$g(N_I)\,\frac{N_I}{N_f} = g(N_f) - g(N_a)\,\frac{N_a}{N_f} - g(U)\,\frac{U}{N_f} - g(N_{s+g})\,\frac{N_{s+g}}{N_f}. \quad (3.2)$$

A high rate of increase in employment in the industrial sector is possible only by the matching high rates of increase (or decrease) in the terms on the right-hand side of (3.2). In the period from 1951 to 1961, $g(N_{s+g}) = 0$ so that this term may be ignored. In 1956, $N_I/N_f = 0.38$, $N_a/N_f = 0.32$, $U/N_f = 0.19$, $N_{s+g}/N_f = 0.11$. It is important, however, to divide the whole period into two parts; from 1951 to 1956 and from 1956 to 1961. Throughout the entire period the high rate of increase in labor force, $g(N_f) = 2$ percent, is the main factor making a high value of $g(N_I) = 6$ possible. But during the period up to 1956 it was particularly rapid as a result of the high birthrate just before the war; whereas after 1957, $g(N_f)$ slowed down reflecting the fall in birthrate during the war. The absolute increase from 1951 to 1956 was about 6 millions and the annual average was 1.2 millions; whereas from 1956 to 1961 the absolute increase suddenly dropped to about 3 millions with an annual average of 0.6 millions. In spite of rapid growth of employment, from 1951 to 1956, N_I increased by about 4 millions and the industrial sector as a whole failed to employ all the new labor force. As a result N_a and U increased during the first half period. Employment in the industrial sector, however, kept increasing at a faster pace in the second half period. The absolute increase in N_I was about 6 millions in this period with the annual average 1.2 millions. This sharp rate of increase was matched not only by the high, though falling, rate of increase in N_f but also by the rapid rate of decrease in N_a and U; $g(N_a)$ in this period was about -3 percent (the absolute number was 2.1 millions), and $g(U)$ was -4 percent (the absolute number was 1.5 millions). Indeed, 60 percent of new industrial workers were absorbed from the reserve army of labor in unemployment and agriculture, which awaited the opportunities of industrial employment since they had received improved training and education, particularly during the first period. This reserve army must still have contained a considerable number of demobilized soldiers and returning emigrants. These groups numbered 5 millions and more than compensated for the loss of 2 million vigorous youth and civilians during the war. Thus we conclude that the most important factor in rapid Japanese economic growth was this ample supply of good quality labor during a limited span of time.

The contribution of this increase of labor to the growth of industrial production can be seen by an identity similar to (1.34). Assume that

$$Y_{ij} = A_{ij} N_{ij}^{1-\beta} K_{ij}^{\beta} \tag{3.3}$$

then, omitting the subscript for simplicity,

$$\frac{\Delta Y}{Y} = \frac{\Delta A}{A} + \frac{\Delta N}{N} + \beta \frac{\Delta(K/N)}{K/N} + \Delta\beta \log \frac{K}{N}. \tag{3.4}$$

This expression partitions the factors contributing to the growth of Y into four parts; the growth of employment $\Delta N/N$, the part attributed to the growth of the capital-labor ratio for given β, the part due to biased technical progress, and the overall increase of efficiency. Notice that if technical progress is "laborsaving," $\Delta\beta > 0$ so that the last term is positive. Note also that (3.4) relates Y to N and K only, but since Y may increase for the same N and K if M/X decreases, this aspect needs some consideration. If M/X decreases or Y/X increases, the growth rate of Y exceeds that of X. The change in the overall efficiency not related to "material-saving" technical progress can be seen by $g(A) - g(Y/X)$.

Table 8–7 shows the percentage contribution of each factor to the total growth rate in each sector. It can clearly be seen that the dominant factor is, as we said above, the very rapid growth of employment in the industrial sector. The second important factor is capital accumulation. In order to exceed the rapid growth of employment and achieve an ever-increasing capital-labor ratio, capital must be accumulated very rapidly. Except for the MS sector a significant part of industrial growth can be attributed to the high rate of capital ac-

TABLE 8-7

Factors Contributing to Industrial
Growth of GNP

	$g(Y)$	$g(N)$	$\beta g(K/N)$*	$\Delta\beta \ log \ K/N$*	$g(Y/X)-g(A)-g(Y/X)$
hL	17.6	6.7	2.4	2.0	-0.9	7.4
ML	15.8	5.6	2.8	.0	0.1	7.3
hS	13.7	6.9	1.2	0.6	-0.4	5.4
MS	12.2	5.0	-0.9	0.1	1.2	6.8
E	7.1	6.0	1.5	-0.9	0.7	-0.2
A	3.8	-1.5	(1.3)	?	-0.3	(4.0)

*The assumed values of β's are: 0.39, 0.45, 0.30, 0.44, and 0.5 in the order of sectors listed in the table. They are computed by the ratios of the arithmetic mean of P_{ij} to that of $P_{ij} + W_{ij}$ over the sample period except for agriculture. 0.5 was simply assumed for agriculture for lack of better information. $\Delta\beta$ was computed by multiplying $g(\pi K/pK)$ [Table 8-6] for each industry group by the corresponding β estimate for that industry group. Since $g(\pi K/pK) = g(\beta) - g(\delta)$, this is only an approximation.

cumulation shown in the third column of Table 8–5. Such an unusually high rate of capital accumulation is surely an important factor in rapid growth, as we shall see in detail later.

The third factor, bias in technical progress, seems to have been important in heavy industry in particular, not so important in other manufacturing. It had an inverse effect in tertiary industry. The remaining part of growth rate may be attributed to the overall efficiency. This part appears to be as important as the growth rate of employment. The only exception was tertiary industry, in which 85 percent of $g(Y)$ was due to $g(N)$. The increase in overall efficiency in all the manufacturing industries is very significant, but this is not too surprising. The first half of the period was still a phase of postwar recovery. Not only were there well-trained workers and administrators but also much unused complementary capital equipment and social capital which must have made the marginal productivities of labor and capital, as a result of postwar investment, unusually high. The following Figure 8–2 of capital-output ratios clearly demonstrates a sharp decline in *capital-output ratios* from 1951 to 1956 in most sectors. This may be taken as a manifestation of postwar recovery phenomena. Since this favorable condition gradually disappeared after 1956, $g(A)$ must have receded in the latter half of the period. In fact there was an

FIGURE 8–2.   Capital-Output Ratios in Five Sections.

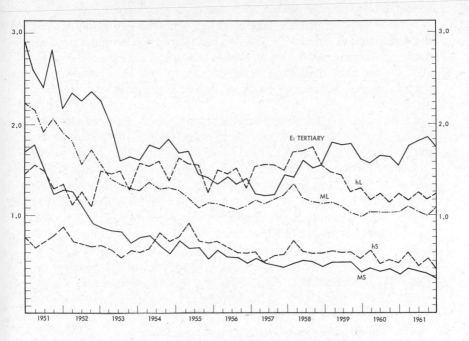

extremely high rate of capital accumulation in all the sectors after 1956 to compensate for the declining trend in $g(A)$. Indeed, $g(K)$ was considerably larger in all sectors after 1956 than it was before.

V. RESOURCE ALLOCATION AND MARKET MECHANISM

The Japanese economy is often cited as a showcase of free enterprise achievement of rapid economic growth. Although it would seem possible to show that labor and capital were utilized more efficiently and allocated more optimally in Japan than in the Soviet Union, this does not imply that resource allocation in Japan was actually optimal. Through simple use of ratios of relevant variables we shall try to analyze this problem.

Observe the third column of Table 8–6. If we could assume that $g(\gamma/\delta)$ is the same for the hL and hS sectors, then it implies that technical progress in the hS sector was more "laborsaving" than in the hL sector. This is hard to believe. In fact, the first column of the same table seems to imply the reverse. Comparison of the first with the second columns leads to suspicion that $g(\delta)$ was larger in the hL sector than in the SL sector; i.e., the degree of competition in the capital market declined for large-scale heavy industry corporations. To the extent that π/p and w/p deviated more from the marginal productivities of capital, allocation of capital was less than optimal. Similar observations are difficult to make for the other manufacturing industry, because of the difference in technical progress in large- and small-scale firms.

If, however, it can be assumed that large and small corporations produce more or less similar products, then it is possible to say something about the force of the market mechanism in allocating resources among different scales of firms in the same industry. Table 8–8 shows that π is higher for small firms, and that capital coefficients, both average and marginal, are consistently lower for smaller firms. Yet there is no indication in the absolute value of investment nor in the growth rates of capital and investment that increasingly more capital is attracted to the hS sector rather than the hL sector. This seems to imply that there was a misallocation of capital toward large corporations. This observation is consistent with the direction of the change in degree of competition or, some may say, degree of monopoly in heavy industry mentioned above.

The same proposition holds for other manufacturing industry. Despite the higher π and lower capital coefficients, capital was not allocated enough to smaller firms in this industry. Tertiary industry consists predominantly of smaller corporations and private businesses in Japan. In this industry $g(K)$ and $g(I)$ are below the values in the hL and M sectors, not to mention agriculture in this connection. Thus

TABLE 8-8

Sectoral Allocation of Capital

	π	K/X (Average)	K/X (1961)	$\Delta K/\Delta X$	$g(K)$ (%)	I (Billion Yen)	$g(I)$ (%)
hL	8.5	1.73	1.31	2.25	12.9	0.57	27.1
hS	11.6	0.75	0.63	0.92	10.9	0.17	16.6
ML	8.6	1.40	1.16	1.42	11.7	0.53	15.3
MS	9.7	0.80	0.49	0.90	1.9	0.20	12.2
E	13.6	1.62	1.88	0.86	9.3	1.34	13.7
A		1.08	0.91	1.92	0.4	0.39	8.9

*$\Delta K/\Delta X$ was computed by $\frac{K}{X}(1 + g(X/K)/g(X))$. The second column is the arithmetic mean of K/X in the period.

it seems conclusive that the capital market was not sufficiently competitive to allocate capital optimally by the market mechanism.

The arguments concerning the allocation of capital among industries is more involved, because demand conditions must be taken into consideration. It seems possible, however, to judge demand and supply conditions in the market by observing $g(p)$ in Table 8–5. In particular the high rate of price rise in tertiary industry and agriculture seems to indicate that there was a need to increase productivity in these two sectors. In the case of tertiary industry π is very high, and the marginal capital coefficient is very low. Nevertheless $g(K)$ and $g(I)$ do not show any significant rise compared with other industries.[12] In the case of agriculture, the marginal capital coefficient is higher than in any other sector, except for the hL sector, which is after all a very capital-intensive industry. But extremely low rates of growth in capital and investment seem to require a careful inquiry into the underlying causes of difficulties in agricultural investment.[13] Thus, even among industries there seems to have been some misallocation of capital during this period.

The allocation of labor can similarly be analyzed. Table 8–9 shows the same kinds of related variables for six sectors. The higher rate of money wages and the higher marginal productivity of labor in heavy industry attracted more labor into large corporations. This desirable direction of allocation of labor among large and small businesses holds also for other manufacturing industry. But the small difference in $g(N)$ between the two scales of industries seems to be a reflection of nonoptimal allocation of capital which we have just discussed. If more capital had been allocated to small businesses, $g(N)$ would have been significantly less in smaller scale enterprise.

The same argument seems to hold for tertiary industry. Since this

---

[12] This must have something to do with the topic often discussed in Japan that the service and distribution industries are especially inefficient. However, as Table 8–13 in the next section shows, postwar Japan inherited an excess capacity of overhead capital. This fact must have made it possible for some industries like transportation or communication to be satisfied with low rates of capital accumulation. The ratio of overhead capital to tertiary industry output declined up to 1957 and then began to rise. It seems, therefore, that the low rate of capital accumulation was not so unusual in the first half of the period as in the latter half.

[13] If we assume the existence of a Cobb-Douglas production function and the β's equal to those in Table 8–7, then the marginal productivity of capital can be computed as $\beta X/K$. They are: hL, 0.23; hS, 0.60; ML, 0.26; MS, 0.61; E, 0.22; a, 0.46. The argument on capital allocation needs no change, except for agriculture. But β is probably less than 0.5 so that 0.46 is an overestimate. If $\beta = 0.4$, in place of 0.46 we have 0.37.

sector had a high rate of w and π combined with low productivity of labor and yet absorbed only labor, but not capital, the substitution of more capital for labor would have made it possible to reduce price inflation in this industry by not bidding up wages so much, particularly in the latter period. The domestic migration of labor out of agriculture is a necessary consequence of the income differential and productivity gap between agriculture and industry, as Table 8–9 shows. Thus, we

TABLE 8-9

Sectoral Allocation of Labor

	w^*	X/N	$X/N(61)$	$(1-\beta)X/N$	$g(N)$	ΔN (Thousand)
hL	0.83	4.46	7.8	2.7	6.7	8.1
hS	0.43	2.44	3.7	1.3	5.6	7.4
ML	0.69	6.50	11.8	4.6	6.9	7.1
MS	0.29	2.14	2.7	1.5	5.0	16.3
E	0.46	1.77	1.9	1.0	6.0	60.3
A	(0.21)	1.55	1.6	1.1	-1.5	-20.0

$^*w$ in A is computed as 70 percent of per capita income in A.
β is assumed to be the same as Table 8-7.

conclude that there is some evidence for capital to have been misallocated among different scales of business as well as among industries, but ample supply of labor alleviated the serious consequences which might have resulted from this faulty allocation.

VI. THE GROWTH OF NATIONAL EXPENDITURE AND ITS COMPOSITION

Now we turn to the demand side of GNP. We have already discussed the high rate of capital accumulation as an important factor in rapid economic growth. This is possible only when the rest of items in national expenditure do not occupy an unusually large proportion. Table 8–10 shows the average composition over the period and the growth rate of each item in national expenditure. It can be seen that fixed-capital formation occupied 24.8 percent, of which 59 percent was private fixed-capital formation. Moreover, the percentage of fixed-capital formation kept on increasing toward the end of this period, and in 1961 it was above 30 percent. Table 8–11 shows the ratio of gross capital formation to GNP and the ratio of residential investment to gross investment in some countries in 1962. Japan's high investment ratio can be readily seen. Such a high rate of capital accumulation was made possible by the items growing less proportionately than national expenditure in Japan. The average growth rate of GNP in real terms was about 9.6 percent, whereas consumption increased at the rate of only 6.9 percent. This is undoubtedly the most important factor in the high rate of capital accumulation. Most of the rest of components grew faster than GNP itself. Particularly significant are private capital formation and exports. They were the leading sectors of rapid growth.

It is of interest to note that some components of inventory invest-ment grew at a slower pace than GNP, but that the predominant part of inventory investment, particularly goods in process and dealers' inventories, grew significantly faster than 15 percent. It is a reflection of inefficiency of tertiary industry in the Japanese economy, which we discussed earlier.

Another reason for high ratio of investment to GNP is the fact that the balance of trade could remain negative almost always in this period. On the average, the propensity to import (12.1 percent) ex-ceeded the ratio of exports to GNP (10.6 percent). This was possible only because of the inflow of foreign capital, which amounted to 1.5 percent of GNP on the average over this period. Were it not for an offsetting reduction in capital formation to match this amount of capital import, the growth rate would have been correspondingly lower. If the ratio of private industrial capital formation to the incre-ment of GNP remained stable, then the decline in growth rate would be computed as approximately 0.9 percent: $1.5 \times (9.6/16) = 0.9$.

One could say, however, that it was rather surprising for the Japa-nese economy with so few natural resources to have become less dependent on imports from abroad despite such an unusually high rate of industrial growth. Having lost 45 percent of its former territory including two main rice-supplying areas, Taiwan and Korea, Japan was able to be almost self-sufficient in food up to the end of this period, thanks to the great achievement of Japanese agriculture dis-cussed in Section III. Imported raw materials, however, have become an increasingly important part of industrial materials. The ratio B_m/M_m has risen at the annual rate of 1.3 percent. On the other hand, the development of new capital goods industry made it possible for the proportion of imported capital equipment to total domestic fixed capi-tal formation B_h/I_p to decline at the rate of 1.2 percent a year.[14]

---

[14] The Japanese balance of trade was helped by the general fall in import prices. $g(p_f^b) = -3.5$, $g(p_h^b) = 3.0$, $g(p_m^b) = -2.9$, $g(p_c^b) = -2.7$. On the aver-age, the annual rate of fall in the import price index is 2.5 percent.

TABLE 8-10

Composition of National Expenditure
and Growth Rates in Its Components

	Composition (%)	Growth Rates (%)
C_f	32.1	4.9
C_t	5.3	9.0
C_o	24.3	9.1
	61.7	6.9
J_{fh}	0.3	15.5
J_{fM}	0.5	4.0
J_m	0.8	6.3
J_p	1.7	20.1
J_d	1.7	15.2
J_A	-0.3	2.0
	4.7	15.1
I_{hL}	2.6	27.1
I_{ML}	2.4	16.6
I_{hS}	0.8	15.3
I_{MS}	0.9	12.2
I_E	6.1	13.7
I_A	1.8	8.9
	14.6	16.0
I_R	2.0	11.1
G_I	8.2	11.3
$G_c + W_g$	10.8	9.7
E_a	0.7	11.1
E_h	3.8	19.4
E_M	6.1	15.8
	10.6	16.8

TABLE 8-10 (Continued)

	Composition (%)	Growth Rates (%)
B_m· · · · · · · · · · · · · · ·	-9.0	15.3
B_f· · · · · · · · · · · · · · ·	-1.4	3.1
B_h· · · · · · · · · · · · · · ·	-0.9	15.5
B_c· · · · · · · · · · · · · · ·	$\dfrac{-0.8}{-12.1}$	$\dfrac{14.9}{13.9}$
Y_G· · · · · · · · · · · · · · ·		9.6

TABLE 8-11

Gross Capital Formation, Its Ratio to GNP,
Share of Residential in Total Investment, 1962

	I (Billion Dollars)	I/Y_G (%)	I_R/I (%)
Japan. · · · · · · · · · · · ·	17.4	35.3	7.2
West Germany · · · · · · · · ·	19.5	25.1	23.3
Italy. · · · · · · · · · · · ·	8.2	23.1	23.6
Sweden · · · · · · · · · · · ·	3.0	22.2	23.1
Canada · · · · · · · · · · · ·	7.7	21.8	18.3
France · · · · · · · · · · · ·	11.2	17.8	22.3
U.K. · · · · · · · · · · · · ·	12.6	16.9	18.1
U.S. · · · · · · · · · · · · ·	82.4	15.8	27.7

SOURCE: UN: *World Statistical Yearbook, 1963.*

The most remarkable characteristic of capital accumulation in Japan is, however, the composition of investment itself. First we note that residential investment occupies a small proportion (say 8.1 percent) of total capital formation. This has been a characteristic of Japanese capital formation, even in prewar years,[15] and the construction cost of simple houses in Japan might have been much cheaper. The proportion is astonishingly small if one remembers that most of the big cities were bombed during the war, and that nearly half a

[15] The percentage of residential investment in gross capital formation in Japan was 9.5 percent in 1934–36; 13.5 percent in 1930.

million people moved from rural to metropolitan areas every year during this period. The second characteristic is that government investment occupies also a relatively small proportion, 33 percent of total gross capital formation or only 56.2 percent of private industrial capital formation. This may, however, not be so surprising, because the overhead capital inherited from the prewar economy must have saved the postwar government investment, particularly during the first half of the period. In this connection Table 8–12 supplements the argument we presented before with reference to the chart of sectoral capital-output ratios and the investment in tertiary industry. The high overhead capital to GNP ratio in the postwar years shows a gradual decline toward the prewar level. This fact is particularly noticeable if we take the ratio of K_g to the level of output in tertiary industry, which includes some industries heavily dependent on overhead capital. K_g/X_E already reached a low value in 1957, from which the ratio K_E/X_E can no longer show any further decline. This must imply that the low ratio of G_I to I_p cannot continue after 1961. In fact this is what has been happening since then.

The last factor to be mentioned as contributing to low G_I/Y_G is the extremely low expenditure for defense. As Table 8–10 showed, government expenditure on national accounting basis accounted for 19 percent of GNP, of which defense expenditure made up only 6.8 percent. Since GNP is 1.23 times as much as national income for this period, the ratio of defense expenditure to national income is 1.6 percent, which should be compared, for example, with Germany's 5 percent, Italy's 4.1 percent, France's 8.1 percent, England's 8.3 percent or U.S.'s 12.5 percent, all in 1958. The effect on Japanese economic growth of more expenditure for defense can be computed if we can accept some assumptions. Suppose, for instance, that the Japanese government had to spend as much as Italy; i.e., 3.3 percent of GNP; the new resources required for defense were realized by decreasing the components of GNP like consumption, inventory investment, private capital formation and imports; and that the ratio of the increment of GNP to private capital formation (0.6) remain unchanged. Then the percentage decline of I_p/Y_G is 3.3 percent $\times$ 0.20 = 0.66 percent, and the fall of $g(Y_G)$ is 0.66 $\times$ 0.6 = 0.4 percent. This gives some idea of how much the Japanese growth was promoted by saving defense expenditure.

For all these reasons the Japanese economy could devote an unusually high proportion of gross national product to productive fixed-capital formation and, allocating them intensively in export industries or capital goods industries, succeed in achieving a high rate of economic growth.

TABLE 8-12

Overhead Capital, GNP, and
Output of Tertiary Industry

	K_g'	Y_G'	K_g/Y_G	K_g	X_E	K_g/X_E	K_E/X_E
1926	3,917	4,446	.88				
1930	4,922	4,589	1.07				
1935	6,132	6,248	.98				
1940	7,151						
1945	6,804						
1948	8,031						
1951	8,861	6,386	1.39	8,843	364.8	24.2	5.2
1952	9,188	7,146	1.29	9,196	645.8	14.2	3.2
1953	9,637	7,830	1.23	9,692	759.2	12.8	3.0
1954	10,100	7,993	1.26	10,245	953.4	10.7	2.5
1955	10,518	8,895	1.18	10,770	1,078.0	10.0	2.3
1956	10,996	9,615	1.14	11,277	1,243.3	9.1	2.2
1957	11,532	10,495	1.10	11,853	1,499.9	7.9	2.1
1958	12,991	10,448	1.24	12,525	1,214.5	10.3	2.8
1959	13,923	12,356	1.13	13,369	1,612.2	8.3	2.4
1960	15,086	14,065	1.07	14,265	2,040.1	7.0	2.1
1961	16,614	16,231	1.02	15,507	2,066.4	7.5	2.3

SOURCE: K_g', Y_G' are taken from data prepared at the Economic Planning Agency; others from S. Ichimura, et al., "A Quarterly Econometric Model of Japan, 1952–1959: Data Appendix," *Osaka Economic Papers*, July, 1964.

Appendix: Statistical Data

Almost all the statistics used in this article are available in Ichimura *et al.*[16] Tables 8A–1 and 8A–2 are some additional data compiled for this paper.

Additional References

S. ICHIMURA. *Japanese Economy in the World*. Tokyo: Chuokoron-Sha, 1966.*

O. SHIMOMURA. *To Accomplish Economic Growth*. Tokyo: Kochikai, 1958.*

M. SHINOHARA. *The Structure of Economic Growth*. Tokyo: Kunimoto Shobo, 1964.*

---

[16] S. Ichimura, *et al.*, "A Quarterly Econometric Model of Japan, 1952–1959: Data Appendix," *op. cit.*

* In the Japanese language.

TABLE 8A-1

Annual Data for Agriculture

	K_A*	I_{Aa}	X_{Aa}	$K_{A,-1}/X_{Aa}$	X_{Aa}/N_{Aa}	K_{Aa}/N_{Aa}	$I_{Aa}/K_{A,-1}$
1950.	15,612						
1951.	15,771	158.6	13,757	1.13	1.00	1.15	1.01
1952.	15,914	143.1	14,293	1.10	1.04	1.16	0.91
1953.	16,088	174.0	13,011	1.22	0.93	1.15	1.09
1954.	16,175	87.1	12,380	1.30	0.89	1.16	0.54
1955.	16,278	102.7	14,934	1.08	1.07	1.16	0.63
1956.	16,350	71.8	14,641	1.11	1.07	1.19	0.44
1957.	16,330	-20.0	15,180	1.08	1.12	1.20	-0.12
1958.	16,344	14.3	15,944	1.02	1.21	1.24	0.09
1959.	16,394	49.8	17,085	0.96	1.35	1.30	0.30
1960.	15,572	177.6	17,307	0.95	1.41	1.35	1.08
1961.	16,789	217.1	18,215	0.91	1.56	1.44	1.31

*K_A: capital stock at the beginning of the year; taken from the unpublished data at the Economic Planning Agency; units, billion Yen. I_{Aa}: net investment in agriculture. X_{Aa}, N_{Aa} are taken from S. Ichimura et al., "A Quarterly Econometric Model of Japan, 1952-1959: Data Appendix," *Osaka Economic Papers*, July, 1964.

TABLE 8A-2

Quarterly Data for Agriculture, Tertiary
Industry, and Government Sector

	I_A	M_A	M_E	p_E^m	I_g	$K_g{}^*$
1951.1.	14.9	793	3,676	0.865	77.2	8,634
2.	77.6	561	3,760	0.961	59.0	8,693
3.	28.9	832	3,919	0.957	71.8	8,765
4.	37.2	1,290	4,597	0.973	78.2	8,843
1952.1.	44.5	907	5,004	1.003	95.6	8,939
2.	114.1	675	5,758	0.970	71.1	9,010
3.	68.6	898	5,560	0.970	88.4	9,098
4.	-84.1	1,585	6,432	0.970	97.5	9,196
1953.1.	115.3	864	5,288	0.990	120.4	9,316
2.	114.3	723	5,425	0.980	107.8	9,424
3.	65.8	981	5,659	1.000	128.0	9,552
4.	-151.4	1,681	6,924	1.02	139.5	9,692
1954.1.	101.2	962	5,931	1.03	173.4	9,865
2.	162.2	771	6,031	1.01	104.0	9,969
3.	53.0	1,071	5,920	0.99	133.5	10,103
4.	-229.3	1,867	7,103	1.004	141.5	10,245
1955.1.	142.6	960	6,230	1.015	172.3	10,412
2.	158.7	841	6,222	0.989	101.0	10,518
3.	27.1	1,386	6,397	0.994	121.0	10,639
4.	-225.7	2,087	7,921	1.001	130.5	10,770
1956.1.	97.4	1,052	6,951	1.017	150.0	10,920
2.	154.2	900	7,390	1.035	114.7	11,035
3.	4.3	1,333	7,377	1.060	118.8	11,154
4.	-184.1	1,952	9,057	1.088	123.1	11,277
1957.1.	84.4	1,053	7,828	1.087	139.3	11,416
2.	169.9	893	8,162	1.100	115.5	11,532
3.	0.8	1,474	8,416	1.086	144.9	11,677
4.	-275.1	2,226	9,283	1.087	176.0	11,853
1958.1.	135.0	1,128	8,040	1.048	190.6	12,044
2.	222.2	880	8,290	1.045	137.5	12,182
3.	1.9	1,509	8,498	1.044	159.4	12,341
4.	-344.8	2,362	9,905	1.053	183.8	12,525
1959.1.	102.4	1,226	8,643	1.048	272.4	12,797
2.	237.6	1,027	9,279	1.071	150.6	12,948
3.	-34.1	1,522	9,574	1.082	191.7	13,140
4.	-256.1	2,577	11,324	1,109	228.9	13,369

TABLE 8A-2 (Continued)

	I_A	M_A	M_E	P_E^m	I_g	K_g*
1960.1.	182.5	1,231	10,120	1.084	294.2	13,663
2.	280.1	1,029	11,946	1.106	181.3	13,844
3.	-24.2	1,908	11,859	1.104	238.0	14,082
4.	-260.8	2,778	13,809	1.135	282.6	14,265
1961.1.	236.8	1,370	11,361	1.102	349.8	14,615
2.	345.7	1,178	12,235	1.143	251.0	14,866
3.	31.9	2,163	12,872	1.162	288.8	15,155
4.	-397.3	3,302	16,073	1.196	352.4	15,507

$*K_g$: social overhead capital, taken from unpublished data at the Economic Planning Agency; units billion Yen; I_g: net government investment.

9 | Patterns and Some Structural Changes in Japan's Postwar Industrial Growth*

MIYOHEI SHINOHARA

This paper is laid out in three parts. In the first part we are concerned with certain analyses in relation to changes in the patterns or phases of postwar industrial growth in Japan. The period is divided into the following four phases: 1946–51, 1951–55, 1955–61, and from 1961 onward. By making these divisions, it is expected that the characteristics of these phases will be clarified to some extent. In the second part, we shall explore the process and significance of the so-called heavy industrialization, which has been realized through the investment superboom and the upsurge in the demand for consumer durables for 1955–61. Thirdly, we will present a hypothesis on the changes in the industrial structure, laying particular emphasis on the increasing degree of fabrication which persisted even in the 1955–61 boom period.

I. FOUR PHASES IN THE 20 POSTWAR YEARS

The characteristics of the four postwar phases already mentioned can be quantitatively explained by constructing Table 9–1 in which the growth rates of the manufacturing and mining sector together with their major subsectors are computed by each phase.

In the first phase (1946–51), the growth rate of every sector is conspicuously high, compared with that of other phases. This indicates quantitatively that the first phase belongs to a genuine postwar rehabilitation period. This can be assumed as a mere reaction to the

---

* I am grateful for useful comments on my paper presented in the Conference, particularly to Professors H. König and Simon Kuznets, although any revisions of my original paper are my own responsibility.

TABLE 9-1

Growth Rates of Industry and Its Subsectors
(Percent)

	1946–51	1951–55	1955–61	1961–65
Manufacturing and mining. .	29.3	11.2	16.8	9.9
Mining.	17.5	1.7	5.4	-0.2
Manufacturing	31.2	12.3	17.4	10.3
Iron and steel.	48.4	9.2	19.3	9.0
Machinery	30.8	10.3	28.6	11.4
Ceramics.	32.1	9.0	14.3	8.9
Chemicals	35.6	15.8	14.9	16.8
Textiles.	32.7	13.5	9.1	8.0
Public utilities.	9.8	7.0	13.3	9.3
Capital goods	31.4	7.8	24.9	12.9
Construction materials. . .	26.7	5.6	13.8	8.4
Consumer durables	29.2	22.9	37.2	5.7
Consumer nondurables. . . .	23.1	15.0	7.9	8.3
Producers' goods.	31.2	10.3	10.2	10.0

NOTE: Each growth rate is computed by finding the annual rates of compund interest that would increase the beginning year of each phase to the value of the terminal year.

drastic decline in production in the immediate postwar years. Industrial production dropped to 27.8 percent of the 1934–36 level in 1946, the volume of exports to 7.5 percent in 1948, the volume of imports to 17.8 percent in 1948, and the level of living in urban households to 55.4 percent in 1947.

The speed of recovery from the postwar trough was naturally very rapid, although hyperinflation prevailed alongside a severe food shortage, a drastic decrease in production, and an extraordinary monetary expansion. The Dodge stabilization plan of 1949 requested the Japanese government to enforce a strictly balanced (actually a surplus) budget, to set up a single exchange rate ($1 = ¥360) and to eliminate subsidies to key industries which were used to cover costs in excess of controlled prices. The deflationary effect of this stabilization program, however, was temporary owing to the outbreak of the Korean War in June, 1950. Thus, the Japanese economy during 1946–51 was in a situation in which postwar inflationary pressures strongly persisted.

Yet, the tempo of postwar rehabilitation was very rapid in this period consistent with and as a result of (1) a general empirical law (which has held true among various countries) showing an inverse relationship between the degree of decline and the speed of recovery in industrial production,[1] (2) U.S. aid, especially food imports, which amounted to 70 percent of total imports from September, 1945 to 1948, (3) the strategic promotion of key industries, such as coal, electricity, iron and steel, fertilizer, etc., through the priority rationing of necessary funds and basic materials to them, and (4) the provision of a price subsidy for these basic industries in order to hold down the purchase prices of coal, steel, fertilizer, etc., used by other industries.

The second phase (1951–55) was a period in which the growth rate slowed down. In terms of the real national product (before revision),[2] the growth rate was reduced to 7.5 percent in the second phase from 11.2 percent in the first phase. In terms of manufacturing and mining production, it decreased from 29.3 percent to 11.2 percent. In this period, the growth rates for iron and steel, machinery, and ceramics were even less than those for textiles and chemicals. The slowing down of the speed in heavy industrialization and private fixed investment was one of the most important aspects of the second phase.

What accounts for the decline in the growth rate and the stagnation of the rate of increase in investment in the second phase? We will consider four explanations:

1. Before the Dodge plan could be implemented to obtain a far-reaching rationalization of Japanese industries, the Korean War broke out; so it was necessary for the Japanese economy, which was in transition from an inflationary to a stable phase, to have a moderate braking action applied. Particularly, since the Japanese economy had already passed through the phase in which a large amount of price subsidy funds had been given to basic industries, it was necessary for corporations (in the coal, and iron and steel industries, especially) to wipe out their deficits. In such a situation, passive remedies to improve business conditions were favored over aggressive investment projects.

2. During the period of the Korean War, private fixed investment increased tremendously. According to the *Quarterly Corporate Enterprise Survey* of the Ministry of Finance (for corporations whose paid-in capital was ￥2 million and over), fixed investment in January–June

---

[1] Miyohei Shinohara, *Growth and Cycles in the Japanese Economy* (Tokyo: Kinokuniya Bookstore, 1962), p. 8.

[2] The revised estimate is available only after 1951, and it is impossible for us to make a comparison between the first and second periods with the new data.

of 1950 was ¥89.2 billion (about 5 percent of their sales), but it increased to 349.2 billion (about 3.9 times as high as the former, and 9.1 percent of their sales) in October, 1951–March, 1952. After that, however, the increase in fixed investment became persistently stagnant, and even in the July–December period of 1955, it remained at the level of 303.2 billion yen, lower than during the Korean booms. We may interpret this to mean that, as a reaction to the excessive increase in the fixed-investment sales ratio in the period of the Korean War, an adjustment process continued for four years during which the fixed-investment ratio for corporate enterprises declined from 9.1 percent to 4.2 percent, by the end of 1955. We see here an example of a longer adjustment process for fixed investment than for inventory investment. The adjustment followed a jump in the fixed-investment ratio, which came about as a result of excess demand during the Korean boom.

3. The third factor may not be so important. It is based on the observation that there was underutilization of equipment during the second period. According to the data of the Ministry of International Trade and Industry, the utilization ratio for mining and manufacturing was 53.1 percent in March, 1950, 73.4 percent in March, 1951, and 79.4 percent in March, 1955. Of course, this does not mean that fixed investment decreased for this period, but it may reasonably be imagined that the economy still had fairly ample capacity and that this deterred fixed investment.

4. The fourth factor lies in the fact that the economy had been strongly influenced by the high level of the "special procurement demand" of the U.S. Armed Forces. In 1951, the proportion of foreign currency receipts from "special procurement demand" was 26.4 percent. It increased to 36.8 percent in 1952 and 38.1 percent in 1953, although it fell to 25.8 percent and 20.8 percent in 1954 and 1955, respectively. These high ratios of "special procurement demand" indicate that the economy could raise the balance-of-payments ceiling without relying as much as in other periods upon exports. The receipt of foreign currency without fixed investment or rationalization in export or export-affiliated industries seems to have obstructed the propensity of entrepreneurs to invest to that extent. Furthermore, since the proportion of "services" in "special procurement demand" contracts amounted to 42 percent for 1951–55, we can see that the effect of "special procurement demand" in inducing investments was much lower than would have been the case for an equivalent expansion of exports.

After the four-year stagnation in investment, we had an extraordinary investment boom, 1956–61. Private fixed investment increased from ¥944.1 billion in 1955 to about ¥4.53 trillion in 1961, an increase of 4.5 times in only six years!

If we compare the two periods of high-growth rates, 1946–51 and 1955–61, in Table 9–1 and Figure 9–1, we observe that growth rates in the subsectors are less uniform and more concentrated in heavy industry in 1955–61 than in 1946–51. In the 1946–51 period, the growth rate was pushed up in every industry, but in the 1955–61 period a disproportionate growth pattern oriented to heavy industry prevailed.[3] In 1946–51, every industry experienced excess demand,

FIGURE 9–1.   Interindustry Differences in Industrial Growth Rates by Subsector in the Two High-Rate Growth Periods.

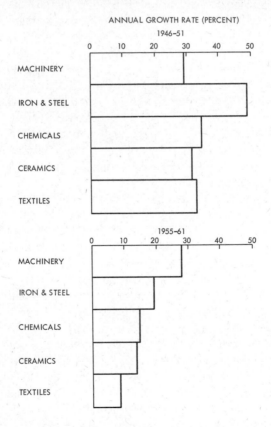

ANNUAL GROWTH RATE (PERCENT)

---

[3] By heavy industry, we mean here metals, machinery (in a wider sense) and chemicals (including coal and petroleum products), according to the conventional usage. It includes not only capital goods, but also consumer durables.

but there was, at the same time, unused capacity, so the mere acquisition of raw materials made it possible to expand production in every sector. This was a typical growth pattern of a postwar rehabilitation period.

Compared with this, the growth pattern during 1955–61 was highly investment or heavy industry-oriented. In machinery, the growth rate was 28.6 percent; in iron and steel, it was 19.3 percent; and in chemicals, 14.9 percent, on the one hand, but in textiles, it was only 9.1 percent. The growth rate in capital goods was 24.9 percent and that in consumer durables 37.2 percent, while that in consumer nondurables was only 7.9 percent. The 1946–51 period was one of a proportionate high-pitched growth, while the 1955–61 period was one of a disproportionate high-pitched growth. The former period was so, because production increases in every industry were made possible by a rapid rise in the rate of utilization, while the growth pattern in the latter was disproportionate because excess demand and the full utilization of capacity coexisted. In order to increase capacity further, it was necessary to increase fixed investment relative to sales, with a particular industrial concentration. Another point to be remembered is that in this period an extraordinary expansion of consumer durables, e.g., television sets, refrigerators, etc., proceeded in parallel with the investment boom. Table 9–2 indicates the disproportionate growth pattern, with an emphasis upon investment goods and consumer durables.

In the 1956–61 period, technological innovation proceeded in various fields of industry. For example, mass production was introduced into the automobile industry to such an extent that the monthly production of passenger cars per factory and per kind of car amounted to 8,000 by 1961, which means that the industry had already passed beyond the sharpest part of its decreasing-cost curve. In the petrochemical industry, the mushroom appearance of petrochemical combinations in various places became an object of heated discussion, in which there was apprehension that there would be obstacles to the expansion of the industrial scale to an international level. However, in May, 1962, the average annual production capacity of ethylene per plant reached 61,000 tons, which approached the 66,000 ton level of West Germany and surpassed the 30,000 tons produced in France, although it was less than the 103,000 tons of the United States, and the 98,000 tons of the United Kingdom. Furthermore, in the iron and steel industry, the number of hot strip mills in Japan was 8 in July, 1962, but was 45 in the United States, 6 in the Soviet Union, 4 in the

TABLE 9-2

Production of Major Commodities, 1961
(Ratios to 1955 Production)

Electric refrigerators . .	50.48	Bicycles.	2.84
Television sets.	33.64	Aluminum.	2.65
Passenger cars	12.31	Steel vessels (started) . .	2.58
Chassis for trucks and		Electrolytic copper	2.44
buses.	11.59	Cement.	2.33
Synthetic fabrics.	11.37	Paper pulp.	2.29
Synthetic fibers	9.72	Carbide	2.25
Radio receivers.	7.60	Woven woolen fabrics. . . .	2.19
Corrugated cardboard . . .	6.40	Electricity	2.11
Machine tools.	6.33	Crude oil	2.08
Standard induction motors.	6.28	Foreign style paper	2.07
Plastics	5.71	Sheet glass	2.00
Standard transformers. . .	5.26	Caustic soda.	1.84
Heavy oil.	5.24	Sewing machines	1.72
Electric washers	4.69	Woolen yarn	1.72
Hot roll special steel		Rayon filament yarn	1.59
products	4.60	Looms	1.44
Steel frames	4.42	Sulfuric acid	1.42
Auto tires and tubes . . .	4.13	Cotton fabrics.	1.34
Paperboard	3.52	Cotton yarn	1.33
Pig iron	3.03	Rayon staple fabrics. . . .	1.30
Crude steel.	3.00	Coal.	1.28
Watches and clocks	2.97	Rayon fabrics	1.23
Gasoline	2.95	Ammonium sulfate.	1.18
Hot roll ordinary steel		Rayon staple yarn	1.09
products	2.94	Raw silk.	1.08
Telegraph wire and cable .	2.93	Calcium super phosphate . .	1.05
A.C. generators.	2.91	Silk fabrics.	1.00

United Kingdom, 3 in West Germany, and 2 in France. Japan now holds second place in the number of hot strip mills. In the 1950's, the price of Japanese steel was comparatively high, but as a result of rapid technological progress and capital expansion, the relative price of Japanese steel was greatly lowered and its international competitive power strengthened.

Together with the expansion in output of industrial products, an explosive boom in the production and consumption of consumer durables resulted in this historical epoch. Table 9–2 already indicated this.

The highly investment-oriented growth pattern of 1955–61 could not continue after 1962. In 1955, private fixed investment (excluding residential construction) as a percentage of GNP was 10.7 percent, which was too low for maintaining the 10 percent annual growth rate in GNP for 1955–61. Therefore, private fixed investment as a percentage of GNP rose to 21.9 percent in 1961. It was, at the same time, self-evident that the maintenance of the private fixed-investment ratio at a level of 22 percent would be too high for a continuation of the 10 percent growth rate after 1962. A continuation of a high fixed-investment ratio would result in a buildup of excess capacity. Even if we assume a balanced growth process between demand and capacity, a drastic decline in the growth rate of private fixed investment would still be inevitable as compared with that of 1955–61. Such was this writer's view expressed in 1961–62, and he emphasized a transition in economic growth from a pattern of excess demand to a pattern of excess capacity, predicting that private fixed investment for 1961–65 would be ¥4 trillion per annum on the average, and that the investment superboom of 1955–61 would end. Actually, private fixed investment in 1960 prices was ¥4,051.2 billion (1961), ¥3,940.1 billion (1962), ¥4,192.8 billion (1963), ¥4,731.5 billion (1964), and ¥4,510.8 billion (1965, preliminary). The five-year average was ¥4,285 billion, my prediction being an understatement by 6.7 percent.[4] Although my prediction was a bit low, a transition in private fixed-investment behavior, is now apparent.

A decrease in the increased rate of fixed investment, however, does not stand for a halt in economic growth when its level is very high. Although excess capacity will emerge, the continuation of private fixed investment on a level of ¥4,000–4,500 billion, on the average, would have brought about a huge expansion of high-grade efficient equipment for these five years.

The proportion occupied by the petrochemical industry in the total output of the chemical industry was 8.1 percent in 1961, but in 1965 it had increased to 22.6 percent. The increased rate of petrochemical products in real terms was 60.8 percent, 51.8 percent, 33.1 percent, and 32.2 percent, respectively, for 1962–65. The capacity to produce ethylene jumped from 438,300 tons to 839,500 tons between March, 1964 and March, 1965. The number of petrochemical combinations, whose annual capacity for ethylene production exceeded 100,000 tons, totaled 4 units in 1965, but it was supposed to increase to more than 10 units by 1966. Thus, petrochemical combinations have now

---

[4] This conclusion depends upon the revised national income estimate. Since the new estimate is 4.9 percent higher than the old estimate for private fixed investment for 1961–64, my prediction for the five-year period as a whole was closer to the actual figure.

reached a scale equal to or in excess of those in advanced countries, although fears have sometimes been expressed over the mushroomlike expansion of its small-scale units.

We may take up another growing industry, the automobile industry. The production of passenger cars increased by 12 times at its highest point for 1955–61, while it continued to grow by 2.8 times for the next five years, 1961–65. The annual rate of increase was 52.2 percent for the former period, but it was still 29.4 percent in the latter period. The volume of production of passenger cars in 1965 was 696,176 units, ranking seventh in the world. However, total production of automobiles, including trucks, buses, etc., was 1,876,000 units in the same year, and this was the fourth highest in the world. Automobile plants, with a monthly production level of more than 10,000 units per plant per one kind of car, began to emerge and have almost successfully absorbed most of the advantages of cost reductions through mass production. Further, the automobile industry entered an export expansion phase from a state of defense against imported cars. The exports of passenger cars were 20,010 in 1962, 36,622 in 1963, 79,848 in 1964, and 110,840 in 1965.

In the iron and steel industry, however, the production of crude steel increased by three times in 1955–61, but only 1.46 times in 1961–65, and this reveals a decline in its annual growth rate from 20.1 percent to 9.9 percent. Although the GNP growth rate fell to 8 percent per annum in 1961–65, the growth rate of steel production decreased by half, reflecting the tapering-off of fixed investment. Investment in machinery facilities was depressed drastically, but this was mitigated to some extent by an increase in construction investment, e.g., the construction of factories, hydroelectric dams, buildings, and harbor facilities. Nevertheless, the transition of the economy from a situation of short to excess capacity is clearly indicated in these changes in the iron and steel industry.

The stagnation in the increase of fixed investment has, thus, affected the increase of production in the iron and steel industry. The reduction of the growth rate by half in this industry has played a great role in pushing down fixed investment in the iron and steel industry itself below the 1961 peak. According to the *Quarterly Corporate Enterprise Survey* of the Ministry of Finance, corporate fixed investment in the iron and steel industry was ¥420.5 billion (100) in 1961, ¥345.1 billion (82.1) in 1962, ¥272.5 billion (64.8) in 1963, ¥299.5 billion (71.2) in 1964, and ¥297.2 billion (70.7) in 1965.

A similar decline emerged in the cement, machine tool, and other machinery industries. In addition to these, we find a decline in the rate of increase in the production of consumer durables (television sets, refrigerators, washing machines, etc.) as a result of a gradual approach to saturation demand, following a brisk expansion. Table 9–3 indicates how the annual growth rate decreased from the 1955–61 to the 1961–65 period.

The tapering-off of fixed investment as an aftermath of the investment superboom for 1955–61, as well as the saturation of demand for consumer durables, has retarded expansion since 1962. We might characterize the period since 1962 as the excess capacity phase, although fairly high-economic growth still continued to persist in the economy as a whole, at least before 1964.

Thus, Japan's 20-year postwar economic growth has so far exhibited a dynamic rhythm, which consists of four phases, the *first phase* (1946–51) being a genuine postwar period of rehabilitation, coupled with hyperinflation and some chaos, the *second phase* (1951–55) being one of relative stabilization of inflation and investment growth, the *third phase* (1955–61) an investment superboom, highly oriented toward a disproportionate expansion of production of capital goods as well as consumer durables and rapid heavy industrialization, and, lastly, the *fourth phase* (1961–65) of excess capacity and investment stagnation as an aftermath of the preceding investment boom. In this phase the growth rate of GNP fell to 8 percent.

Our four-phase divisions of the postwar era, however, may be debatable, for Ohkawa and Rosovsky conclude in their paper that the period of postwar rehabilitation ended between 1952 and 1954. I do not strongly disagree with their opinion, but I would like to emphasize that the characteristics of 1946–51 and 1951–55 are extremely different, and that from the viewpoint of the medium-term fixed investment cycle, very clearly shown in Figure 9–2, our division is also

TABLE 9-3

Annual Growth Rate of Production of Consumer Durables
(Percent)

	Electric Washers	*Refrigerators*	*Television Sets*
1955-61.	29.3	92.2	79.7
1961-65.	1.5(6.5)	10.3(27.6)	-2.4(4.5)

NOTE: Figures in brackets represent annual growth rate for 1961-64.

FIGURE 9–2.   Private Fixed Investment—GNP Ratio for the 1946–66 Period.

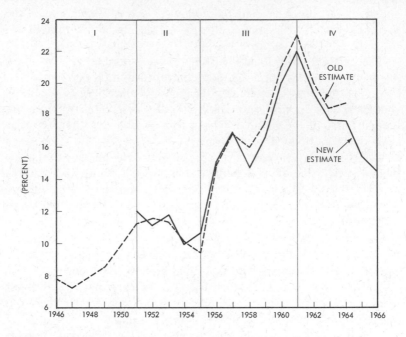

useful in understanding the phase differences in postwar economic growth.

II. HEAVY INDUSTRIALIZATION: PRESENT AND FUTURE

After passing through the high-growth period, 1955–61, Japanese manufacturing production advanced from sixth rank in the world in 1958 to third in 1963.[5] In 1958, the international cross-section index of the volume of industrial production indicates that Japan was 15.6 percent of the United States, but in 1963, its position had risen to 26.1 percent of the United States. With the United States equal to 100, the Soviet Union = 70.6 percent, Japan = 26.1 percent, West Germany = 23.5 percent, France = 20.5 percent, the United Kingdom = 17.5 percent, and Italy = 17.4 percent. On a per capita basis,

---

[5] M. Shinohara, *International Comparison of Industrial Levels* (Tokyo: Institute of Asian Economic Affairs, 1965), in Japanese. This is summarized in my paper, "Japan's Industrial Level in International Perspective," issued by the Ministry of Foreign Affairs, Japan, in March, 1966.

however, Japan was still 16th (51.6 percent) and lower than most of the advanced industrial countries of the West.

Accompanying the increase in Japan's international ranking in the level of industrial production, there was a spectacular acceleration in heavy industrialization as a consequence of the investment super-boom of 1955–61 and the extended production of consumer durables. Table 9–4 indicates the ratios for heavy industries (chemicals, metals, and machinery) in terms of value added in selected industrial countries, and suggests that Japan's heavy industry ratio was 61.2 percent in 1961, exceeding the ratios of the United Kingdom (59.3 percent), the United States (54.4 percent), and West Germany (54.6 percent). We may assume, therefore, that Japan's heavy industry ratio, reached in 1961, was probably one of the highest in the world, except for the Socialist countries. If so, this may be one of the most conspicuous structural changes the Japanese economy has attained in the postwar period.

Of course, if the value added in heavy industry is deflated by the national income, Japan's ratio may not be the highest, since we can enumerate various industrial countries in which the proportion of manufacturing in national income is higher than Japan's. Moreover,

TABLE 9-4

Heavy Industry Ratio in Terms of Value Added
(Percent)

		Chemicals	*Metals*	*Machinery*	*Total*
Japan	(1957).	11.6	17.8	26.5	55.9
	(1961).	11.8	17.1	32.3	61.2
W. Germany	(1954).	11.7	18.1	24.8	54.6
U.S.	(1958).	10.5	14.9	29.0	54.4
U.K.	(1958).	9.4	14.4	35.5	59.3
Denmark	(1959).	8.5	7.7	28.8	45.0
Norway	(1958).	10.6	17.0	21.5	49.1

SOURCES: Japan, *Kōgyō Tōkeihyō* (Census of Manufactures), *1957* and *1961*, Ministry of International Trade and Industry, Nikkan-kogyo Shimbunsha, Tokyo; West Germany, *Statistisches Jahrbuch für die Bundesrepublik Deutschland, 1960*, Statistisches Bundesamt, Verlag: W. Kohlhammer GMBH, Stuttgart und Mainz, 1960; U.S., *Census of Manufactures*, 1958, Bureau of the Census, U.S. Department of Commerce, U.S. Government Printing Office, Washington, D.C., 1961; U.K., *Census of Production*, 1958, Board of Trade, Her Majesty's Stationery Office, London, 1960; Denmark, *Industriel Produktionsstatistik, 1959*, Det Statistiske Departement, København, 1961; Norway, *Statistisk Årbok for Norge, 1960*, Statistisk Sentralbyrå, Oslo, 1960.

it should be pointed out that in Japan the relative prices of products in the light industries are comparatively lower than those in advanced industrial countries, so its apparently high, heavy industry ratio conceals within it the comparatively high-relative prices of its heavy industrial products. In this respect, the heavy industry ratio in terms of the number of employees would be also useful as a reference, as indicated in Table 9–5. When the heavy industry ratio is computed in terms of employees, Japan's ratio falls to 48 percent, which is about the same as the U.S. ratio (47.8 percent), but considerably lower than those in the United Kingdom (54.9 percent) and West Germany (58.9 percent). Taking this fact into account, the statistical conclusion that Japan has the highest heavy industry ratio should be accepted only provisionally. However, the fact that Japan's heavy industry ratio was pushed up to a level comparable with those in advanced countries through the process of the high-pitched growth is to be borne in mind, particularly because it was not only a consequence but also one of the causes of the high-pitched growth.

Heavy industrialization seems to have a close connection with economic levels in various countries, and it can be easily demonstrated by constructing Table 9–6 from United Nations' data. These show an international comparison of the proportion of metal and machinery industries in the value added in manufacturing. We have excluded here the chemical industry, simply because in the less developed countries the relatively high proportion occupied by the oil and fat industry will mislead us in understanding the role of the modern chemical industry. From this cross-section observation, it is almost evident that the more industrialized the economy is, the higher is the heavy industry ratio, in general, although there seems to be an upper limit to it.

The same conclusion can be reached by considering the relatively higher income elasticities for metals, machinery, and chemicals than for other industrial products, as suggested by the well-known computations of Chenery and Maizels. For instance, according to A. Maizels,[6] the elasticity of real value added per capita in each industry with respect to per capita real national income for 1899–1957 was 1.26 for manufacturing as a whole, 1.52 for basic metals, 1.96 for metal products and machinery, and 2.44 for chemicals for 7–10 countries on the average. Taking into further consideration the very low income elasticities for textiles (0.59) and food and tobacco (0.78), heavy

---

[6] Alfred Maizels, *Industrial Growth and World Trade* (Cambridge University Press, 1963), p. 53.

TABLE 9-5

Heavy Industry Ratios in Terms of Employees
(Unit: Thousand Men)

	Manufacturing	Chemicals	Coal and Petroleum Products	Metals	Machinery	Heavy Industry Ratio
Japan (1961). . . .	8,188.5	457.1	34.2	1,142.0	2,299.2	48.0%
U.S. (1958). . . .	15,393.8	699.2	179.2	2,154.4	4,324.9	47.8
U.K. (1958). . . .	7,781	444		1,040.4	2,789.3	54.9
W. Germany (1961). . . .	7,623	494.3	37.0	1,472.4	2,485.6	58.9
Norway (1953). . . .	350.7	19.3	0.5	36.7	68.6	35.7
Denmark (1959). . . .	71.4	8.2	0.8	14.3	13.2	51.1

SOURCES: Japan, *Kōgyō Tōkeihyō* (Census of Manufactures), *1957* and *1961*, Ministry of International Trade and Industry, Nikkan-kogyo Shimbunsha, Tokyo; West Germany, *Statistisches Jahrbuch für die Bundesrepublik Deutschland, 1960*, Statistisches Bundesamt, Verlag: W. Kohlhammer GMBH, Stuttgart und Mainz, 1960; U.S., *Census of Manufactures, 1958*, Bureau of the Census, U.S. Department of Commerce, U.S. Government Printing Office, Washington, D.C., 1961; U.K., *Census of Production, 1958*, Board of Trade, Her Majesty's Stationery Office, London, 1960; Denmark, *Industriel Produktionsstatistik, 1959*, Det Statistiske Departement, København, 1961; Norway, *Statistisk Årbok for Norge, 1960*, Statistisk Sentralbyrå, Oslo, 1960.

TABLE 9-6

International Comparison of the Proportion
of Metal and Machinery Industries, in 1958
(In Terms of Value Added)

40% and over.....	U.K. (48.1%), Sweden (45.8%), U.S. (43.4%), Australia (42.0%), Japan (41.5%)
30-39%..........	Norway (38.2%), Italy (36.6%), Denmark (36.2%), Netherlands (35.4%), West Germany (34.5% in 1954), Canada (33.5%), Union of South Africa (30.8%)
20-29%..........	Rhodesia-Nyasaland (29.1%), India, 20 employees and over (28.2%), Israel (26.3%), Brazil (26.5%), Singapore (25.6%), Finland (25.4%), New Zealand (24.7%), Ceylon, large factories (23.6%), Kenya (21.5% in 1957), Morocco (20.4%)
10-19%..........	Greece (14.9%), Ireland (14.3%), Korea (14.1%), Peru (14.1%), Turkey (13.6%), Puerto Rico (13.0%), Philippines (11.9%), Pakistan (11.7%), Malta (11.6%), Indonesia (10.9%), Malaya (10.2% in 1959)
Less than 10%....	Jordan (9.8% in 1959), Trinidad-Tobago (9.6%), Ghana (9.3%), Tanganyika (8.9%), U.A.R. (8.4%), Jamaica (7.1%), Mozambique (6.5%), Nigeria (5.4% in 1957), Guatemala (3.9%), Honduras (2.8%)

SOURCE: United Nations, *The Growth of World Industry 1938-1961* (New York, 1963).

industrialization itself seems to be a normal process accompanying economic growth in general. Particularly, if one country specializes in heavy industrial products in its exports, it is probable that its export growth rate will be favorably influenced. Studies by Tyszinsky, Cairncross and Maizels made it clear that heavy industrialization exists not only in the relative composition of manufacturing output but also in that of manufacturing commodity exports. According to their studies, the share of metals and machinery in the total exports of manufacturing commodities increased from 30.3 percent in 1899 to 59.0 percent in 1959, and the share of textiles decreased from 40.6 percent in 1899 to 11.1 percent in 1959. This indicates to us that the export growth rate of the economy will increase, other things being equal, according to the extent that the economy is oriented to the export of heavy industrial products. However, as concerns chemical products, we must bear in mind that although its growth rate in terms of *physical volume* of production or exports is very high, its proportion in output as well as in export *value* will not increase so sharply, owing to the decline of its relative price.

Insofar as heavy industrialization is, thus, a long-term trend, we might speculate on the one hand, that an unnecessary hesitation in transforming the industrial structure may bring about a stagnation in the economic growth of the economy. On the other hand, those economies which have succeeded in the transformation with a high capacity or have the flexibility to transform will certainly realize a high-rate economic growth. The so-called secular stagnation of the British economy in the 1920's and 1930's seems to have been closely associated with an unwillingness to transform its industrial structure, then basically oriented toward light industry, to one oriented toward heavy industry. Since it was then menaced by an export expansion of light industrial products by latecomers like Japan and Germany, a wise policy, if any, should have consisted of a smooth transformation of its production structure toward heavy industrialization. This point was once emphasized by I. Svennilson in *Growth and Stagnation of the European Economy* (United Nations, 1954). The preservation of dominance for light industry made for a rapid narrowing of foreign markets for British textiles, etc., and this brought about a conspicuous stagnation of the domestic economy for almost 20 years.

Let us compare the above experience, with Japan's postwar development, particularly during 1955–61. Since the speed of the transformation of its industrial structure was swift, it might have contributed to an unprecedented high-pitched growth, although causation may also be the other way round. Let us assume that it is correct to say that the stagnation of the British economy in the 1920's and 1930's was closely associated with an extremely low willingness to transform its industrial structure, on the one hand, and that the phenomenal growth of the postwar Japanese economy was closely linked with its aggressive propensity to introduce foreign technology and to change its industrial structure in a flexible way so as to accelerate heavy industrialization. This picture gives us two opposite cases in the United Kingdom and Japan although our interpretation is purely imaginative and hypothetical, without support of a detailed analysis.

We may speculate in another way about the pattern of the future course of Japanese heavy industry, based on an observation in international perspective. Figure 9–3 depicts the relationship between the proportions of heavy industry in value added in manufacturing, on the one hand, and the proportions of heavy industrial products in the exports of manufactured commodities, on the other, for six countries; the United States, the United Kingdom, West Germany, France, Italy, and Japan, and also for six years; 1900, 1913, 1928, 1938, 1958, and 1959. From this relationship we may formulate a hypothesis that the heavy industrial countries that first went ahead, e.g., the United States,

FIGURE 9–3.   Heavy Industry Ratios of Output and Exports (1900–1959).

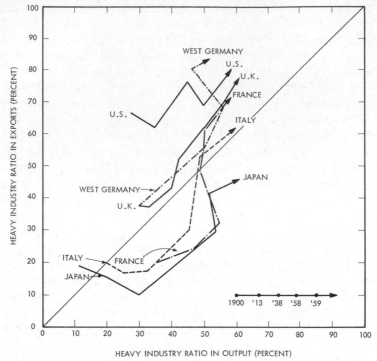

HEAVY INDUSTRY RATIO IN OUTPUT (PERCENT)

Source: Ministry of International Trade and Industry, *Tsushō Hakusho* (White Paper for International Trade) (1961), p. 310.

Germany, and the United Kingdom, were located on the chart far beyond the 45° line at an early stage, but that the heavy industrial countries who were latecomers, e.g., Italy, France, and Japan, were first located below the 45° line and then shifted upward in the later period. This means that in the "going-ahead" countries the heavy industry ratio in terms of exports was higher than in terms of output, reflecting their strong competitive positions in the world market. In the "late-coming" countries the former ratio is lower than the latter ratio, reflecting unfavorable competitive positions in the world market. The tendency to have a poor competitive position was sometimes intensified by a protection of domestic industries in the late-coming countries.

At the present time, in most European industrial countries, the heavy industry ratio in exports is generally higher than the ratio in output. However, in Japan, the opposite relation prevails. The heavy industry ratio in output surpasses the other ratio. One interpretation of this phenomenon was provided by the Ministry of International Trade and Industry.[7] They contended that although heavy industry expanded tremendously in the period of high-pitched growth, its competitive position in the world market remains inferior. This is reflected in the higher heavy industry ratio in output than in exports. A rapid heavy industrialization in a relatively closed system before trade liberalization brought about this discrepancy between the two ratios. In the opinion of the Ministry of International Trade and Industry, heavy industry needs to be strengthened by policy measures. As a result of this opinion the so-called "industrial structure policy" was set up, which aims at fostering expansion in strategic export industries and realizing economies of mass production which would be adequate to bring these industries to an internationally competitive position.

Once it is realized that the rise of the heavy industry ratio in output is to precede that in exports in the historical process of heavy industrialization of latecomer countries, we may conjecture that, after a big wave of heavy industrialization in output, another wave in exports will follow. This reminds us of the proposition of Professor K. Akamatsu[8] (the "Wild-Geese-Flying Pattern of Growth") in his analysis of the industrial development of Japan since the Meiji period. He pointed out that in light industries, particularly in the textile industry, we can find a succession of big waves of imports, domestic production, and exports, with some time lags. A wave of imports of textiles preceded that of the domestic production of textiles, and after a rise of the latter another bulge in its exports followed. In other words, first there must be a formation of a minimum domestic market through an expansion of imports to serve as a prerequisite for the expansion of new domestic industries. Second, domestic industries should grow to an extent that they can reduce their costs and compete effectively in the world market. Then we have conditions favorable for the expansion of their exports.

His "Wild-Geese Formation" of industrial development seems to fit not only the pattern of light industry development in the past, but also to explain the coming sequence of Japan's heavy industrial-

---

[7] Sangyō-Kōzō Chōsakai (Research Committee for Industrial Structure), *Nihon no Sangyō-Kōzō* (Industrial Structure in Japan), Vols. I and III, 1964.

[8] K. Akamatsu, "Synthetic Dialectics of Industrial Development in Japan," *Journal of Nagoya Higher Commercial School,* July, 1937, (in Japanese). See also his article, "A Theory of Unbalanced Growth in the World Economy," *Weltwirtschaftliches Archiv,* Band 86, Heft 2, 1961.

ization. If so, the process in which heavy industrialization in exports will replace that in output can come about in the future not only as a result of an economic policy for strengthening the international competitive power of heavy industry, but also as a necessary link in the causal chain of industrial development. The heavy industry ratio in output already reached 61.2 percent (the highest in capitalist countries) in 1961, and there is considerable uncertainty whether or not this ratio can be maintained in the future. However, if we can rely on the empirical law for heavy industrialization in output and exports as a long-term trend, we may be optimistic about the future and presume that after we have had heavy industrialization in output, we shall have heavy industrialization in exports as a historical sequence.

The investment superboom of 1955–61 has been undergoing a period of adjustment and shifting from a capacity shortage to an excess capacity phase since 1962. This may be a medium-term aftermath of the unprecedented investment boom. From the viewpoint of the longer term structural change, we should anticipate that Japan's postwar heavy industrialization will be completed by a rise in the exports of heavy industrial products.

It is likely that heavy industry in the future will be supported by the following three factors: (1) export expansion of heavy industrial products, a preview of which can already be seen in the recent rapid expansion of steel, automobiles, and similar products; (2) a long-run increase in the relative share of consumer durables in the machinery industry. This will, to some extent, mitigate the unfavorable effect of the cessation of the investment superboom and the medium-term leveling-off of heavy industrialization. It should be pointed out, however, that the life cycle effect of consumer durables brought about a decline in their growth rate for the past few years;[9] (3) the proportion of construction in total investment will increase and moderate the instability in the heavy industrialization process. Construction activity often moves in a countercyclical pattern. If construction were stimulated by government policy, the decline of the heavy industry ratio would not be as significant as it otherwise might be.

Although I have been using the "conventional" concept, heavy industry, there remain some problems in this connection. In the Conference, Professors S. Kuznets and H. König pointed out the weakness

---

[9] See Y. Shionoya, "Patterns of Industrial Growth in the United States and Sweden—A Critique of Hoffmann's Hypothesis," *Hitotsubashi Journal of Economics,* June, 1964. He pointed out the long-run stability of the proportion of capital goods production in the final output in manufacturing, despite the long-term trend of heavy industrialization.

in its definition. It includes not only capital goods but also consumer durables and chemicals, as well as some intermediate goods. This makes it a heterogeneous concept. While I recognize the relevance of their criticism, I have been in favor of the heavy industrialization that the Japanese economy has actually experienced, simply because heavy industrial products seem to satisfy the following important conditions in general; (1) higher income elasticity; (2) a higher rate of technological progress; (3) higher backward and forward linkage effects. I do not maintain that every item of the so-called heavy industrial products has these three properties, but that the predominant portion of heavy industrial products do.

Even if some of the heavy industrial products with high-income elasticities do not have a comparative cost advantage at a particular point of time, the relatively higher rate of technological progress, if it is realized, may give them comparative cost advantage.

In 1965, the labor productivity indices (1960 = 100) of the Japan Productivity Center for the subsectors of manufacturing are as follows:

Iron and steel	163.0	Textiles	141.9
Nonferrous metals	151.7	Leather	140.1
Machinery	154.9	Rubber	111.1
Chemicals	188.6	Lumber	107.0
Petroleum products	196.0	Food	100.5
Coal products	197.0	Tobacco	132.5

Even in the fourth phase in which the investment boom leveled off, it can be seen that increases in labor productivity are higher in heavy industry. It is also of interest that the gross fixed-capital–output ratios estimated by the Economic Research Institute of the Economic Planning Agency indicate the following results:

	1955	*1963*
Food	0.67	0.99
Textiles	2.74	2.83
Chemicals	3.63	2.14
Metals	2.64	2.38
Machinery (including electrical machinery)	1.13	0.96
Transportation equipment	2.47	1.44

The fixed-capital–output ratio decreased in heavy industry, indicating a higher investment efficiency, but it increased in light industry.

A casual look at these and the Chenery-Watanabe computation of the backward and forward linkage effects[10] provides convincing evidence that the industries which satisfy these three criteria were, by and large, the so-called heavy industries. According to Chenery and Watanabe, the machinery industry (in a wide sense) has high backward linkage effects, but lower forward linkage effects. However, if we take into account the capacity-increasing effect of machinery and equipment, the machinery industry has both linkage effects of a relatively high order. What is important is not that the industries we are concerned with belong to heavy industry, but that they satisfy our three criteria.

Finally, in this section, it seems useful to add some words about the limitation of heavy industrialization in understanding the future course of industrial structure and in constructing economic policy. In Table 9–6, we found some relationship between the heavy industry ratio and the per capita income of different nations. We must not, however, overlook the fact that the heavy industry ratio of the United States is a little lower than that of the industrial countries of Europe. This suggests that there seems to be a strong positive relationship between the two magnitudes up to the income level of the European industrial countries, but that after that level the relationship fades and the economy may grow without increasing the heavy industry ratio.

As concerns Abramovitz's comment on whether or not my proposition will hold true even when all countries follow the course of heavy industrialization, I simply answer that many of the present developing economies still lack capability to realize the second criterion, i.e., the enhancement of the rate of technological progress in the sphere of heavy industry.

III. INDUSTRIAL GROWTH AND THE DEGREE OF FABRICATION

In my analysis, I came across an interesting fact that merits further consideration.

Table 9–7 indicates the increases in value added (or shipments) and employment in various sectors of manufacturing for 1955–61

---

[10] H. B. Chenery and T. Watanabe, "International Comparisons of the Structure of Production," *Econometrica*, October, 1958. Albert O. Hirschman, *The Strategy of Economic Development* (New Haven, Conn.: Yale University Press, 1958). Y. Hayamizu pointed out to me that the concept of the linkage effects will be useful in explaining the relation between heavy industrialization and the high rate of growth.

TABLE 9-7

Value Added, Shipment and Employment in Sectors of Manufacturing

	Establishments with 40 Employees and Over				Establishments with 30 Employees and Over	
	Value Added		Employees		Shipment	Employees
	1961 1955	1961 1951	1961 1955	1961 1951	1965 1955	1965 1955
Food.	2.10	5.48	1.45	2.04	3.77	2.45
Textiles.	1.90	2.53	1.21	1.25	2.32	1.23
Apparels.	2.50	4.10	1.61	1.95	5.94	2.56
Lumber and wood products.	2.49	4.50	1.37	1.45	5.04	2.05
Furniture and fixtures. .	3.17	7.54	1.64	2.33	9.50	2.97
Paper and pulp.	3.92	3.92	1.41	1.95	3.87	1.89
Printing and publishing .	2.10	4.77	1.35	1.85	4.00	1.74
Chemicals	2.44	4.34	1.30	1.35	3.91	1.47
Petroleum and coal products.	2.64	3.93	1.19	1.25	6.55	1.42
Rubber products	2.87	6.46	1.93	2.14	3.75	2.01
Leather and leather products.	2.51	4.19	1.60	1.95	4.97	2.73
Ceramics.	2.60	5.30	1.56	1.86	4.46	2.04
Iron and steel.	3.43	5.18	1.73	1.68	4.14	1.78
Nonferrous metals	2.68	3.70	1.79	2.36	4.22	1.82
Metal products.	3.91	8.17	2.08	3.00	6.87	2.95
Machinery	4.77	7.97	2.27	2.36	7.97	2.67
Electrical machinery. . .	5.88	11.94	3.34	4.27	9.45	3.95
Transportation equipment.	4.21	8.21	1.73	1.90	7.94	2.16
Instruments and related products.	3.49	9.39	2.13	3.15	7.30	2.79
Others.	3.46	10.59	1.91	3.15	9.37	3.08

Sources: The Ministry of International Trade and Industry, *Kōgyō Tōkeihyō* (Census of Manufactures), Ministry of International Trade and Industry, Nikkan-kōgyō Shimbunsha, Tokyo.

and 1951–61 (establishments with 40 employees and over) and for 1955–65 (establishments with 30 employees and over). On the whole, the trend of heavy industrialization can still be observed, even for the 1955–65 period in which the effect of the fixed-investment adjustment in 1962–65 is involved, if the relative price decline of chemical products is taken into consideration.

We find, however, a tendency for the relatively more fabricated commodities to manifest higher rates of increase. In the 1955–65 period, shipments by the textile industry increased by 2.32 times, but those by the apparel industry by 5.94 times. For the same period, the lumber and wood products industry showed an increase of 9.50 times.

The iron and steel and nonferrous metals industries show an increase of about four times, while the metal products industry an increase of 6.87 times and other machinery industries an increase of 7–9 times. The miscellaneous industries, which may consist of fabricated commodities, showed an increase of 9.37 times. Similar results can also be derived for the 1955–61 and 1951–61 periods. In other words, the statistical figures in the *Census of Manufactures* clearly indicate that increasing production has proceeded with a relatively higher speed in those industries whose degree of fabrication is relatively higher. Although these results must be accepted with some reservation because of changes in relative prices, the great differences in the increases in shipments are strong pieces of evidence in favor of an empirical law.

Since those industries whose degree of fabrication is relatively higher are mostly labor-intensive, we have, in effect, bilateral industrial developments in the national economy: (1) the growth of more capital-intensive industries (extension of mass production, surrounding the big plants); (2) the growth of more fabricated commodity production with relatively more labor-intensive technology (expansion of more elaborate-type commodity production, in conformity with the diversification of consumers' demand structure, by medium-sized or below medium-sized plants). Naturally, each development may entail an advance in technology which will save labor, but the former may continue to be relatively more capital-intensive than the latter at every instant of the growth process.

When I undertook the compilation of the intercountry index of industrial production, I was surprised to see the statistical figures on shipments in the *Census of Manufactures* in three countries: the United States, the United Kingdom, and Japan in 1958 (Table 9–8).

TABLE 9-8

Relative Magnitudes of Shipments
between Textiles and Apparel in 1958

	Textiles		*Apparel*
U.S.	100.0	vs.	109.1
U.K.	100.0	vs.	39.8
Japan.	100.0	vs.	8.9 (13.5)

NOTE: 13.5 in parentheses is an adjusted estimate which amends the downward statistical bias in the Japanese statistics.

It is surprising to see that the difference in the ratios between textiles and apparel are so great among these three countries, and one may wonder about the reliability of the statistics.[11] Nevertheless, I believe that most of these differences may reflect the difference in the degree of fabrication associated with the stages of economic growth of the three countries. In other words, as the economy grows, human desires may become diversified and the degree of fabrication will accordingly be raised. This will necessarily increase the ratio of the more fabricated commodities to the relatively more primary or basic commodities in manufacturing production.

If this is a phenomenon associated with industrial growth, it is evident that the intercountry cross-section index of the volume of industrial production, which I have computed mostly depending upon basic-type commodities, may have an upward bias for the relatively lower countries. Since Japan has developed rapidly in the postwar period and has placed strong emphasis upon increases in basic commodities, like iron and steel, ethylene, etc., there is a possibility that the production of fabricated commodities may be delayed in comparison with other advanced countries. If so, my computed result, that Japan advanced to the third industrial level in the world in 1963, should be discounted.

Our finding points to another implication, because the increase in the degree of fabrication may have something to do with the Leontief paradox.[12] Leontief found that the United States exports relatively labor-intensive commodities, on the one hand, and imports relatively capital-intensive commodities, on the other. This finding, which seems to contradict common sense in international economics, is, however, reasonable if we take into account the increasing degree of fabrication coupled with growth. The United States exports a considerable amount of machinery, automobiles, etc., which are essentially labor-intensive, compared with other industries.

The increasing degree of fabrication has also been found in the fast growth process of postwar Japan, and we should not overlook this point. Probably, the heavy industrialization of the past several years has contributed to the rapid industrial development of Japan, but the matter of the increasing degree of fabrication in the changing industrial

---

[11] The extremely high ratio of the apparel industry in the United States may have something to do with its high dependency upon imports for intermediate textile products.

[12] W. Leontief, "Domestic Production and Foreign Trade, American Capital Position Re-examined," *Proceedings of the American Philosophical Society,* September, 1953.

structure will play a much more important role in the coming decades, when the pace of heavy industrialization slows.

IV. CONCLUSION

1. In its postwar economic growth, the Japanese economy has shown a dynamic rhythm, consisting of four phases: a postwar rehabilitation period, coupled with hyperinflation (1946–51), a period of stabilization of inflation and investment tranquility (1951–55), investment superboom together with heavy industrialization (1955–61), and excess capacity and investment stagnation (1961–66). The characteristics of each phase have been analyzed in some detail.

2. As a consequence of the investment superboom and the expansion of consumer durables production, the heavy industry ratio in terms of value added reached 61.2 percent in 1961, the highest in the capitalist world. Even if this ratio declined to 57.8 percent in 1965, it is expected that future heavy industrialization in exports will follow the heavy industrialization in output. This is the sequence suggested by an empirical law governing industrial development. Three things will play a role in future expansion of Japanese heavy industry. They are expansion of exports of heavy industrial products; a rising portion of consumer durables in the output of the machinery industry; construction activity.

3. In parallel with heavy industrialization, there has been a tendency for the shipment of more highly fabricated commodities to increase in importance, reflecting the diversification of human desires. Thus, economic growth can be assumed to be a joint development of both mass production with capital-intensive techniques, on the one hand, and of more fabricated commodity production with relatively greater labor-intensive techniques (however, with more elegant designs, more advanced devices, and more modern technology), on the other. From this point of view, the implications of the Leontief paradox can easily be understood. Japan, which attained the highest heavy industry ratio in 1961, is expected, from now on, to place more emphasis on increasing the degree of fabrication in manufacturing.

10 | Economic Growth and Exports*

HISAO KANAMORI

I. A POSTWAR CONTROVERSY

After World War II, there was a controversy on how to reconstruct the Japanese economy, whether through trade expansion leading to a greater division of labor among nations (the foreign trade method), or through the development of domestic resources leading to increased self-sufficiency (the domestic development method).[1]

Advocates of domestic development argued that it would be dangerous to depend too heavily on trade, and that effort should be directed toward an effective utilization of domestic resources. They reasoned as follows:

1. The world economy is vulnerable to great changes such as war and panic.
2. The loss of colonies by the war meant the loss of the source of cheap food supply and the loss of the market for Japanese industrial products.
3. A forced trade expansion may lead to disadvantageous terms of trade, i.e., low export prices and high import prices.
4. Export expansion may require wage reduction.

* I have received useful comments from many individuals on this paper, but I am particularly grateful to M. C. Kemp and M. Shinohara. The original draft was substantially revised according to their comments, and the first two sections were added as a result of suggestions by Dr. Shinohara.

[1] Professor Ichiro Nakayama was the chief advocate of the foreign trade method, and Professor Shigeto Tsuru, of the domestic development method. See Ichiro Nakayama, "Bōekishugi to Kokunai Kaihatsushugi" ("Foreign Trade Method and Domestic Development Method"), *Nihon Keizai no Kao* (*Aspects of Japanese Economy*) (Tokyo: Nihonhyōronsha, 1953), and Shigeto Tsuru, "Boekimondai no Shoten" ("Highlights of Trade Problems"), *Heiwao Motomeru Nihonkeizai* (*Japanese Economy Seeks Peace*) (Tokyo: Kōbundo, 1951).

II. WERE THE ADVOCATES OF DOMESTIC DEVELOPMENT RIGHT?

The subsequent trend of the Japanese economy revealed that their judgment was not right in many respects. Despite the high economic growth rate of 11.1 percent per annum in real GNP for the period 1951–65, Japan's international balance of payments has not deteriorated. This is, however, not because the Japanese economy has become more self-sufficient and less dependent on imports. After the war, the ratio of imports to gross national product decreased drastically compared with the prewar years, but within the postwar period, "nominal" dependence has remained more or less constant at about 10 percent, while "real" dependence (the ratio of imports to gross national product in 1960 prices) has increased slightly (see Table 10–1). The reason is that although the dependence on imports decreased in commodities like foodstuff, raw cotton and wool, it increased in iron ore, lumber, petroleum, processed foods, etc.

Thus, Japan achieved a high rate of economic growth with a proportionate increase of imports and needed at least a corresponding growth of exports. As shown in Table 10–2, real GNP of 1965 is

TABLE 10-1

Shifts in the Dependence on Imports
(Percent)

	Nominal Dependence*	Real Dependence†
1952.	12.1	7.4
1953.	12.5	9.3
1954.	11.1	9.0
1955.	10.4	8.4
1956.	12.2	9.7
1957.	13.9	10.7
1958.	9.6	8.7
1959.	10.1	9.9
1960.	10.6	10.6
1961.	11.3	12.0
1962.	9.7	11.0
1963.	10.4	12.3
1964.	10.3	12.2
1965.	9.7	12.1

*Nominal dependence = $\dfrac{\text{Imports (customs statistics)}}{\text{GNP}}$.

†Real dependence = $\dfrac{\text{Imports (customs statistics) in 1960 prices}}{\text{GNP in 1960 prices}}$

TABLE 10-2

Rates of Increase: GNP, Exports and Imports

	1965 Indexes (with 1951 as 100)	Annual Rate of Increase in Percent (1951-65)
Nominal		
GNP.	720	15.1
Export	624	14.0
Import	410	10.6
Real		
GNP.	436	11.1
Export	893	16.9
Import	557	13.1

SOURCE: Exports and imports are based on customs statistics and the Finance Ministry's export and import volume indexes.

about 4.4 times that of 1951 and imports 5.6 times, but exports have increased as much as 8.9 times. This remarkable increase of exports enabled Japan to achieve a high economic growth rate with little strain on the balance of payments. Why did pessimistic predictions about exports turn out to be wrong? Let us consider briefly each of the arguments mentioned earlier.

1. The Danger of War and Panic

The postwar world economy was not disturbed by war or panic. Despite some international conflicts such as the Korean War of 1950, the Suez dispute of 1956; the Vietnam War of the 1960's and three U.S. recessions (1954, 1957, and 1960), the world economy has, on the whole, flourished. Table 10–3 indicates that during 1951–65 the volume of world trade has expanded at an average annual rate of nearly 6 percent, which is well above the rate for the years before World War I when world trade was on an increasing trend, to say nothing of the rate for the 1930's when world trade was depressed. Naturally, this favorable trend in the world economy helped to promote Japanese exports.

2. The Loss of Colonies

In prewar years (1934–36), trade with colonies (Korea and Formosa) accounted for 25 percent of Japan's total exports and 27

TABLE 10-3

World Trade and Japanese Exports
(Average Annual Increase Rate of Export Volume)
(Percent)

	1881–85 ~ 1911–13	1911–13 ~ 1938	1951 ~ 1965
World *(a)*.	3.2	0.5	5.9
Japan *(b)*.	7.5	5.2	16.9
(b)/(a).	2.3	10.4	2.9

SOURCES: World: For 1881-85~1911-13, F. Hilgerdt, *Industrialization and Foreign Trade;* for 1938, League of Nations, *Review of World Trade* (Geneva, 1938); for postwar years, UN, *Monthly Bulletin of Statistics.*
Japan: For prewar years, *Nihon Boeki Seiran* (Tokyo: Toyokeizai, 1935); for postwar years, Ministry of Finance, Tokyo, *Monthly Bulletin of Foreign Trade Statistics,* January, 1966.

percent of its imports. Therefore, the loss of colonies meant damage to one quarter of its market. After the war, trade with the former colonies did indeed shrink, but new markets were opened in the United States, Europe, and other regions of the world (see Table 10–4). A comparison of the prewar (1934–36) and the postwar (1965) years reveals that the percentage of total exports going to Korea and Formosa has decreased from 25 to 5 percent, while the percentage going to the United States has increased from 6 to 30 percent and the percentage going to Europe from 8 to 15 percent, respectively. Percentages of exports going to Africa, Oceania, and South America have also increased.

In 1965, the value of Japanese exports increased sixfold over 1951, a gain of about $7.1 billion. Exports to the United States accounted for one third of this increase; those to Europe, 16 percent; to Southeast Asia, 15 percent; and to the former colonies, only 5 percent. Thus the acquisition of new markets amply compensated for the loss of colonies.

3. The Terms of Trade

The pessimists' fear that the terms of trade may be adversely affected by export expansion proved to be groundless. As shown in Table 10–5, export prices dropped by about 20 percent from 1952 to

TABLE 10-4

Weights of Various Regions of the World
in Japanese Trade and Its Export Increase
(Percent)

	1934~36		1951		1965		Export Increase Rate 1965 (1951=1)	Rate of Contribution to Export Increase 1951 ~ 1965
	Export	Import	Export	Import	Export	Import		
Asia.	64	53	52	29	33	33	3.9	28.9
Korea and Formosa .	25	27	8	3	5	2	6.1	4.7
China	18	10	-	1	3	3	3.6	2.5
Southeast Asia . . .	19	17	41	20	19	14	2.9	15.1
North America . . .	17	25	16	46	35	37	13.8	38.3
U.S.	6	24	14	34	30	29	13.4	32.3
Europe.	8	10	11	8	15	12	8.9	16.2
South America . . .	2	2	6	5	3	5	3.1	2.4
Africa.	6	3	8	4	10	4	7.3	10.0
Oceania	3	7	8	8	5	8	3.8	4.2
Total	100	100	100	100	100	100	6.2	100.0

SOURCE: See Table 10-3.

TABLE 10-5

Changes in Terms of Trade
(Indexes with 1952 as 100)

	Unit Export Price (a)	Unit Import Price (b)	Terms of Trade (a)/(b)
1952. . . .	100	100	100
1953. . . .	95	87	109
1954. . . .	92	85	109
1955. . . .	86	85	101
1956. . . .	89	89	100
1957. . . .	92	96	96
1958. . . .	88	80	109
1959. . . .	87	76	115
1960. . . .	89	77	116
1961. . . .	87	76	114
1962. . . .	85	75	113
1963. . . .	84	76	111
1964. . . .	83	78	107
1965. . . .	82	79	103

SOURCE: Ministry of Finance, *Gaikoku Boeki Geppo* (Monthly Bulletin of Foreign Trade Statistics).

1965, but as the import price fell to the same extent, the terms of trade have remained more or less constant. It is true if we compare 1965 with 1959, the terms of trade have deteriorated, for import prices stopped falling after 1959, while export prices continued to fall. A little deterioration, however, is natural because the rate of productivity increase is much higher in Japanese industrial exports than in imported foodstuffs and raw materials.

4. The Danger of Wage Reduction

The fall of export prices, shown in Table 10–5, is mainly due to increased labor productivity, and *not* to wage reduction as the advocates of domestic development had feared. As shown in Table 10–6, unit labor costs have decreased by 5 percent in the past 10 years (1955–65), while the nominal wage in 1965 rose by a factor of 2.2 over 1955 and the real wage by a factor of 1.5. Increased productivity permitted export prices to fall at the same time that wages were rising.

TABLE 10-6

Wage, Labor Productivity, and Export Price

	Wage (in Manufacturing Industries) (w)	Labor Productivity (e)	Unit Labor Cost (w)/(e)	Export Price	Real Wage
1952. . . .	100.0	100.0	100.0	100.0	100.0
1953. . . .	112.2	118.2	94.9	94.5	105.3
1954. . . .	118.1	122.8	96.2	91.7	104.1
1955. . . .	122.7	129.3	95.0	85.9	109.4
1956. . . .	134.1	146.9	91.4	88.6	119.0
1957. . . .	138.7	158.1	87.7	92.0	119.5
1958. . . .	142.0	157.5	90.2	87.6	122.9
1959. . . .	152.6	177.4	86.0	87.4	130.6
1960. . . .	164.7	200.4	82.2	89.4	136.1
1961. . . .	183.9	220.8	83.3	86.9	144.2
1962. . . .	201.2	227.1	88.7	84.7	147.6
1963. . . .	221.9	248.5	89.3	83.7	151.4
1964. . . .	246.0	283.4	86.8	82.8	161.8
1965. . . .	268.4	298.4	90.0	81.7	163.9

SOURCE: For labor productivity up to 1955, Ministry of Labor, Tokyo, *Maigetsu Kinro Tokei*; after 1955, Japan Productivity Center, Tokyo, *Quarterly Bulletin of Labour Productivity*.

III. CAUSES OF THE EXPORT EXPANSION

1. Advantage in Price Competition

How, then, did Japan succeed in increasing its exports and thereby maintain a high economic growth without entailing wage reduction or a deterioration in the terms of trade?

Some reasons have already been given. They are the Japanese participation in the growth of world trade, the maintenance of the terms of trade, and the reduction of unit labor costs through increased productivity. Japan remained competitive in world trade. Between 1958 and 1965, export prices of European countries, except in the case of Italy, have increased (see Table 10–7). According to the table, the smaller the increase in export prices, the greater the increase in export volume; there is a clear negative correlation between the two. Thus we may conclude that the comparatively low price of Japanese exports was an important reason behind its export growth.

TABLE 10-7

International Comparison of Production, Labor Productivity
and Labor Cost in Manufacturing Industries

	Annual Increase Rate for 1958-65				Indexes for 1965 with 1958 as 100	
	Production	Labor Productivity	Wage	Export Volume	Labor Unit Cost	Export Price
Japan.	15.1	9.4	9.5	17.8	101	94
Italy.	8.9	7.5*	8.7	16.7	108	95
West Germany	7.1	5.6	8.7	9.3	121	104
U.S.	6.4	4.2	3.1	6.2	93	106
U.K.	4.3	3.9	5.9	3.8	115	109

SOURCES: UN *Monthly Bulletin of Statistics;* and National Institute of Economic and Social Research,
Economic Review, May, 1966, London.
*January-June.

2. Change in the Commodity Composition of Exports

Lowered export prices do not provide the sole explanation of the export increase; another important factor was the change in the composition of Japanese exports.

During 1950–65, Japanese exports grew at an accelerated pace. There was an increase of $1,183 million from 1950 to 1955, $2,044 million from 1955 to 1960, and $4,397 million from 1960 to 1965. Contributions of various commodities to this increase are listed in Table 10–8. During 1950–55, the main contributors were textiles and sundry goods; during 1955–60, machinery and textiles; and during

TABLE 10-8

Ratios of Contributions to Export Increase

	1950-55	1955-60	1960-65	1950-65
Total value of export increase	100.0	100.0	100.0	100.0
Food.	7.1	5.9	2.0	3.8
Fishery products.	4.0	4.8	1.3	2.6
Fibers and textiles	29.6	23.2	8.2	15.5
Raw silk.	0.9	0	Δ0.8	Δ0.3
Cotton textile.	2.0	5.9	Δ1.2	1.3
Silk fabric	Δ0.5	1.8	Δ0.4	0.2
Woolen textile.	2.4	1.3	Δ0.8	1.1
Synthetic textile	...	1.6	3.5	2.4
Rayon fabric.	1.9	Δ0.2	0.3	0.4
Staple fiber fabric	6.0	1.8	Δ0.6	1.0
Clothing.	7.1	5.6	1.5	3.5
Chemicals	6.6	4.0	8.3	7.0
Chemical fertilizer	3.2	0.8	0.6	1.1
Nonmetallic mineral products.	4.6	4.1	2.2	3.1
Porcelain	2.0	1.3	0.4	0.9
Metals and their products	19.8	8.9	26.1	20.5
Iron and steel.	15.8	6.3	20.5	16.0
Metallic products	3.3	4.6	3.4	3.7
Machinery	13.9	33.3	39.0	33.6
Textile machine	1.4	1.0	0.8	0.9
Sewing machine.	2.2	0.6	0.5	0.8
Radio set	0.1	7.0	1.6	2.8
Automobile.	0.5	3.5	3.6	3.1
Motorcycles	...	0.4	3.2	2.0
Ship.	4.4	10.3	9.7	9.0
Sundry.	20.0	20.4	14.3	16.5
Veneer.	3.0	1.3	0.05	0.8
Optical instruments	1.8	2.6	2.4	1.4
Toy	2.5	2.3	0.2	1.1

1960–65, machinery and metals. In the first five-year period, the contribution of textiles and sundry goods was 50 percent but their contribution dropped to 23 percent in the last five-year period, while those of machinery and metals rose to 65 percent. If we turn to individual items, we find that the largest contributors in the first period were iron and steel (15.8 percent), clothing (7.1 percent), staple fiber fabric (6 percent), ships (4.4 percent), fishery products (4 percent) and veneer (3 percent); in the middle period, ships (10.3 percent), radio sets (7 percent), iron and steel (6.3 percent), cotton textile (5.9 percent), clothing (5.6 percent), fishery products (4.8 percent) and metallic products (4.6 percent); and in the last period, iron and steel (20.5 percent), ships (9.7 percent), automobiles (3.6 percent), synthetic texiles (3.5 percent), metallic products (3.4 percent) and motorcycles (3.2 percent). Thus the predominance, in the first period, of light-industry products such as clothing and staple fiber fabric was replaced, in the last period, by products of heavy and chemical industries. Without this change in composition, Japanese exports probably would not have achieved the spectacular increase of 17 percent per year.

2.1. Overseas Factors in the Changed Commodity Composition

Japan's traditional export commodities consisted mainly of items whose overseas demand was increasing slowly; therefore it was necessary for export promotion to shift toward commodities with fast-growing demand. As world income rises, the focus of demand shifts from textiles and ordinary nondurable goods to luxuries and products of heavy and chemical industries. This tendency is clearly revealed in the national export statistics of the Organization for Economic Cooperation and Development (O.E.C.D.) and the United Nations, during 1955–64. When 70 major industrial commodities of the world are classified into five groups according to the rate of export increase, high rates are observed for machinery (business machines, recording machines, electric machinery, metal-processing machinery, automobiles, and motors), chemicals (synthetic textiles, organic compounds, and plastics) and luxuries (fur and precious stones). Corresponding rates are low for traditional textiles (cotton and others), veneer, porcelain, and fertilizers. The rate for business machines (a fourfold increase in 10 years) or for synthetic textiles (more than threefold) contrasts strikingly with the increase of 3 percent for cotton textiles.

In 1955, as shown in Table 10–9, Japan's exports contained few growing and many stagnant items. Fast-growing items (those belonging to maximum and large export-growth groups) constituted only 20 percent of the total exports, while static and stagnant items amounted to over 60 percent. By contrast, in West Germany, the United Kingdom and Italy, approximately 50 percent of total exports were in the fast-growing category. In one decade, however, Japan managed to raise the ratio of growing items substantially; in 1964, the percentage of maximum export–growth goods reached 26 percent, surpassing corresponding percentages for West Germany or the United Kingdom. In 1955, Japan's share of maximum growth goods in the world export total was low (see Table 10–10), but in 1964 it ranked fourth, after the United States, West Germany, and the United Kingdom.

In terms of the world demand pattern, the composition of Japanese exports was, at the outset, unfavorable for growth, but Japan's success in transforming the commodity composition accounts to a large extent for its subsequent export expansion. If it had persisted in exporting more traditional items, with stagnant demand, export prices would have had to be drastically lowered, leading to a deterioration of the terms of trade. This may, have led to the "immiserizing growth"[2] that the advocates of domestic development had feared.

2.2. Domestic Factors in the Changed Commodity Composition

Domestic circumstances provided the second reason for the need to change the composition of exports. Compared with other industrial nations, Japan had abundant labor but insufficient capital, and the interindustrial differences in wages were great. The products of low-wage industries enjoyed comparative advantages in export.[3]

---

[2] Immiserizing growth refers to the case where an exporting country is worse off after growth than before, because the deterioration of the terms of trade, resulting from export increase, exceeds the profit from increased productivity. See J. Bagwatish "Immiserizing Growth: A Geometrical Note," *Review of Economic Studies,* Vol. 25 (1958).

[3] There are two views on the relative importance of the effect of interindustrial wage differentials on trade composition. Taussig, MacDougall and Kravis deny the importance because the pattern of interindustrial differentials is similar from one nation to another. Forchheimer, Shinohara and Tsukuda emphasize the importance. Although the pattern is similar in all nations (high wage in chemicals and metals, low in clothing and spinning, etc.), the differen-

TABLE 10-9

Rates of Export Increase and Ratios of World Industrial Products in Exports
(Percent)

	Rates of Increase of Exports from Industrial Countries 1964/1955	Ratios in Exports, Industrial Countries		Japan		West Germany		U.K.		Italy		U.S.	
		1955	1964	1955	1964	1955	1964	1955	1964	1955	1964	1955	1964
Maximum export--growth goods. .	210	16	23	10	26	21	24	17	21	18	31	17	26
Large export--growth goods. .	147	29	34	9	15	33	41	32	39	26	30	42	42
Medium export--growth goods. .	94	14	13	17	15	16	13	15	14	22	15	13	12
Export static goods. .	76	30	24	43	37	22	18	25	20	26	20	22	16
Export stagnant goods	21	10	6	21	8	7	4	12	6	8	4	7	5

SOURCES: OECD, *Statistical Bulletins, Foreign Trade*, Series IV, 1955, and *Commodity Trade*, Series B, January-December, 1964; and UN, *Commodity Trade Statistics*, January-December, 1955. For the rates of increase (1964/1955) of the individual commodities, see *1966 Economic White Paper*, page 112.

TABLE 10-10

Shares of Selected Industrial Nations in
Exports of Industrial Products
(Percent)

	Industrial Products		Maximum Export-Growth Goods		Large Export-Growth Goods		Medium Export-Growth Goods		Export Static Goods		Export Stagnant Goods	
	1955	1964	1955	1964	1955	1964	1955	1964	1955	1964	1955	1964
Industrial nations.	100	100	100	100	100	100	100	100	100	100	100	100
Japan	5	8	3	9	2	4	6	9	7	12	10	11
West Germany.	11	19	20	20	17	23	17	19	11	14	11	14
Italy	3	6	4	8	3	6	5	7	3	5	3	5
Holland	4	5	6	7	2	3	4	6	4	4	5	5
Sweden.	3	3	2	3	2	3	2	2	4	6	2	2
Belgium and Luxembourg. . . .	6	6	3	3	3	5	6	7	9	9	10	12
France.	9	9	7	8	6	7	11	11	11	10	9	8
U.K.	19	13	19	12	20	15	20	14	15	11	22	14
U.S.	28	22	29	24	39	28	24	20	20	15	19	17

SOURCE: See Table 10-9.

As a result of subsequent economic growth, however, surplus labor was absorbed. The wage level in low-wage industries began to rise and interindustrial differentials narrowed. This reduced the advantage of low-wage industries, and it became imperative to shift production in favor of goods requiring advanced techniques and more capital.

This is evident from Table 10–11. Here 55 Japanese manufacturing industries are divided into 5 groups (11 industries in each group) according to the ratio of exports to production. The average wages, rates of wage increase, and rates of export increase are compared among groups. Naturally, some industries depend heavily on exports, others on the domestic market. In 1955, some of the industries exporting more than 50 percent of their production were matting, toys, sewing machines, clothing, and porcelain. Some of those catering almost exclusively to the domestic market and exporting less than 5 percent of production were plastics, business machinery, dynamos, motors, automobiles, and radios and TVs. Between these extreme groups, with an export ratio of approximately 10 percent, there were such items as bicycles, cement, chemical fertilizers, and iron and steel. If we examine, in Table 10–11, the relation between the amount of annual cash wages per worker and the degree of dependence on export, we find that in 1955 the average annual wage of group I industries (those most heavily dependent on exports) was ¥105,000, which is less than half the ¥216,000 of group V industries (those least dependent on exports). This suggests that low wages were important in determining the comparative advantage of Japanese industries in export trade (see Table 10–12). During the process of economic growth, the demand and supply of labor became more balanced, and

---

tials, in the case of Japan, were so great as to be significant (see Table 10–12); in 1956, the hourly wage in the Japanese clothing industry was one-twelfth that of the American figure; whereas the average for Japanese industries was only one-eighth that of the United States. We believe that such excessive wage differentials gave advantage to Japanese low-wage industries in export competition. See F. W. Taussig, *International Trade* (New York, 1927); I. B. Kravis, "Availability and other Influences on the Commodity Composition of Trade," *Economic Journal,* September, 1952; K. Forchheimer, "The Role of Relative Wage Differences in International Trade," *Quarterly Journal of Economics,* November, 1947; Miyohei Shinohara, *Shotokubunpai to Chinginkōzō (Income Distribution and Wage Structure)* (Tokyo: Iwanami Shoten, 1955); Chikao Tsukuda, "Chinginsuijun to Yushutsu" ("Wage Level and Export"), *Quarterly Economic Analysis* (issued by Economic Research Institute of Economic Planning Agency), No. 3 (1960).

For details, see Hisao Kanamori, *Nihon no Boeki (Japanese Trade),* Chap. 2, "Chinginkakusa to Yushutsukosei" ("Relative Wage Differentials and Export Composition") (Tokyo: Shiseido, 1965), Part II.

TABLE 10-11

Wages and Exports

Classification According to the Export Ratio of 1955	Export Ratio of 1955	Annual Cash Wage per Worker (Unit = Y10,000)			Rates of Increase of Imports (Percent)			Rates of Increase of Exports (Percent)			Ratio of Contribution to Export Increase (Percent)		
		1955	1960	1964	1955 -60	1960 -64	1955 -64	1955 -60	1960 -64	1955 -64	1955 -60	1960 -64	1955 -64
I. Industries most heavily dependent on exports.	44	10.5	15.1	25.9	7.5	14.4	10.6	12	4	8	32	10	20
II. Industries heavily dependent on exports	23	15.7	21.9	35.1	6.9	12.5	9.4	18	12	15	22	19	20
III. Industries moderately dependent on exports.	11	18.4	24.0	38.8	5.5	12.8	8.6	112	14	13	10	14	12
IV. Industries with little dependence on exports.	7	18.2	26.5	41.3	7.8	11.7	9.5	12	21	16	15	33	25
V. Industries least dependent on exports	4	21.6	26.8	42.0	4.4	11.9	7.7	51	21	37	22	24	23

SOURCE: Ministry of International Trade and Industry, Kōgyō Tōkeihyō (Census of Manufactures, 1955, 1960, and 1964, Tokyo. For iron and steel, figures in 1955 were abnormal due to U.S. steel strike; so 1954 data were used.

TABLE 10-12

International Comparison of Wage Differentials
(For 1956, Unit: Shilling per Hour)

	Japan	U.K.	U.S.	U.K. Japan	U.S. Japan
Clothing.	0.89	3.26	10.3	3.7	11.6
Textile	1.11	3.78	10.4	3.4	9.4
Lumber.	1.12	4.26	12.6	3.8	11.2
Leather	1.51	3.78	10.7	2.5	7.1
Foods	1.56	3.64	13.2	2.3	8.5
Metallic products	1.65	4.32	14.8	2.6	9.0
Machinery	2.03	4.60	15.5	2.8	7.6
Paper	2.08	4.70	13.9	2.3	6.7
Chemicals	2.34	4.45	15.0	1.9	6.4
Tobacco	2.44		10.3		4.3
Primary metals.	2.65	5.25	16.9	2.0	6.4
Average for all industries. .	1.80	4.32	14.2	2.4	7.9

SOURCE: For Japan, Labor Ministry, *Maigetsu Kinro Tokei*
(Monthly Labor Survey); for U.K. and U.S., ILO, *Yearbook of
Labour Statistics* (1957).
    The comparison between Japan and the United States was easy
because their industrial classifications were the same, but for
England, which has a different system of classification, *similar*
industries were compared.

by 1964, interindustrial wage-differentials narrowed considerably. The
average wage for group I was 60 percent of that for group V.

    The composition of Japanese exports underwent changes in re-
sponse to these domestic economic changes. The industries that depended most heavily on exports in 1955 have increased their exports
at the rate of only 8 percent per year, against a figure of 37 percent in
those industries that formerly depended least on exports. Nearly half
Japan's export increase between 1955 and 1964 occurred in industries
that had scarcely depended on exports in 1955. This indicates that
export growth was accompanied by a rapid compositional change—a
replacement of the traditional industries based on low wages by new,
more promising, industries.

3. *Is It an Export-Led Growth?*

    Increased competitive strength and a capacity for compositional
transformation, enabled Japan to increase its exports and simultane-

ously achieve a high rate of economic growth. Is its postwar economic growth a so-called "export-led growth"?[4] This term is used in many senses, but if we define it as the type of growth where (1) the primary autonomous stimulus to economic development comes from abroad and (2) exports rise in response to this stimulus, then Japan's economic growth is not an export-led type.[5] The causes of its export increase—increased competitive strength and a change in commodity composition—were made possible by domestic factors such as increased domestic investment and an enlarged home market.

We mentioned earlier that increased competitive strength was due to cost reduction resulting from increased labor productivity. Productivity increase, in turn, is closely related to an increase in the scale of output (see Table 10–7), presumably because a manufacturing industry whose production scale is rapidly expanding adopts new techniques and methods with higher productivity. The pressure for wage increases is always strong in any industrial economy, whether labor productivity is increasing or not. Unless the scale of production increases rapidly, unit labor costs tend to rise, thus reducing competitive strength in international trade. England is a case in point. In Japan, by contrast, an increasing scale of production, giving rise to improved labor productivity, has strengthened its competitive position.

The change of composition of exports too would have been impossible without the growth of domestic demand and investment. Japan's postwar economy is characterized by a remarkably rapid increase of investment, but the rate of increase differs considerably among industries. Among the 55 industries studied earlier, those in which fixed-capital formation increased sharply during 1955–64 comprise many of the new industries such as organic medicines, metal-processing machinery, automobiles, business machinery, and radios and TV. A number of traditional industries such as electric bulbs, cotton yarn and textiles, woolen yarn and textiles, lumber, porcelain, wood products, and footwear showed a low rate of increase. In Table 10–13, these industries are classified into five groups according to the rate of increase in equipment investment. The relation of this rate to the rates of increase in domestic demand, exports, and labor productivity (value added per worker) can be seen from the table. Although the order is reversed in groups III and IV, there is a

---

[4] This term was introduced by C. P. Kindleberger, *Foreign Trade and the National Economy* (New Haven, Conn.: Yale University Press, 1962), chap. 12.

[5] This definition was given by M. C. Kemp in the Conference discussion.

TABLE 10-13

Relations between Equipment Investment,
Domestic Demand, and Exports
(Average Annual Rate of Increase, 1955-64)

Classification According to the Rate of Increase in Equipment Investment	Equipment Investment	Rates of Increase (Percent)		
		Domestic Demand	Export	Labor Productivity in Value Added (Nominal)
I. Maximum investment-increase industries	39.9	26.9	21.1	12.3
II. Large investment-increase industries	27.3	19.7	19.1	10.5
III. Medium investment-increase industries	24.8	12.6	13.8	9.9
IV. Low investment-increase industries	19.8	15.1	17.8	10.3
V. Lowest investment-increase industries	12.5	9.1	4.5	7.4

tendency for the higher rates of investment increase to be associated with the higher rates of increase in domestic demand and exports. Significantly, in groups I and II, where investment increased the fastest, domestic demand grew faster than exports. This suggests that Japan's export growth was supported by growing domestic demand and investment. If the domestic demand for a product increases, it attracts new investment, and mass production reduces costs. This strengthens the competitive position of the product in the international market. The relation between investment increase and labor productivity (value added per worker) is shown in the right column of Table 10–13. In general, there is a positive relationship.

Similar correlations are observed when the 55 industries are classified into five groups according to the rate of increase of exports during 1955–64. High rates are observed in radios and TV (annual increase of 87 percent), business machinery (49 percent increase), automobiles (45 percent increase), and construction machinery (31 percent increase). Low rates are observed in many of the traditional industries such as tea (15 percent decrease), raw silk (7 percent decrease), lumber (3 percent decrease), cotton yarn (0.4 percent increase), rolling stock (1.7 percent increase), and cotton textiles (3.4 percent increase). Table 10–14 shows that the higher rates of export increase are associated with the higher rates of increase of investment and rates of increase of domestic demand. These correlations are particularly marked for the period 1955–60. Can we not conclude then that the expansion of domestic demand during this period stimulated mass production, which reduced costs, and led to the subsequent growth of export? New and fast-growing export commodities such as TV sets, automobiles, and construction machinery were not originally produced for export. Increased domestic demand strengthened their competitive position and enabled them to advance in the international market.

Table 10–15 shows the relative weight of the export and the domestic demand increase during 1955–64 for the 55 goods studied in Table 10–11. The goods are classified into four groups: I, goods with increasing domestic demand and increasing exports (both increasing at an annual rate of over 15 percent); II, export-centered goods (export increase rate in excess of 15 percent and domestic-demand increase rate below 10 percent); III, domestic-demand-centered goods (export increase rate below 10 percent and domestic-demand increase rate in excess of 15 percent); and IV, goods with stagnant domestic demand and exports (the rates for both below 10 percent). This table reveals the following points:

TABLE 10-14

Relation between Exports and Domestic Demand
(Annual Rate: Percent)

Classification According to the Export Ratio of 1955-64	Exports			Rate of Increase Domestic Demand			Investment		
	1955 -60	1960 -64	1955 -64	1955 -60	1960 -64	1955 -64	1955 -60	1960 -64	1955 -64
Export stagnant industries.	5	Δ3	1	11	9	10	17	12	15
Export static industries.	12	5	9	13	16	14	27	8	18
Medium export-growth industries	15	17	16	14	13	13	41	8	25
Large export-growth industries.	27	19	23	24	12	18	36	15	26
Maximum export-growth industries.	61	26	44	30	17	24	41	20	31

SOURCES: Ministry of Finance, *Nihon Boeki Geppyo* (Monthly Bulletin of Foreign Trade Statistics) and Ministry of International Trade and Industry, *Kogyo Tokeihyo* (Census of Manufactures, 1955, 1960, and 1964, Tokyo). For details of industrial classification, see *1966 Economic White Paper*, page 212.

TABLE 10-15

Classification of Goods According to the
Rates of Increase of Exports and Domestic Demand
(Annual Rate for 1955-64)

I. Goods with increasing domestic demand and increasing exports
                        (Export   rate > 15 percent
                        Domestic demand   rate > 15 percent)

Radios and TV sets	Metal-processing machinery
Business machinery	Watches
Pulp and paper manufacturing	Dynamos and electric motor
machinery	Motors
Automobiles	Optical instruments
Bearings	Inorganic chemicals
Sporting goods	Wooden products
Plastics	Metallic products
Organic medicines	Artificial and synthetic fibers
Insulated electric wire	Textile machinery
Oil products	Lace
Tile	
Pump	

II. Export-centered goods
                        (Export   rate > 15 percent
                        Domestic demand   rate < 10 percent)

Footwear

III. Domestic-demand-centered goods
                        (Export   rate < 10 percent
                        Domestic demand   rate > 15 percent)

Sewing machines	Aluminum
Porcelain	Rolling stock
Veneer	Precious stones

IV. Goods with stagnant domestic demand and stagnant exports
                        (Export   rate < 10 percent
                        Domestic demand   rate < 10 percent)

Woolen textiles	Cotton yarn
Chemical fertilizers	Raw silk
Cotton textiles	Tea
Cement	

NOTE: See also Table 10-11.

First, 23 items, around 40 percent of the total studied, belong to group I. Many, though not all, are products of heavy and chemical industries such as machinery and chemicals.

Second, group IV also contains a fairly large number of items, many of which are traditional products such as woolen yarn and textiles, raw silk, and tea.

Third, only one item, footwear, belongs to group III.

Thus the case of a stagnant domestic demand coupled with increasing exports is rare. Increased exports, after the war, of rubber-soled shoes and sandals for the American market accounts for this one item, but in terms of monetary value it is insignificant. In most cases, the expansion of domestic demand was at the root of export growth.

Once the expansion of domestic demand and investment begins to promote exports, a kind of circular action begins. An industry whose market was enlarged through growing exports attracts more investment and thus strengthens its competitive position. This is suggested by the figures in Table 10–16. Although the correlation is not perfect, there is a general tendency that, in industries with growing exports, both capital shares and productivity increased rapidly. This indicates that these industries enjoyed a favorable circle; they attracted new capital, which raised productivity and led to further growth in exports.

TABLE 10-16

Rates of Increase of Wages, Capital Shares and Productivity
(Annual Rate for 1955-64: Percent)

Classification According to the Rate of Increase of Exports during 1955-64	Cash Wages per Worker	Productivity (Value Added per Worker)	Capital Shares
I. Export stagnant industries. . .	9.3	8.0	Δ0.7
II. Export static industries. . . .	9.9	8.6	Δ0.7
III. Medium export-growth industries	9.0	9.8	0.5
IV. Large export-growth industries.	8.3	10.8	3.3
V. Maximum export-growth industries.	7.8	10.4	1.0

SOURCE: Ministry of International Trade and Industry, *Kogyo Tokeyiho* (Census of Manufacturing).

IV. SUMMARY AND CONCLUSION

Contrary to the pessimistic view that had been held about Japan's capacity to increase its exports after the war, a spectacular growth in exports has been achieved. This was partly due to the favorable trends of the world economy, but a more important reason was Japan's success in changing its commodity composition of exports and fostering new export industries while gaining strength in international price competition. The composition of Japanese exports immediately after World War II had been shaped by the old demand pattern and the abundant labor which then characterized the Japanese economy. Since then, the world demand pattern and the balance between demand and supply of labor in Japan underwent great changes. Without a successful adaptation of export composition to these external and internal changes, Japan could not have attained its rapid growth of exports.

Yet, despite this remarkable increase in exports, Japan's economic growth is not a so-called export-led growth, since domestic factors played important parts in sustaining the export increase. As a result of economic growth, domestic demand increased; this encouraged investment and helped to foster new export industries capable of competing in the international market. Once a new export commodity begins to sell well, it attracts new investment of capital. In the light of this growth pattern, both the development method and the trade method proposed immediately after the war seem to have been one-sided. High-economic growth prompted a compositional change which led to increased exports, which, in turn, accelerated economic growth. This favorable circle provides a key to the understanding of Japan's high economic growth rate.[6]

---

[6] I am grateful to Messrs. Saburo Kawanishi, Masaaki Kusakabe and Tadaaki Ito, staff members of the Research Section, Economic Planning Agency, for their assistance in preparing the tables for this paper. Tables 10–7, 10–9, 10–10, 10–11, and 10–16 are taken from the *1966 Economic White Paper*, Part II, Section 3. For details of classified commodities, etc., see *1966 Economic White Paper*, pp. 210–13.

11 | The Financing of the Public Sector in Postwar Japan*

HUGH T. PATRICK

Resource allocation at the macro level is a major concern of government fiscal policy in Japan as in other nations. Three interrelated types of resource allocation problems may be distinguished. One is to ensure that labor and capital resources are fully used—the compensatory finance problem of balancing aggregate demand with full capacity supply consonant with price level stability objectives. While primarily a business cycle problem it also has implications for growth.

A second problem is to determine and provide for the proper allocation of resources between the public sector and the private sector. Essentially it involves the tradeoff between the provision of public goods and private goods. Related to this, third, is the problem of the allocation of resources between consumption and investment. This is essentially the issue of the optimum rate of growth. The government influences not only private consumption, saving, and investment but, of course, determines the rate of public consumption, saving, and investment. The government has a variety of instruments to implement its policies—taxation, expenditures (on goods and services, and on transfer payments), and borrowing and lending.

The purpose of this paper is to focus on the somewhat more narrow problem of financing of the government sector in postwar Japan, and particularly external financing, rather than directly examining these broad issues. Nonetheless, the analysis is predicated upon this broader policy framework, and will tackle various facets of the broader problems, albeit from occasionally indirect approaches. The main emphasis

* I wish to thank Ohara Kenichiro for research assistance and the Guggenheim Foundation for financial support of this research.

326

is on net relationships—government investment and its financing—with little discussion of government transfer payments or current purchases of goods and services.

I first present and discuss the data on public sector investment and its financing. Following a brief excursion into intragovernmental financing, I turn to certain contemporary policy issues emanating from the government's investment program and its financing. Throughout I use the Japanese national income definition of the government sector, which includes central and local (prefectural and municipal) governments and, at each level, general government and government enterprise. "Government" is thus synonymous with "public sector," though in terms of policy making it refers mainly to the central level. Less use is made of the Ministry of Finance legalistically motivated budget classification of general account, special accounts, and government corporations, since they involve considerable overlapping and duplication on a nonconsolidated basis. The new national income estimates are used wherever possible.[1] Data are in current prices, unless otherwise noted.

I

As indicated in Table 11–1, government investment has grown rapidly in the postwar period (increasing eightfold between 1952–65, and about five times in real terms), with some cyclical and erratic fluctuation. Moreover, the investment share in the government's total purchase of goods and services has risen dramatically from 39 percent in 1952 to approximately 53 percent in the mid-1960's. Because GNP and gross domestic investment have also grown rapidly and with cyclical swings, the share of government investment in them has been rather more stable. Since 1957, however, the trend of the government investment/GNP ratio has been strikingly upward, rising from 6.7 percent to 10.7 percent.

For the postwar period as a whole private aggregate demand, based on booming private fixed-investment demand, has been sufficiently strong that the government has not needed to use compensatory fiscal policy to generate demand through deficit spending. Consequently, public sector demand for resources has been competitive with private demand. The exceptions have been the recession periods of 1954, 1957–58, 1962, and 1965, but these represent deliberate restrictions of aggregate demand to restore balance-of-payments equilibrium.

---

[1] As published in Economic Planning Agency, *Annual Report on National Income Statistics, 1966* (Tokyo, 1966).

TABLE 11-1

Government Gross Investment and Saving
(Current Prices, Amounts in Billion Yen)

Calendar Year	Investment (I)					Savings (S)					I-S
	Amount	Annual Rate Increase	% Govt. Purchase Goods and Services	% GNP	% Gross Investment	Amount	Annual Rate Increase	% Govt. Revenues	% GNP	% Gross Saving	
1952	398.8	---	38.8	6.6	25.0	527.4	---	40.4	8.7	33.0	-128.6
1953	525.2	31.7	41.3	7.5	32.4	480.7	-8.9	33.4	6.9	29.6	44.5
1954	595.2	13.3	41.7	7.6	31.6	458.4	-4.6	29.2	5.9	24.4	136.8
1955	747.9	25.7	45.7	8.8	34.0	464.6	1.4	28.2	5.4	21.2	283.3
1956	666.7	-10.9	42.1	7.0	24.7	619.3	33.3	33.9	6.5	23.0	47.4
1957	742.3	11.3	42.6	6.7	20.6	848.3	37.0	39.3	7.7	23.6	-106.0
1958	891.2	20.1	44.4	7.9	27.3	714.2	-15.8	31.5	6.3	21.9	177.0
1959	1,080.2	21.2	47.7	8.4	26.6	898.7	25.8	35.7	7.0	22.1	181.4
1960	1,294.4	19.8	49.4	8.5	24.1	1,301.1	44.7	41.5	8.6	24.3	- 6.7
1961	1,532.0	18.4	49.7	8.3	21.1	1,786.3	37.3	45.5	9.7	24.7	-254.3
1962	2,085.4	36.1	53.7	10.0	27.4	1,971.8	10.4	44.2	9.5	25.9	113.6
1963	2,353.2	12.8	52.3	10.0	28.6	2,156.7	9.4	41.8	9.2	26.2	196.5
1964	2,692.5	14.4	52.8	9.7	26.0	2,106.4	-2.3	35.6	7.6	20.3	586.1
1965	3,219.4	19.6	52.5	10.7	31.3	2,359.6	12.0	36.3	7.8	22.2	859.8

NOTE: Saving includes central and local government enterprise capital consumption allowances.

SOURCE: Economic Planning Agency, *Annual Report on National Income Statistics, 1966* (Tokyo, 1966); and *National Accounts Statistics Quarterly*, No. 12 (July, 1966).

The government reaction to the public-private competition in the use of resources at full-capacity levels and rates of growth of output has been, at least until 1963, to give top priority to the private sector, notably business fixed investment. This was a major feature of the government's great emphasis on the goal of economic growth relative to other objectives.[2] Government total purchases of goods and services as a proportion of GNP (17–19 percent) did not display any rising trend, unlike that in many other industrial nations. The government also encouraged by fiscal and financial means the relative shift within the private sector from personal consumption to business investment, in order to promote growth.[3]

Given the vigorous private investment demand, government expenditure policy thus contributed to the growth process in three major ways. First, as noted above, public sector expenditures were not a particularly large proportion of GNP, nor did they grow more rapidly than the growth of aggregate demand. Second, government consumption expenditures decreased and government investment expenditures increased relative to GNP and to each other. Third, until recently government investment was allocated in large part to areas complementary to private investment and production of goods and services, rather than to the provision of public facilities for consumers—such as housing, urban water and sewage systems, and roads. In other words, the government restricted its own consumption and investment expenditures for the provision of public consumption goods more than it restricted private investment and production of consumer goods.

A further implication of strong private aggregate demand and of the government's policy to give it high priority was that the government had to finance its own investment by the least demand-creating method. Governments can pay for their gross investment (and other expenditures) by fiscal means through internal financing (gross saving) or by financial means through external borrowing from households, private financial institutions, the central bank, or from abroad. Government saving out of tax and nontax revenues is the least demand-creating method, followed in order by borrowing from indi-

---

[2] I do not consider here the welfare implications of this policy; some Japanese economists, notably Professor Ryutaro Komiya, apparently feel that the output mix should have included more public services even at the expense of a somewhat slower growth rate.

[3] The expansive monetary policy of the Bank of Japan (with full governmental support) at the least abetted private investment demand, and was instrumental in allowing it to be made effective.

viduals, from financial institutions, and from the central bank.[4] In Japan, the domestic demand effect of government foreign borrowing is the same as borrowing from the Bank of Japan, since the government converts the foreign exchange received into yen by selling either the foreign exchange or foreign exchange bills to the central bank.

As is clear from Tables 11–1 and 11–2, in Japan the government has relied heavily on its own saving to finance its investment (I).[5] In the early postwar years, government saving was greater than investment; inflation came not from government expenditures but from the central bank-financed lending of government financial institutions. Thereafter government investment has grown more rapidly than government saving. Indeed, the overall public sector has been in a deficit position since 1962, and the gap between government saving and investment has been widening substantially. Both saving and investment are highly influenced by the business cycle. Government saving has risen rapidly in boom periods because government revenues increased more than expected and therefore more than budgeted current account expenditures. Thus, as indicated in Table 11–2, the I–S gap disappeared in the late stages of the 1955–57 and 1959–61 booms, and increased in recession. The 1964 experience is significant in that the I–S gap widened rather than narrowed. Cumulatively, government saving financed 88.7 percent of government investment between 1952–65, but declined to 83.0 percent for 1962–65.

An extremely important reason for this high share of internal financing despite rapid growth of investment is that the government's tax system is highly elastic relative to the growth of GNP.[6] This has enabled the government to follow simultaneously several politically attractive courses: regular tax rate reductions and increases in ex-

---

[4] If we assume that any increase in aggregate demand from the financing of government investment in a full-resource employment economy tends to increase private demand relative to public and to increase total consumption relative to investment, then this same sequence applies to these allocations as well.

[5] Government saving consists of the surplus on current account (tax and nontax revenues including government enterprise profits less current purchases of goods and services, subsidies, and transfer payments) and capital consumption allowances of government enterprise.

[6] It is difficult to obtain precise elasticity estimates, since the government changes tax rates virtually every year. Ishi estimates a weighted average elasticity to national income of direct taxes of 1.58 and indirect taxes of 0.990; cf., Ishi Hiromitsu, "Sozei Danryokusei no Ichi Keisoku" (A Measurement of Tax Elasticity), *Hitotsubashi Ronso*, Vol. 52, No. 5 (November, 1964). In addition, income has shifted relatively to corporate business, which has a higher tax rate.

TABLE 11-2

Government Investment-Savings Gap
(Current Prices, Amounts in Billion Yen)

Calendar Year	National Income Estimate I-S	National Income Estimate I-S / I	Flow of Funds Estimate* I-S	Discrepancy Amount	Discrepancy % of I
1954.	136.8	23.0%	165.5	-28.7	-4.8
1955.	283.3	37.9	183.9	99.4	13.3
1956.	47.4	7.1	- 8.7	56.1	8.4
1957.	-106.0	-14.3	- 98.5	- 7.5	-1.0
1958.	177.0	19.9	25.0	152.0	17.1
1959.	181.4	16.8	78.4	103.0	9.5
1960.	- 6.7	- 0.5	-102.5	95.8	7.4
1961.	-254.3	-16.6	-192.5	-61.8	-4.0
1962.	113.6	5.4	180.4	-66.8	-3.2
1963.	196.5	8.4	288.0	-91.5	-3.9
1964.	586.1	21.8	639.1	-53.0	-2.0
1965.	859.8	26.7	872.1	-12.3	-0.4

*Net financial surplus or deficit.

NOTE: Complete flow of funds data are available only on a calendar year basis, and only from 1954.

SOURCES: Table 11-1 and Bank of Japan flow of funds data, adjusted as indicated in notes to Table 11-3.

emptions; increases in current expenditures; increases in investment; and little obvious increase in borrowing (until 1966). The government's propensity to save out of its actual current revenue (T) has been high, despite reductions in tax rates. A simple least squares regression using the new national income data for 1954–64 provides the following results:

$$S = 6.267 + 0.3974T \qquad R^2 = .911$$
$$(0.0375) \qquad d = 1.060.$$

In other words, the government's marginal propensity to save is almost 40 percent, after taking tax reductions into account.

Thus, between 1952–65, only 11.3 percent of government investment had to be financed from external sources. In other words, the government relied only to this extent on the net voluntary transfer of claims on resources from outside the public sector. The amount and degree of external financing are measured by the investment-savings gap in the first two columns of Table 11–2.[7] Two points should be made. First, consolidated at all levels the government has been a net borrower continuously (with cyclical exceptions only) since 1952. Second, the amount of government borrowing has been rising sharply since 1962, culminating in the 1965 decision to sell new issues of government debentures to households and financial institutions starting in early 1966. This more recent trend is clearly related to the increased share of government investment in GNP.

One way to estimate government reliance on external borrowing is to regress the net issue of government securities (Y) on government investment and saving:

$$Y = a_0 + a_1 I + a_2 S \, .$$

Two estimates were made. The first (Y_1) had as the dependent variable net long-term bond issues (mainly local governments and government corporations), while the second (Y_2) included in addition central government short-term bills. The results were:

$$Y_1 = -50.685 + .0932 \, I + .02943 \, S \qquad R^2 = .860$$
$$ (.0494) \quad (.0535) \qquad\quad d = 2.45$$
$$Y_2 = -8.566 + .6932 \, I - .7038 \, S \qquad R^2 = .695$$
$$ (.1746) \quad (.1894) \qquad\quad d = 2.43.$$

The coefficients in the first equation are not really significant, especially for S, despite the good fit. The sign for S seems wrong. This, however, may be explained by the tendency for investment by local government and government enterprise, together with the bond issues to finance the investment, to grow most rapidly in a boom, when S also is growing rapidly, and to slow down together with S in a recession.

The second equation looks much better. However, S and I are highly correlated and have virtually the same coefficients; this equation really indicates that government security issue increases by 0.7 times the increase in the I–S gap. But the implied causal relationship is probably spurious. Most of the change in government security issue is in short-term bills. At the height of a boom the I–S gap narrows (Table 11–2) because of the officially unanticipated increase in saving. Coincidentally the government loses foreign exchange reserves

---

[7] The flow of funds data, which provide an alternative estimate of the I–S gap from the net financial deficit of the public sector, underestimate the gap relative to the national income data for earlier years, but overestimate for 1961–64. It is unclear as to which is the better estimate; fortunately, the divergence has been decreasing.

due to balance-of-payments problems; it can therefore reduce its foreign exchange bill sales to the Bank of Japan. The opposite happens both to saving and to foreign reserves in a recession.

The external sources of the financing of government investment are estimated from flow of funds data, and appear in Table 11–3. Of the cumulative total borrowed by the government between 1954–65, 74.2 percent came from the private sector, 34.4 percent from the Bank of Japan (mainly in 1964), and −8.6 percent from abroad (i.e., the government was a net foreign lender). Within the private sector the government borrowed on a net basis from households and financial institutions, while lending to corporate business.

Government borrowing from the Bank of Japan is measured by direct transactions.[8] Hence, government borrowing from the private sector which is in effect financed by central bank credit to the private sector is excluded. (It would be fruitless to include it, since in that case all government domestic borrowing could be regarded as central bank financed). Government direct reliance on central bank credit has been short-term, relatively small, and seasonal or cyclical in nature. The government is legally restricted in its borrowing from the Bank of Japan to short-term bills. Much of the borrowing has been to finance increases in government purchases of domestically produced rice; this seasonal phenomenon results in increased net borrowing on a calendar year basis in years of good rice crops. The government was able to pile up sufficient liquidity during 1960–62 from the small I-S gaps and increasing net borrowings from the private sector that it could finance its own activities and pay off bills held by the Bank of Japan as they matured. In 1964 it financed the sharply widening I-S gap by increased bill sales to the Bank of Japan, but in 1965 relied primarily upon funds from the private sector (mainly postal savings and public corporation and local government bond issue).

I was surprised to find that the government has been a net foreign lender rather than borrower. I estimate that the government's net foreign debt has declined from about ¥184 billion ($501 million) at the end of 1953 to ¥13 billion ($40 million) at the end of 1965.[9] On a gross basis the central government, a few local governments (Tokyo,

---

[8] Government foreign exchange holdings and their financing are consolidated with the Bank of Japan sector in order to focus on government borrowing for purposes other than holding foreign exchange.

[9] The foreign borrowing estimates are the least reliable, though I regard them as reasonably accurate. The Bank of Japan does not make available sectoral foreign asset and liability stock figures, though some flow data are published.

TABLE 11-3

External Sources of Government Finance, 1954-1965
(Billion Yen)

	1954	1955	1956	1957	1958	1959	1960	1961	1962	1963	1964	1965
From private sector (A)	77.5	20.5	59.1	23.3	- 37.1	- 18.9	25.1	31.0	169.5	256.3	187.8	712.0
Households												
Receipts from. . .	143.9	140.7	175.2	181.2	176.5	238.3	272.0	294.9	391.1	396.0	467.0	655.8
Loans to	59.7	36.6	51.0	66.8	89.8	84.8	90.0	103.2	120.2	114.2	150.9	158.3
Net	84.2	104.1	124.2	114.4	86.7	153.5	182.0	191.7	270.9	281.8	316.1	497.5
Corporate business												
Receipts from. . .	2.9	3.9	- 5.1	2.7	16.9	10.8	33.3	53.1	79.8	74.2	73.6	60.4
Loans to	102.1	90.3	84.9	122.3	124.0	147.8	166.4	210.5	267.6	285.0	418.9	425.9
Net	-99.2	-86.4	-90.0	-119.6	-107.1	-137.0	-133.1	-157.4	-187.8	-210.8	-345.3	-365.5
Financial institutions												
Receipts from. . .	50.9	56.1	68.1	48.2	29.1	50.2	94.3	128.3	144.0	267.8	302.6	586.0
Loans to	-41.6	53.3	43.2	19.7	45.8	85.6	118.1	131.6	57.6	82.5	85.6	6.0
Net	92.5	2.8	24.9	28.5	- 16.7	- 35.4	- 23.8	- 3.3	86.4	185.3	217.0	580.0
From Bank of Japan (B)	170.7	261.8	-74.4	-146.0	77.1	120.6	-117.6	-220.1	- 19.6	20.2	444.3	181.4
From abroad (C). . .	-82.7	-98.4	6.6	24.2	- 15.0	- 23.3	- 10.0	- 3.4	- 30.5	11.5	7.0	- 21.3
Total (A + B + C). . .	165.5	183.9	- 8.7	- 98.5	25.0	78.4	-102.5	-192.5	180.4	288.0	639.1	872.1

NOTE: The government sector includes central and local government, government enterprises, and government finan-cial institutions, but excludes government holdings of foreign exchange and coin production (both of which are con-solidated into the Bank of Japan sector).

SOURCE: Based on Bank of Japan flow of funds data plus Ministry of Local Autonomy worksheet data on local government loans and equity to private business corporations.

Osaka), and government agencies (Japan Development Bank, Nippon Telephones & Telegraph Public Corporation) have borrowed long-term funds abroad by loans from the World Bank, and the U.S. Export-Import Bank, and by bond issues. Concomitantly the central government and its agencies have lent long-term even more abroad, mainly loans by the Export-Import Bank of Japan (which increased by ¥508 billion—$1,411 million—between the ends of 1953 and 1965) and subscriptions to such international organizations as the International Monetary Fund (IMF), World Bank, and International Development Association (IDA).

The net flows between government and the private sector summarize and mask somewhat the much larger gross flows, which are extensive and complicated. The government, in addition to its current spending, investing, and saving activities, is a large financial intermediary, operating through a variety of government financial institutions. In some items it may be possible to trace government borrowing directly to those units engaging in government investment; examples are debentures sold by central government public corporations to financial institutions and to individuals and business corporations using their services, and local government bond sales to and loans from financial institutions. Most, however, become mingled with other funds and pass through several intermediaries before investment expenditures actually occur.

The most notable example is individual postal savings and post-office annuities and life insurance. These net flows are the largest single and most routine source of government borrowing. The administrative procedure is to mingle the postal savings with other funds administered by the Trust Fund Bureau. These funds, along with postal annuity and life insurance funds, welfare pension taxes, and others, are then used to finance the government's Investment and Loan Program. The program consists of transfers to local governments and central government enterprise activities by means of loans and bond purchase, and loans to the private sector through government financial institutions and bond purchase.

However, there is a surprisingly close correlation between the net flow of postal savings, annuities and life insurance (P) and net government loans (L) to corporate (and to a lesser extent unincorporated) enterprise.

Using 1954–64 flow of funds data,

$$L = -64.3 + 1.19\,P \qquad R^2 = .9106$$
$$(0.0155) \qquad d = 1.524.$$

This implies that government lending activity depends mainly upon the inflow of postal savings and life insurance; of course campaigns to encourage postal deposits may have been geared to lending programs. The statistical relationship suggests that Ministry of Finance decision makers employ, perhaps not explicitly, some such rule-of-thumb criterion in preparing the Investment and Loan Program. If so, then government financial intermediation is separated from the operation of fiscal policy. We might also note that since government financial institutions lend primarily to big business, in this way saving of small savers is channeled on a preferential basis to large-scale enterprises.

As indicated in Table 11–3, the government is a net borrower from households and private financial institutions and a net lender to corporate business. Relative to its total net cumulative borrowings (including credit from the Bank of Japan) between 1954–65, the government's gross borrowings from households was 160.2 percent and from financial institutions 82.8 percent, while its gross credit to corporate business was 110.9 percent. In other words, the government borrowed considerably more for purposes of relending than for financing its own investment. On a gross basis the central government sold virtually none of its bills or bonds to the private sector; it was legally restricted in its bond issue, and kept its bill rate uncompetitively low since it could rely upon their purchase by the Bank of Japan. The most important flows between private and government sectors have been postal savings and life insurance, public corporation and local government bond issues, government loans to business, and govern-purchase of bank bonds.

Analysis of the effects of government financial intermediation on the amount of private saving and on the composition of the total allocation of investment funds is beyond the scope of this paper. We may note that the net increase between 1954–65 in government loans to corporate enterprise and households was only 11.8 percent of the loan increase by private financial institutions. Government loans have been concentrated, however, in relatively few industries; for example, the electric power industry received 35 percent of its loans from the Japan Development Bank, the shipping industry (probably the most unprofitable industry in postwar Japan) 57 percent, and coal mining (another sick industry) some 39 percent.

II

Thus far I have treated the government as a single homogeneous unit. In terms of the locus of decision making on tax, expenditure, and financial policies this is reasonable, since the central government strongly influences, if it does not actually determine, local government policies as well as those of government enterprises. Much of the power on these matters is concentrated in the Ministry of Finance.

An important reason for such concentration of power at the central level is the imbalance between expenditures and internal sources of financing of local governments and government enterprises. While in aggregate the public sector may finance most of its investment from its own saving, when disaggregated into the four components of the public sector (central general government, local general government, central government enterprise, local government enterprise) only the central general government has had a large surplus of revenues over expenditures. Local general governments have excess expenditures, and both central and local government enterprise investment has grown more rapidly than has their internal generation of funds. The intragovernmental financing problems that hence arise may be considered in terms of the central-local and general government-government enterprise relationships.

The drastic central-local government revenue-expenditure imbalance is clear from the data in Table 11–4.[10] More detailed data on the level of government investment and their sources of financing are provided in Table 11–5.[11] The central government engages in 40–45 percent of total public sector investment, but finances 55–60 percent of it.[12] These are net flows; gross flows are even larger since local governments finance portions of certain central government investment projects. More important, central government financing is underestimated since certain tax receipts which actually were collected at the central level are attributed to local governments.

As is implicit in Table 11–4, local governments finance only approximately half their consolidated expenditures from within. Their need for external funds is great. Most come from the central govern-

---

[10] The national income statistics are inadequate for this breakdown because they attribute to the central government much investment actually done at local levels. I calculate central government investment in the old national income statistics to be overestimated by approximately 45–50 percent, with a corresponding underestimate of local government investment. The underestimate in the new national income statistics is about 35–40 percent.

[11] Percentages for investment by central government differ slightly from Table 11–4 because inventory investment is excluded and there are slight differences in coverage.

[12] This tends to understate the flows from central to local government, since central government enterprise investment is large and is financed at the central level. For general (nonenterprise) government investment, the central government does about 23 percent and finances about 46 percent.

TABLE 11-4

Share of Central Government in Total Government
Revenues and Expenditures
(In Percent of Total)

Fiscal Year	Revenues	Expendi- tures	Purchase of All Goods and Services	Invest- ment
1952.	73.6	41.5	35.5	39.7
1953.	71.8	42.0	36.5	34.8
1954.	70.8	41.4	36.2	31.3
1955.	70.2	51.9	44.9	49.3
1956.	71.9	49.2	41.7	41.0
1957.	71.9	50.0	41.8	40.2
1958.	71.7	48.7	41.2	40.7
1959.	72.0	50.6	43.0	43.2
1960.	72.6	50.3	42.1	41.9
1961.	73.0	50.6	42.6	42.3
1962.	71.8	49.7	42.0	40.8
1963.	71.6	47.8	39.5	41.2
Cumulative average .	72.0	48.6	41.0	41.1

NOTE: Including government enterprise saving and investment.
SOURCE: My work sheets from forthcoming study on the public
sector in postwar Japan. Expenditures (notably the investment
component) are adjusted to the level of government where they
actually occurred.

ment, through a complex variety of channels. In brief, they are:[13]
automatic allotment of specified percentages of certain taxes collected
at the central level;[14] central government grants for specified local
expenditures, such as compulsory education, health facilities, and
disaster relief; central government loans and purchases of local government bond issues (mainly from Trust Fund Bureau and postal annuity
and life insurance funds), usually related to specific investment
projects; and bond sales to and loans from the private sector and from
abroad. Only a few large municipalities and prefectures have sufficiently high-credit ratings to be able to issue bonds publicly.

The separation of functions—with the central government collect-

---

[13] Ministry of Home Affairs, *The Local Finance System in Japan,* n.d.
(1965).

[14] 28.9 percent of personal income, corporation and liquor taxes. Allotment,
while automatic to local governments as a group, is discretionary for individual
local units, depending on their financial needs and local tax base.

TABLE 11-5

Gross Fixed Investment Expenditures and Its Financing
by Level of Government
(Percent of Total)

Fiscal Year	*Share*	*Central*	*Prefec- ture*	*Munici- pality*
1958.	Investment by	39.9	30.6	29.5
	Financed by	56.5	19.8	23.7
1959.	Investment by	42.3	30.6	27.1
	Financed by	58.7	20.0	21.3
1960.	Investment by	42.3	31.1	26.6
	Financed by	58.0	21.9	20.9
1961.	Investment by	46.2	29.8	24.0
	Financed by	59.8	21.0	19.2
1962.	Investment by	41.4	33.6	25.0
	Financed by	55.4	24.3	20.3
1963.	Investment by	44.0	31.2	24.8
	Financed by	57.1	22.7	20.2

NOTE: Includes government enterprise, which is financed primarily at same level of government. Central government financing
is probably underestimated.

SOURCE: Computed from Jichicho (Ministry of Local Autonomy),
Todōfukenbetsu Gyōsei Tōshi Jisseki Chōsa Hōkoku (Report on the
Actual Results of Administrative Investment by Prefecture) (Tokyo,
1963 and 1965 issues), plus adjustments for excluded central government enterprise investment.

ing most of the taxes and the local government doing most of the purchases of goods and services (including investment)—poses some
interesting issues of efficiency. I am not aware of studies of the relative
efficiency (cost, degree of evasion, etc.) of collection of different kinds
of taxes at various levels of government, or of the relative efficiency
of different types of expenditures. I hypothesize that the central
government is more efficient in collection of most kinds of taxes, due
to economies of scale and the advantages of having identical rates
throughout the country. For expenditures the picture is much less
clear, depending greatly on the type of expenditure.

Efficiency is not the sole, nor necessarily the most important, criterion for evaluating central-local relationships. Clearly political and
social objectives loom heavily (for example, the desired degree of de-
centralized governmental decision making, or of voter identification
with and participation in local politics). Whatever may have been
early postwar reform objectives, the degree of actual fiscal dependence

of local on central government severely circumscribes the independent power and decision-making ability at the local level.

While central government revenue surpluses have been used to pay for local government expenditures, they also have gone in large part to finance investment by central and local government enterprises. Indeed, except for 1953–55 and again in 1965 (reflecting the policy of deficit spending to pull the economy out of recession), the general government has generated a fairly large saving surplus (Table 11–6).[15] On the other hand, government enterprise investment has grown rapidly, far beyond their depreciation allowances. More than three quarters of government enterprise investment has been growth oriented, in areas complementary to private investment—notably transport, communications, electricity, and industrial water. In other than recession years, the general government surplus of saving over its investment was sufficient to cover the government enterprise gap of investment in excess of saving. This pattern ended, as we know also from Table 11–2, in the boom following the 1962 recession. The locus of the public sector *I-S* gap which has developed since then has clearly been in the large government enterprise investment program.

III

The events of the past few years—the relative rise in government investment, the greater relative decline in private demand (as business fixed investment demand first leveled off, and then declined somewhat, as a percent of GNP), the increased reliance by government on borrowing to pump-prime and to finance government investment, and the lowering of interest rates—attest to the changes evolving in public-private sector relationships. While some of these represent new trends and new problems, some probably are of only a temporary nature, and certain old problems are likely to come once again to the fore. In this section I consider three policy issues: the major questions of the financing of future government investment and of interest rate policy, and the lesser issue of whether the public or private sector is entitled to the initial claim on resources generated from expansion of central bank credit. My time horizon is on the order of five to eight years.

---

[15] This is true no matter how government enterprise profits are treated. It could be argued that for purity's sake general government revenues from government enterprise should include only that portion (roughly one-half) that is equivalent to corporate taxes and dividend payments, with the remainder being included in government enterprise saving.

TABLE 11-6

Gross Investment and Saving, General
Government and Government Enterprise
(Billion Yen)

Fiscal Year	General Government			Government Enterprise			Reference: Government Enterprise Profits†
	I	S	S-I	I	S*	S-I	
1951	231.5	501.3	269.8	114.7	39.7	- 75.0	
1952	310.6	431.7	121.1	148.9	57.1	- 91.8	
1953	425.5	389.4	-36.1	164.1	66.7	- 97.4	
1954	427.7	373.3	-54.4	155.8	69.5	- 86.3	
1955	375.0	364.2	-10.8	338.7	82.9	- 255.8	11.4
1956	395.2	588.9	193.7	222.0	86.7	- 135.3	23.3
1957	495.3	750.1	254.8	317.7	96.7	- 221.0	80.3
1958	559.7	653.7	94.0	384.7	104.7	- 280.0	101.2
1959	661.7	867.3	205.6	448.3	113.1	- 335.2	82.5
1960	798.6	1,304.4	505.8	516.9	123.5	- 393.4	142.2
1961	1,015.8	1,766.3	750.5	701.1	169.6	- 531.5	208.8
1962	1,318.5	1,791.7	473.2	874.1	172.8	- 701.3	143.7
1963	1,453.2	1,988.9	535.7	994.2	202.0	- 792.2	197.9
1964	1,684.5	2,035.9	351.4	1,105.2	251.4	- 853.8	53.6
1965	1,959.2	1,889.9	-69.3	1,512.4	268.2	-1,244.2	

*Capital consumption allowances only; see notes below.

†Excluding Japan Monopoly Corporation profits transferred as general account revenues.

NOTES: Government enterprise profits are included in general government revenues (and hence saving) in order to provide data for more years. Attribution of part or all of these profits to government enterprise does not alter the underlying pattern.

SOURCES: Economic Planning Agency, *Annual Report on National Income Statistics, 1966* (Tokyo, 1966); and *National Account Statistics Quarterly*, No 13 (September, 1966). 1965 investment divi- sion and capital consumption allowances are rough estimates based on 1963-64 ratios.

A basic assumption is that the share of government investment in GNP (and in gross domestic investment) will continue to rise somewhat. The lag in government social overhead investment has produced a strong pent-up demand for public provision of certain consumer services which is being reflected through the political process.[16] These pressures are likely to remain extremely strong for at least another five years. They will induce a considerable shift in the allocation of investment from private production of goods and services to public production. Let us examine the nature of these pressures briefly.

Demand focuses mainly on urban housing and roads, and to some extent on urban environmental sanitation (water and sewage systems). The housing shortage—variously estimated as involving 17–33 percent of the population—is both a legacy of World War II destruction and low priority for housing in the 1950's and a consequence of dynamic factors (rising incomes, urbanization, family formation, etc.). While more than 90 percent of housing investment is in the private sector, approximately one third of that involves some government financing. The need is particularly great for relatively low-priced urban dwelling units, an area in which government investment has concentrated. High urban land prices, high interest rates, need for large-scale investment, and lack of private financial institution support[17] on the one hand, and government experience in such large-scale projects, ability to subsidize through low interest rates and other measures, ability to obtain land through condemnation processes, and a feeling by citizen and bureaucrat that housing is a governmental responsibility on the other hand—all argue for a considerably greater government housing investment as well as financing program.[18]

The demand for investment in roads is also very strong, and will rise rapidly. It is not limited to consumers. As industries find urban land and other production costs rising, they increasingly diversify geographically. Truck transport, over even terrible roads, has accordingly grown rapidly and will continue to grow. Most important, perhaps, is the growth of the automobile industry and reliance upon it as one of the major leading sectors for future growth of the economy.

---

[16] Indeed, the government plans (income doubling between 1961–70, and medium term for 1964–68) and, more important, annual budgets have already been responsive to these problems and no doubt will continue to respond.

[17] This could change fairly rapidly if alternative lending opportunities dry up and interest rates continue to decline.

[18] Economic Planning Agency, *Economic Survey of Japan, 1964–1965* (Tokyo, 1965), pp. 99–105.

Without a substantially better road system than Japan has today, the cars to be produced will have no way of being used.

While such government social overhead investment will expand rapidly, government investment to complement private production more directly will not slow down substantially. Further improvements in the national railroads and especially in harbor facilities are needed. Regional dispersion of industry will generate new demands for government complementary investment.

The evaluation of the policy issues depends on whether it is assumed that demand in the economy is deficient relative to supply capacities, as was the case from early 1965 into the summer of 1966, or whether aggregate demand is equal to or in excess of supply. In a demand deficient situation a large expansion of government spending financed by borrowing is not competitive with private sector demand for resources, so a vigorous government investment program has little social cost.

Evaluation of future policy issues has to be made in light of the present (1965–66) recession. Its immediate cause was similar to previous recessions; restrictive monetary policies were undertaken to restrict investment (and hence aggregate) demand in order to restore balance-of-payments equilibrium. However, the reaction of the economy to the easing of monetary tightness, once the balance-of-payments crisis was over, has been substantially different from earlier recessions. Easy money since early 1965 has not set off a fixed-business investment boom; the overhang of excess capacity and reduced profit margins has been too great. The government rather quickly recognized the unresponsiveness of private investment demand, and also acted rather quickly, in July, 1965. However, it apparently underestimated the amount of additional spending that was needed to attain reasonably full-capacity operation, and also underestimated the rapidity and degree of improvement in the balance of payments. Hence, its increase in demand during 1965 only balanced decreases in private investment demand; much of the net growth in demand came from abroad. Preliminary evidence for the spring of 1966 indicated growing success in government compensatory fiscal measures, but output was still considerably below the full-capacity level. GNP can grow rapidly without substantial new private investment until the capacity limits are reached.

Eventually, however, the very success of compensatory fiscal policy in generating aggregate demand to a full-capacity level of output will once again place the Japanese economy in its postwar pattern of full demand, with the attendant financial problems of the past. At that point, any further relative increases in government investment (or consumption or transfer payments) will have to be at the expense of private demand.

The Financing of Government Investment

The rising share of government investment in GNP will probably be financed increasingly from external sources, both before and after a full-aggregate demand economy is reached. This judgment is based on the following reasoning. The government has the objective, though not always achieved, to limit tax and nontax current revenues to 20 percent of GNP. Strong political pressures to continue the annual practice of reducing tax rates and increasing exemption levels will make it difficult to raise the tax share substantially above 20 percent.[19] Government current expenditures are unlikely to fall much relative to GNP.[20] In fact, rising private wage rates and increases in the consumer price index will place pressure on the government to continue to raise government salaries, so that the government's wage bill will probably increase more rapidly than GNP. With revenues constant and current expenditures and investment rising relative to GNP, the *I-S* gap will widen, as indeed it already has in 1964–65; accordingly government will rely more on borrowed funds. The government will increasingly substitute financial for fiscal means of obtaining the saving of the economy.

The government could try to increase its net foreign borrowing. The sole justification for foreign borrowing is to increase the supply of resources available to the economy as reflected in the balance of payments—to pay for additional imports, to build up foreign exchange reserves, or to engage in foreign investment. This justification of course has been and will continue to be important for Japan.[21]

---

[19] The ratio reached a peak of 21.8 percent in 1962, and has declined steadily since then to 20.9 percent in 1965.

[20] An only moderate expansion of Japan's defense capabilities, due to changing governmental policies as Japan's security position and potential international power are perceived and acted upon, would increase government current expenditures substantially.

[21] For the periods (most of the postwar) in which aggregate demand has been strong and the balance of payments a substantial constraint upon even more rapid growth, government foreign lending under the export financing program of the Export-Import Bank of Japan has been rather expensive. It has deprived the economy of resources for domestic use or foreign exchange from direct cash sales, and has not yet been a substantial net earner of foreign exchange (new loans each year being greater than repayments). Supporters of this policy have not demonstrated that it sufficiently developed new markets

The government will rely mainly upon domestic borrowing to finance the rising *I-S* gap. *Ceteris paribus,* government borrowing directly from the central bank rather than from the private sector results in a greater increase in aggregate demand because there is no direct decline in private liquidity and spending. However, it is analytically useful to examine fiscal and monetary policies on a consolidated basis in terms of their overall effects. If the central bank has certain liquidity and expenditure targets for the private sector which it can achieve on its own after taking fiscal actions into account, then there is no difference between government borrowing from the private sector or from the Bank of Japan. For example, if the government borrows from the private sector, the Bank of Japan can replenish the liquidity drain by loans to or security purchases from private financial institutions.[22] On the other hand, if the government were to borrow directly from the Bank of Japan and thereby to generate excess (inflationary) aggregate demand, the Bank of Japan could reduce private sector liquidity by reducing its loans to the private sector.

In practice, policies are unlikely to be implemented this way. Government direct borrowing from the Bank of Japan is probably relatively more expansive, especially in periods when the Bank of Japan would prefer not to have liquidity eased. The basic reason is that Bank of Japan's independence from government policy is limited. Past experience with direct borrowing from the Bank of Japan by the government and government agencies indicate how powerless the Bank of Japan may be in such direct relationships. The law prohibiting direct purchase of government long-term securities by the Bank of Japan seems well justified.

Whatever restrictive power the Bank of Japan has is more effective against private financial institutions. Given its large portfolio of short-term loans to banks, the Bank of Japan operates from a position of considerable strength. It can take the initiative in deciding to restrict credit. Ironically it is more effective for the Bank of Japan to hold loans than government securities. The imperfections of Japan's capital

---

not otherwise obtainable or generated new technologies and economies of scale in domestic production (i.e., infant industry arguments) to have been worthwhile. In recession periods, such as 1965–66, the expansion of export related loans is socially not very costly; indeed it is one good way to generate additional demand.

[22] This is the present system. The Bank of Japan lends mainly to the private sector, and most of the government's borrowing is from the private sector. Apparently, the Bank of Japan has in effect underwritten the recent government bond issues by informally guaranteeing private financial institutions all the liquidity they need, through loans or security purchase.

market, and the political and administrative pressures of the government, restrict the Bank of Japan's freedom to engage in open market bond sales for restrictive purposes.

So long as demand is deficient it does not really matter whether the government borrows from the private sector or from the Bank of Japan. In either case the Bank of Japan's policy supports high liquidity in the private sector. The problem arises once sufficient demand has been generated through fiscal policy, and yet the government needs additional financing to cover a portion of the *I–S* gap.[23] At that point government investment becomes competitive with private spending. To prevent inflation, any borrowing to finance government investment must be offset by reductions in private liquidity to contract private spending by an amount equal to the government investment. As argued above, government borrowing from the private sector, without support by the Bank of Japan, most nearly achieves this, though further adjustment of private liquidity may be necessary to leave aggregate demand unchanged. This is the most efficient way—aside from taxation—to finance the desired shift of resources to the government from the private sector without generating inflation. However, since lending within the private sector is mainly to finance investment, government borrowing only transfers saving, while government internal financing from taxation of private consumption (through personal income or indirect taxes) increases the economy's aggregate saving rate.[24]

Initial Claim on Bank of Japan Credit

The question of whether the government should borrow from the private sector or from the Bank of Japan raises a long-run (non-Keynesian) issue as to whether the government or the private sector is entitled to the initial claim[25] on resources equal to the amount of

---

[23] This presupposes that government investment demand will not be fully satisfied by the amount of expenditure provided for by compensatory finance. There is no particular reason to believe that the *I–S* gap will always be just filled by the amount of deficit financing (borrowing) needed to obtain full employment of resources. This might be the case for a short period, but not once private demand again grows fairly rapidly.

[24] This does not apply to taxes on corporate profits, since the corporate sector has a much higher marginal propensity to save than the government, while the household propensity is somewhat lower.

[25] There is, in addition, a secondary claim on resources which occurs when private financial institutions increase loans and deposits by the multiple of the initial expansion of "high-powered" money. This I assume is done by the private financial system.

expansion of Bank of Japan credit.[26] The Bank of Japan's cumulative credit increase between 1954–65 was 8.3 percent of the increase in GNP, a not inconsequential claim on resources.

Of this, the government received 36.6 percent, but most of it in 1964 (Table 11–3). Central bank credit has gone mainly to private financial institutions. By rediscounting rather than lending to the government, the Bank of Japan has delegated the resource allocation function to the commercial banks rather than to the government. This, however, has been mitigated by the private sector's lending to the government. Indeed, it is misleading to say that the Bank of Japan has not allocated its credit to the government; it has, but by the indirect process of loans to the private sector and of private sector loans to the government. If these transactions had been carried out in a competitive market situation one could argue that the linkage was rather weak, since the private sector was free to choose between private and public debt. But in fact the new issues of local government and public corporation bonds—the major form of government borrowing through the marketplace—have been forced upon private financial institutions at uncompetitive terms by government administrative suasion. An implicit arrangement seems to have been that any funds that financial institutions used for such purposes would be more or less replenished, if indirectly, by Bank of Japan loans.

This suggests that the issue as to whether the government or the private sector receives the initial claim on resources by the Bank of Japan's credit expansion can be misleading and is perhaps inconsequential. It is misleading if measurement is on the basis solely of the direct flow of credit. It is inconsequential if the decision on the public-private decision on the allocation of resources has already been made and implemented by other fiscal and financial measures. However, fiscal-monetary policy decision making is not so well articulated and coordinated in Japan that Bank of Japan allocations have no effect.

Interest Rate Policy

The prospect of future government investment being financed increasingly by borrowing has major implications for policies concerning the level and term structure of interest rates. The current levels of

---

[26] This issue has been raised in certain underdeveloped countries such as India, where it is argued that the claim on resources represented by an increase in currency in circulation (which is one form of financial asset in which the private sector puts its saving) should go to the government as noninflationary borrowing from the central bank.

short-term and long-term interest rates are atypical of the postwar period in that many rates on loans and bonds are close to or at equilibrium levels.

Almost all interest rates have been kept abnormally low throughout the postwar period by a combination of legal and administrative restraints by the Ministry of Finance and the Bank of Japan.[27] Official short-term rates have fluctuated slightly over the course of the cycle, but yields on all new bond issues have remained virtually unchanged at artificially low levels for a decade regardless of changes in demand and supply. Evidence on the degree of tightness of funds and on market levels of interest rates is provided by the actual call market rates and the effective yields on transactions in bonds sold by the Japan Telephone & Telegraph Company (*den-den sai*) to·new users of telephone services. The call rate has been subject to wide fluctuation (4.75–21.90 percent for unconditional loans); the data on average call rates are poor, especially for the period June 1957–62 when the Bank of Japan applied official calling rates which were not fully observed.[28] For only brief periods of very easy money has the call rate been below official long-term interest rates. (Even bank average effective short-term lending rates have tended to be above the long-term bond rates). The *den-den* yields ranged between 7.5–15.0 percent for the period 1958–65. While the market is narrow, the *den-den* rates reflect better than any other available data the level of long-term rates and their changes.

Only when easy money policies have been pursued (notably in recessions) have short-term rates gone substantially below officially determined long-term rates. The disastrous easy money policy of 1963 to reduce short-term interest rates sufficiently below long-term rates to establish a market equilibrium term structure should serve as warning to those who anticipate that a market-determined level and structure of rates is always consistent with a low-interest rate policy. The money supply increased 17 percent (seasonally adjusted[29]) in

---

[27] For greater detail, see Hugh T. Patrick, "Japan's Interest Rates and the 'Grey' Financial Market," *Pacific Affairs,* Winter, 1965–66. Effective interest rates, changed in part by varying the compensatory deposit ratio, are somewhat less rigid than nominal rates.

[28] The call rate does not correlate well with the Bank of Japan discount rate; see Hannan Ezekiel, "The Call Money Market in Japan," International Monetary Fund, *Staff Papers,* Vol. 13, No. 1 (March, 1966). However, Ezekiel uses official statistics rather than actual call rates. Regressions which I estimated relating the call rate to growth of GNP (quarterly change over same quarter of the previous year) also showed little correlation; while estimates of actual call rates were used, they were probably not very accurate.

[29] Adjusted also for the surfacing of hidden loans (*fukumi kashidashi*) and hidden deposits.

the first half of 1963 and 27 percent for the year. This creation of money did bring the call rate down from a 1962 tight money peak of about 14 percent to a 1963 low of 7.3 percent and the *den-den* rate from 14.016 percent to 8.440 percent (still well above official rates). It also generated high corporate liquidity, a new round of expenditures, and an abortive boom leading to renewed balance of payments problems. Of course call and *den-den* rates once again rose as the boom developed.

The present situation is different from 1963 in that private demand for funds and for investment is relatively slack while monetary policy is and can be easy, so that equilibrium as well as official interest rates have declined to postwar lows. Thus, a market level and structure of rates is being approximated. This offers the policy makers a real opportunity to establish viable and strong capital and money markets by ending the restrictions on interest rates and market transactions.[30]

The sale to the private sector of central government bonds in early 1966 for the first time since 1947, and at a yield (6.795 percent) attractive in relatively liquid financial markets, provides a good vehicle for establishing real issue and secondary markets in debentures. Apparently individual purchasers have been guaranteed a high degree of liquidity for their bonds; the securities companies from which they purchase the bonds agree to repurchase them at a slight discount (0.4 percent).[31] The decision to sell government bonds had to overcome a large psychological block in Japan, since it ended the fiction that the government maintains a balanced budget and does not borrow on more than a seasonal basis.[32] Some fear lingers that government bond issue *must* lead to inflation—a simplistic and misleading view.[33]

---

[30] The arguments concerning the resource allocation and welfare benefits of reliance on markets and prices (interest rates) for fund allocation in place of controls are well known and are not repeated here.

[31] In late 1966, central government bonds were listed on the exchanges for the first time postwar.

[32] As we have seen (Table 11–3), this is a fiction because the government has been a net borrower almost every year. However, the borrowing was in a sense disguised (postal saving, local governments, public corporations); it was, and is, possible to maintain a surplus in the general account with overall central government deficits, since it covers only a part of central government expenditures.

[33] However, it may not be unreasonable to think that once the government begins government bond-financed deficit spending it will not stop even when aggregate demand is sufficient. On the other hand, restriction of government bond issue does not guarantee that fiscal policy will result in price stability. For example, if private demand were relatively strong, the government could readily generate inflationary pressures (as perhaps in 1963 and 1964) without government bond issues by financing a widening *I–S* gap through increased local government and public corporation bond issue, and use of government financial institutions to finance government rather than private investment.

If government bonds lead the way to a relatively free market in all kinds of financial assets, considerable adjustments among rates will take place both in the short-run and long-run. In the short-run, the most important adjustment could be between government bonds and financial institution savings and time deposit rates. If bonds are highly liquid and maintain their present yield considerably above deposit rates, individuals will be induced to switch from deposits to bonds.[34] Substantial switching would put competitive pressure on banks to raise deposit rates.[35] This would be healthy; depositers now subsidize big business borrowers. An increase in bank deposit rates in turn would generate pressure to raise postal-savings deposits rates.[36]

The longer run effects of a market-determined level and structure of interest rates have far greater implications. It is useful to distinguish between two phases: the present with inadequate aggregate demand, and that period in the future when successful fiscal policy restores the economy to the high-aggregate demand condition prevalent throughout the postwar period.[37] As deficit spending progresses, the economy will move continuously from the first into the second phase.

The first phase, until its later stages, will not pose serious interest rate problems. Rates will rise only slightly above present levels, since the Bank of Japan will continue to support compensatory fiscal policy with easy money policy. However, as the rise in demand moves the

---

[34] Much of course depends on expectations concerning bond prices. I would not be surprised to see develop a *de facto* floor price, as apparently exists at present, being supported directly by the monetary authorities or indirectly by forcing financial institutions to support the market by purchases.

[35] So far this has not been a serious problem for banks. The lack of success of bond investment trusts, despite their high liquidity and yield, is one indication of individual unwillingness to hold bonds. Nonetheless, some city banks are considering the issue of certificates of deposit, in small as well as large denomination, having higher interest rates than time deposits.

[36] The government can justify postal-savings rates somewhat below government bond yields on grounds of convenience and divisibility.

[37] While pump-priming may be needed for a year or two because of a slowdown in business investment, I anticipate a new round of expanded business investment thereafter, in substantial part due to the very success of fiscal policy. Of course, the increase in private demand does not have to come from business investment; the only necessary condition is that it come from somewhere in the private sector. I assume that, while bothered by continued rises in consumer prices, the government will still place sufficient emphasis on full use of resources and growth to take the fiscal actions necessary to generate a fairly high level of demand (though perhaps below that of the 1961–64 level). Finance Minister Fukuda feels a 7–8 percent growth rate is feasible, and that deficit financing will have to continue vigorously for three years before slacking off. See "Sato Government's Fiscal Policy—Fukuda-Higo Forum on Fiscal Problems," *Oriental Economist,* April, 1966.

economy into the second phase, financial markets will begin to tighten and market-determined interest rates will begin to rise.

In the second phase—when the Japanese economy is once again in a boom, with demand pressing against supply capacities—government spending (investment) will once again be competitive with private spending. Fiscal-monetary policy will have to end its ease in order to forestall the emergence of inflationary and balance-of-payment problems. With financial markets accordingly tight, interest rates will rise substantially. Because few financial markets have been free, past experience provides little information as to how high market-determined short-term and long-term interest rates would rise. The call and *den-den* rates are indicators, but their markets are narrow, so that they probably exaggerate the magnitude of changes. Call rate data are poor and do not correlate well with other variables.

Den-den rates (D), lagged six months, regressed on the rate of growth of GNP over the same quarter for the previous year provide the following results:[38]

$$D = 7.77 + 0.1727 \, GNP_{-2} \qquad R^2 = .296$$
$$(0.0504) \qquad\qquad d = 1.6625.$$

In other words a 10 percentage point increase in the quarterly growth rate would increase the *den-den* rate by 1.73 percentage points. Quarterly growth rates vary much more widely than annual rates, ranging between -7.3 and 26.1 percent. Whatever evidence we have does suggest a considerable rise in market-equilibrium interest rates in a boom from present levels.

The important question is how will the government respond to an increase in the general level of interest rates, and in particular to the price decline of outstanding government bonds and the higher requisite yield for new government bond issues. Will the government allow the market forces to work themselves out in higher interest rates? Or will the government restore controls over interest rates (especially long-term rates), set rates low relative to their equilibrium level, try to halt trading in bonds, and once again emasculate the nascent capital market? What alternative paths are open to the government?

One alternative would be to have the Bank of Japan support the

---

[38] Fitted only to the upswing phase the results are:

$$D = 7.37 + 0.1616 \, GNP_{-2} \qquad R^2 = .517$$
$$(0.0391) \qquad\qquad d = 0.6932.$$

While this result shows higher correlation, the Durbin-Watson statistic indicates an autocorrelation problem.

bond market by direct or indirect purchases (loans to financial institutions on condition that they support the bond market). This would clearly be inflationary, and eventually self-defeating. I regard it unlikely as a major action, though interim support may occur.

A second alternative would be for the government to have a more restrictive fiscal policy by increasing the share of taxes in GNP or, more politically likely, by reducing government expenditures, notably investment. This would both apply the necessary restriction to demand and reduce the government's need to borrow. But much depends on the size of the I-S gap and the government decision as to whether its investment program should be carried through. It is very likely that a full demand condition will be restored before the government has built sufficient houses, roads, waterworks, sewage systems, harbors, etc. The government may be unwilling to restrict its investment program (reduce the government's share of total resources) sufficiently for purposes of compensatory finance.

A third alternative is for the government to continue its investment program, and to finance the I-S gap by competing with private borrowers in the private sector market for funds. It would, in effect, bid away resources from private users. This, plus appropriately restrictive monetary policy, would offset the increases in demand generated by the government investment expenditure. It would have the advantage of allowing money and capital markets to flourish and permit interest rates to carry out their proper allocative functions. This would thus appear to be the economically most efficient method.

A fourth possibility is for the government to borrow directly from the Bank of Japan and thereby through its expenditures generate excess private demand. The Bank of Japan would have to reduce its loans to the private sector sufficiently to reduce private demand in equal amount. Fiscal policy under this circumstance would continue to be expansive. The system would rely even more upon the Bank of Japan than it has in the past 15 years to curb credit to the private sector by tight money measures sufficiently to absorb the government-generated excess demand. The Bank of Japan is unlikely to accomplish such a policy adequately. The result would be inflation. Probably the laws restricting government direct borrowing from the Bank of Japan will not be changed, in which case this is a less feasible alternative.[39]

---

[39] It is not, however, a technical or political impossibility. For example, in early 1966, the government (Trust Fund Bureau) arranged to sell some of its holdings of long-term credit bank bonds to the Bank of Japan, in order to use the proceeds to subscribe to new central government bond issues. This is about

The government would not be happy with a price decline sub-stantially below par in its already issued bonds, and would be reluctant to see its interest cost of funds raised very much. The government arguments appear to be founded on bookkeeping, legalistic, and status, pride, or other psychological criteria rather than on economic reason-ing. Thus, the final alternative is that the government will restore interest rate ceilings and other controls in order to keep interest rates below equilibrium levels. In other words, the government will revert to the control system used throughout the postwar period. Credit rationing and administrative guidance would once again force private financial institutions (and to some extent indirectly the Bank of Japan) to finance the government's borrowing at artificially low-interest rates. For reasons of prestige, the government might well dis-continue financing the *I-S* gap with government bond issues.[40] Instead it would arrange the issue of local government and public corporation bonds and, by shifting flows through government financial inter-mediaries to finance goverment investment, divert postal savings and life insurance more into government investment. While this too will sop up private funds, reliance will also have to be placed upon Bank of Japan restrictive credit policies. If this alternative were selected, the nascent capital market would once again whither away, and the efficacy of interest rates in the allocation process would be reduced.

Which among these alternatives will the government choose when the success of present fiscal policy restores growth, and market-determined interest rates rise? My prediction is that while the govern-ment will make marginal adjustments among the first four alternatives to reduce the aggregate demand pressure, its main adjustment will be to restore administrative controls over financial markets and ceilings

as direct a form of indirect central bank purchase of government bonds as is possible.

[40] The outstanding government bonds held by individuals and others over whom the government could exert only a small degree of suasion would con-stitute a vexing problem, since some such holders might wish to sell. Mainte-nance of the issue price, by direct or indirect Bank of Japan support, would simply make it attractive and possible for holders to sell, as well as being inflationary. Alternatively, the Bank of Japan could focus any expansion of credit it deemed necessary by purchases of individually held bonds in the open market. The government would probably object because of the decrease in government bond prices in an open market; the city banks would object because they are used to being the prime recipients of central bank credit. A third possibility, suggested by Professor Komiya is that city banks and other financial institutions will be required to hold government bonds as secondary reserves, thus inducing them not only to maintain present holdings but to buy up those sold by individuals and to support renewed government sales at a low-interest rate.

on interest rates. The attempt to establish a real long-term capital market and a market-determined structure of interest rates will be aborted. Perhaps the most interesting question is how high—7 percent?, 7½ percent?—will the government allow the market yield on government bonds to rise before it clamps on controls once again.

IV

Several conclusions emerge from this study.

In aggregate, the public sector has financed most of its investment internally, from tax and nontax current revenues and from government enterprise depreciation allowances. This was a consequence of the policy decision to give first priority to private demand, especially business investment, in a period when it was very strong. Thus, in order to restrain inflationary pressures and to increase gross saving, the government had to finance its own expenditures in this manner.

Since 1962, however, the gap between government investment and saving has been widening, forcing greater reliance on external sources of finance. These sources, on a net basis, have been entirely domestic —mainly households, private financial institutions, and to some extent the Bank of Japan. In boom years 1963–64, government demand for resources was in direct competition with the private sector. Since then, as business investment demand has slowed down, there has been little competition; it has been more a matter of restoring full use of resources.

The government's policy to allow private business investment a relatively free rein has resulted in an unbalanced pattern of economic growth. Until the early 1960's, private investment to expand capacity and provision of private consumption goods took precedence over public social welfare investment and provision of public consumption goods. Since then, with the slackening of private investment demand, government investment to improve public services has become relatively more important. Continued effort will be needed to achieve a balance between public and private goods, particularly if housing is considered a public responsibility. It is not clear that such an unbalanced growth pattern has been undesirable. My guess is that this pattern has resulted in a higher overall rate of growth than would have occurred otherwise. The increases in output may well have more than compensated for the welfare distortions that this pattern produced.

The public sector's cumulative gross borrowing from the private sector has been 3½ times as large as its total net cumulative borrowings, including those from the Bank of Japan. In this quantitative sense, the government's role as financial intermediary is much larger than its role as borrower for its own investment. Government financial institutions collect savings (notably from small savers via postal-savings deposits) and re-lend them mainly to large corporate business enterprises.

The smallness of the *I-S* gap for the public sector on a consolidated basis masks large *I-S* gaps among component government units. The central general government generates a large-saving surplus; this is used to finance the saving gaps of local general governments and central and local government enterprises. The mechanisms for such intragovernmental financial flows are diverse and complex. These *I-S* gaps reinforce the power of the central government.

If my assumption is correct that the next several years will see a continued effort by the government to increase the supply of public goods (including housing) through its investment (and/or lending) programs, then the government will have to finance a greater proportion of its investment externally. I expect the ratio of government investment to GNP, and hence of government total claim on resources, to rise somewhat while the revenue ratio lags. The increasing *I-S* gap will be financed from private sector saving directly, or indirectly by Bank of Japan credit. No substantial problems will arise so long as private aggregate demand is weak relative to the supply capabilities of the economy. During 1965–66, Japan has had the standard compensatory finance problem of an economy with insufficient demand.

However, financing problems for the government will inevitably arise out of the very success of compensatory fiscal policy. Once the economy emerges from recession and resumes rapid growth, aggregate demand will eventually push against aggregate supply. At this point the competition between the public and the private sectors for resources will become severe. How the government finances its *I-S* gap will be important for control of inflation and for efficiency of resource allocation.

Although there are a variety of alternatives, essentially they reduce to a choice between free or controlled money and capital markets in Japan. Free markets would be more efficient; present conditions make it feasible to establish and develop them. Indeed a number of progressive steps have already been taken. However, once financial markets begin to tighten as resources are fully utilized, market-determined interest rates will rise and bond prices will fall. I predict that the government will resist these market pressures by restoring administrative controls over financial markets and interest rates.

12 | The Role of the Government in the Postwar Economic Development of Japan*

SHUNTARO SHISHIDO

I. INTRODUCTION

Japan's fast rate of postwar economic growth has been characterized by an extremely high rate of investment. The most dynamic factor in this has been private fixed investment in the industrial sector, based on rapid technological progress; a relatively abundant labor supply; increased efficiency in the utilization of resources as a result of trade liberalization, etc. The price level, especially consumer prices, started rising rapidly at about 1960, indicating a labor shortage, wage pressure, and a restrictive food supply.

As for the role of government in this period of fast economic growth, it is generally believed that the corporate tax system has been stimulating private investment and that monetary policy has favored growth, particularly in private fixed investment, though in a way that is peculiar to Japan.[1] An evaluation of fiscal policy seems to lead to different appraisals of government's role. Some credit the principle of a balanced budget for its effect on increased saving; others criticize the rigidity of fiscal policy in managing aggregate demand.

In the present paper we shall focus our attention first on the role of fiscal policy in postwar economic growth to see whether it was intended to promote growth and how effective it was toward this end. Problems connected with our corporate tax system and monetary

---

* The views expressed in this article are entirely personal and do not represent any view of the government. The author is indebted to Professors L. R. Klein and H. Rosovsky and Mr. I. Miyazaki for useful comments and Messrs. S. Kuribayashi, S. Nagaya and A. Saito for research assistance.

[1] R. Tachi, "Fiscal and Monetary Policy," *The Postwar Economic Growth,* ed. R. Komiya (in Japanese) (Tokyo: Iwanami, Ltd., 1963).

policy, including government financial activities, will be dealt with only in connection with our main subject. Next, we shall discuss government measures for price stability associated with growth. The effectiveness of government structural policy will be discussed. In conclusion, we shall give an overall evaluation of the policies for growth and price stability.

II. THE ROLE OF FISCAL POLICY

First, we shall discuss the extent to which Japanese fiscal policy has influenced the high rate of growth and investment.

We will use new data on the national accounts for the period 1951–64 which were released by the Economic Planning Agency (EPA) in April, 1966. These contain the most substantial revisions made in the 20 years since 1947 in terms of concepts and estimation techniques. For instance, the level of GNP was increased by about 10 percent and the proportion of private consumption in GNP was raised by 3 to 4 percent over the past 14 years; the rate of growth of GNP in real terms was also revised on the basis of the newly estimated price deflators. Since the conceptual framework is now almost completely in accord with the O.E.C.D. and the UN accounting system, its comparability has been greatly improved over previous series.

1. Government Account for 1951 to 1964

During the past 14 years, GNP in real terms rose by nearly 10 percent annually, and in 1964 it reached a level 3.3 times that of 1951. Among the components of real GNP, fixed investment, both private and public, indicates the highest rate of increase while consumption expenditures, in particular government consumption, increased at the lowest rate, as shown in Table 12–1(A). Thus, the share of government purchases of goods and services, i.e., government consumption and investment as a whole, indicates a slightly declining tendency, though somewhat modified, if those expenditures are indicated in money terms as shown in (III), Table 12–1(A). This implies that government influence on aggregate demand through public expenditure has not been strong enough, and it is mostly due to low-tax revenues, increases in the relative price of public expenditure and the balanced budget principle, as we shall see later.

Components of government revenue as a percent of the GNP are indicated in Table 12–1(B). The percent of total current revenue remains fairly stable, i.e., at approximately 20 to 21 percent of GNP

TABLE 12-1

GNP and Government Account
(Percent--Fiscal Year)*

A. GNP AND ITS MAJOR COMPONENTS AS PERCENT OF GNP

	1951	1952	1953	1954	1955	1956	1957	1958	1959	1960	1961	1962	1963	1964
I. Growth rate of GNP in 1960 prices		11.3	8.8	2.8	12.1	8.5	9.7	3.5	13.4	14.3	14.5	4.3	12.8	9.9
II. Components in 1960 prices														
1. Private consumption expenditure. . .	57.6	60.4	61.2	62.4	60.7	59.8	58.0	60.1	57.9	55.0	52.8	54.9	53.2	52.6
2. Government consumption expenditure. .	13.8	13.4	12.9	12.6	11.2	10.3	9.8	9.9	9.1	8.5	7.9	8.1	7.8	7.6
3. Government fixed investment . .	5.5	6.6	7.8	7.7	6.8	6.2	7.1	8.0	8.0	8.0	8.7	10.3	9.9	9.3
(Government purchases = 2 + 3)	19.3	20.0	20.7	20.3	18.0	16.5	16.9	17.9	17.1	16.5	16.6	18.4	17.7	16.9
4. Private fixed investment in equipment . .	12.1	11.3	12.2	10.9	11.4	14.5	16.3	14.5	16.5	20.4	22.4	20.8	20.3	20.5
5. Private residential construction . .	2.5	3.2	3.0	3.4	3.3	3.4	3.5	3.7	3.8	3.8	3.8	4.1	4.6	4.8
III. Components in current prices														
1. Private consumption expenditure. . .	54.2	63.1	63.7	64.9	62.1	59.6	57.5	59.9	56.9	53.8	51.5	54.2	53.4	52.8
2. Government consumption expenditure. .	10.0	10.9	11.1	10.9	10.3	9.6	9.3	9.0	9.0	8.8	8.4	9.0	9.0	9.2
3. Government fixed investment . .	6.0	7.0	8.2	7.6	6.7	6.6	7.3	8.0	8.1	8.0	9.0	10.5	10.1	9.7
(Government purchases = 2 + 3)	16.0	17.9	19.3	18.5	17.0	16.2	16.6	17.6	17.1	16.8	17.4	19.5	19.1	18.9
4. Private fixed investment in equipment . .	12.1	11.2	11.8	10.1	10.7	15.0	17.0	14.8	16.6	20.3	22.0	19.3	18.4	17.9
5. Private residental construction . .	2.1	2.8	3.0	3.2	2.9	3.2	3.3	3.5	3.7	3.9	4.3	4.5	5.0	5.3

*Based on fiscal year starting April 1.
SOURCE: Economic Planning Agency, *Annual Report on National Income Statistics, 1966* (Tokyo, 1966).

TABLE 12-1 (Continued)

B. GOVERNMENT ACCOUNT, AS PERCENT OF GNP

	1951	1952	1953	1954	1955	1956	1957	1958	1959	1960	1961	1962	1963	1964
1. Direct taxes on households, etc.	7.1	7.1	6.7	6.6	6.4	6.4	5.5	5.7	5.4	5.9	6.1	6.8	7.0	7.2
a. Social security contributions	1.8	2.0	1.9	2.2	2.2	2.3	2.3	2.5	2.5	2.6	2.7	2.9	2.9	3.0
b. Other direct taxes	5.3	5.1	4.8	4.4	4.2	4.1	3.2	3.2	2.9	3.3	3.4	3.9	4.1	4.2
2. Direct taxes on corporations	4.4	3.8	3.3	3.1	2.7	3.1	3.8	3.3	3.7	4.2	4.4	4.5	4.2	4.1
3. Indirect taxes	9.2	9.8	9.5	9.4	8.5	8.6	8.7	9.0	8.7	8.9	8.8	8.4	8.2	8.2
4. Income from property and entrepreneurship	0.0	0.5	0.5	0.9	0.7	0.8	1.3	1.5	1.2	1.5	1.6	1.3	1.5	0.8
5. Current transfers from households, etc.	0.7	0.9	0.9	0.9	0.9	0.9	1.0	1.0	1.0	1.0	1.0	1.1	1.0	1.1
6. Current transfers from the rest of the world	0.7	0.0	0.0	0.0	0.0	0.1	0.0	0.0	0.0	0.0	0.0	0.0	0.0	0.0
7. Total current revenues (= 1 + 2 + 3 + 4 + 5 + 6)	22.0	22.1	20.9	21.0	19.2	19.9	20.3	20.4	20.1	21.4	21.9	22.1	21.8	21.6
8. Government consumption expenditure	10.0	10.9	11.1	10.9	10.3	9.6	9.3	9.6	9.0	8.8	8.4	9.0	9.0	9.2
9. Subsidies	0.6	0.9	1.0	0.4	0.1	0.1	0.1	0.1	0.1	0.2	0.3	0.4	0.4	0.5
10. Interest on the public debt	0.1	0.6	0.6	0.6	0.6	0.6	0.5	0.5	0.5	0.4	0.3	0.3	0.3	0.3
11. Current transfers to households, etc.	2.1	2.8	2.8	4.3	4.0	3.6	3.4	3.8	3.7	3.6	3.5	3.8	4.0	4.2
12. Current transfers to the rest of the world	0.0	0.0	0.0	0.0	0.1	0.1	0.3	0.8	0.2	0.2	0.2	0.2	0.1	0.1
13. Total current expenditure (= 8 + 9 + 10 + 11 + 12)	12.8	15.2	15.5	16.2	15.1	14.0	13.6	14.8	13.5	13.2	12.7	13.7	13.8	14.3
14. Net saving of the general government	9.2	6.9	5.3	4.8	4.1	6.0	6.7	5.7	6.5	8.2	9.2	8.5	8.1	7.2
15. Depreciation of government enterprises	0.7	0.9	0.9	0.9	0.9	0.9	0.9	0.9	0.8	0.8	0.9	0.8	0.8	0.9
16. Gross fixed government investment	6.0	7.0	8.2	7.6	6.7	6.6	7.3	8.0	8.1	8.0	9.0	10.5	10.1	9.7
17. Increase in stocks	0.4	-0.1	-0.1	-0.2	1.4	0.3	-0.1	-0.1	0.2	0.2	-0.1	-0.1	-0.2	0.2
18. Net balance* (= 14 + 15 − 16 − 17)	3.5	0.4	-1.9	-1.7	-3.1	0.0	0.4	-1.6	-1.0	0.8	1.2	-1.1	-1.0	-1.8

*Net financial surplus of general government and public enterprises before adjustment of net purchase of land and used assets.

SOURCE: Economic Planning Agency, *Annual Report on National Income Statistics, 1966* (Tokyo, 1966).

in current prices. Among components, there is a marked increase in the share of contributions to social security while the share of indirect taxes indicates a slight decline in recent years. The share of personal tax gradually declines in the 1950's and starts rising slowly afterward. The share of corporate taxes fluctuates according to business conditions and the tax system. Although there have been several reductions in the corporate tax, most of the changes in this table can be attributable to the changes in the share of corporate profits in GNP. As for transfer payments, the share in GNP rose during the early 1950's and then remained at an almost constant level of about 3 to 4 percent, the lowest level by Western standards, as discussed later.

The net savings of general government, defined as a difference between current revenue and current expenditures of the general government, indicate a fairly high proportion of the GNP, which fluctuates from 4 to 8 percent according to business conditions. The net balance of the government sector, i.e., the difference between gross saving and gross government investment, also fluctuates widely, with a surplus in boom years and a deficit in recession years. To a limited extent, therefore, no one can deny the existence of a built-in stabilizer in Japanese fiscal policy. Generally, however, the balance in Table 12–1(B) indicates a deficit trend, although interrupted by boom years, such as 1951, 1957, 1960, and 1961. In view of the fact that a substantial amount of fixed investment of government enterprises is included in this balance and an adjustment is also needed in regard to depreciation allowances and net purchase of land and used assets, the net balance of the general government in a narrower sense of the term may indicate a smaller amount of deficit, or even a little surplus in certain years. An argument that a strict adherence to a balanced budget by fiscal authorities and the "natural" increase of tax revenues due to high economic growth causes a constant surplus in the government account, thus promoting investment and growth, seems to be the case only with the central government.[2] Local governments have always suffered from a serious deficit and have had to rely heavily on borrowing from external sources. This would imply that the financial effect of general government in Japan has been almost neutral on the average in supplying or absorbing money from private sectors. But recently there is a growing deficit in the government account due to increased government investment, especially in a recession year.

---

[2] P. A. Samuelson, "The New Look in Tax and Fiscal Policy," *Federal Tax Policy for Economic Growth and Stability,* Joint Economic Committee on Economic Report (Washington, D.C.: U.S. Government Printing Office, 1955), pp. 229–34; Tachi, *op. cit.*

In the pages to follow, we shall further discuss these features of the Japanese government sector using an international comparison with Western countries.

2. International Comparison

Professor Komiya made an interesting analysis of Japanese fiscal policy, based on our old national income estimates and UN data.[3] Our analysis is based mostly on the latest O.E.C.D. data and our new national account estimates.

As shown in Table 12–2A, the pattern of Japanese growth in terms of GNP is characterized by a low proportion of private and government consumption and a high proportion of gross fixed investment. A low share of government consumption reflects, no doubt, an extremely low proportion of military expense and also a small share of civil expenditure. As indicated before, this low share has continued to decline in the past. If we compare the trend of government consumption between 1950 and 1960 in terms of both current and constant prices, we obtain the following interesting result on the share in GNP.

1. European O.E.C.D., combined:*

	(A) 1950	(A) 1960	(B) 1950	(B) 1960
a) Military expenditure	4.7	4.4	5.0	4.1
b) Civil expenditure	8.5	9.8	8.9	8.9
c) Total government consumption	13.2	14.2	13.9	13.0

2. Japan (FY basis):†

	(A) 1951	(A) 1960	(B) 1951	(B) 1960
a) Military expenditure	1.7	1.0	1.7†	1.0†
b) Civil expenditure	8.3	7.8	12.1	7.5
c) Total government consumption	10.0	8.8	13.8	8.5

* (A) = current prices, (B) = 1954 prices for Europe and 1960 prices for Japan.
† Deflated by an implicit deflator of GNP.

The difference between current and constant price statistics probably reflects a rising trend in the relative price level of civilian government activity. The price increase occurs when there is a decline in military expenses. There is a sharp contrast in the case of civilian ex-

---

[3] R. Komiya, "Tax Burden, Size of Fiscal Budget and National Debt Policy," *Economic Growth and Fiscal and Monetary Policy,* ed. R. Tachi and T. Watanabe (in Japanese) (Tokyo: Iwanami, Ltd., 1964).

TABLE 12-2A

International Comparison of GNP and Its Major Components, 1960
(GNP Components)*

	Aus-tria	Bel-gium	Canada	Den-mark	France	Ger-many
1. Private consumption expenditure.	59.5	68.4	65.0	65.3	63.9	56.8
2. Government consumption expenditure.	12.9	12.1	14.4	12.6	13.3	13.6
a. Military.	(1.2)	(3.2)	(4.6)	(2.5)	(5.3)	(3.2)
b. Civil	(11.7)	(8.9)	(9.8)	(10.1)	(8.0)	(10.4)
3. Gross fixed capital formation.	22.7	18.6	22.7	19.5	18.6	24.0

	Greece	Ice-land	Ire-land	Italy	Nether-lands	Norway
1. Private consumption expenditure.	75.2	66.9	75.3	61.4	56.8	57.6
2. Government consumption expenditure.	12.6	8.7	12.0	14.5	13.5	14.6
a. Military.	(5.0)		(1.1)	(2.9)	(3.8)	(3.2)
b. Civil	(7.6)		(10.9)	(11.6)	(9.7)	(11.3)
3. Gross fixed capital formation.	25.9	30.0	13.0	22.3	23.4	27.5

	Portugal	Sweden	U.K.	U.S.	Japan†
1. Private consumption expenditure.	76.6	58.8	65.7	63.9	54.9
2. Government consumption expenditure.	11.9	17.7	16.6	18.1	8.8
a. Military.	(3.9)	(4.7)	(6.2)	(9.3)	(1.0)
b. Civil	(8.1)	(13.0)	(10.3)	(8.9)	(7.8)
3. Gross fixed capital formation.	18.2	21.9	16.1	16.4	32.2

*Military expenses for Italy and Netherlands are estimated from UN *Statistical Yearbook, 1965,* and *Yearbook of National Account Statistics, 1965* (New York, 1966).
†Fiscal year basis.
SOURCE: OECD, *Statistics of National Accounts, 1951-1960* (Paris, 1964), and Economic Planning Agency, *Annual Report on National Income Statistics, 1966* (Tokyo, 1966).

penditures. European countries raised their share of civilian expenditure, and it remains at the same level in both current and constant prices. In Japan, however, the share of civilian expenditure declined slightly in current prices and dropped sharply in constant prices.

The components of gross fixed investment are given in Table 12–2B as average percentages of GNP during 1950 to 1963 for selected countries. Although there are conceptual difficulties, it is obvious that Japanese investment on the part of general government is the highest in the group, while the share of investment by government enterprises and public corporations varies according to institutional differences. The high rate of general government investment in Japan is no doubt closely related to the rapid economic growth and the high frequency of natural disasters. If these elements are taken into account, the Japanese investment ratio by the general government will be below average, as suggested by Table 12–2C.

The share of government purchases in GNP, defined as a sum of government consumption and investment shares, is also indicated at the bottom of Table 12–2B. For convenience, we use two concepts: (1) purchases of goods and services by the general government, and (2) purchases by the public sector as a whole, including the general government, government enterprises, and public corporations. In this table, purchases by the government sector as a whole are the lowest in Japan and those by the general government fall in the lowest group. This implies that an extremely low-government consumption offsets a relatively high rate of government investment in Japan.

This tendency toward low-government expenditures is closely connected with a traditional requirement of a budget balance and a low-tax burden. These features become notable when we look at transfer payments and current revenues. In Table 12–3A, shares of total current expenditure, defined as government consumption plus transfer payments, is compared with data from other countries. The share of transfer payments in Japan is notably low, reflecting the backwardness of its social security system. Thus, the total share of current expenditures at about 13 percent is again the lowest among the developed countries cited here.

For the revenue side in Table 12–3B, there is a similar tendency, for low ratios of personal tax, social security contributions and indirect taxes. Here, too, we notice again the lowest Japanese share of total current revenue of only 21.5 percent. The most important aspect in this regard is the low rate of the Japanese personal tax, which indicates an excessive tax reduction as discussed later. For instance, in most developed countries the personal tax burden tends to increase

TABLE 12-2B

Composition of Gross Fixed Capital
Formation and Government Purchases
as Percent of GNP for 1950-63

	Austria	*Belgium*	*Canada*
1. Gross fixed capital formation	22.2	18.2	22.2
a. Private enterprises.	13.0	I	16.7
b. Public corporations.	3.3	16.2	I
c. Government enterprises	1.8	I	2.7
d. General government	4.1	2.0	3.8
2. Government consumption.	13.2	11.8	14.4
3. Government purchases on goods and services by general government only*.	17.3	13.8	18.2
4. Government purchases on goods and services by government sector as a whole†.	22.4		20.9

*Defined as a sum of I(d) and 2.
†Defined as a sum of I(b), I(c), I(d) and 2.
SOURCE: OECD, *Statistics of National Accounts, 1951-1960*
(Paris, 1964), and Economic Planning Agency, *Annual Report on
National Income Statistics, 1966* (Tokyo, 1966).

because of the slower pace of tax reduction and of the growing demand for increased public wants.[4] As indicated in Table 12–4, in most
countries, except Austria and Belgium, the personal tax burden as
well as contributions to social security have increased.

With regard to the net balance for the government sector, we mentioned that it has been almost zero but recently showed a deficit.
Money flow account data in Table 12–5 indicate a deficit tendency
in Japan, the United States and a great deficit in the United Kingdom,
while a surplus is noted in Germany and France in the last five years.
It is likely that a country like Japan with low-tax revenues will have a
deficit balance in the public sector. This does not contradict a common notion concerning the surplus budget of the central government,
as noted before.

We now tentatively characterize our recent fiscal policy as (*a*) a
small-sized budget with low-tax revenues, (*b*) an extremely low
proportion of current expenditure in the GNP, (*c*) lagging public

---

[4] A. Maddison, *Economic Growth in the West* (New York: The Twentieth
Century Fund, and London: George Allen and Unwin Ltd., 1964), chap. 6.

France	Germany	Italy	Nether-lands	Norway	Sweden	U.K.	U.S.	Japan
19.4	23.3	21.6	23.5	29.8	21.5	15.4	16.5	29.7
			15.6	21.7	13.1	8.7	13.8	21.1
17.0	20.0	19.0	1.3	3.5	1.8	3.1	0.4	3.6
			2.3		3.3	2.0		
2.4	3.3	2.5	4.2	3.4	3.3	1.6	2.4	5.0
13.5	14.0	14.0	14.3	14.0	17.5	16.9	18.2	9.3
15.9	17.3	16.5	18.5	17.4	20.8	18.5	20.6	14.3
			22.1	20.9	25.9	23.6	21.0	17.9

investment behind fast economic growth, and (*d*) neutral or, sometimes, a tendency toward deficits in the government balance. In other words, there has been no significant effort to raise tax revenue by taking advantage of a fast rise in total income so as to meet pressing demands for public wants due to rapid growth and structural changes.

3. Simulation of Fiscal Policy

In the following we shall discuss the effects of an alternative fiscal policy on the basis of the international comparison in the previous section.

Had we experienced a higher tax burden and greater government current expenditure as in Europe, what would have been the effect especially on our growth rate? We use here the revised Medium-Term Macromodel, based on semiannual data of 1954–64, and consisting of 42 equations.[5]

First, we will examine the effect of higher rates of personal tax, social security contribution and indirect taxes as in Europe. For con-

---

[5] Economic Planning Agency, *Econometric Models for Medium-Term Economic Plan, 1964–1968,* A Report by the Committee on Econometric Methods (Tokyo: Government Printing Office, 1965); M. Tatemoto, T. Uchida, and T. Watanabe, "A Stabilization Model for the Postwar Japanese Economy: 1954–1962," *International Economic Review,* Vol. 8, No. 1 (February, 1967).

TABLE 12-2C

Rate of Fixed Investment of General Government
and Growth Rate of GNP for 1950-1963

		Austria	Bel- gium	Canada	France	Ger- many	Italy
A.	Rate of investment . . .	4.1	2.0	3.8	2.4	3.3	2.6
B.	Rate of growth	4.3	2.8	3.9	4.5	7.9	5.6
	A ÷ B.	95	72	97	53	42	46

		Nether- lands	Norway	Sweden	U.K.	U.S.	Japan
A.	Rate of investment . . .	4.2	3.4	3.4	1.6	2.4	5.0
B.	Rate of growth	4.8	3.7	3.3	2.8	3.3	9.7
	A ÷ B.	87	92	103	57	73	51

NOTE: A relates to the average for 1950-63, B relates mostly to the average for 1950-60, except Japan (1951-64) and Belgium (1953-60).

SOURCE: UN, *Yearbook of National Account Statistics, 1965* (New York, 1965), and Economic Planning Agency, *Annual Report on National Income Statistics, 1966* (Tokyo, 1966).

venience, we use the German tax rate in 1960 except for personal tax. As indicated below, column (1) relates to the original tax burden in 1960 and column (2) to the alternative tax burden based on the German tax system in the same year. Adjustment ratios in column (3) were used to adjust tax ratios for years other than 1960. For personal

	(1) *Original Tax Burden, 1960*	*(2)* *Alternative Tax Burden Based on the German Tax System*	*(3)* *Adjustment Ratio* $[=(2) \div (1)]$
1. Contributions to social security, as percent of personal income	3.9	14.9	3.82
2. Indirect tax, as percent of GNP	9.6	14.8	1.54

TABLE 12-3A

International Comparison of Government Account
(Components of Government Expenditure and Saving, as percent of GNP, 1960)

	Austria	Belgium	Canada	Denmark	France	Germany	Greece	Iceland
1. Government consumption expenditure	12.9	12.1	14.4	12.6	13.3	13.6	12.6	8.2
2. Subsidies.	1.6	1.1	0.7	0.3	1.6	0.5	0.5	8.5
3. Interest	0.8	2.5	3.0	1.1	1.3	0.6	0.3	0.2
4. Transfers to household	10.0	10.6	8.7	7.4	13.2	12.4	6.4	6.5
5. Transfers to the rest of the world	0.1		0.2	0.2	1.5	1.9	0.1	
6. Total current expenditure. . . .	25.4	26.4	27.0	21.7	30.8	28.9	19.9	23.4
7. Saving	5.1	-0.4	1.7	5.8	3.6	7.8	2.4	15.8

	Ireland	Italy	Nether-lands	Norway	Portu-gal	Sweden	U.K.	U.S.	Japan*
1. Government consumption expenditure	12.0	14.5	13.5	14.6	11.9	17.7	16.6	18.1	8.8
2. Subsidies.	3.0	1.8	1.2	3.9	0.7	1.2	2.0	0.1	0.2
3. Interest	2.8	1.9	2.8	1.0	0.8	1.9	4.1	1.5	0.4
4. Transfers to household	5.8	9.7	9.8	7.9	2.8	8.5	6.5	5.2	3.6
5. Transfers to the rest of the world	0.3	0.1	0.2	0.1	0.1	0.1	0.4	0.4	0.2
6. Total current expenditure. . . .	23.8	28.0	27.5	27.5	16.4	29.4	29.5	25.4	13.2
7. Saving	0.6	3.2	5.5	6.8	3.2	7.3	1.7	2.6	8.2

*Fiscal year basis.
SOURCE: OECD, *Statistics of National Accounts, 1951-1960* (Paris, 1964), and Economic Planning Agency, *Annual Report on National Income Statistics, 1966* (Tokyo, 1966).

TABLE 12-3B

Components of Government Revenues, as Percent of GNP, 1960

	Austria	Belgium	Canada	Denmark	France	Germany	Greece	Iceland
1. Personal tax and social security contributions.	14.3	12.1	7.6	11.9	15.0	16.5	7.7	9.3
2. Corporate tax.	2.1	1.6	4.4	1.2	2.4	3.1	0.4	6.6
3. Indirect taxes	14.2	11.4	13.2	12.2	16.3	14.3	12.2	29.1
4. Income from entrepreneurship, etc.	0.8	0.9	2.9	1.8	0.5	2.0	1.4	0.9
5. Transfers from household . . .			0.4	0.4		0.1	0.4	
6. Transfers from the rest of the world.	0.1		0.2		0.1	0.8	0.3	
7. Total revenues	31.5	26.0	28.7	27.5	34.4	36.8	22.3	39.2

	Ireland	Italy	Nether- lands	Norway	Portu- gal	Sweden	U.K.	U.S.	Japan*
1. Personal tax and social security contributions.	4.3	15.1	17.0	17.5	5.7	18.1	11.5	14.0	5.9
2. Corporate tax.	1.5	6.0	3.2		3.6	2.4	2.8	4.4	4.2
3. Indirect taxes	16.2	13.6	9.9	14.4	8.2	11.5	13.3	9.5	8.9
4. Income from entrepreneurship, etc.	2.3	2.1	2.5	1.2	1.6	3.4	3.5	1.5	1.5
5. Transfers from household . . .		0.6		1.2	0.5	1.3	0.1		1.0
6. Transfers from the rest of the world.	0.1		0.5		0.1			0.1	0.0
7. Total revenues	24.3	31.2	33.0	34.2	19.6	36.8	31.2	28.0	21.5

*Fiscal year basis.

SOURCE: OECD, *Statistics of National Accounts, 1951-1960* (Paris, 1964), and Economic Planning Agency, *Annual Report on National Income Statistics, 1966* (Tokyo, 1966).

TABLE 12-4

Direct Taxes on Household as Percent of GNP, 1950 and 1960

	Austria		Belgium		Canada		France		Germany		Italy	
	1950	1960	1950	1960	1950	1960	1950	1960	1950	1960	1950	1960
1. Direct taxes on households	15.0	14.3	11.3	12.1	4.8	7.6	13.1	15.0	13.9	16.5	12.4	15.1
2. Total contributions to												
social security	5.4	6.2	5.1	6.3	1.4	2.0	9.4	11.3	8.0	9.8	7.4	9.1
3. Other direct taxes	9.7	8.1	6.2	5.8	3.4	5.5	3.7	3.7	5.9	6.7	5.0	6.0

	Netherlands		Norway		Sweden		U.K.		U.S.		Japan*	
	1950	1960	1950	1960	1950	1960	1950	1960	1950	1960	1950	1960
1. Direct taxes on households	13.3	17.0	15.4	17.5	10.8	18.1	11.1	11.5	9.5	14.0	7.1	5.9
2. Total contributions to												
social security	4.2	7.9	1.8	4.9	0.7	3.9	3.3	3.6	2.4	4.1	1.8	2.6
3. Other direct taxes	9.2	9.1	13.5	12.5	10.1	14.2	7.7	7.9	7.1	10.0	5.3	3.3

*Fiscal year basis.

SOURCE: OECD, *Statistics of National Accounts, 1951–1960* (Paris, 1964), and Economic Planning Agency, *Annual Report on National Income Statistics, 1966* (Tokyo, 1966).

TABLE 12-5

Financial Surplus or Deficit by Sector, Average 1960-64

	Japan	U.S.	U.K.	Germany	France
Government	-190	-5.0	-767	6.9	0.1
Household.	1,868	13.7	587	19.0	14.4
Private corporation. . .	-1,832	-8.2	214	-25.1	-16.2
Oversea.	154	-2.0	94	-0.8	1.7
Statistical discrepancy.		1.5	-128		

NOTE: Japan......billion yen   U.S.......billion dollars
        U.K........million pounds   Germany...billion marks
        France.....billion francs

SOURCE: Bank of Japan, *Economic Research Bulletin*, January, 1966.

tax, we assume no tax reduction during the past 10 years.[6] This implies that there is a tendency for the average tax ratio to increase from 7.2 percent in 1954 to 10.7 percent in 1964 as percent of personal income. It should be noted that on this assumption the average personal tax burden in the past 10 years is 8.4 percent, which is still a little below the German ratio of 9.3 percent in 1960.

Obviously this policy of tax increases causes deflationary pressure throughout the economy. The result is given in column(B) of Table 12-6. The real GNP is reduced by ¥4.88 trillion in 1964, implying that growth fell from 9.8 to 7.4 percent during the past 11 years. Among GNP components, private fixed investment was most greatly affected by the lower rate of economic activity. The rate of increase of private consumption was also reduced as a result of the higher tax

---

[6] Instead of the original formula in the Medium-Term Macromodel, we used a personal tax function with the following specification, i.e.,

$$T_p + R = -97.0 + 0.1247 \, Y_p + 0.2893 \, Z$$
$$(0.0025) \quad (0.1031)$$
$$\overline{R}^2 = 0.992 \qquad \overline{S} = 23.8 \qquad d = 2.39$$

where T_p = personal tax, R = personal tax reduction accumulated since 1953, Y_p = personal income, Z = dummy variable with the first-half year = 0 and the second-half year = 100, $\overline{R}^2$ = adjusted coefficient of determination, $\overline{S}$ = adjusted standard error of estimate, d = Durbin-Watson ratio. Thus, R indicates a shift of the constant term of the tax function. The higher marginal tax ratio in this function gives a relatively low multiplier effect although the assumption of constancy of the marginal ratio may be subject to criticism.

TABLE 12-6

Effects of Increase in Taxes and Government Current Expenditure, 1964 (Fiscal Year)*

	Standard Simulation A	Effect of Tax Increase B	Effect of Increase in Current Expenditure C	Alternative Fiscal Policy D (=A + B + C)
1. GNP† (1,000 billion yen)	22.32	-4.88	5.17	22.61
2. Private consumption expenditure† (1,000 billion yen)	10.54	-3.46	3.00	10.09
3. Private fixed investment† (1,000 billion yen)	5.20	-1.87	1.62	4.95
4. GNP in current prices (1,000 billion yen)	26.24	-8.44	8.98	.26.77
5. General deflator (1960 = 100)	117.6	-15.5	16.3	118.4
6. Consumer price deflator (1960 = 100)	126.3	-22.8	24.1	127.6
7. Wage rate (= wages and salaries per employee) (1,000 yen)	417	-13.3	140	424
8. Net exports in current prices, accumulated for 1954-64 (1,000 billion yen)	-0.21	4.90	-5.72	-1.04
9. Net balance of the government accumulated for 1954-64 (1,000 billion yen)	-4.40	12.75	-12.85	-4.50
10. Accumulated private fixed investment†, 1954-63 (1,000 billion yen) .	22.77	-7.63	7.01	22.15

*Figures are subject to rounding errors.
†Indicates values in 1960 prices.

burden and the lower rate of economic growth. This type of deflationary tendency is also indicated in terms of aggregate money income. GNP in money terms is more sharply reduced by this tax increase than is real GNP, reflecting the lower levels of prices and money wages. It must be noted, however, that price levels in terms of both general and consumer prices still continue to rise, though at a much slower rate, since they are as low as 92 to 94 in 1954. This indicates a strong downward rigidity of prices and wages, suggesting the necessity of employing a structural policy toward specific sectors. The real wage also declined from ¥330,000 to ¥274,000 per annum, i.e., from 5.1 percent to 3.1 percent in terms of an annual rate of increase.

There are four types of serious imbalance in this simulation: (*a*) an enormous trade surplus, (*b*) an increase in the government surplus, (*c*) unused capacity, and (*4*) increased unemployment. The export surplus is mostly due to the decline of the growth rate; whereas the increased surplus of the government is caused by the tax rate increase and the suspension of personal tax reduction amounting to ¥665 million since 1954, though the increase in tax revenue is partly cancelled by the reduced rate of growth of total income. The degree of idle capacity can hardly be measured by the model itself, but a crude check on the relation between accumulated investment and output indicates the existence of large unused capital stock in 1964. With regard to unemployment, the result of our simulation is subject to a wide margin of error and does not indicate a sizable increase in unemployment despite a sharp drop in GNP. This rise in "open unemployment," however, clearly reflects a fair amount of increase in "hidden unemployment" in agriculture and small business.

In summing up, the tax increase to European standards causes a much lower rate of increase of the aggregate demand, but the rate of growth is still higher than that of the European countries, while there are serious deflationary gaps which need to be filled by increased government expenditures.

We have thus to turn our subject to the expenditure side of fiscal policy. Here again we use the German expenditure pattern as below:

	(*1*) *Original Ex-* *penditure* (%)*	(*2*) *Alternative Ex-* *penditure* (%)*	*Adjustment* *Ratio* [= (2) ÷ (1)]
1. Transfer payment	3.6	12.4	3.46
2. Government current expenditure	8.8	13.6	1.54

* Valued as percent of GNP in 1960.

The increased government consumption and transfer payments undoubtedly have expansionary effects on the economy, thus offsetting the contractions resulting from the tax increases. As can be easily understood, the increased government expenditure in column (C) of Table 12–6 raises total demand and prices and also absorbs foreign trade surplus and idle capacity to a great extent. It also produces a favorable effect on employment. If these two opposite effects are taken together, the joint effects are mostly canceled with each other as shown in column (D). It is rather striking that the adoption of the European-type fiscal policy to Japan does not affect the high rate of economic growth. Strictly, there is a slight decline of private consumption and investment, but it is offset by a substantial increase in government consumption, thus giving a slightly higher level of total demand. The proportion between private and public consumption is now substantially changed from 84:16 to 77:23. Although there is hardly any difference in net balance of the government, net balance of foreign trade deteriorates to some extent, due to a slightly higher level of aggregate demand.

As for price and wage levels, there is also no significant difference between the standard and alternative simulation in column (D). However, the latter has a little stronger effect on prices and wages due to its larger aggregate demand and its higher rate of capacity operation as indicated in the ratio of item 1 to item 10 in column (D). In this respect the lower private fixed investment in column (D) mostly reflects a higher indirect tax rate used in our alternative simulation. For real wages, column (D) indicates a slight increase as compared with our standard simulation, while the level of total employment also returns to about the same level.

Thus, it can be said as a tentative conclusion (a) that the adoption of the European fiscal structure for Japan tends to cause a lower share of private expenditure for both investment and consumption and a higher share of public expenditures through a greater tax burden on private business and households, but it does not significantly affect the overall growth rate and the net balance of the government, (b) that such policy usually produces a more favorable effect on social welfare through increased expenses for social security, education and research, public health, etc., which are essential to sustained high-economic growth and the resulting changes in economic and social structure, as discussed later, and (c) that a fiscal or monetary policy dealing with total demand does not help to reduce price rises without employing a drastic deflationary policy.

III. THE ROLE OF STRUCTURAL POLICY FOR PRICE STABILITY

Our last problem is concerned with a compatibility between growth and price stability, since price levels, especially consumer prices, started rising at a faster pace in recent years, thus becoming one of the most serious obstacles for further economic growth. There is a growing possibility that a spiral of consumer price and wage levels would eventually cause a rise in wholesale prices which have been stable ever since 1951, thus affecting the international balance of payments. As mentioned in our fiscal policy simulation, it proved to be extremely difficult to check such a rising tendency by suppressing aggregate demand through fiscal or monetary measures because of a downward rigidity of the price and wage levels in recent years.[7] Thus we shall focus our attention on structural change in the economy, such as in agriculture, and the labor market, rather than on management of aggregate demand by fiscal and monetary policy.

1. *Submodels of Prices and Wages*

Our model experiment in this problem is not one related to "incomes policy," but one which affects the supply side of the economy with the aim of raising the efficiency of resource allocation. As a typical example for this we shall take up the liberalization of food imports. Since the rise in prices of food in recent years accounts for nearly half the rise in consumer prices, a policy that liberalizes food imports will no doubt affect the rising trend of consumer prices. Another important aspect of such a policy is the promotion of labor mobility from agriculture to industry. A substantial encouragement of growth in nonagricultural sectors would promote expansionary tendencies, thus compensating for the discouraging effect on marginal producers in agriculture. In the following pages we shall analyze effects of structural policy on output, price and wage levels. Here again we employ a simulation approach, which is designed to provide only a crude estimate of the effects of the structural policy.

Since there are no such variables in our present model as food

---

[7] T. Watanabe, "Price Changes and the Rate of Change of Money Wage Earnings in Japan, 1955–1962," *The Quarterly Journal of Economics,* Vol. 53 (February, 1966); P. A. Samuelson and R. Solow, "Problem of Achieving and Maintaining a Stable Price Level—Analytical Aspects of Anti-Inflation Policy," *American Economic Review,* May, 1960.

price, food import, agricultural employment, etc., we shall use the approach of adjusting the constant terms of the relevant functions dealing with consumer price deflator, wage rate and commodity imports on the basis of a submodel accounting for these variables.[8] The relevant equations are based on quarterly data from 1953 to 1964.[9]

$$\dot{p}_{wf(t)} = 2.600 + 0.820\, \dot{C}_{f[(t-5)+(t-6)]/2} - 1.435\, M_f/C_{f(t-2)} \quad (1)$$
$$(0.119) \qquad\qquad (0.289)$$
$$+ 0.197\, \dot{p}_{wr(t-1)} + 0.091\, \dot{p}_{mf(t-2)} - 0.056\, T_{e(t-2)}$$
$$(0.045) \qquad\qquad (0.029) \qquad\qquad (0.049)$$
$$R^2 = 0.788 \quad S = 1.633\ (\%) \quad d = 1.455.$$

$$\dot{p}_{cf(t)} = -2.017 + 0.536\, \dot{w}_{s(t)} + 0.226\, \dot{p}_{cr(t)} - 0.194\, \dot{x}_{v(t)} \quad (2)$$
$$(0.081) \qquad\quad (0.102) \qquad\quad (0.050)$$
$$+ 0.459\, \dot{p}_{wf}$$
$$(0.157)$$
$$R^2 = 0.740 \quad S = 2.284\ (\%) \quad d = 1.262.$$

$$\dot{w}_{(t)} = -5.291 + 0.310\, \dot{p}_{c(t)} - 8.162 \sum_{i=2}^{5} u_{(t-i)}$$
$$(0.141) \qquad\quad (1.863) \qquad\qquad\qquad (3)$$

$$+ 0.354 \sum_{i=0}^{3} l_{a(t-i)} + 1.086\, y_{c(t)}$$
$$(0.141) \qquad\qquad (0.161)$$
$$R^2 = 0.846 \quad S = 1.68\ (\%) \quad d = 1.95.$$

An overhead symbol . indicates an annual percentage rate of increase (e.g., $\dot{p}_{wf(t)} = [p_{wf(t)} - p_{wf(t-4)}]/p_{wf(t-4)}$).$p_{wf}$ is the wholesale price index for food, C_f is private consumption expenditure for food; M_f is import of food; p_{wr} is producer's price of rice fixed by the government; p_{mf} is import price of food; T_e is temperature; p_{cf} is consumer price for food; w_s is wage rate in small enterprises; p_{cr} is consumer's price of rice fixed by the government; x_v is shipment of vegetables to Tokyo and Osaka; w is wage rate; p_c is implicit deflator for consumer price; u is unemployment rate; l_a is share of agricultural employment in total labor force; y_c is share of corporate profit in national income before inventory valuation adjustment.

In equation (1) the long-term movement of wholesale prices of

---

[8] We might have rebuilt a complete new global model including these additional variables, but time did not permit this effort. The adjustment of constant terms is merely a matter of convenience aiming at a rough approximation of the policy implications of our present study.

[9] The author is particularly indebted to Messrs. A. Saito and S. Nagaya for research assistance in estimating these equations.

food is accounted for mostly by demand for food with a lag exceeding one year, government-fixed price of rice and food imports. This wholesale price is included in equation (2) as an explanatory variable so that the government policy on food imports and price of rice have indirect effects on consumer price. The consumer price of food is also explained by other factors such as wages in small business, distribution and transportation policy for vegetable supply to large cities and policy on the consumer price of rice. Equation (3) differs from that in our Medium-Term Macromodel, in that we now include variables that measure labor mobility from agriculture to industry and profit share in national income.

In our experiment on the liberalization of food import, we assume that during the past 10 years there has been a gradual increase in additional imports of food which amount to $1 billion in current prices in 1964. Thus, the ratio of imports to private consumption of food is assumed to rise gradually from 6.6 to 7.7 percent in 1955, and from 9.2 to 15.8 percent in 1964. In view of the fact that the actual values of this ratio were about 6 to 9 percent for the past 10 years as indicated here, it is clear that this assumption would have significant effect on food prices and agricultural production. Our preliminary calculation of the direct effect on prices based on the equations (1) and (2) indicates that the wholesale price of food would decline about 5 percent annually, so that the gap between domestic and international price levels (c.i.f. value) would be narrowed greatly in 1964. For the rate of increase in consumer prices as a whole, our estimate of the direct effect of the food imports indicates a decline from 3 to 1.4 percent per annum during our period.

Secondly, we assume that the price of rice is fixed by the government at the 1954 level in terms of both wholesale and consumer prices. This assumption has a negative effect on the rise of consumer prices as a whole of about 0.4 percent per annum.

In Table 12–7, a summary of these direct effects of trade liberalization and the stabilization of rice price are indicated, distinguishing between the first and second half of our observation period.

The increased food imports give rise to other important effects in addition to those on consumer and wholesale prices: (*a*) an increase in total imports and a decline in the trade surplus, (*b*) a decline in related domestic production and employment, (*c*) a mitigation of wage pressure due to increased nonagricultural employment. The first effect can be dealt with in our model by changing the constant term of the import function. For the second effect, input-output

TABLE 12-7

Direct Effect of Food Imports and
Stabilized Rice Price on Consumer Price
(Percent)

		1955-59	1960-64	1955-64
1.	Increase in food imports. . . .	-0.9	-1.6	-1.2
2.	Stabilization of rice price at 1954 level.	.0	-0.8	-0.4
3.	Total direct effect	-0.8	-2.4	-1.6

NOTE: 1. Average annual percentage rate of increase during the period.
2. Subject to rounding error.

analysis was employed to estimate the reduction of related output and employment.[10] In terms of value added by agriculture, the increased food imports would have reduced the growth rate of agriculture in the past from 4.4 to 3.5 percent per annum, while in terms of employment the rate of decrease would have been accelerated from 2.6 to 4.4 percent per annum. With regard to the third effect related to the wage level, the reduced agricultural employment was introduced in equation (3) to provide a crude estimate of the change in wage levels. The result indicates that an additional decline in the share of agricultural employment would have lowered the rate of increase in the money wage rate from 8.2 to 7.1 percent annually during the past 10 years. As in the case of consumer prices, the negative effect on the wage increase is higher in the second half of our observation period.

2. Simulation of Structural Policy

Now we can do an overall simulation by taking into account all of these direct effects derived from our submodel. We adjusted the constant terms of the import function, consumer price function, and wage determination function in our global model, and then made an experiment on the basis of the alternative fiscal policy simulation in

---

[10] First the effect of the increased food import on the value added in agriculture was estimated by employing input-output matrix multipliers, and the result was then applied to a production function for agriculture in the EPA, Long-Term Model II to obtain the effect on agricultural employment. Economic Planning Agency, *op. cit.*

column (D) of Table 12–6.[11] The results are indicated in columns (E), and (F) in Table 12–8. In view of the deflationary effect of food imports, we made an additional simulation that included a gradual reduction of the interest rate so as to bring about a long-term expansionary effect, as shown in column (G). In column (H), joint effects of our alternative simulation of fiscal and structural policy are indicated in terms of levels instead of differences.

We readily note that the direct effect of food imports in column (E) causes a contraction in most of the items in this table, although prices and wages decline only slightly, as in the case of the tax increase. The deficit in the balance of foreign-trade increases, but by less than the original increase in food imports, implying that a decline of total demand diminished induced imports. The change in the parameters of consumer price and wage functions in column (F) indicates a similar tendency except for private consumption, prices, wages, and balance of payments. The rise in private consumption in real terms clearly reflects the stabilization of consumer prices, especially food prices. It is interesting to note that this rise in private consumption is higher than the reduction resulting from the higher tax burden in our previous simulation, thus suggesting that the higher tax burden can be compensated by stabilization of relative prices for consumption with the aid of the appropriate structural policy based on this increased tax revenue. Unlike the results of other types of simulation, a sharp drop in both general and consumer prices is shown in this column. It should be noted that this drop is even greater than that in column (B) of Table 12–6 based on a tax increase despite the fact that the decline in real GNP is less than one tenth of that due to a tax increase. The rise in the balance-of-payments surplus mainly reflects a decline in imports resulting from a slight drop in GNP.

Our last simulation in column (G) relates to the gradual reduction of the interest rate, starting from zero in 1954 to 10 percent in 1964, so that the interest rate in 1964 turns out to be 7.2 percent instead of the original 8 percent. Needless to say, this effect is expansionary on both total demand and price and wage levels. Though the effect on the accumulated balance of payments is negative,[12] a substantial financial

---

[11] Strictly, we should also take into account the direct effect of food imports on wholesale prices and supply of total labor force (e.g., retirement of female employment from agriculture, etc.). But they are omitted from the present study in the interests of simplicity for illustration.

[12] Since there is a possibility that increased imports might stimulate exports through improved balance-of-payment positions of foreign countries and that resource allocation might turn to the advantage of the industrial sectors and

TABLE 12-8

Effects of Additional Food Imports

	Alternative Fiscal Policy D	Change in Import Function E	Change in Consumer Price and Wage Functions F	Effect of Cut in Interest Rate G	Alternative Fiscal and Structural Policy H (= D + E + F + G)
1. GNP* (1,000 billion yen)	22.61	-.55	-.33	.56	22.29
2. Private consumption expenditure* (1,000 billion yen)	10.09	-.14	.93	.0	10.87
3. Private fixed investment* (1,000 billion yen)	4.95	-.14	-1.17	.67	4.30
4. GNP in current prices (1,000 billion yen)	26.77	-.98	-5.58	1.76	21.98
5. General deflator (1960 = 100)	118.4	-1.4	-23.3	4.8	98.5
6. Consumer price deflator (1960 = 100)	127.6	-2.5	-35.3	4.9	94.7
7. Wage rate (= wages and salaries per employee) (1,000 yen)	424	-16	-91	29	346
8. Net exports in current prices, accumulated for 1954-64 (1,000 billion yen)	-1.04	-1.16	.15	-.67	-2.72
9. Net balance of the government accumulated for 1954-64 (1,000 billion yen)	-4.50	-.93	-.96	1.07	-5.32
10. Accumulated private fixed investment*, 1954-63 (1,000 billion yen)	22.15	-.77	-2.25	3.06	22.19

*Indicates values in 1960 prices.
NOTE: 1. Columns E, F, and G relate to differences, while columns D and H to levels.
2. Figures are subject to rounding errors.

surplus is indicated in the government balance, which will enable government investment to be increased. This may suggest that for promoting growth the government surplus caused by an easy money policy needs to be large enough to finance further government investment in order to keep up with increased private investment, and that a higher tax burden would be a prerequisite for such a policy.

Finally, if we compare our final result of fiscal and structural policy in column (H) with the standard simulation in column (A) of Table 12–6, the following remarks can be made: (*a*) with the aid of an appropriate policy mix the value of real GNP remains almost at the same level as in the standard simulation even after significant fiscal and structural policy, (*b*) stabilization of price levels has been achieved as a result of appropriate increases in food imports, (*c*) private consumption becomes a little higher due to lower consumer prices even though it is affected by a substantially increased tax burden, (*d*) private investment declines because of reduced inflationary tendencies so that the incremental capital-output declines slightly, (*e*) the balances of both government and foreign trade indicate an increased deficit, the latter being greater.

IV. CONCLUDING REMARKS

Now we can summarize the features of postwar growth policy of the government and make some suggestions about future policy-making efforts.

As mentioned earlier, the government has been actively engaged in promoting private investment through corporate tax, monetary policy, and government financial activities. For private consumption, government policy has been oriented towards stimulating it through continuous and excessive tax reduction. Thus the overall tax burden to the GNP has been kept at an extremely low level by Western standards. There has been no effort to increase the tax burden by taking advantage of the high-economic growth rate. This relatively low tax revenue was connected with the traditional balanced budget principle until 1965, and it is our impression that the flexibility needed for countercyclical policy has been quite limited and that there has been a continuous lag of public investment, and shortages of government consumption and expenditure for social security. As for the government balance, a neutral or inflationary tendency has been found

---

their exports, this negative effect on our balance of payments might be exaggerated to a certain extent.

in the past, if central and local governments are combined together. There has been no effort to create a substantial surplus in the budget to strengthen the financing of private investment. Thus, we say that the imbalance in promoting growth between the private and public sectors is the most basic feature of our fiscal policy.

The small-sized budget has also been closely connected with a serious lag in structural policy in particular for the stability of prices. The backwardness of social overhead, housing investment, and social security due to a limited government budget have been great impediments for raising productivity, labor mobility, and efficiency in resource allocation, thus leading to a continuous price rise in low-productivity sectors under government protection. The quick rise in food prices in recent years is one of the typical examples of this deficiency in dynamic structural policy. Such a policy is essential to a fast-growing economy, where rapid changes in economic and social structure are taking place.

Our simulation approach in the previous two sections provides several suggestions for a possible future in growth policy. As noted already, the adoption of the European-type larger sized fiscal budget does not itself affect our overall growth rate and price levels, though the share of private consumption tends to decline. With this expanded fiscal policy, it becomes feasible to employ a structural policy to stimulate competition in low-productivity sectors, such as agriculture, and to stabilize price levels through increased imports, as indicated in the previous section. Actually, in the course of these structural changes the increased tax burden will be largely compensated for by the rise in disposable income and consumption in real terms, which follows from stabilized consumer prices. Furthermore, in view of a possible fast increase in imports, the government measures to strengthen the international competitiveness of leading manufacturing sectors will also be needed through more active private and government financing, as shown in our last simulation of interest rate. A recent trend of a growing trade surplus in the balance of payments appears to make it easier to utilize our policy measures as compared with the past decade.

To summarize, our desired long-term policy mix for growth and price stability should be a combined effort (*a*) to expand the size of government budget based on higher tax revenues, (*b*) to stimulate competition in the private sector by lifting various protective devices, particularly import barriers and (*c*) to strengthen leading sectors especially through financial measures.

PART III

Summary Remarks

13 | Notes on Japan's Economic Growth

SIMON KUZNETS

I. INTRODUCTION

The papers in this volume provide new and valuable long-term records, and additional insights into many aspects of a strategically important case of economic growth. But neither the papers nor the discussion at the Conference revealed fully the problems of analyzing and explaining Japan's economic growth—and naturally so: the quantitative basis for a complete formulation, which lies in comparative analysis, has become available only recently and still lacks some crucial components. The reflections presented below emphasize, by design, the limitations of hypotheses commonly advanced to explain Japan's impressive growth record. Even if the results are more unanswered questions, such a critical and seemingly destructive enterprise may still be a help in clearing the path to a more productive view of the analytical problems.

By way of introduction we begin with Table 13–1. It could easily be expanded to provide more detail for Japan, and to add more developed countries to the comparison. But the import of the table is clear enough as it stands, and would not be affected by expansion. Even after downward revision of the Japanese growth rates derived from the original series published in 1957, the rates—for both total and per capita product—are at the upper end of the range for developed countries. Only the aggregate product growth rate of the United States and the per capita product growth rate of Sweden approach those of Japan. Nor is there any indication that the rate is declining in Japan. Despite the inclusion of World War II in the longer period in Table 13–1, the rate is somewhat higher than in

TABLE 13-1

Aggregate Rates of Growth, Japan and Other Selected Countries
(Percentages per Decade)

	1870-79 to 1925-29			1870-79 to 1960-64		
	Total Product (1)	Population (2)	Per Capita Product (3)	Total Product (4)	Population (5)	Per Capita Product (6)
1. Japan (initial period, 1874-79) . . .	42.3	11.3	27.8	44.7	12.2	29.0
2. United Kingdom (excluding Ireland before the 1920's).	19.3	9.5	9.0	19.9	7.6	11.4
3. France (constant boundaries, initial period, 1871-80).	20.9	1.3	19.4	19.5	2.4	16.7
4. Germany (West Germany after 1936) .	22.7	10.6	11.0	30.4	11.3	17.2
5. Italy (initial period, 1890-99) . .	23.1	6.6	15.6	27.4	6.8	19.3
6. Sweden.	30.3	6.6	22.2	36.2	6.5	27.9
7. United States	41.0	19.8	17.7	38.0	17.3	17.7
8. Australia	31.1	25.7	4.3	32.7	22.2	8.6

NOTES: Based on revised estimates prepared for republication of the series of papers entitled "Quantitative Aspects of the Economic Growth of Nations," in *Economic Development and Cultural Change*. Product is either GNP or GDP.

The Hitotsubashi revised series for Japan was extended back by a combination of the agricultural series, in Volume 9 of *Estimates of Long-Term Economic Statistics of Japan since 1868*, with the Shionoya index of manufacturing output--on the assumption that the ratio of output in the S sector to the sum of the outputs of the agricultural and industrial sectors was the same in 1874-78 as in 1879-83 (in constant prices).

the shorter period—an acceleration that is found in several other countries but not in all (compare columns 4 and 1 and columns 6 and 3). If further revisions of the long-term series for Japan still leave the rate of growth of its total and per capita product at the upper end of the range among the developed countries—and it is difficult to assume otherwise—the question is as to the major factors that would explain this high growth record.[1] These factors, once

---

[1] The discussion in the Appendix to my paper, "Trends in Level and Structure of Consumption," Chapter 7 of this book, indicates that with the maximum allowance for the effects of the new series, the rate of growth in PCE per capita for 1879–83 to 1924–28 becomes 16.2 percent per decade, compared with 26.8 percent for the series used in the paper (see Table 7A–1, lines 19 and 20, column 3, entries in parentheses); for the full period, 1879–83 to 1962–64(F), the growth rates per decade are 17.4 and 24.8 percent, respectively (see page 237).

In considering what the new series would mean for the growth rate of total product, we *cannot* assume that the "residual" (see Table 7–1), i.e., the difference between PCE and GDP, largely government consumption and capital formation, expressed as a fraction of GDP, can remain the same. This assumption would imply *proportional* revisions in the combined total of government consumption and capital formation as large as those suggested for PCE by the new series—and since both capital formation and governmental consumption are directly derived from a variety of data, it is highly unlikely that further work would yield major revisions. It seems more realistic to assume for the present that the absolute values for the "residual" would remain about the same.

Using this assumption, the shares of the "residual" in GDP in Table 7–1 (derived directly from column 4), and the proportional difference between the new and the old series on personal consumption expenditures in constant prices (from Table 7A–1, line 8), we can secure a new set of indexes of GDP per capita for 1879–83, 1924–28, and 1962–64(F), as follows:

	Proportion of "Residual" to PCE, from Table 7–1 (1)	Proportion, Reflecting Shinohara Series (2)	PCE per Capita, Reflecting Shinohara Series (3)	GDP per Capita (based on Shinohara) (4)
1879–83	21.0/79.0 = .2658	21.0/(79.0 × 1.79) = .1485	50.9	50.9 × 114.85 = 5846.
1924–28	26.4/73.6 = .3587	26.4/(73.6 × 1.21) = .2964	100.0	100 × 129.64 = 12964.
1962–64(F)	44.3/55.7 = .7953	same as col. 1	190.0	190.0 × 179.53 = 34111.

From the last column we derive growth rates, per decade, of 19.4 percent for 1879–83 to 1924–28, 29.7 percent for 1924–28 to 1962–64(F), and 23.9 percent for the full period; which compare with 28.9, 31.8, and 30.2 percent,

identified, would also implicitly explain how Japan could have grown at all, i.e., at rates that were *within* the representative range (which, for per capita product, was between 12 and 18 percent per decade for some 16 developed countries). But the attempt to account for a rate of growth higher than average puts an extra burden on the explanatory hypotheses; and there is some value in doing so, because attention to the more extreme cases (whether high, such as Japan and Sweden for per capita product, or low, such as Australia and the United Kingdom) would facilitate the explanation of the mechanism of economic growth within the central range.

The discussion below touches upon two groups of factors commonly associated with the high rates of growth in Japan—its late entry into modern economic growth and great economic backwardness at the initial stages; and its dual structure. We also comment on the presumptive importance of foreign trade—the major mechanism by which a less developed country secures the means of modernization, particularly economic. These three broad topics all refer to the overall high rate of growth in Japan over the full period—but with particular relevance to the subperiod before the 1920's or 1930's. Another topic that calls for brief comment is the apparent major break in structure after the 1920's—especially in the allocation of product between consumption and capital formation. This topic is particularly relevant to the post–World War II period when the Japanese record of savings and capital formation proportions is striking and distinctive.

II. BACKWARDNESS AND BACKLOG

It need hardly be urged that Japan's case is exceptional, both because it is the only country of non-European background and

---

respectively in the paper (see Table 7–1, lines 22–24, column 2). Thus for the two long periods above (they are slightly different from those used here, because of the need to make the latter comparable with those easily available for other countries), use of the revised series reduces the rate of growth of per capita GDP about a third for the first 45 years, and about a fifth for the full period.

If we apply these adjustments to the growth rates for per capita GDP, given in Table 13–1, 27.8 and 29.0 percent per decade for the earlier and full period, we get 18.5 and 23.2 percent, respectively (suggesting a much more conspicuous acceleration in the later part of the long period). For total GDP the rates, which are given as 42.3 and 44.7 percent respectively, become 31.9 and 38.2 percent. Even with this reduction, the growth rates for per capita product are matched only by Sweden (now exceeded by the latter), and those for total product are matched only by the United States and Sweden.

origin that managed to join the economically developed group, and because it began with a per capita product that was far lower than that of the other developed countries *before* their industrialization. If we can accept the rough estimates now available, the per capita product of Japan in the late 1870's was between a half and a third of that of most European developed countries before their entry into modern economic growth, at dates ranging from the late 18th to the late 19th century. If, as a reflection of the low per capita product, savings and capital formation proportions were correspondingly low in Japan, it is all the more analytically challenging to find that the growth rate of its aggregate product (with rather moderate growth of population) was at the upper end of the range.

Yet a lower per capita product, greater economic backwardness, means a greater backlog of unexploited technology, material and social; and the possibility of utilizing this vast stock of tested but still unused knowledge leads to the notion that a more backward country might grow more rapidly on this borrowed knowledge than the less backward areas that entered modern economic growth earlier, but with a scantier stock of knowledge. This association between backwardness and rapidity of ensuing growth is strongly suggested by Henry Rosovsky in his excellent summary of Professor Gerschenkron's thesis as applied to Japan, when he writes: "Industrialization seems more promising in proportion to the backlog of technological innovation which the country can borrow. Thus, industrialization is based on borrowed technology assuring a *high speed* of development."[2] A similar point is made in the Watanabe paper (Chapter 4) in this volume which deals with "a synthetic hypothesis which can explain rapid industrialization" and then, as one central thesis in the hypothesis, stresses the role of Japan as a "latecomer," the achievement of technological progress by means of imported or borrowed technology, and "the rate of adoption of this imported technology has been quite high." A line of association is thus drawn between low per capita product, "late arrival," greater backlog, borrowed or imported technology, and a high rate of growth.

A closer examination of the hypothesis reveals three sets of implications, which must be specified in distinctive ways to yield the suggested association. (*a*) The first refers to the character of the backlog of technology, from which the backward country can borrow once it initiates its growth process. (*b*) The second concerns concomitants and consequences of economic backwardness, *other* than the avail-

---

[2] See Henry Rosovsky, *Capital Formation in Japan, 1868–1940* (New York: The Free Press, 1961), p. 57 (italics mine).

ability of a larger technological backlog to borrow from. (*c*) The third sharpens the bearing of the first two sets of implications, stressing that the higher growth rates to be explained are long term and relate to the economy as a whole—not to some "modern" sector.

a) That a greater backlog of unexploited technology means a higher rate of growth implies some specific patterns of technological as well as of economic growth. This can be demonstrated by formulating, for illustrative purposes, patterns of additions to the stocks of technology and of economic growth in which the expected association is *not* given.

Consider the case in which new technology shifts from one sector to another, being limited first to sector A, then to sectors B, C, D, etc., without significant spread effects from one sector to another. Assume that economic growth also follows a distinct sectoral sequence, so that any given phase, the "catching up," the shift from premodern to modern, is accomplished sector by sector, from A to B, to C, etc. Under these assumptions a leading developed country has only modern sectors, and new technology is being pursued in a completely new sector Z (say atomic energy); and a most backward country has only the premodern sectors, and there is no sign of Z (or of any other "new" sector).

Under these conditions, the economic growth of the most backward country, once initiated, will be concentrated first in A, then in B, then in C, etc.; whereas the growth of a less backward country, but still a follower, will be concentrated in D, E, F, etc. Unless the relative backlog in D, E, F, etc., is smaller, thus implying a lower growth rate than the backlog in A, B, C, etc., we cannot assume that the growth of the most backward country, once initiated, will be at a higher rate than that of a less backward country that began its growth earlier. Indeed, there is no reason to assume that the rate of growth will be higher in the follower countries than in the pioneer country, since we cannot specify that the technical advance and economic expansion are relatively more limited in Z than they were in the now complete and technologically stagnant sectors A, B, C, etc. (up to but not including Z). Clearly, this model denies any association between the rate of growth and the magnitude of the technological backlog, barring, as it does, the possibility of cumulative growth of technology within any single sector, and limiting the sector-sequence in the process of growth and borrowing to one sector at a time.

The illustration is unrealistic in several respects. While at any given period technological progress and innovation do tend to be concentrated in a few sectors, innovations and progress are not necessarily completely absent in the other sectors; and progress in sector K or L may well affect productivity in sectors A, B, etc. The recent concentration of technological progress in the United States on atomic energy, electronic computers, and space did not mean stagnation in the technology of agriculture or of textile manufactures—to name the older sectors. Thus, the spread of computers has raised productivity in almost all sectors of the economy. Hence, even if the sectoral sequence in the process of economic growth were as rigid as suggested in the illustration, the latecomers with their backward technology would enjoy the comparative advantage of a greater backlog of unexploited technology in *any* sector, no matter how old, greater than was available to the earlier entrants with their lesser backwardness. Likewise, it is unrealistic to limit the mechanism of economic growth to one sector at a time. Indeed, in view of the interrelations among sectors, such limitation would be incompatible with sustained growth. But this means that the backlog would be greater in the sense that advanced modern technology characterizes many more sectors when entry into the growth process is later than when it is earlier.

Yet there is sufficient realism in the illustration to suggest caution in evaluating the technological backlog presumably available to the backward country. Although economic growth does not follow a rigid sectoral sequence, atomic bombs are not put ahead of more productive agriculture except when perversions are introduced by militant nationalism; nor does advanced electronic technology assume importance before a relatively secure foundation has been laid in the basic consumer and producer goods industries. Hence, much of the stock of technology accumulated with the passage of time in developed countries may not be relevant to the needs of the backward latecomer; and in that sense, while possibly borrowable, will not add to the capacity for growth for a long time. Another part of the stock of technology may not be easily borrowable because it is not suited to the conditions of the backward country (e.g., laborsaving devices of Western agriculture, for land-saving requirements of intensive monsoon agriculture). Borrowing in such cases may require the capacity for substantial modifications, and this capacity is not likely to be attained until the backward country has advanced sufficiently in the process of its growth. Thus *relevance* of the existing stock of unexploited technology may change over time in the process of growth itself—increasing because the once backward country acquires greater capacity for modification, or because its scale of priorities shifts toward the more advanced components of technology. But, in application to our hypothesis, this means that late entry and greater backwardness, while implying a greater *total* stock of unexploited technology, do not necessarily imply a greater *relevant* stock—compared with an earlier entrant country with less backward status. If the hypothesis is to hold, we must argue that the relevant borrowable technology is, in the long run, greater for a country that comes in late and starts low, than for a country that comes in early and with less backwardness—an argument that, given the special sets of priorities and the greater costs of technological borrowing for a truly backward country, is not immediately convincing for comparisons between late and early followers. At any rate, the argument calls for a more systematic examination of the concept of the relevant stock of technology, and greater attention to the factors involved in the capacity to borrow and to transform—a point that leads us to the second set of implications, related to the "other" concomitants of backwardness.

b) A country's late entry into modern economic growth, largely or partly the reason for its greater economic backwardness, must, in turn, be due to some obstacles to economic modernization. If these obstacles vanish the moment growth begins, we need only consider the greater technological backlog for borrowing, the factor discussed above. But if the obstacles tend to persist—at full, or even reduced, strength—for a long period following initiation of economic growth, they must affect the growth rate attained.

The interrelation between lateness of entry, degree of backwardness, and magnitudes of the obstacles to growth that may *survive* for the long term, is of cardinal importance to the hypothesis under examination. If lateness of entry, and the resulting greater backwardness, imply greater obstacles to modern economic growth, and if such obstacles survive for a long period, then, *despite* the greater technological backlog available for borrowing, growth rates may not be any higher than for earlier entrants, with smaller technological backlogs but also with lesser obstacles to growth.

Indeed, it is not difficult to construct a model in which the association between late entry and greater backwardness, on the one hand, and greater stock of borrowable technology *and* greater surviving obstacles to growth, on the other hand, results in the *same* growth rates, at least for all follower countries. Thus assume $n-1$ follower countries, all equally aware of the potentials of economic growth demonstrated by the leader, but all facing obstacles to growth of different weight—and designate these weights W_2, W_3 . . . W_n in order of increasing burden. These follower countries will then enter modern economic growth only when B_t, B_{t+1}, etc., which represent the borrowable technology that increases over time, and thus exerts an increasing pull on would-be followers, reach levels significantly above W_2, W_3, etc., and thus overcome the obstacles represented by the latter. *If* the rate of survival (or reduction) of the obstacles, once growth begins, is proportionately the same (or the same, subject to only chance variations), the long-term growth rates of the different countries, which are functions of (B_t, W_2), (B_{t+1}, W_3) . . . , should not differ significantly for follower countries.

It follows that the hypothesis under examination can be retained only if we deny any association between the degree of backwardness at the beginning of growth and the strength of the surviving obstacles to long-term growth; or reduce the parameters of the surviving obstacles to insignificance, compared with the presumptive advantages of a greater backlog of borrowable technology. Thus, association between late entry and greater obstacles to growth would not hold if knowledge of and contact with development potentials is not fully and equally available to all would-be followers, but is a matter of historical chance determined partly by changes in transportation and communication. Japan's entry was delayed, not because, presumably fully informed since the late 18th century of the potentials of economic growth, it labored under the handicap of particularly severe obstacles, but because it was historically and geographically isolated. Once the contact was established, even if by outside aggression, Japan could grow rapidly because its late entry was *not* ascribable to some major entrenched obstacles to economic modernization. Alternatively, it may be argued that even if the association exists, even if late entry does usually signify greater obstacles to the *initiation* of modern economic growth, the rate of resistance or survival of these obstacles is low, compared with the presumptive advantages of a greater borrowable stock of unexploited technology.

The validity of all these arguments would differ with the degree of generality claimed—so that broadly valid associations would still permit conspicuous exceptions, of which Japan would be one. But whatever the judgment, if it is claimed that late entry and greater backwardness are connected with a higher growth rate once growth is initiated, it must also be demonstrated that the country's institutions and historical heritage, connected with greater backwardness and possibly responsible for the delay in entry, do *not* constitute major growth obstacles, the survival of which would reduce the long-term growth rate. The resulting shift in emphasis in analysis from the presumed dominance of a greater backlog of borrowable technology to the country's institutions and organizational endowment, seems to me crucially important. In the light of this shift, Japan's late entry and the decades of growth that ensued must be examined in terms of the political, social, and economic structure that was a concomitant—if not a cause of—this late start. The backlog aspects of late entry, while important, may be far less relevant analytically than the capacity of Japan's political and social structure for rapid modernization without a breakdown, than the technological potential that existed within Japan's traditional agriculture, than the education and skills of its labor force.

Unfortunately, even if these aspects of preindustrial Japan are relevant, we have no tested theory of economic growth that clearly identifies the social, political, and even economic variables that are obstacles to economic growth, those that are inducements, and those that are neutral; and there are always questions of degree that are not easily ascertainable. For example, too much political stability in the sense of rigidity can be as deadly to economic growth as too much political instability and turmoil. But can one specify how much is "too much" *ex ante* by objective tests? Yet, difficult as it is to quantify these and other domestic variables in premodern Japan, and establish in comparative analysis that, in this particular case, historical heritage and endowments were or were not clearly superior to those of many other would-be late or earlier comers (in imposing lesser or greater obstacles to a high and sustained growth rate in the future), we have no choice but to follow this difficult path. The alternative, to rely on an assumed lack of association between greater backwardness and greater obstacles to growth, would be to take as valid a hypothesis that is patently unrealistic.

c) In considering backlog as an inducement and backwardness as an obstacle to economic growth, it must be stressed that growth refers to the long period and the total economy. This long-time and wide economy perspective affects our view, particularly with respect to the greater technological backlog thesis. Two illustrations may suffice.

The first refers to the wide differences possible among different sectors of the economy in transferability of modern technology—particularly as between agriculture and nonagricultural industry. In the case of agriculture, which reflects the specific natural endowments, so different in many Asian and African countries from those of the temperate West, transfer of modern technology may be far more difficult, and directly less effective, than in the case of modern manufacturing which is less dependent on land, soil, and climate. The weight to be assigned to the technological backlog may be much greater for the growth of modern manufactures than for the growth of the economy as a whole—including agriculture and other major traditional sectors. Unless we can assume an automatic and significant backward linkage between modern manufacturing and traditional agriculture, growth of modern industry may contribute little to the growth of the total economy. And experience, in both recent and past decades, shows that growth of modern industry—up to a rather large share in the national output—cannot be counted upon, in and of itself, to have much effect on the agricultural sector of developing countries.

The second illustration refers to the long span of time over which the high rate of growth is observed and is to be explained. Table 13–1 suggests that the high rate of growth of Japan is long term; and while the details are not given there, we can assume that the growth rate for both total and per capita product, has been at the upper end of the range throughout—so that if we calculate it for four-decade spans, the result for 1920 to 1960 is as high (relative to most other developed countries) as that for 1870 or 1880 to 1910 or 1920. But if the high rate of growth is to be explained by the greater technological backlog at the beginning of growth, a continuation of this high rate for say four decades should imply a *reduction* in the backlog, if the latter is represented, as it well may be, by the spread between per capita levels of the leader and the follower countries. If the United States has been the leader, and if from the 1870's to the 1920's the per capita product of Japan grew at a rate that was distinctly higher than the rate for the United States, the respective per capita products would have converged, implying a reduction in the total technological backlog, and also a tendency for the Japanese growth rate to move toward that of the United States, with the excess of the former being reduced. No such convergence appears to have occurred in the later part of our period.

Of course, in our discussion above of the concept of technological backlog, arguments were adduced to explain the persistence of the relevant or borrowable backlog, even after the passage of decades in which high growth rates might have reduced the proportional weight of the total backlog. But it is useful to add here that the fact that the time span over which growth rates are observed is long reinforces the earlier critical comments on the concept of the technological backlog and hence on its relevance to the explanation of high growth rates. It may have greater relevance to the explanation of a short-lived, decade spurt than to an advantage in growth rates that persists over long periods for almost a century.

III. DUAL STRUCTURE

"Dual structure" may refer to the contrast between traditional and modern sectors, or between labor-surplus and labor-requiring sectors, or between small- and large-scale industries, or between capital-intensive and labor-intensive sectors, or between low-product-or-income per worker and high-product-or-income per worker sectors. Of course, these dichotomies or dualities overlap—in that the traditional sector is also likely to be the labor-surplus, small-scale, labor-intensive, and low-product-or-income per worker sector; whereas the modern sectors are likely to display the opposite characteristics. We are not concerned here with niceties of definition, and proceed on the assumption that we can agree on the meaning of dual structure in its broad spectrum and also on the fact that this dual structure is often assigned an important role in the economic growth of Japan, where it is claimed to be particularly conspicuous.

Of course, with a wide spectrum in the meaning of dual structure, the nature of its contribution to growth (and by implication of a more "dual" dual structure, *ceteris paribus,* to a higher rate of growth) can also vary. Thus in a country where duality means the existence of a large traditional sector that can satisfy persisting and growing domestic demand for its goods, and does so with increasing effectiveness using abundant traditional resources, the rate of growth would be higher than in a country where the demonstration effect on consumption is so strong that it raises the real costs of consumption and reduces the potential for domestic savings. Likewise, if duality means the existence of a large traditional sector, capable of generating a large export flow with efficient use of abundant traditional resources, its contribution to growth via foreign trade would be greater than in cases where the traditional sector is not an active member of a "duality" in which the other member is the modern sector of the *rest of the world.*

But we are concerned here with the more commonly assumed contribution of dual structure to growth, that suggested in the Lewis-Ranis-Fei models. These stress the argument that the traditional, labor-surplus, low-wage-and-product sector provides cheap labor to the labor-requiring, capital-intensive, high-profit-and-big-savings modern sector—both within the same country; and that the contribution at a low (and for a long period unchanging) rate of compensation of sustained volumes of labor by the traditional to the modern sector enhances the possibility of profits, high-savings rates, and rapid capital accumulation in the modern sector—without adversely affecting the output of the traditional sector that is only shedding its surplus labor.

As Professor Abramovitz pointed out at the Conference (bearing particularly on the Ohkawa-Rosovsky paper, Chapter 1), a crucial question with respect to this thesis is whether the wage rate is low for the same quality of labor (as between the two sectors in the economy). And there are other related questions ranging from one as to the existence of labor surplus in the traditional sector, if its technology is fixed, to the one of the relevance of cheap labor supply to modern sectors which are usually characterized by limited labor requirements and demands for highly specific labor skills. But we are less concerned here with a general discussion of the various aspects of what is essentially a quantitative problem than with the empirical data usually adduced to reveal and measure the duality of structure in the meaning just suggested—in Japan and elsewhere.

Two sets of statistical data are usually employed. (*a*) One type— used in Chapter 1—relates to the product (or compensation) per worker in major sectors within the economy—particularly agriculture, on the one hand (standing for the traditional, small-scale, low product, etc., sector), and manufactures or all nonagriculture, on the other (standing for the more modern, larger scale, higher product or compensation per worker sector). (*b*) The other type of data—that employed in the Watanabe paper—measures size differentials within a given sector, usually manufactures, and in particular the scale differentials in compensation and product per worker. With either set of data, difficulties arise in linking the statistical evidence with an interpretation of the bearing of the differences revealed by the data upon the growth rate of an economy; and it is our purpose here to illustrate the difficulties in the hope that data more relevant to the dual structure thesis (as specified above) can be found.

a) In the first illustration we compare intersectoral differences in product per worker, for selected years within an 80-year period, for Japan and the United States (Table 13–2). Several conclusions stand out clearly.

First, whether we measure intersectoral differences in product per worker in terms of current or constant prices makes little difference in the trends, and even in the levels, of the A/M or A/N ratios that we are comparing (lines 1–16, columns 2 and 3, and 4 and 5). In Japan, where the dual structure, the contrast between labor-surplus agriculture and labor-demanding modern sectors, is presumably much sharper than in the United States, the A/M ratios are only slightly lower than those in the United States, and the A/N ratios are not

TABLE 13-2

Intersectoral Differences in Product per Worker, Japan and the United States

A. DIFFERENCES BASED ON LABOR FORCE AS GIVEN

| | Share of A Sector in Labor Force (%) (1) | Ratios of Product per Worker | | | |
| | | A/M | | A/N | |
		Product in Current Prices (2)	Product in Constant Prices (3)	Product in Current Prices (4)	Product in Constant Prices (5)
Japan, GDP, 1880–1960 (Constant Prices to 1934–36 Base)					
1. 1880	82	0.43	0.44	0.40	0.40
2. 1890	76	0.375	0.37	0.35	0.34
3. 1900	70	0.36	0.36	0.36	0.36
4. 1910	63	0.44	0.44	0.38	0.38
5. 1920	54	0.38	0.38	0.39	0.39
6. 1930	50	0.26	0.26	0.25	0.25
7. 1960	35	0.29	0.30	0.33	0.34
United States, NNP, 1839–1919 (Constant Prices to 1860 Base)					
8. 1839	66	0.38	0.53	0.39	0.42
9. 1849	61	0.34	0.37	0.36	0.41
10. 1859	57	0.42	0.40	0.37	0.36
11. 1869	53	0.46	0.47	0.43	0.39
12. 1879	50	0.49	0.49	0.39	0.36
13. 1889	42	0.34	0.35	0.31	0.31
14. 1899	38	0.39	0.37	0.35	0.31
15. 1909	31	n.a.	0.34	n.a.	0.31
16. 1919	27	n.a.	0.34	n.a.	0.32

B. EFFECT OF DIFFERENCES IN STRUCTURE OF LABOR FORCE

	Ratio of Share in Labor Force, Adjusted to Unadjusted			Adjusted Ratios of Product per Worker (Constant Price Base)	
	A Sector (1)	M Sector (2)	N Sector (3)	A/M (4)	A/N (5)
Japan, 1920-1960					
Excluding all women					
17. 1920.	0.90	1.06	1.12	0.45	0.49
18. 1930.	0.87	1.10	1.12	0.33	0.32
19. 1960.	0.79	1.13	1.10	0.43	0.47
Excluding women in agriculture					
20. 1920.	0.74	1.32	1.31	0.68	0.70
21. 1930.	0.72	1.28	1.28	0.46	0.45
22. 1960.	0.58	1.20	1.20	0.62	0.71
Excluding unpaid family labor					
23. 1960.	0.55	1.25	1.22	0.68	0.76
United States, 1869-1919 and 1960					
Excluding all women					
24. 1869.	1.10	n.a.	0.90	n.a.	0.32
25. 1879.	1.09	n.a.	0.91	n.a.	0.30
26. 1899.	1.11	n.a.	0.93	n.a.	0.26
27. 1919.	1.13	n.a.	0.95	n.a.	0.27
Excluding women in agriculture					
28. 1869.	0.97	n.a.	1.04	n.a.	0.42
29. 1879.	0.96	n.a.	1.04	n.a.	0.39
30. 1899.	0.94	n.a.	1.04	n.a.	0.34
31. 1919.	0.92	n.a.	1.03	n.a.	0.36
Based on net product, current prices					
32. 1960, unadjusted.	1.00	1.00	1.00	0.54	0.53
33. 1960, excluding all women.	1.35	1.12	0.97	0.45	0.38
34. 1960, excluding women in agriculture.	0.91	1.01	1.01	0.59	0.58
35. 1960, excluding unpaid family labor.	0.95	1.01	1.00	0.57	0.56

TABLE 13-2 (Continued)

NOTES: *Lines 1-7:* The underlying series on labor force and gross domestic product by sectors are from the Ohkawa-Rosovsky Hitotsubashi tables. The labor force figures are for single years; for gross domestic product they are three-year totals for 1880 and 1960; and five-year totals centered on the other years, to derive sector shares. The A sector includes forestry and fishing; the M sector is limited to mining and manufacturing; the N sector is all except the A sector.

Lines 8-16: The underlying series on labor force and national income (net national product) for 1839-99 are based on Robert E. Gallman and Thomas J. Weiss, "The Service Industries in the 19th Century" (mimeographed paper submitted to the Conference on Research in Income and Wealth in 1967), and on Robert E. Gallman, "Commodity Output, 1839-1899," in William N. Parker (ed.), *Trends in the American Economy in the Nineteenth Century, Studies in Income and Wealth,* Volume 24 (Princeton, N.J.: National Bureau of Economic Research, Princeton University Press, 1960). In the first source the authors give the distribution of total product (Tables 2 and 4, pp. 6 and 13) and of gainfully occupied (Table 7, p. 19) between commodity and service sectors. We broke down the commodity component into agriculture, mining and manufacturing, and construction by applying their shares in commodity product and labor force in the second source (for commodity product, Table A-1, p. 43, variant A for construction; and for labor force, Table 6, p. 30). The construction share was then shifted to limit the M sector to mining and manufacturing.

The shares for labor force and NNP in constant prices were then extrapolated from 1899 to 1909 and 1919 by the movement from 1900 to 1910 and 1920 (for labor force) and from 1894-1903 to 1904-13 and 1914-23 (for NNP), in Simon Kuznets, "Long-Term Changes in the National Income of the United States of America since 1870," in Simon Kuznets (ed.), *Income and Wealth, Series II* (Cambridge: Cambridge University Press, 1952), Table 17, p. 102 (for shares in NNP, 1929 prices) and Table 19, p. 107 (for shares in labor force).

Lines 17-23: The underlying data for distribution of labor force by industrial attachment and sex for 1920 and 1930 are from Irene Taeuber, *The Population of Japan* (Princeton, N.J.: Princeton University Press, 1958), Table 28, p. 87. Those for 1960, both on sex distribution by sector and distribution by labor force status (which distinguishes unpaid family workers) are from United Nations, *Demographic Yearbook, 1964,* Table 12, pp. 404-5. In all cases, the shares are in totals excluding the components unallocated either by industrial attachment or by labor force status.

The ratios in columns (1), (2), and (3) are derived from the shares in labor force before and after adjustment. The entries in columns (4) and (5) are obtained by dividing the entries in lines 5-7, columns (3) and (5), by the ratios of the entries in column (1) to those in columns (2) and (3), in lines 17-23.

TABLE 13-2 (Continued)

Lines 24-31: The distribution of labor force, agricultural, and nonagricultural, by sex is from American Philosophical Society, *Population Redistribution and Economic Growth,* Memoir 45 (Philadelphia, 1957), Reference Table L-4, p. 609. The calculation is similar to that followed for lines 17-23.

Lines 32-35: The distribution of labor force for 1960 is from United Nations, *Demographic Yearbook, 1964* (New York, 1965), Table 12, pp. 392-95 (M was limited to mining and manufacturing). The distribution of net domestic product (in current prices) is based on totals for 1958-62 from United Nations, *Yearbook of National Accounts Statistics, 1965* (New York, 1966).

at all lower.[3] In the United States, product per worker in the A sector (and presumably also compensation per worker) was between a half and a third of that in the M sector, while in Japan it was between four-tenths or more and a quarter. Does this difference signify that the dual structure was strong enough to effect a rate of growth of per capita (or per worker) product in Japan more than one-and-a-half times that of the United States? The comparison of the A/N ratios is perhaps more pertinent here, since N includes such modern sectors as construction, transportation and communication, professional activities, and government, in addition to mining and manufacturing. Yet the A/N ratios are at about the same levels in the United States and Japan. In view of this finding, what particular relevance can this aspect of the dual structure have to an explanation of the high rate of growth in Japan?

Second, it should be noted that the United States is not exceptional with respect to the low levels of the A/M or A/N ratios (despite the discrimination against a large Negro minority in its A sector). Inter-sectoral differences no narrower than those in Japan can be found in several other developed countries. The comparison is confined to the A/N ratios because with M in Table 13-2 limited to mining and

---

[3] The A/M ratios in Table 13-2 differ somewhat from those in the Ohkawa-Rosovsky paper (Table 1-4, last column). For current price volumes, the A/M ratio in the Ohkawa-Rosovsky paper is 0.50 in 1886, ranges between 0.45 and 0.51 through 1917, and declines to 0.20 in 1961. In Table 13-2, the A/M rate ranges from 0.36 to 0.44 between 1880 and 1920, and then drops to 0.29 in 1960 (column 2, lines 1-7). The differences are due to the use in the Ohkawa-Rosovsky paper of revised estimates for both output and labor force. These estimates are not available either for total product (and hence for the A/N ratios), or in sufficient detail for the labor force to permit the analytical adjustments carried through in Table 13-2. While the revised series could not be used, the differences do not affect the relevance of the findings and of the questions that they raise.

manufacturing, comparable data are not at hand. The average A/N ratio for Japan for 1880–1920 is 0.38 (lines 1–5, column 4, for product in current prices); that for Germany (1882, 1895, and 1907) is 0.39; that for Norway in 1910 is 0.35 (and averages 0.34 for 1910, 1930, and 1950); and that for Sweden for 1880–1920 (total population) averages 0.35.[4] To be sure, in several countries the A/N ratio is larger, but there is no clear association between it and the rate of growth.

Third, the comparisons in Panel A are based on labor force as given. But the structure of labor force, with respect to age, sex, occupational status, education, etc., may differ widely not only among sectors within Japan but also between sectors in Japan and in other countries (e.g., the United States). Hence the A/M and A/N ratios may be low for Japan because labor force includes all women in agriculture and all unpaid family labor (which is most dominant in agriculture); whereas in other countries these groups are excluded or are less important. And, of course, other intersectoral differences in quality of labor may be more prominent in Japan than in other developed countries.

The adjustments for sex differences, and for differences in the proportion of unpaid family workers, made in Panel B of Table 13–2 are extreme, in that they exclude *all* women or *all* unpaid family workers, whereas these groups presumably do contribute to output. But since the contribution of women, and of unpaid family workers, is distinctly lower per head than that of full-time wage earners and entrepreneurs, if only because the former may be working fewer hours, some adjustment for differences of this kind is needed.

Although the adjustments in Panel B are maximum, with respect to effects of differences in the distribution by sex and in the relative proportion of unpaid family workers (but reflect no other quality differentials), the findings are highly suggestive and indicate the importance of such adjustments. The effects on the A/N ratios are

---

[4] See my Paper II in "Quantitative Aspects of the Economic Growth of Nations," *Economic Development and Cultural Change,* Supplement to Vol. V, No. 4 (July, 1957), App. Table 6, pp. 100–04.

For the same countries and dates the average A/M ratio (M defined more broadly to include construction and sometimes electric light and power) is 0.65 for Germany, 0.44 for Norway (all three dates), and 0.51 for Sweden. These averages are above that for Japan for 1880–1920, which is 0.40 (Table 13–2, column 2, lines 1–5). Yet the ratios for Norway and Japan are not significantly different, given the approximate character of the estimates. And the telling fact is that the ratio is much below 1 in all these countries—which would suggest that the "dual structure" is as much a factor in them as in the United States and Japan.

far greater for Japan than for the United States—because the relative proportions of women and of unpaid family workers in Japan are so much greater in the A sector than in the other sectors and this is not true of the United States. As a result the adjustment raises the A/N ratios for Japan far more than it does for the United States, and the adjusted ratios suggest a more conspicuous "duality" in the United States than in Japan. A striking illustration is provided for 1960, when the unadjusted A/N for Japan is 0.33 (line 7, column 4), about six-tenths of that for the United States, which is 0.53 (line 32, column 5, also in current prices)—indicating a greater contrast in Japan. With the adjustment to exclude unpaid family labor, A/N in constant prices in Japan more than doubles, rising from 0.34 to 0.76 (line 7, column 5 and line 23, column 5), and the same adjustment applied to A/N in current prices raises it from 0.33 to 0.68. But adjusted A/N for the United States (line 35, column 5) is only 0.56—suggesting a greater "duality" in the United States.

Even more interesting is the effect of the adjustment on the widening of the dual structure in Japan between 1920 and 1960. The unadjusted A/M and A/N ratios, for constant price shares, decline from 0.38 and 0.39 in 1920 to 0.30 and 0.34 in 1960 (lines 5 and 7, columns 3 and 5)—declines of more than a fifth for A/M and of over a tenth for A/N. Adjusted to exclude women in agriculture—the best approximation of the desirable adjustment to exclude or minimize unpaid family labor—A/M declines from 0.68 to 0.62, or a tenth, and A/N remains about the same, 0.70 and 0.71 (lines 20 and 22, columns 4 and 5). Obviously, much of the widening of intersectoral differentials in product per worker in Japan was associated with an increased proportion of women and of unpaid family labor in agriculture, relative to their proportions either in the M or in the N sectors. How much similar widening in other quality differentials contributes to the general widening of the intersectoral differentials in product or income per worker is a matter that warrants further exploration.

b) Turning now to dual structure in Japan within a single sector, particularly manufacturing, reflected in the contrast between small- and large-scale plants, we find that two aspects of such dualism are usually stressed. One is that in manufacturing, the share of small-scale plants in total employment (or product), is still quite large, compared with that in other countries. This may well be so, since it reflects the continued importance of traditional sectors in Japanese manufactures, and these are usually small-scale operations. In a recent study in which the distribution of employees by size of plant is shown for 32 industries in Japan (for 1956), the industries with the highest proportions of employees in the smallest size class (1–19 employees) are seafood (canning, packing, etc.)—59 percent; knitting mills, and apparel—45 percent each; grain products—51 percent; sawmills and planing mills—58 percent; wood containers—72 percent; and hardware—56 percent.[5] By contrast, in the nontraditional modern industries, the share of the smallest scale group in total employment is minuscule, e.g., steel works—none; petroleum refining—1 percent; aircraft—less than 1 percent; explosives—2 percent; pulp mills—4 percent; and rubber products—6 percent. That the persistence of demand for traditional products—whether agricultural, manufactured, or services—has been a source of strength in the economic growth of Japan, minimizing the adoption of far more costly Western consumer goods while increasing efficiency and utilizing established skills and supplementing labor with relatively inexpensive adaptations of modern power and technology, is a plausible hypothesis; and it has been stressed in the writings of Ohkawa and Rosovsky on the economic growth of Japan. But it was not the present dualism—a large proportion of small-scale manufacturing—that contributed so positively to the past economic growth of Japan. It was rather the persistence of demand for traditional goods, and the feasibility of raising productivity within these traditional branches without heavy material capital investment, that made the contribution in the past decades—*before* the emergence of modern industries such as steel, petroleum, and cement made for dualism. Thus, while the greater dualism of Japanese industry in post–World War II years can be demonstrated, it is not the dualism but the persistence of traditional manufactures with their rising productivity that is relevant to Japan's economic growth, particularly for the long period before current dualism emerged.

The other measure of dual structure in manufacturing—scale differentials in wages or product per worker, like those used in the Watanabe paper in this volume (and in a recent monograph by Seymour Broadbridge, *Industrial Dualism in Japan* [Chicago, 1966]) does present statistical problems. Since the data are treacherous, and I am not too familiar with the Japanese material, only brief comments are appropriate; but answers to the questions implied in these comments are indispensable, if the data and findings are to be used in comparative analysis.

First, scale wage differentials for manufacturing as a whole, like those used in Table 4–5 of Watanabe's paper (Chapter 4), may also

---

[5] Joe S. Bain, *International Differences in Industrial Structure* (New Haven, Conn.: Yale University Press, 1966), Table A–7, pp. 177–79.

reflect interindustry differentials, and in changing degree as time passes, with obvious effects on any conclusions concerning widening or narrowing "duality." This interindustry component in scale comparisons may explain, in good part, the narrow scale differentials shown in Table 4–5 for 1909 and 1914, in comparison with those in the post–World War II years. If before World War I, the largest plants in Japan's manufactures were, let us say, in textiles, with their high proportion of female employees, while the smallest plants were in apparel, again with a high proportion of females, the scale differential for total manufacturing in 1909 and 1914 would not have been affected much by the interindustry differential. But if after World War II, the largest plants were in petroleum refining, or in paper, with their heavy capital investment and practically no female labor, while the small plants were still largely in apparel, a large interindustry differential is a component of the scale differential for total manufacturing for the post–World War II years.

Second, this argument also applies to scale comparisons for narrower subdivisions of manufacturing, so long as they comprise rather distinct subbranches. This is certainly true of many divisions in Table 4–6, where broad categories such as foods, textiles, etc. may include individual industries that are different in average scale, quality of labor, and degree of organization (and hence monopolistic elements in compensation) of the latter.

On the other hand, if an industry is defined fairly precisely, the statistical reliability and analytical usefulness of the *range* in scale— between the smallest and the largest scale groups—are badly affected. When the percentage of employment in the smallest (or the largest) scale group becomes tiny, a range measure is erratic; more important, the measure loses its significance. Of what importance is a scale differential of 300 or 400, when one term in the comparison represents 0.7 percent of total employment in an industry and the other term accounts for only 10 percent?

Finally, it is disturbing to find that while the ranks of industries with respect to the magnitude of scale differentials are significantly associated for 1909 and 1914, or 1954 and 1960, no such association is found when we compare the pre–World War I with post–World War II years. Thus Spearman's coefficient of rank correlation, calculated from the data in Table 4–6 of the Watanabe paper, is +0.55 for the 19 industries in 1909 and 1914, and +0.90 in 1954 and 1960, but it drops to +0.03 for 1909 and 1954. Even in Watanabe's Table 4–7, with industries more narrowly defined, the association between 1909 and 1954 is not significant (+0.28), while that between 1954 and 1960 is significant (+0.83). These measures suggest that the universe of scale duality is different in the post–World War II years from what it was in pre–World War I. This may be partly due to the use of daily wage rates for the earlier years, and of total payroll divided by number of employees for the later years. But, at any rate, a question as to comparability over time reduces the significance of the widening of the scale shown even for the more narrowly defined industries in Table 4–7.

We conclude these comments on the dual structure reflected in scale differentials in Japan's manufacturing industries, viewed either as a contribution to growth or as productive of problems resulting from it (survival of low-productivity pockets, etc.), with the impression that the data and analysis available raise more questions than they provide answers. More detailed data and closer analysis seem badly needed to minimize confusion and to provide more illumination of an important and changing aspect of Japan's economic structure.

IV. FOREIGN TRADE

The effect of foreign trade on economic growth could be measured if exports and imports could be revalued in terms of their contributions to the country's economic growth. We could then estimate the excess of growth-inducing gains from imports over growth-limiting losses from exports in terms directly relevant to economic growth. If exports, or resources embodied in them, had a value of X_g—the lower subscript referring to the contribution of X to the economic growth of the exporting country (say the percentage growth that they would contribute if they, or the resources embodied in them, were retained for domestic use); and if imports had a value of M_g—the contribution of imports to growth of GNP of the importing country, $M_g - X_g$ would then directly measure the percentage by which the balance of exports and imports induced growth of total product. But usually we have only the money magnitudes of X, M, and GNP, and a variety of detail on the economic classes within each; and our notions regarding the relation between growth and the supply of these various goods are very rough.

In some extreme cases, it is clear that what might be called the growth-inducing balance of trade must be large. Thus, if exports draw upon a country's natural resources, but leave an adequate supply for subsequent domestic use when development warrants it, if such resources are exported without any additional drain on the country's growth-promoting factors, and if in return for such exports—a large proportion of total product—imports are structured to maximize or enhance sustained growth within the country, then, of course, foreign trade should make a considerable contribution to growth. This is a clear case of export-led growth, since by definition exports are initiated by exogenous forces suggested by the low value of the resource within the exporting country; and since the imports made feasible are assumed to be growth-inducing.

There is the opposite extreme case in which exports represent a real drain upon a resource otherwise useful for economic growth— as may have been the case with several world-product booms in Brazil which drained labor from more continuous and productively cumulative uses—and the imports received in return are used either to expand exports until the export boom collapses and the investments are lost; or to purchase luxuries, or for a flight of capital from the country, or for ill-chosen infrastructure at home.

But we cannot *measure* the contribution of foreign trade to growth in the former case, or the loss of potential growth in the latter case, since we cannot estimate the specific growth-inducing or growth-limiting weights of imports and exports; and this is all the more true of the majority of the cases which are less extreme. Needless to say, these weights or effects depend upon the relative size of the country, its specific factor endowments, and the stage of its development. The smaller the country, the more indispensable for growth is foreign trade and the greater its benefits. The country's specific factor endowments will determine the structure of its exports, and, to a more limited extent, of its imports; and imports will be affected by the changing final demand structure that is part of a country's economic growth.

These rather obvious comments are needed to emphasize that the available and otherwise valuable data on foreign trade relative to total product, and on structure of exports and imports by classes, do not permit an adequate analysis of the relation of foreign trade to growth, let alone of the contribution to the high growth rate of Japan. Consider the data on commodity foreign-trade proportions for Japan, compared with those for several other developed countries (Table 13–3). In the early period, the relative importance of trade of Japan, barely 10 percent of its gross domestic product, was lower than for any other country listed (column 1). Yet this does not mean that foreign trade did not have a *greater* effect on Japan's total product and its growth, for clearly the low proportion reflected the recency of

TABLE 13-3

Commodity Foreign Trade Proportions, Japan and Other Developed
Countries, Selected Periods, 1870's to Date

Country and Product in Denominator	1870's to 1880's (1)	Eve of World War I (2)	1920's or Late 1920's (3)	Recent Period (4)
1. Japan, GDP.	10.3	29.5	35.5	19.4
2. United Kingdom, GNP . . .	40.7	43.5	38.1	30.4
3. France, NNP	32.4	35.2	n.a.	n.a.
4. Germany, total uses . . .	36.7	38.3	31.4	34.6
5. Italy, national income plus depreciation	21.3	28.1	26.3	25.0
6. Denmark, GDP (general trade).	52.0	69.1	61.6	53.9
7. Sweden, GDP	35,5	40.4	31.9	36.5
8. United States, GNP. . . .	12.9	11.0	10.8	7.9
9. Canada, GNP	30.9	32.2	41.5	31.2
10. Australia, GNP.	36.2	38.9	35.8	26.9

NOTES: For column (1) the dates for Japan are 1878-87, for the
United States, 1879-88 (to avoid effects of the Civil War) and for the
other countries around 1870-80. For column (2) the dates are usually
from 1909 or 1910 through 1913. For column (3) the period is usually
from 1925 to 1929, with the full decade of the 1920's for some countries.
For column (4) the period is usually 1957-63, but for Canada it is 1956-
60, and for Germany, 1960-63.
    The foreign trade proportions are from Simon Kuznets, Paper X in
"Quantitative Aspects of the Economic Growth of Nations," *Economic Development and Cultural Change*, Vol. 15, No. 2, Part 2 (January, 1967),
App. Tables I.1, 1.2, 1.3, 1.6, 1.7, 1.9, 1.10, 1.11, 1.12, 1.13, pp.
96-120 (with omissions). For Japan we also used the Ohkawa-Rosovsky
Hitotsubashi tables.

Japan's shift from isolation to participation in international trade; with
its greater economic backwardness, Japan may have gained so much
more from its imports than it lost from its exports, that the net growth-
inducing contribution of foreign trade may have made for a higher
growth rate than was true of the other developed countries with
higher foreign-trade proportions. Conversely, the much greater rise
from the late 1870's to the eve of World War I in Japan's foreign-
trade proportion than in the proportion for any other developed
country, is not necessarily evidence of a causal relation with a higher
rate of growth of total product in Japan. The rise in the proportion
may have been accompanied, as a result of economic development
and reduction of economic backwardness, by a rapid fall in the

growth-inducing coefficients of the balance of exports over imports. And if this growth-inducing contribution may not have been any less proportionately in Japan in the 1870's, despite its low foreign-trade proportion, it also may not have grown any faster despite the greater rise in the foreign-trade proportion. These, of course, are hypothetical statements, not assertions of substantive value; but they indicate the present limitations of our knowledge.

In short, statements concerning presumptive effects of foreign trade on economic growth are only plausible *obiter dicta;* and despite their plausibility and any attempts to establish common patterns, they are likely to remain so until our analysis distinguishes the specific growth contributions of the major classes of exports and imports, in comparison with similar categories of goods in domestic production and use. However, even preliminary judgments are of some use as long as it is remembered that they are suggestions, not tested assertions. Thus it is plausible to argue that for Japan, removed from isolation and facing the need for modern economic growth, if only to retain its political independence, foreign trade was of cardinal importance; and that in the early periods the greater growth-inducing properties of imports compared with growth-limiting losses via exports, must be assigned a large weight in any attempt to allocate economic growth among various sources. And it can also be plausibly argued that this growth advantage of foreign trade must have been significantly greater for Japan for some decades after initiation of growth than for the more developed and less backward countries—once allowance is made for the effects of size on foreign-trade proportions. If so, foreign trade must have contributed to the higher growth rate of Japan, at least in the earlier subperiods.

But if this is so, we are only saying that in this case the greater technological backlog of the more backward country is exploited partly through the mechanism of foreign trade, i.e., via the greater growth advantage of the exchange of exports for imports, assuming imports are chosen to enhance growth. Consequently, all that we suggested with reference to the concepts of total and relevant technological backlog and the persistence of that backlog over time, and to the interplay between backwardness and its concomitants and consequences also applies to the foreign-trade mechanism by which the presumptive advantage of backwardness is utilized. The change in the foreign-trade proportion of Japan was probably paralleled in several other less developed countries—a rapid rise from low to substantial levels (e.g., in many Latin-American countries)—but it did not lead to the kind of sustained growth at high rates that characterized Japan. If so, foreign trade should be construed as a permissive condition, which requires a variety of concomitant domestic factors that were operative in only a few cases.

V. CAPITAL FORMATION AND SAVINGS PROPORTIONS

Much of the preceding discussion dealt with the possible factors in Japan's high growth rate that would explain a low capital-output ratio, i.e., a capacity to generate a high rate of growth *despite* the limited proportion that domestic savings and imported capital constitute of total product. But, of course, Japan's capital formation and savings proportions may have been higher than those of other countries—so that Japan's high growth rate could have been attained even with the same capital-output ratios as in other developed countries. If this were so, the burden of analysis would shift toward explaining how a higher domestic savings rate or more foreign capital were secured, and there would be less emphasis on higher returns to the same inputs of capital; the factors noted, such as greater backwardness, dual structure, and gains from foreign trade, would assume a somewhat different role, in their bearing upon capital and savings proportions.

Because of data problems for earlier decades, it is best to begin the brief discussion with the recent years for which revised official data are now at hand. This post–World War II period merits emphasis on its own because the position of Japan, with respect to capital formation and savings proportions, is so conspicuous in these years relative to other developed countries. Then, after having discussed the recent years, we may ask how they appear in the light of a long-term perspective, and consider the long-term trends in the capital formation and savings shares.

a) In Table 13–4, we limit the measures to the 10-year span, 1955–64, in order to omit the immediate postwar years. The evidence shows that, compared with other developed countries (we omit the Communist countries because of the incomparability of measures and of underlying social and political structures), Japan's capital formation proportions—35 and 26 percent for gross and net proportions, respectively—are much higher than those for other countries, ranging from 18 to 29 percent for gross and from 10 to 21 percent for net. The rate of growth of aggregate product for Japan, almost 11 percent per year, is also much above those for the other countries, which range from 3.1 to 6.4 percent per year. And the incremental capital-output ratios for Japan, at 3.2 for gross and 2.4 for net, are lower than those

TABLE 13-4

Capital Formation Proportions, Rates of Growth of GNP, and Incremental C/O Ratios,
Japan and Other Developed Countries, 1955-1964

	Share of GNCF in GNP (%) Current Prices (1)	Share of GNCF in GNP (%) Constant Prices (2)	Annual Rate of Growth of GNP (%) (3)	Gross C/O Ratio (2)/(3) (4)	Share of Capital Consumption in GNP, Current Prices (%) (5)	Share of NNCF in NNP, Constant Prices (%) (6)	Net C/O Ratio (6)/(3) (7)
1. Japan.	33.6	34.6	10.8	3.2	11.3	26.3	2.4
2. West Germany . . .	28.2	26.4	5.7	4.6	9.3	18.9	3.3
3. Netherlands. . . .	27.2	27.0	4.6	5.9	9.4	19.4	4.2
4. Finland.	27.8	28.6	5.6	5.1	9.3	21.3	3.8
5. Italy.	22.2	22.1	6.4	3.5	9.3	14.1	2.2
6. United Kingdom . .	17.2	17.8	3.1	5.7	7.6	11.0	3.5
7. Belgium.	19.6	20.6	3.7	5.5	9.6	12.2	3.3
8. France	21.3	21.3	5.1	4.2	8.9	13.6	2.7
9. Denmark.	20.0	19.8	5.2	3.8	7.8	13.0	2.5
10. Norway	27.9	27.9	4.1	6.8	12.8	17.3	4.2
11. Sweden	22.5	22.1	4.2	5.3	n.a.	n.a.	n.a.
12. Switzerland. . . .	26.4	24.5	4.9	5.0	9.1	16.9	3.4
13. United States. . .	18.6	18.7	3.2	5.9	9.6	10.1	3.2
14. Canada	21.7	22.1	3.5	6.4	12.0	11.5	3.3
15. Australia.	24.2	24.6	4.1	6.0	7.5	18.5	4.5

NOTES: Data for Japan for fiscal years are the latest revisions of national accounts given in the Bank
of Japan, *Supplement* to *Hundred-Year Statistics of the Japanese Economy*; for all other countries from United
Nations, *Yearbook of National Accounts Statistics, 1965* (New York, 1966), (with adjustment for West Germany
to include the Saar and West Berlin before 1960).

The percentage shares in columns (1), (2), and (5) are averages of shares calculated separately for
1955-59 and 1960-64. The rate of growth in column (3) was computed from the totals of GNP in constant prices,
for 1955-59 and 1960-64, respectively.

Column (5) was derived from totals in current prices, and column (6) was calculated from columns (5) and
(2).

The ratios do not check because of rounding.

for other countries, which range from 3.5 to 6.4 for gross and from 2.2 to 4.5 for net.

It is the combination of a high capital formation proportion with a low capital-output ratio that yields the high growth rate of Japan's total product for 1955–64; and according to Table 13–4 the combination is unique to Japan. In some other countries the capital formation proportions are not much below those for Japan: in West Germany, the Netherlands, and Finland (that for Norway is known to be affected by overinclusion of maintenance), they range from 26 to 29 percent, gross, and 19 to 21 percent, net. But in these three countries the capital-output ratios are also high, from 4.6 to 5.9 for the gross ratios and from 3.3 to 4.2 for the net ratios. On the other hand, some countries have a fairly low incremental capital-output ratio—Italy, with a gross ratio of 3.5 and a net of 2.2; Denmark, with a gross ratio of 3.8 and a net of 2.5; and France, with a gross ratio of 4.2 and a net of 2.7. But in these three countries the capital formation proportions are relatively low, ranging from 20 to 22 percent for gross and 13 to 14 percent for net.

Table 13–4 raises two distinct, if related, questions. First, how did Japan, with its much lower income per capita, manage to attain in 1955–64 a much higher gross or net *national* capital formation proportion, i.e., a gross or net national *savings* proportion, than the other developed countries? Second, how, despite the large volume of capital investment (proportionately to its product), did Japan manage to attain a lower capital-output (or higher output-capital) ratio than most other developed countries? The questions are distinct, because the former is involved with the sources of savings, and the latter emphasizes the types and uses of capital investment. But they are related, because sources of savings are not unresponsive to growth of product, total and per capita, and thus to a high output-capital ratio; and returns to capital investment in the way of growth are not independent of the origin of savings, which may partly determine how effectively savings are channeled into growth-producing capital investment.

The second question, that relating to the incremental capital-output ratio, requires more information on structure of production and capital investment than is easily available, and more familiarity with the data for Japan and other countries than I have. The readily available data on the distribution of capital formation by type of capital good are not much help. In general, one would expect high proportions of construction, particularly of residential buildings, to lead to high capital-output ratios, and high proportions of producers' equipment (and inventories) to lead to low capital-output ratios. The share of residential construction in gross domestic capital formation in Japan, for 1955–64, is quite low, 12.7 percent in constant price volumes (separate estimates of other construction and producers' equipment are not available, judging by the revised national accounts given in the source cited in Table 13–4). For Italy and Denmark, the two countries in Table 13–4 with relatively low incremental capital-output ratios, the shares of residential construction are 25.8 and 15.6 percent, those of other construction are 28.7 and 26.5 percent, and those of producers' equipment are 41.3 and 50.1 percent (all of these and the percentages below are for volumes in constant prices except for Germany, and are averages of percentages calculated for the two quinquennia). And for Germany and the Netherlands, the two countries with high capital-output ratios, the shares of residential construction are 19.7 and 17.1 percent, of other construction 24.7 and 28.8 percent, and of producers' equipment 47.5 and 46.6 percent. No association is thus found between the structure of total domestic capital formation by these broad types of capital goods and the incremental capital-output ratio. Nor is such association likely to be found with the conventional distribution of capital formation among user sectors.[6] It may be that a meaningful analysis of the connection between capital investment and the incremental capital-output ratio would require the study of *growth potentials* of various capital uses, and these are not clearly distinguished in the standard classifications by type of capital good and by user sectors. At present, nothing useful can be added here to this complicated problem, except to urge that it merits detailed comparative analysis.

The first question, that relating to sources of national savings, can be explored more effectively; and Table 13–5, based on readily available sources, provides illuminating information. To minimize data problems, the table is limited to six countries, in addition to Japan; but they include countries with high and low capital formation proportions and countries directly affected by World War II and those only indirectly affected. To provide a more careful comparison, the decade 1955–64 was subdivided into three unequal periods.

The following findings may be noted.

(*i*) Japan's high capital formation proportion, higher even than those for countries like Germany, the Netherlands, and Finland, emerges *after* 1955–56. In the European higher capital formation and

---

[6] See my Paper V in "Quantitative Aspects of the Economic Growth of Nations," *Economic Development and Cultural Change*, Vol. VIII, No. 4, Part II (July, 1960), pp. 60–68.

TABLE 13-5

Structure of Gross National Capital Formation Financing,
Japan and Selected Developed Countries, 1955–1964
(Percentages; Underlying Totals in Current Prices)

	Share in Gross National Product					Share of NNCF in NNP (6)	Share of Household Savings in Disposable Income (7)
	Capital Consumption Charges (1)	Government Savings (2)	Private Corporation Savings (3)	Household Savings (4)	GNCF (5)		
Japan (fiscal years)							
1. 1955–56.	10.4	5.1	3.1	9.7	28.4	20.1	13.6
2. 1957–60.	10.7	6.9	5.0	10.9	33.5	25.5	15.8
3. 1961–64.	12.3	8.1	4.6	11.8	36.9	28.1	17.8
West Germany (public corporations with private)							
4. 1955–56.	8.3	7.8	2.0	8.8	26.9	20.3	12.9
5. 1957–60.	8.7	6.7	2.0	9.7	27.2	20.3	14.2
6. 1961–64.	9.7	7.5	1.3	8.5	27.0	19.2	12.8
Netherlands							
7. 1955–56.	9.1	4.0	5.0	7.8	26.0	18.6	11.6
8. 1957–60.	9.5	5.1	5.0	8.4	28.0	20.4	12.6
9. 1961–64.	9.3	4.9	3.8	8.8	26.8	19.3	13.0
Finland (public corporations with private)							
10. 1955–56.	7.4	9.5	4.4	6.2	27.5	21.7	9.2
11. 1957–60.	9.5	9.7	3.1	5.4	27.7	20.1	8.3
12. 1961–64.	10.0	7.4	2.3	8.4	28.2	20.2	12.5

	(1)	(2)	(3)	(4)	(5)	(6)	(7)
Switzerland							
13. 1955-56. . . .	8.6	6.3	4.7	4.3	23.9	16.7	6.0
14. 1957-60. . . .	8.8	5.3	4.4	5.6	24.2	16.9	7.8
15. 1961-64. . . .	9.6	5.5	4.1	7.7	27.0	19.2	10.9
United States							
16. 1955-56. . . .	9.0	2.6	3.4	4.4	19.3	11.3	6.5
17. 1957-60. . . .	9.6	1.3	2.7	4.2	17.8	9.1	6.1
18. 1961-64. . . .	9.9	1.4	2.8	3.8	17.9	8.9	5.7
Canada							
19. 1955-56. . . .	11.9	3.7	3.6	4.3	23.6	13.3	6.4
20. 1957-60. . . .	12.1	2.0	2.6	4.7	21.4	10.6	6.7
21. 1961-64. . . .	12.0	2.3	2.3	5.5	22.1	11.5	7.9

NOTES: The percentage shares are calculated from totals for the periods.
Household savings usually include savings of nonprofit private associations and corporations.
Unless otherwise indicated the savings of public corporations and government enterprises are included with government savings.
The sum of columns (1-4) should equal column (5). Discrepancies are due to rounding.
Column (6) is calculated from columns (1) and (5).

SOURCES: Bank of Japan, *Supplement to Hundred-Year Statistics of the Japanese Economy*; and United Nations, *Yearbook of National Accounts Statistics, 1965* (New York, 1966).

savings proportion countries, as well as in the other developed countries, the shares do not rise much after 1955–56, but in Japan the rise after 1955–56 is quite substantial.

(*ii*) If we limit our comparison to the period after 1955–56, average the two periods that follow, and group capital consumption charges with the savings of private corporations (because between 75 and 95 percent of these charges are assigned in the more detailed classification to "private enterprises"—even though the latter include households as owners of housing), the following summary of Table 13–5 points up the findings:

	Share in GNP, 1957–64 (%)			Share of Household Savings in Disposable Income (%)
	Government	Private Enterprises	Households	
Japan	7.5	16.3	11.4	16.8
Germany	7.1	10.8	9.1	13.5
Netherlands	5.0	13.8	8.6	12.8
Finland	8.5	12.4	6.9	10.4
Switzerland	5.4	13.5	6.6	9.4
United States	1.3	12.5	4.0	5.9
Canada	2.2	14.5	5.1	7.3

(*iii*) The sources of savings that contribute to the higher proportions in Japan differ in different ways from those for other developed countries. Thus, in comparison with Germany, the excess in Japan is largely in the savings of the private enterprise sector. In the comparison with Finland, the largest difference is in savings of households. In comparison with the United States and Canada, the excess in Japan is substantial for both the government sector and households. And, of course, if we compared Japan with a variety of developed countries, the magnitude of the difference for each of these three major sources of savings would vary from country to country and source to source. Significantly, all three sources contributed to the overall high savings rate of Japan—in the sense that all three shares in GNP are large, although each can be matched in some other country. But no other country has large shares for all three sources—just as no other country has the combination of a high capital formation-savings proportion with a low capital-output ratio.

(*iv*) The personal savings propensity is also higher in Japan than in any other country in Table 13–5 and would indeed be higher than in any country on the longer list in Table 13–4. In a few countries, like Germany and particularly the Netherlands, the ratio of household savings to disposable income barely approaches that observed in Japan (e.g., 14.2 percent in Germany compared with 15.8 percent in Japan in 1957–60; or 13 percent in the Netherlands, compared with 17.8 percent in Japan in 1961–64).

Partly as a matter of curiosity, and partly in an attempt to check the consistency of the Japanese estimates of personal savings used in Table 13–5 (a residual item in the national accounts), I tried to combine data on savings-disposable income proportions of urban employees and farm households (derived from family expenditure sample studies) with those on aggregate personal savings proportions (Table 13–6). The combination, together with the distribution of personal (and, on the basis of additional assumptions, disposable) income, yields the savings presumably derived from disposable income other than that of employees and unincorporated farm entrepreneurs—largely incomes of unincorporated nonfarm entrepreneurs, transfers, and returns on personal property. With these items allocated on some reasonably plausible assumptions, we can derive the savings-disposable income proportion for the remaining group—nonfarm entrepreneurs and property income recipients—which works out to between 24 and 32 percent.

Three findings of Table 13–6 deserve explicit mention. First, the derived savings-disposable income proportions for the nonfarm entrepreneurs and property income recipients are not unrealistically high. Even in the United States, the savings proportions of nonfarm entrepreneurs are high compared with the nationwide personal savings-income ratios, or with those of employees and farm entrepreneurs. The proportions in lines 17–18—twice or less than twice the national average—are compatible with a judgment that the national savings proportion is not inconsistent with the information available in the sample studies of family expenditures. Second, the rise in the personal savings-income proportion during the decade 1955–64 appears to have been due primarily to a substantial rise in the savings-income proportion for urban employees; to some extent, to the rise in the savings-income proportion for farm proprietors; and only slightly to the decline in the share in total personal income of farm entrepreneurs, with their below national average savings-income proportion. The remaining group—nonfarm entrepreneurs and property income recipients—apparently contributed nothing to this rise. Finally, the savings-income proportions in 1961–64, 16 percent for urban employees, 13 percent for farm entrepreneurs, and between 26 and 30 percent for the remaining group, were probably higher than those for the corresponding groups in other developed countries.

TABLE 13-6

Personal Savings Proportions to Three Types of Factor
Income, Japan, 1955-1964

	1955-56 (1)	1957-60 (2)	1961-64 (3)	1955-64 (4)
Share of Savings in Disposable Income (%)				
1. National.	13.07	15.86	18.37	16.31
2. Urban wage and salaried workers	10.49	13.48	16.31	14.01
3. Farm households	7.57	7.87	13.11	9.90
4. Ratio, line 2 to line 1 . . .	0.803	0.850	0.888	0.859
5. Ratio, line 3 to line 1	0.579	0.496	0.714	0.607
Distribution of Personal Income (%)				
6. Comp. of employees.	50.8	54.3	56.8	54.6
7. Net transfers	5.0	4.9	5.2	5.1
8. Unincorporated entrepreneurial income, farm.	19.4	15.8	11.9	14.9
9. Unincorporated entrepreneurial income, nonfarm	17.9	16.0	15.2	16.1
10. Property income	6.9	9.0	10.9	9.3
Distribution of Disposable Income (net transfers allocated to compensation of employees; property incomes combined with incomes of unincorporated enterprises, nonfarm; tax burden assumed double for "other" group)				
11. Employees, lines 6 and 7, adjusted (E).	57.0	60.4	63.5	61.0
12. Farm entrepreneurs (F)	19.8	16.1	12.2	15.2
13. Others (O).	23.2	23.6	24.3	23.8
Distribution of Disposable Income (transfers, property income, and taxes distributed proportionately to basic factor incomes)				
14. (E)	57.7	63.1	67.8	63.8
15. (F)	22.0	18.3	14.1	17.4
16. (O)	20.3	18.6	18.1	18.8
Share of Savings in Disposable Income, O Group (%)				
17. Based on lines 11-13.	24.0	27.4	26.4	26.3
18. Based on lines 14-16.	26.3	31.8	30.2	30.1

NOTES: Detail does not check because of rounding.

The data for lines 1 and 6-10 are from revised national accounts in the Bank of Japan, *Supplement* to *Hundred-Year Statistics of the Japanese Economy*.

The data for lines 2 and 3 are from Bank of Japan, *Hundred-Year Statistics of the Japanese Economy*, Table 130, pp. 356-57 for urban worker households (savings proportions are the ratio of balance between income and expenditure to disposable income), and Table 131, pp. 358-61 for farm households (savings proportions are ratios of surplus to disposable income defined as the sum of expenditures for living and the surplus). For lines 1-3 and 6-10 the shares were computed for each calendar year and averaged.

TABLE 13-6 (Continued)

For lines 11-13 we assume that transfer payments go to recipients of compensation of employees, and that personal property income goes to nonfarm unincorporated entrepreneurs. The direct tax burden for the latter group was assumed to be twice that of farmers and employees; and the tax deductions were derived annually from the national share of disposable in total personal income, and the distributions of total personal income underlying lines 6-10. In lines 14-16 transfers, taxes, and personal property income were distributed proportionately among compensation of employees, income of farm entrepreneurs, and income of nonfarm entrepreneurs.

Line 17 is derived from lines 1, 4, 5, and 11-13 (the products of lines 11 and 4 and 12 and 5 respectively are the shares of the E and F groups in *savings*); the residual, the share of the O group in savings, divided by its share in disposable income (line 13), yields the ratio of the savings proportion of the O group to the national savings proportion; and this ratio, multiplied by the national savings proportion in line 1, yields the savings proportion of the O group in line 17. For line 18 the calculation is similar, except that the shares of the E, F, and O groups in lines 14-16 are used.

Clearly, a closer analysis of the sources of savings in Japan in the last decade—particularly of personal and business savings—in comparison with those in other developed countries, would be promising. It might reveal some distinctive aspects of the Japanese economic and social structure that would explain these high savings ratios—whether they are linked to pressure for internal capital funds rather than external credit, pressure that to some extent reveals a weakness in financial institutions; or to duality in the sense of contrast between traditional consumption and modern production, or to patterns of income distribution over time. And it might distinguish the effects of these aspects from the more general connection between very high rates of growth of per capita income, characteristic of Japan, and allocation of income between consumption and savings.

b) In turning now to the long-term record of capital formation and savings proportions, we must remember that the revisions, still in work, may affect the presently available series markedly. We therefore pick our way cautiously, and limit our statements to findings that are not likely to be contradicted even by the most substantial revisions.

The unrevised estimates suggested proportions of gross national capital formation (including military investment) to gross national product varying from 1887–96 to 1922–31 between 9.5 and 17.2 percent, with a fairly distinct upward trend; the domestic capital formation proportions varied between 12 and 18.5 percent for the same period.[7] It is only in the 1930's, with the decided shift to investment in and production of war matériel, that these capital formation proportions, domestic or national, rose to about 25 percent. The revision, embodied in the Hitotsubashi tables for the Ohkawa-Rosovsky study in Chapter 1, relates to gross domestic capital formation proportions alone, and for the period 1887–1931 yields a range from 13 to 19 percent based on constant price volumes; and a range from 15 to 21 percent, based on current price volumes; and the revisions are subject to further change. No data are presently available that would make it possible to allocate domestic or gross national capital formation among sources of savings along the lines followed in Table 13–4.

It is reasonable to conclude that the capital formation proportions of Japan for 1955–64 were much higher than those in the decades between the late 1880's and the 1930's, and presumably also for the one or two decades preceding the late 1880's. Even in the 1930's, the gross domestic or national capital formation proportion (including military investment), about 25 percent, was distinctly below the 33.6 percent shown for 1955–64 in Table 13–4; and the difference would be much wider in the comparison with earlier decades. This most recent decade is also probably distinctive with respect to its low incremental capital-output ratio. With a rate of growth of total product shown in Table 13–1 of 42.3 percent per decade, or 3.6 percent per year, even the low capital formation proportion of 13 percent would yield a capital-output ratio of 3.6, compared with 3.2 for 1955–64; and this ratio would probably have risen as the capital formation proportion rose from 13 to 19 percent. (We are using only gross capital formation proportions, because it is difficult to estimate capital consumption for earlier decades comparable with that for the post–World War II years.) Finally, the personal savings-income ratios were probably not as high in the pre-1930 decades in Japan (and possibly even in the 1930's) as in 1955–64; but it would require further evidence, not at hand now, to check this guess.

The more interesting question here is in regard to the long-term, pre-1930 record of the capital formation and savings proportion in Japan, compared with other developed countries. Allowing for possible revisions, one may still advance two tentative conclusions. First, if the gross capital formation proportion (including military investment) in Japan, in current or constant prices, domestic or national, ranged from 13 to 19 percent between the late 1880's and the 1930's, it was not significantly lower than those for many other developed

---

[7] See Rosovsky, *op. cit.*, Table 3, p. 9.

countries (even if it was distinctly below the proportion of 20 percent or more for the United States). If later revisions confirm this fact, we shall again be confronted with the question as to how Japan, with its much lower per capita income, achieved this high proportion. Or, to return to our main theme—the factors that made for a higher long-term growth rate of Japan—the conclusion suggests that among these factors some should explain how Japan, despite its greater economic backwardness reflected in its much lower per capita income, generated a volume of savings and capital formation that was no lower relative to product than in most other, economically richer developed countries.

The second tentative conclusion is that *if* the gross capital formation proportion in the long run before the 1930's was no *larger* in Japan than in other developed countries, whereas the growth rate of Japan's total product was distinctly higher (except in comparison with countries like the United States and Canada, which grew almost as rapidly, but with a much higher growth rate of population and a lower growth rate of per capita product), then the long-term level of the incremental capital-output ratio must have been distinctly lower in Japan than in other developed countries. The difference between Japan and the older developed countries of Europe lay in a higher growth rate of Japan's total product, with about the same gross capital formation proportions; between Japan and the United States and Canada, with the growth rates of total product about the same, the difference lay in the lower capital formation proportions (relevant to this argument, i.e., domestic) in Japan than in the United States or Canada.

If these two conclusions—the higher capital formation proportions viewed as a savings rate and the low incremental capital-output ratio —hold, two aspects of the factors used to explain Japan's higher growth rate should always be considered: their contribution to an explanation of the relatively high savings rate, and their contribution to an explanation of the low incremental capital-output ratio.

The above notes dealt quite briefly with several factors commonly referred to in discussions of the high rate of growth of Japan, probing them as empirically testable hypotheses; and dwelt, at some length, on the capital formation and savings proportions in the recent decade, against a background of long-term trends in these proportions—still to be confirmed by revisions now being made of the underlying long-term series. The questions to be answered were more complex than they seemed at first glance; and we were unable to explain satisfactorily the differences in the rate of growth between Japan and other developed countries. By inference, this also reflects our limited ability to explain any economic growth at all, by Japan—if by the latter we mean a rate *sufficiently high and sustained* to transform the traditional and economically backward Japan of the 1870's to the industrialized Japan of the 1960's.

This is not surprising because no adequately tested, quantitatively specified, theory of economic growth has yet been formulated; because comparative quantitative analysis, one of the requirements for such a theory, is in its early stages; and because the evidence for the few disparate cases of modern economic growth now at hand may be an inadequate basis for such a theory. In that sense, conclusions similar to those suggested above in the examination of the case of Japan would be reached if any other country were being examined—except that Japan is a particularly intriguing case because its initial economic level was so low and its historical heritage and background were so different from those of all other currently developed countries.

One final point: the critical examination and stress on the lack of tested explanation are not without value, if they help to eliminate or reduce the use of vague hypotheses and point clearly at lines of further quantitative analysis that might help to fill the most crucial gaps. To recognize the limitations of our knowledge and understanding is not to depreciate what little we know; but rather to urge its greater value when and if it is supplemented in the proper directions.

Program of the Conference

September 5

MORNING

Chairman: M. Abramovitz

Paper: T. Watanabe, "Industrialization, Technological Progress, and Dual Structure"

Discussant: G. Ranis

AFTERNOON

Chairman: K. Ohkawa

Papers: (1) Y. Hayami and S. Yamada, "Technological Progress in Agriculture"; (2) Y. Shionoya, "Patterns of Industrial Development"

Discussants: (1) D. W. Jorgenson and G. Ranis; (2) Y. Yasuba and H. König

September 6

MORNING

Chairman: S. Tsuru

Paper: K. Nakagawa, "Organized Entrepreneurship in the Prewar Japan"

Discussant: Y. Horie and H. Rosovsky

AFTERNOON

Chairman: M. C. Kemp

Papers: (1) S. Fujino, "Construction Cycles and Their Monetary-Financial Characteristics"; (2) M. Baba and M. Tatemoto, "Foreign Trade and Economic Growth in Japan: 1858–1937"

Discussants: (1) R. C. O. Mathews; (2) S. Tsuru and K. N. Raj

September 7

MORNING

Chairman: K. N. Raj

Paper: K. Ohkawa and H. Rosovsky, "Postwar Japanese Growth in Historical Perspective: A Second Look"

Discussant: M. Abramovitz

AFTERNOON

Chairman: H. König

Papers: (1) S. Ichimura, "Factors for Rapid Economic Growth: A Social Accounting Approach"; (2) T. Uchida, "Structural Characteristics of Japanese Economy"

Discussants: (1) H. Patrick, and (2) L. R. Klein

September 8

MORNING

Chairman: R. C. O. Mathews

Papers: (1) M. Shinohara, "Patterns and Some Structural Changes in Japan's Postwar Industrial Growth"; (2) S. Kuznets, "Notes on Consumption: Trends in Level and Structure of Consumption"

Discussants: (1) H. König, and (2) M. Shinohara

September 9

MORNING

Chairman: M. Shinohara

Papers: (1) H. Kanamori, "Economic Growth and Exports"; (2) K. Tsujimura, "Rapid Industrialization of Dual Economy"

Discussants: (1) M. C. Kemp, and (2) D. W. Jorgenson

AFTERNOON

Chairman: T. Watanabe

Papers: (1) H. Patrick, "The Financing of the Public Sector in Postwar Japan"; (2) S. Shishido and I. Miyazaki, "The Role of the Government in the Postwar Economic Development of Japan"

Discussants: (1) R. Komiya, and (2) H. Rosovsky

September 10

MORNING

Chairman: S. Okita

Paper: S. Ishikawa, "Net Resources Flow between Agriculture and Industry"

Discussant: K. N. Raj

AFTERNOON

Chairman: S. Ichimura

General comments: S. Kuznets